Understanding
Data
Communications
4th Edition

Understanding

Data Communications

4th Edition

Second, Third, and Fourth Editions Revised by: Gilbert Held

**First Edition by: George E. Friend, M.S.; John L. Fike, Ph.D., P.E.;
H. Charles Baker, Ph.D., P.E.; and John C. Bellamy, Ph.D. With
Contributions by Gerald Luecke and Charles W. Battle**

SAMS
PUBLISHING

A Division of
Macmillan
Computer Publishing
201 W. 103rd St.
Indianapolis, Indiana
46290 USA

Overview

Contents

Preface

The communication of information of all kinds by means of binary signals—the ones and zeros that are used by computers—has gained such an important place in American society that it is fair to say that successful operation of the U.S. economy would be impossible without it. Information sent using data communications controls a major portion of the long-distance telephone network, enables the rapid authorization of credit purchases and cashing of checks, and provides for the inventory and ordering of goods in stores of all kinds, from fast-food franchises to photo finishers. Data communications technology allows the simultaneous printing in widely separated cities of national magazines and newspapers, whose entire text and picture copy is transmitted from a central source to the city in which the publications are to be printed on a daily basis.

A basic knowledge of such a pervasive force in our lives is as necessary for all of us as some knowledge of the working of another transportation system—the automobile. The authors have attempted to cover the basic principles of data communications and to explain those areas of application that have a daily impact: communications between terminals and computers, including local area networks and packet networks; communication of telephone conversations and control of the telephone network; and the use of light rays and satellites for carrying the ever-increasing volume of data that helps make our lives more comfortable and sometimes a great deal more confusing.

This book is arranged somewhat like a textbook. Each chapter starts by saying what it covers, ends by saying what has been covered, and provides a short multiple-choice quiz on the chapter's contents. Like other books in the series, this book builds understanding step-by-step. Try to master each chapter before going on to the next one.

If your objective is to obtain general information about the subject, the more detailed portions of the text and the quiz can be bypassed. This will enable you to absorb the information more easily and, hopefully, enjoy the style of presentation. If you need more basic information about the telephone system and telephone electronics, a companion book in the series titled *Understanding Telephone Electronics* should be helpful. For more detailed and more advanced information about data communications, refer to the books listed in the bibliography.

G.H.

An Overview of Data Communications

About This Book

This book is intended to explain how data communications systems and their various hardware and software components work. It is not intended to tell you how to build the equipment, nor will it tell you how to write computer programs to transmit data between two computers. What can be learned is a basis for understanding data communications systems in general, as well as some tips for setting up your own system to communicate between your personal or professional computer and another personal computer, a database service, an information utility, or an electronic bulletin board.

To understand data communications, it is necessary to have some understanding of the telephone channel, because it is the medium used by most data communications systems to move information from one place to another. Therefore, part of this book is devoted to describing the public telephone network and the equipment used to interface between it and a computer.

About This Chapter

This chapter presents some history of data communications and a general description of a data communications system. Explanations of bits, bytes, two-state communications systems, and codes help lay the foundation for further discussions in the remainder of the book.

What Is Data Communications?

Data communications is the process of communicating information in binary form between two or more points. Data communications is sometimes called computer communications because most of the information interchanged today is between computers, or between computers and their terminals, printers, or other peripheral devices. The data might be as elementary as the binary symbols 1 and 0, or as complex as the characters represented by the keys on a typewriter keyboard. In any case, the characters or symbols represent information.

Data communications is often referred to as computer communications due to the ever-increasing use of computers and their support equipment.

Why Is Data Communications Important?

It is important for us to understand data communications because of its significance in today's world. Data communications is commonly used in the world of business, and it is being used more and more in homes as well. Whether it is the transmission of bank-account information from a central computer to a convenient electronic teller machine, the selection of a pay-per-view cable TV program, or the downloading of a video game from a computer bulletin board to a home computer's memory, data communications is becoming an integral part of our daily activities. In fact, for many readers, hardly a day goes by without their being the recipient of an activity performed or enhanced through the use of data communications. For example, many traffic lights are controlled via the transmission of signals from computer systems, and large retailers routinely transmit sales information that allows timely distribution of warehouse inventory to retail locations. Thus, the more modern a society, the more dependent that society is on data communications.

The First Data Communications Systems

Modern data communications involves the use of electrical or electronic apparatus to communicate information in the form of symbols and characters between two points. Because electricity, radio waves, and light waves are all forms of electromagnetic energy, it is stretching things only a bit to say that early forms of communication, such as the puffs of smoke from the Indian's signal fire (see Figure 1.1), or reflections of sunlight from a hand-held mirror, also were forms of the same type of data communications. To carry this idea further, think of the puffs of smoke as discrete symbols, just as the symbols used in today's communications systems are discrete.

The first data communications did not rely on electricity.

Early Uses of Electricity

The discovery and harnessing of electricity introduced many new possibilities for communications codes beyond the smoke signals, mirrors, signal flags, and lanterns in use in the 18th and 19th centuries.

One of the early proposals, submitted to a Scottish magazine in 1753, was simple but had profound implications for hardware. This idea was to run 26 parallel wires from town to town, one wire for each letter of the alphabet. A Swiss inventor built a prototype system based on this 26-wire principle, but the technology of wire making at that time eliminated that idea from serious use.

In 1833, Carl Friedrich Gauss used a code based on a 5-by-5 matrix of 25 letters (*I* and *J* were combined) to send messages by deflecting a needle from one to five times, right or left. The first set of deflections indicated the row; the second, the column.

●
Originally, data communications depended on codes transmitted by visual systems such as mirrors, flags, and smoke. Electrical data communications systems transmit codes by switching electrical current.

The Telegraph

The next notable development in data communications occurred in the 19th century when an American, Samuel F.B. Morse, invented the electric telegraph. Although other inventors had worked on the idea of using electricity to communicate, Morse's invention was by far the most important because he coupled the human mind (intelligence) with the communications equipment.

Samuel F.B. Morse perfected the telegraph, the first mass data communications system based on electric power.

A basic telegraph system is diagrammed in Figure 1.2. When the telegraph key at station A was depressed, current flowed through the system, and the armature at station B was attracted to the coil, clicking as it struck the stop. When the key was released, it opened the electrical circuit, and the armature of the sounder was forced to its open position by a spring, striking the other stop with a slightly different click. Thus, the telegraph sounder had two distinctive clicks. If the time between successive clicks of the sounder was short, it represented a dot; if longer, a dash. Morse developed a code, similar to the one shown in Figure 1.3, to represent characters by a series of these dots and dashes. The transmitting operator converted the characters in the words of a message to be sent into a series of dots and dashes. The receiving operator interpreted those dots and dashes as characters; thus, the information was transmitted from point A to point B.

FIGURE 1.2.

Basic telegraph system.

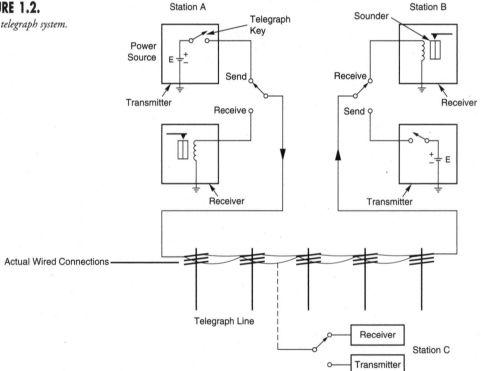

When Morse developed his code, legend has it that he examined the quantity of type in boxes a typesetter used for storing English characters and digits. Morse assigned short codes to frequently occurring characters and digits, whereas longer codes were assigned to less frequently occurring characters and digits. This explains why a dot was assigned to the letter E, which is the most frequently occurring character in the English language, and a dash was assigned to the letter T, which is the second most frequently occurring character.

Telegraph Characters

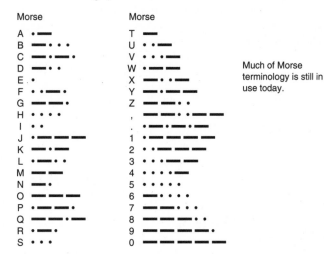

Much of Morse terminology is still in use today.

FIGURE 1.3.

International Morse code.

Morse first developed the telegraph in 1832, but it wasn't until much later that he successfully demonstrated its use. The best-known demonstration took place in 1844, when Morse transmitted over a wire from Washington to Baltimore the message, "What hath God wrought!"

Because mail delivery by the Pony Express was the typical means of communication before the telegraph, the telegraph quickly became a success because of its much greater speed. The equipment was simple and rugged; the key and the sounder each contained only one moving part. Both the system's strength and its weakness (and its only real complexity) was the human mind—the transmitting and receiving operators. By the time of the Civil War, a telegraph line spanned the continent, crossing the prairies and deserts to connect California with the rest of the United States. It was from this historic technological breakthrough that the Western Union Telegraph Company made its legacy and indeed was named; its line connected the West with the Union. By the time the telephone was invented some 30 years later, the telegraph industry was large and prosperous, with many companies providing service to almost every city and town in the United States. In 1866, the telegraph connected the nations of the world with the laying of the trans-Atlantic cable between the United States and France.

Two-State Communications Systems

The importance of the Morse telegraph is not just historical; it illustrates the simplicity of a complete data communications system. Much of the terminology that developed around the Morse system still is in use today. For example, consider the terms *mark* and *space*. If a device were arranged so that paper continually moved under a pen attached to the telegraph sounder armature, a mark would be made on the paper when the armature was

●
The telegraph was the first electrically based communications system to connect the east and west coasts of the United States and both sides of the Atlantic.

●
Much of the telegraph's terminology and many of the principles of operation are still used today. The most important of these is the two-state communications system.

attracted to the coil. Thus, we could refer to the state of current flow in the line as the marking state, and the state of no current flow in the line as the spacing state. Worldwide standards for data communications today still use the terms mark and space, with the idle condition on the transmission channel called the marking condition.

The wire (telegraph channel) between the operators, therefore, is in one of two states: either current is flowing, or it is not. This illustrates a simple idea that has been repeated over and over again in the development of data communications systems. A two-state communications system is the simplest, the easiest to build, and the most reliable. The two states can be On and Off (as in the telegraph), Plus and Minus (with current flowing in opposite directions), Light and Dark (like turning a flashlight on and off to send code), 1 and 0 (the concept used in the computer), or some other design with only two possible values. A two-state or two-valued system is referred to as a binary system.

Bits and Bytes

The 0 and 1 are the symbols of the binary system. A binary digit is commonly referred to as a bit. The individual line changes in digital data (such as the mark and space) are called bits, and each bit is assigned a value of 0 or 1.

Transmission codes in the binary system are made up of digits called bits. Each bit can have one of two possible states (high or low, on or off). Several bits combined in a uniform group are called a byte.

The binary system uses positional notation, just as the familiar decimal system does, except that each position has only 2 possible values, rather than 10. For example, the number 345.27 in decimal means three hundreds plus four tens plus five ones plus two tenths plus seven hundredths. The weight of each position is a power of ten, thus:

```
345.27 = (3 x 100) + (4 x 10) + (5 x 1) + (2 x 1/10) +
         (7 x 1/100)
       = 3 x 10² + 4  x 10¹ + 5 x 10⁰ + 2 x 10⁻¹ + 7 x 10⁻²
```

Note the use of positive and negative exponents, and remember the definition that any number raised to the zero power is equal to one. In the decimal system, as shown by the preceding example, 10 is the base, and the weight of each digit position is a power of 10.

Similarly, we can define powers of two in the binary positional system, in which the weight of each position is two times the weight of the one to the immediate right. A table of powers of two can be quite useful when dealing with binary numbers because most of us don't want to memorize them. Table 1.1 is such a table for powers of 2 up to 2^8, which will be sufficient for this book. Using this table makes it easy to convert a binary number to its decimal equivalent; for example:

```
1101001 = 1 x 2⁶ + 1 x 2⁵ + 0 x 2⁴ + 1 x 2³ + 0 x 2² + 0 x 2¹ +
          1 x 2⁰
        = 64 + 32 + 0 + 8 + 0 + 0 + 1
        = 105 decimal
```

Table 1.1. The powers of two.

Power of Two	Positional Weight	9-Bit Binary Number
2^0	1	000000001
2^1	2	000000010
2^2	4	000000100
2^3	8	000001000
2^4	16	000010000
2^5	32	000100000
2^6	64	001000000
2^7	128	010000000
2^8	256	100000000

Computers are more efficient if their internal paths and registers are some power of two in length (2 bits, 4 bits, 8 bits, 16 bits, and so forth). A commonly used grouping is 8 bits, and this 8-bit group is called a byte or an octet. From Table 1.1, you can see that a byte can represent 2^8 or 256 unique sequences of ones and zeros.

Communications Codes

A common characteristic of data communications systems is the use of an intelligent device to convert a character or symbol into coded form and vice versa. In the Morse system, the intelligent "devices" were the telegraph operators who converted the characters into dots and dashes.

Skilled telegraph operators were always in short supply, and the work was difficult and exhausting. An electrical or mechanical means of coding the characters was therefore needed. However, it was essentially impossible to automate the transmitting and receiving operations because of the varying duration of the dots and dashes in the Morse code and the fact that the codes for the characters were made up of different quantities of dots and dashes. Therefore, a code that had the same number of equal duration signaling elements for each character was needed.

Some Definitions

Before we go any further, let's establish the following definitions in order to discuss communications codes:

Codes: Standard (agreed-on-in-advance) interpretations between signaling elements and characters. The key idea is standard. The codes used in data communications systems are already defined, and the code set is built into the

The use of simplified and standardized binary codes allowed information to be encoded and decoded by mechanical or electrical means and made it possible to automate data communications.

A code is a previously agreed-on set of meanings that define a given set of symbols and characters.

equipment. About the only time the user might need to deal with codes is when interfacing two machines (such as computers and printers) from different manufacturers.

Characters: The letters, numerals, spaces, punctuation marks, and other signs and symbols on a keyboard. (Remember that the space character is just as important as any other, even though we tend to think of it as "nothing" or "blank.") For example, "A 7#" is a sequence of four characters. Communication systems also use control characters that do not print, but these characters also must be coded. Some of these (such as Carriage Return or Tab) might be on a keyboard, but many are not.

Signaling Elements: Something that is sent over a transmission channel and used to represent a character. The dots and dashes (or marks and spaces) of the Morse code are signaling elements, as are the ones and zeros in this sequence:

```
01000001010 0000001011 0111011011 0110001001
```

This is the way "A 7#" might look when transmitted between a personal computer and another computer or printer. You will see later that the code is ASCII, with even parity and one start and one stop bit.

The definitions for characters and signaling elements illustrate why machines and people need different ways to represent information. People quickly and reliably recognize printed characters by their distinctive shapes, but that is difficult and expensive for a machine to do. On the other hand, machines can easily handle long strings of two-valued signaling elements such as marks and spaces or ones and zeros, but that is hard for a person to accomplish with any accuracy.

Baudot Code

As stated before, the Morse code was unsuitable for machine encoding and decoding because of the problems caused by the varying lengths of the codes for the characters. Early in the 20th century, when interest developed in replacing human telegraph operators with machines, several suitable codes already existed. The most prominent of these had been invented in the 1870s by a Frenchman named Emile Baudot. Because Baudot's code, similar to the one shown in Figure 1.4, used the same number of signaling elements (marks and spaces) to represent each character, it was better suited to machine encoding and decoding.

Unfortunately, the number of signaling elements was limited to five by problems in timing the electromechanical devices. The five-bit code could generate only 32 possible combinations, fewer than was needed to represent the 26 characters of the alphabet, the 10 decimal digits, the punctuation marks, and the space character. To overcome this limitation, Baudot used two shift-control characters—the letters (LTRS) shift and the figures (FIGS) shift—to permit the code set to represent all the characters that seemed necessary at the time. The shift codes do not represent printable characters; they select one of two character sets, each composed of 26 to 28 characters.

Characters are the letters, signs, and symbols on an input device's keyboard; some are used to control the system.

Signaling elements are the representations of characters that are transmitted over transmission lines. It is easier to design and build machines to recognize signaling elements than to build them to recognize characters.

Emile Baudot developed one of the more successful codes suited for machine encoding and decoding. However, it was limited because it used only five signaling elements per character.

FIGURE 1.4.

Five-level teleprinter code.

Code Signals •Denotes Positive Current							LTRS Shift	FIGS Shift	
								CCITT Standard International Telegraph Alphabet No. 2 Used for Telex	North American Teletype Commercial Keyboard
Start	1	2	3	4	5	Stop			
	•	•				•	A	—	—
	•			•	•	•	B	?	?
		•	•	•		•	C	:	:
	•			•		•	D	Who Are You?	$
	•					•	E	3	3
	•		•	•		•	F	Note 1	!
		•		•	•	•	G	Note 1	&
			•		•	•	H	Note 1	#
		•	•			•	I	8	8
	•	•		•		•	J	Bell	Bell
	•	•	•	•		•	K	(	(
		•			•	•	L	)	)
			•	•	•	•	M	.	.
			•	•		•	N	,	,
				•	•	•	O	9	9
		•	•		•	•	P	0	0
	•	•	•		•	•	Q	1	1
		•		•		•	R	4	4
	•		•			•	S	,	,
					•	•	T	5	5
	•	•	•			•	U	7	7
		•	•	•	•	•	V	=	;
	•	•			•	•	W	2	2
	•		•	•	•	•	X	/	/
	•		•		•	•	Y	6	6
	•				•	•	Z	+	"
						•	Blank		
	•	•	•	•	•	•	Letters Shift (LTRS)		
	•	•		•	•	•	Figures Shift (FIGS)		
			•			•	Space		
				•		•	Carriage Return		
		•				•	Line Feed		

Notes:
1. Not allocated internationally; available to each country for internal use.

Receipt of the letters shift (11111) code causes all following codes to be interpreted as letters of the alphabet; receipt of the figures shift code (11011) causes all the following characters to be interpreted as numerals and punctuation marks. Notice that the LTRS and FIGS codes, as well as the other control codes and the space character, always have the same interpretation no matter which shift mode the machine is in. Although Baudot's invention did not immediately revolutionize telegraphy (because of the difficulty that human operators had in sending equal length codes), it did provide a basis for the later development of the teleprinter.

Modern Codes

●
There was a need
for new codes that
could represent all
characters, check
for errors, and
leave room for
further expansion.

The Baudot code and variations of it were the backbone of communications for almost half a century, but they clearly left much to be desired. Those in the newspaper industry found the lack of differentiation between upper- and lowercase letters to be a problem. They devised a six-level code to designate the difference between upper- and lowercase letters. This was just one example of general need; modern communications required a code that could represent all printable characters and still leave room for error checking. The code had to permit decoding without reliance on correct reception of previous transmissions, and also had to permit decoding by machine. Perhaps most important of all, the new code needed to be expandable.

During the 1960s, a number of data transmission codes were developed. Most of these have fallen by the wayside, leaving three predominant codes: a single five-bit code (CCITT International Alphabet No. 2) still used for telex transmission; the Extended Binary-Coded-Decimal Interchange Code (EBCDIC, pronounced "eb-see-dik") developed by IBM and primarily used for synchronous communication in systems attached to large mainframe computers; and the American Standard Code for Information Interchange (ASCII, pronounced "as-key") code defined by the American National Standards Institute (ANSI) in the United States and by the International Organization for Standardization (ISO) worldwide.

EBCDIC

●
EBCDIC is a
modern code using
eight bits to
represent 256
characters. It was
developed by IBM
to provide a
standard code for
its own products.

When a clear need arises for standardization, standards come into existence in two ways. In one way, a single manufacturer (especially a dominant one) can define a standard for its own products, and the rest of the industry can follow. This is what IBM did. It created the EBCDIC five-bit code, allowing 256 characters to be represented. The world would probably be better off if EBCDIC had become the standard, because it included enough unique characters to allow almost any representation. However, only IBM and firms that build IBM-compatible equipment adopted EBCDIC. Because EBCDIC is primarily used in large IBM-compatible computing systems, it is not used in most of the examples in this book.

ASCII

●
ANSI developed
the seven-bit ASCII
data communications code that is in
general use today.
It can represent
128 characters.

The other, more common method of creating a standard is through a committee, which serves as a forum for examination of needs, discussion between interested parties, and compromise. This process produced the ASCII seven-bit code, formally known as ANSI Standard X3.4-1977. ASCII can depict 128 characters, but not all of them represent printed symbols. Included in the character set are all the letters of the English alphabet (both uppercase and lowercase), the numerals 0–9, punctuation marks, and many symbols. This standard code set is used in virtually all small computers and their peripherals, as well as in large computers in most of the world.

A variation of ASCII, commonly referred to as "extended ASCII," gained wide acceptance with the introduction of the IBM Personal Computer of 1981. The IBM PC supports an eight-bit code, with the first seven positions supporting the ANSI standard. The additional bit position extends the computer's ASCII, enabling an additional 128 characters to be represented. This extension enables software developers to use extended codes for such functions as end-of-paragraph markings and bold printing indicators in a word processing system.

Figure 1.5 shows the ANSI standard ASCII characters and their associated codes. Compare this chart to the Morse code in Figure 1.3 and the five-bit teleprinter code in Figure 1.4. The Morse code had a varying number of elements (dots and dashes) for each character and was quite restricted—only letters, numerals, and a few punctuation marks. The five-bit code had a constant number of elements and a few more special characters, but still couldn't distinguish between upper- and lowercase letters.

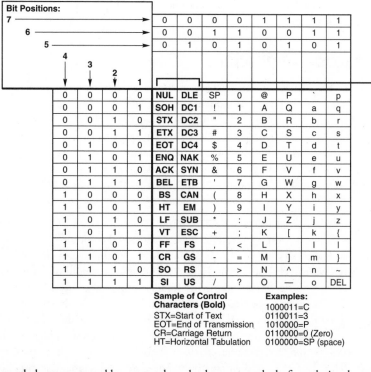

FIGURE 1.5.

American Standard Code for Information Interchange (ASCII).

—— Nonprintable Control Characters

Sample of Control Characters (Bold)
STX=Start of Text
EOT=End of Transmission
CR=Carriage Return
HT=Horizontal Tabulation

Examples:
1000011=C
0110011=3
1010000=P
0110000=0 (Zero)
0100000=SP (space)

● The ASCII format is arranged so that lowercase letters can be changed to uppercase by changing only one bit. Bits 4 through 7 of the numeric characters also are the BCD value of the number.

ASCII not only has upper- and lowercase, but also has a great deal of regularity that might not be readily apparent. For example, to convert any uppercase alphabetic character (A through Z) to lowercase, it is only necessary to change bit 6 from zero to one! Another feature is that bits 4 through 7 of the numeric characters (0, 1, 2, 3, 4, 5, 6, 7, 8, and 9) are the binary-coded-decimal (BCD) value of the character. Another advantage of standard

ASCII is that 128 different characters can be represented by the seven bits used in the code, rather than only 32 characters from the five-bit code.

● ASCII also has several control codes that, in addition to their defined control functions, have been used by some manufacturers to represent specialized functions.

The two leftmost character columns in the chart of Figure 1.5 represent the nonprinting control characters that can be used to control the operation of the receiving device. For example, the control codes for carriage return (CR) and linefeed (LF), which are commonly used on a typewriter, are shown. Other control codes include formfeed (FF), bell (BEL), horizontal tab (HT), and vertical tab (VT). These control codes were designed for printing or display devices, although some manufacturers have used the control codes for all manner of special functions. Also, some codes control how a receiving device will interpret subsequent codes in a multiple-character function or command. Two shift characters, called Shift In (SI) and Shift Out (SO), are used to shift between ASCII and character sets other than those used in English. ANSI standards X3.41-1974 and X3.64-1979 expand the definition of the escape (ESC) control code for even greater flexibility. Other control codes delimit text, such as start of text (STX) and end of text (ETX). These codes are used primarily in block or synchronous data transmission. You'll see more of them in later chapters.

The Escape Character

● Escape sequences are code sequences made up of noncontrol characters that are to be interpreted as control codes.

The escape (ESC) character designates that the codes that follow have special meaning. Characters received in an escape sequence are not interpreted as printing characters, but as control information to extend the range of the "standard" character set by allowing other definitions. The escape character has the effect of making all character codes available for control of a device. Graphics characters, foreign-language character sets, and special applications sets have been developed that are accessible via escape character sequences; thus, they permit a much richer variety of displayed symbols than is otherwise normally possible.

The CRT terminal and later the personal computer monitor are two hardware devices that have benefited most from the escape sequence. The serial communications link to these terminals and personal computers is the same as for a teleprinter, and ordinarily, any characters received via this channel are displayed on the terminal or monitor screen, as expected. But the people who developed the ASCII standard did not foresee (thus did not make provision for) capabilities for character and line deletion and display enhancements that are available on the CRT terminal and computer monitors, such as inverse video, underlining, and blinking. Unfortunately, little standardization of these sequences existed until the ANSI X3.64 standard came out in 1979. Before then, and without standardization, designers felt free to exercise their creativity. For example, one major feature now found on most video display terminals is absolute cursor positioning. The computer can send a command to the terminal that will place the cursor anywhere on the screen. This capability is important for many types of form-filling operations. Unfortunately, there are almost as many escape sequences to do cursor positioning as there are terminal manufacturers. Even different models in a manufacturer's line might use different escape sequences to perform the same action.

The result of this "creativity" with the character set is that some manufacturers' equipment will not operate correctly with that of most of the rest of the world. An example is a printer that automatically inserts a linefeed after receiving a carriage return. Because most computers send both a carriage return and a linefeed in response to only a carriage return input, the printout will not be spaced as desired because of the extra linefeed supplied by the printer.

To promote compatibility, many terminal and personal computer manufacturers provide implicit or explicit support of the ANSI standard. Explicit support of that standard includes those terminals and personal computers designed explicitly to support the ANSI X3.64 standard. Implicit support is provided by terminals and personal computers that have the capability to load a program and read the contents of a predefined memory area or memory cartridge to enable support of the ANSI X3.64 standard.

Perhaps the most commonly available device capable of supporting the ANSI X3.64 standard is the IBM PC and compatible personal computers. Those computers, which use the Microsoft MS-DOS or PC DOS operating system, can be configured to use device driver ANSI.SYS. ANSI.SYS is a file on the operating system diskette that will be loaded into memory during subsequent startups after it's specified. On most MS-DOS or PC DOS computers with a hard drive, you would add the statement DEVICE = C:\DOS\ANSI.SYS to your CONFIG.SYS file to automatically execute the ANSI.SYS device driver on a power-on or system reset, assuming that it is stored under the DOS directory on drive C. The execution of that file results in the personal computer becoming an ANSI-compatible terminal, including support for standardized escape code sequences.

Teleprinters

The teleprinter was the next major step after the telegraph in data communications. Teleprinter equipment has been the backbone of nonvoice business communications for over half a century. As recently as the mid-1970s, a teletypewriter (TTY), which is a teleprinter with a keyboard for input, was the standard terminal for small- and medium-sized computers. Many companies have nationwide and even worldwide private teleprinter networks, although the fax machine and public and private computer-based electronic mail systems have significantly reduced their use. Two nationwide public teleprinter networks are the TWX and TELEX services. Several common carriers will transmit telex messages to any teleprinter in the United States, and companies called "international record carriers" will deliver them to any teleprinter in the world. A company's telex number can be found in a directory similar to a telephone directory.

> ●
> The technology and techniques used in teleprinting have provided the basis for asynchronous data communications.

Like the telegraph, teleprinters are important not only in their own right because they were the principal data communications method for almost 50 years, but also because most of the standards and terminology for low-speed or asynchronous data communications came from the world of teleprinters. We'll discuss asynchronous transmission more thoroughly in Chapter 2, "Terminal Devices." For now, it is sufficient to realize that the transmission of each of the coded characters begins with a "start" symbol and ends with a "stop" symbol. Although this technique permitted synchronization of teleprinter equipment thousands of miles apart, it also added to the already high overhead (in terms of extra time) required for transmission of each character.

Teleprinter equipment was inherently limited to slow transmission speeds because it was electromechanical: solenoids had to be energized to attract armatures; motors had to start, turn, and stop; and clutches had to engage and disengage. All of these mechanical operations limited the maximum speed at which teleprinters could operate reliably to fewer than 30 characters per second. International telex operates even slower—fewer than 10 characters per second! Either speed is much too slow for a computer to communicate efficiently with another computer, or even with a modern printer or CRT terminal.

Data Communications in Computing

The introduction of the electronic computer provided greater speed and capabilities to the data communications system.

Further improvements in data communications were necessitated by the widespread use of electronic computers, introduced in the early 1950s. These computer systems were capable of storing large quantities of information and processing it quickly. Input and output equipment were much improved over the teletypewriter and teleprinter, so they could operate much faster. As more computers were used, it became necessary for computers to communicate with each other. Because this communication did not need any electromechanical equipment, data transfer theoretically could occur at extremely fast rates. Practically, however, data transfer rates are limited by the transmission medium—primarily the public telephone network.

The 1950s

The first computer systems had little need for data communications because they were located close together, I/O was usually direct, and information was processed in discrete batches.

The typical computer system of the 1950s, shown in Figure 1.6, used punched cards for input, printers for output, and reels of magnetic tape for "permanent" mass storage. There was little or no data communications in these systems because the input devices, output devices, and computer were all located close together and were directly connected by short cables. Information was processed on a "one job at a time" or "batch" basis.

For example, a wholesale grocery company would receive orders by mail and telephone during the day. At the end of the day, these would be collected and punched into cards, which were then assembled as a batch. The data on the cards were read into the computer for processing at night. During the processing, the computer would do such things as check the customer's credit. If the credit was satisfactory, the computer would generate a pick list for the warehouse so that the order could be filled and shipped the next day. The quantity ordered for the different types of items would be deducted from the quantity on hand, and the invoices and various warehouse tickets would be printed. This system worked well except that the person taking the order from the customer during the day, whether on the phone or at the customer's premises, was never certain whether the ordered items were available in the warehouse. Although an updated inventory report was available each morning, a running inventory was not kept during the day as orders were received.

FIGURE 1.6.

Typical data processing system of the 1950s.

The 1960s

Batch processing systems such as the one just described are the most efficient in the use of computer time and equipment. However, they are relatively inefficient in the use of the order clerks, salespeople, and other resources of the company. While the costs of employing people were increasing, the solid-state revolution caused the cost of computer logic and memory to decrease sharply. This meant that companies could invest in more computer equipment to reduce the costs of personnel, as well as to make themselves more competitive in business.

In the 1960s, batch processing was largely replaced by online processing (see Figure 1.7). In the example of the wholesale grocery company, the clerks took the orders over the phone and used online terminals to enter the orders into the computer at the same time. Some of these terminals were directly connected to the computer by parallel communication channels, but many of the terminals were teleprinter devices that used serial data communications over dedicated private cables to the computer.

In the 1960s, the use of outlying online terminals required communications links to connect them to the main computer.

As the order was entered, the computer checked the inventory to see whether the goods were on hand. If so, the customer was given a delivery date; if not, he was told that the goods were out of stock and was given the option of placing a back order or selecting another item. Although more expensive than batch processing in terms of computer time and equipment, this method of doing business made the wholesale grocery company more competitive because it gave the customer better service.

FIGURE 1.7.

Typical data processing system of the 1960s.

The 1970s

The 1970s changed this process still further (see Figure 1.8). Other computers, sometimes called minicomputers, could communicate with the larger computer in the wholesale grocer's central office. The online order terminals were not necessarily in the room next to the computer; they might have been on a different floor, in a different building, or even in a different city. Toward the end of the decade, even smaller computers, called microcomputers or personal computers, began to be seen not only in the homes of some of the employees, but also on their desks at the office. Sometimes the employees would communicate with the main computer through these smaller computers. The company salesmen began carrying portable computer terminals with them on their sales calls. They could enter their orders from the customers' offices directly into the main computer over a standard telephone line.

In the 1970s, the introduction of the minicomputer and the very portable microcomputer required that these units have increased communications with their mainframe computer.

True data communications was everywhere in the system. There was more equipment around than anyone would have thought possible in the 1950s—more computers, more terminals, more communications channels—and businesses were run more efficiently because of it.

FIGURE 1.8.

Typical data processing system of the 1970s.

The 1980s

As the wholesale grocery company grew, it decided to produce some of the food products that it sold, so it set up producing operations in California, Texas, and Florida. Because its wholesale business is primarily in the northeast, it has major warehouse facilities in New Jersey, Pennsylvania, and Ohio, and sales offices in Chicago, Philadelphia, and New York City. The company headquarters is also in New York City.

With the expansion to the south and west, the company's data communications system also needed expansion. The company decided to use the relatively new satellite communications to tie the New York office with the Texas and California operations. (Satellite communications are discussed in later chapters.) The satellite could be used for other points as well, but the company (for various reasons) uses leased terrestrial circuits to the Florida, Chicago, and Philadelphia sites. The smaller sales offices in the states where the company operates are tied together with a network of low-speed teletypewriter-like terminals that allow order entry and some communication with the home office. The company's sales-men still carry portable terminals, but advances in technology have reduced the size of the terminal while increasing its capabilities. A typical terminal is shown in Figure 1.9.

As low-cost personal computers became more widely available during the mid-1980s, many managers acquired them for departmental use. Although the original intention was to use the local processing capability of personal computers for such tasks as budgeting with

●

Advances in technology increased the capabilities of computers, reduced the size and power requirements of computers, and provided a new communications link—the satellite.

spreadsheet programs and word processing, corporate managements quickly began to integrate personal computers into their company communications networks. Some personal computers replaced CRT terminals and served as both terminals and local processing devices. Other PCs were linked into a local area network, which enabled users to share peripheral devices and provided the capability of sending electronic messages to other users on the network.

FIGURE 1.9.

*TI 703KSR
teleprinter.*

Introduced in mid-1981, more than 10 million IBM PC and compatible computers had been manufactured by 1987, when the Personal System/2 Model 30 computer replaced the IBM PC. Figure 1.10 illustrates the major components of an IBM PC computer system. Today, the personal computer is as prevalent in many organizations as was the office typewriter.

FIGURE 1.10.
IBM PC system.

The 1990s

The growth in the distribution of personal computers throughout organizations during the 1980s was linked to a requirement to provide communications capability between these devices. In addition, many personal computer uses required access to corporate mini- and mainframe computers, further increasing requirements for communications between different types of computers.

For the grocery company previously discussed, personal computers were installed in the sales offices in Chicago, Philadelphia, and New York City. The PCs were initially used for a variety of functions ranging from what-if computations using spreadsheets to word processing and the maintenance of small databases of sales and marketing information. Eventually, however, it was recognized that productivity could be increased by providing a capability for various PC users within each office to communicate with one another. Through the installation of an appropriate adapter card in each personal computer (see Figure 1.10), as well as cabling and software, local area networks (LANs) were installed in each sales office. This specialized type of network enabled persons within a building or campus to communicate with one another, share peripheral devices such as laser printers and plotters, and share access to common software programs and database information residing on special types of personal computers known as file servers.

As the grocery company continued to grow, it was recognized that LANs were essentially islands of information isolated from one another. Commencing in the late 1980s and gaining momentum in the 1990s, vendors introduced several internetworking products consisting of software and hardware that enabled diverse LANs to be connected to one another and information to flow between devices connected to one another and between devices connected to different LANs and other computer systems. Taking advantage of this technology, the wholesale grocery company installed devices known as gateways, bridges, and routers.

GATEWAYS

Gateways enabled personal computers on selected LANs to access a corporate mainframe computer. Here the corporate mainframe acted as a central repository for large databases and intensive computing programs that are not suitable for execution on personal computers. For example, database information, including inventory, customer accounts, and historical ordering and pricing information, could require billions of characters of storage, whereas most personal computers are limited to hundreds of millions of characters of storage. Concerning intensive computing applications, the grocery company now used the mainframe for execution of linear programs that optimize delivery schedules based on an analysis of thousands of variables. Although personal computer users can access the linear programming results produced on the mainframe via gateways, the execution of this type of program on a personal computer might require 10 or 20 hours, whereas the execution might take 15 minutes when performed on a mainframe.

BRIDGES

Bridges enable data to be transmitted between two LANs supporting the same transmission protocol, allowing electronic messages, data files, and programs to be sent between users on different networks. A bridge examines the destination address of data flowing on a LAN to determine whether its destination is on that LAN. If it is, the bridge simply functions as a transparent device and allows the data to continue to flow on the LAN to its destination. If the data destination is a different LAN, the bridge then transmits the data via a communications facility to a distant LAN where another bridge functions in a similar manner.

ROUTERS

With a need to add automation to the company's warehouse facilities, also served through the installation of LANs, sales personnel on occasion found it necessary to access information from personal computers connected to warehouse LANs. In fact, the number of LANs installed within the grocery company would have required the establishment of a mesh network with many long-distance lines if only bridges were used. Fortunately, the development of routers, which examine data destination addresses and route data over different circuits based on those addresses, enabled a smaller number of lines to be used for interconnecting many LANs.

Figure 1.11 illustrates in a block diagram format the relationship of bridges, routers, and gateways for internetworking. In this example, a pair of bridges interconnects two sales office LANs, and a router is used to provide a link from one LAN to many warehouse LANs. The gateway provides a mechanism that enables LAN users to access the mainframe computer. In fact, when sophisticated hardware and software are used, it might be possible for a PC user attached to the LAN at the top of Figure 1.11 to be "bridged" to the second LAN and provided, via the gateway, access to the mainframe—a key goal of internetworking. As we move toward the year 2000, it can be reasonably expected that this broad term that defines the connection of diverse equipment and network facilities will represent the method by which organizations integrate their data transmission requirements.

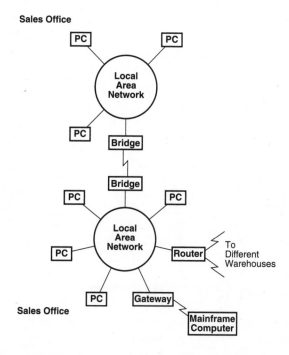

FIGURE 1.11.

Internetworking using bridges, routers, and gateways.

Although the use of LANs by business, government, and academia represents one of the fastest growing areas in the field of data communications, a second rapidly expanding area concerns the use of the personal computer as a multifunctional terminal. In this role, the addition of hardware and software turns the PC into a LAN workstation, a conventional mainframe computer terminal, a fax machine, or another type of communications device. Through the use of modern graphical user interface (GUI) operating systems, such as Microsoft's Windows and IBM's OS/2, you can readily switch from one application to another and, in the case of OS/2, execute two or more applications simultaneously due to the operating system's multitasking capability. For example, under OS/2, you can execute a spreadsheet program while transmitting or receiving a fax.

The key to the capability of the personal computer to function as a multipurpose terminal was the development of specialized microprocessors and integrated circuits. This technology enabled functions that previously required tens to hundreds of individual computer chips to be performed by one or a few chips. This in turn enabled vendors to design adapter cards for insertion into an expansion slot in the system unit of a personal computer, which added the functionality of a standalone device to the PC. Figure 1.12 shows a modem/fax adapter card that enables a personal computer to transmit and receive faxes as well as communicate with other computers, bulletin board systems, and information utilities when used as a data modem.

FIGURE 1.12.

A fax/modem adapter card for insertion into a PC. (Courtesy Practical Peripherals, Inc.)

Changes in the Industries

The hardware and software are not the only things changing. Both the computer industry and the communications industry have changed in ways that would have been unimaginable 20 years ago. The rise of the minicomputer, and later the microprocessor in personal computers, and programmable controllers for equipment, created a situation in which computing power was rather inexpensive. The suppliers of mainframe computers, such as IBM, UNISYS, and Amdahl, were joined by companies such as Texas Instruments, Apple, Radio Shack, and Commodore that had not previously made computers. With many more computers used by many more people to create and use much more data, interest in data communications increased. In communications, the advent of satellites followed by optical-fiber transmission offered the promise of far greater bandwidths (range of usable frequencies), thus, faster data transmission speeds.

The revolution in computing and data transmission was paralleled by an upheaval in the structure of the communications industry. The telephone company's monopoly of almost a century disappeared forever, beginning in the late 1960s and accelerating until the Bell System was broken up in 1984. For the first time, other firms not only could compete with the telephone companies in offering long-distance service, but they also could sell equipment, including data communications devices, to be connected to the telephone network.

These two forces, the advent of the microprocessor-based personal computer and the increase in competition in both the computing and the communications industries, brought about dramatic changes and accelerated technological advances in the communications field. They also brought communications and computing closer together. In the example wholesale grocery company of the 1980s, it is hard to say where communications stops and computing begins. Is the sales person's portable terminal or the manager's personal computer a communications device or a computer? The answer, of course, is that they are both, because they do whatever combination of tasks is required for the job at hand.

By examining current and evolving computer-based applications, we can predict to a fair degree of accuracy future developments in communications. For example, in a LAN environment, many organizations are replacing mainframe computers through the use of client-server applications, a process referred to as downsizing. In addition, these organizations are adding graphical applications in the form of images stored within a database; using multimedia for training employees in which voice, data, and video are merged for instruction; and using digitized voice messages to add verbal information to electronic mail.

Each of these emerging applications has one common feature: a requirement to transmit and store information many orders of magnitudes above conventional text-based applications. Thus, a screen filled with text data is represented by 80×24 or 1920 eight-bit characters, whereas an image on a VGA monitor displayed in a resolution of 640×350 pixels in 256 colors would require 640×350×8/8 bits per byte, or 224,000 characters of storage. This means that the transmission of the previously described image would require more than 100 times the time for the transmission of a screen of text data. Because the patience of persons cannot be expected to grow by a factor of 100 as applications use images and as digitized audio and video are developed, you can reasonably predict the development of new types of communications systems to accommodate emerging computer-based applications.

In fact, this is exactly what is happening in both local and wide-area networking. Concerning LANs, the recent introduction of Fiber Distributed Data Interface (FDDI) enabled organizations to construct LANs that operate at 100 Mbps in comparison to the current popular operating rates of 10 Mbps for Ethernet LANs and 16 Mbps for token-ring LANs. In the wide-area networking environment, which can be defined as the infrastructure that connects geographically separated areas, a new technology referred to as Asynchronous Transfer Mode (ATM) is expected to be widely available by the year 2000. ATM is designed to transport voice, data, and video at operating rates of up to 2.488 Gbps.

● Besides affecting the technological revolution, the breakup of the Bell System changed the way business used and paid for communications.

● The merging of voice, video, and data into computer-based applications requires the transmission of information several orders of magnitudes beyond text-based data, providing the driving force for the development of high-speed communications.

In modern computer-communications systems, we can interconnect equipment of many different sizes and capabilities from various suppliers. One of the purposes of this book is to explain how to interconnect, or interface, these different kinds of equipment so that it all works together in a system.

General Description of a Data Communications System

A data communications system can be described simply in terms of three components: the transmitter (also called the source), the transmission path (usually called the channel, but sometimes called the line), and the receiver (occasionally called the sink). In two-way communications, however, the source and the sink can interchange roles; that is, the same piece of equipment can transmit and receive data simultaneously. Therefore, it is easier to think of a data communications system between point A and point B (see Figure 1.13) in terms of the Universal Seven-Part Data Circuit, which consists of the following parts:

> The most accurate way to separate a data communications system's parts is in terms of the Universal Seven-Part Data Circuit.

1. The data terminal equipment (DTE) at point A.
2. The interface between the DTE and the data circuit-terminating equipment or data communications equipment (DCE) at point A.
3. The DCE at point A.
4. The transmission channel between point A and point B.
5. The DCE at point B.
6. The DCE-DTE interface at point B.
7. The DTE at point B.

In the Seven-Part Data Circuit, the DTE can be a terminal device or computer part; DCE can be a modem if an analog channel is used or a Data Service Unit (DSU) if a digital channel is used.

The function of the various parts of the data communications system, both hardware and software, now can be described more easily. The DTE is the source, the sink, or both in the system. It transmits and/or receives data by utilizing the DCE and data transmission channel. Don't be misled by the name "data terminal equipment"; these could indeed be CRT or Teletype terminals, but they also might be personal computers, printers, front-end processors for mainframe computers, or any other device that can transmit or receive data. The whole purpose of the data communications system is to transmit useful information between point A and point B; the information can be used directly by the DTE, or the DTE can process and display the information for use by human operators.

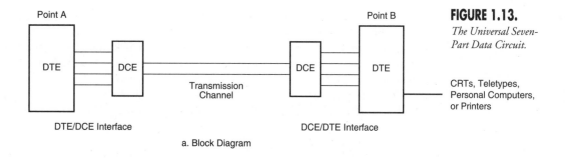

FIGURE 1.13.

The Universal Seven-Part Data Circuit.

a. Block Diagram

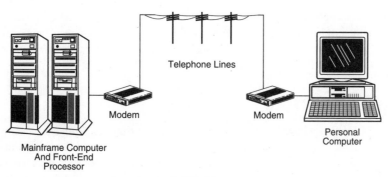

b. Pictorial

Form and Content of Information

The DCE and the transmission channel perform the function of moving the data from point A to point B. In general, they neither know nor care about the content of the information transmitted; it could be stock market quotations, a display for a video game, or recipes for Aunt Martha's fudge.

This brings us to an important point about data communications—the difference between the form and the content of the information transmitted. The form of the information might be English language text represented by code for a telegram; the content might advise you that a rich uncle has just left you a million dollars. Clearly, the ordinary user of data communications is much more interested in the content of the information and really is not concerned about the mechanics of the communication process as long as the information is received correctly. It would be rather disappointing if, in fact, your uncle had left you only $100.00, but because of errors in transmission, the telegram you received stated that you had inherited $1,000,000.00.

●
The data communications system is concerned only with the correct transmission of data, in its coded form, between two points.

The data communications system itself is concerned only with the correct transmission between points A and B of the information given it; the system does not operate on the content of the information at all. This means that where we talk about the "correctness" of the transmitted information in this book, we mean only that the information received has the identical form as the information transmitted. If someone gave a message to the telegraph operator stating that your uncle had left you a million dollars, when he had left you only a hundred dollars, the inaccuracy of that information would probably not be the fault of the telegraph operator or the data communications equipment.

Protocol is the name given to the hardware and software rules and procedures for making sure that any transmission errors are detected. These might be as simple as transmitting an extra bit of information in each character to detect errors, as used with personal computers, or as complex as some systems use for satellite data communications. The satellite system sends extra information not only to allow the receiver to detect transmission errors, but also to correct the errors and to make the receiver appear to be in the room next to the DTE, rather than about 50,000 transmission miles away.

DTE-DCE Interface

The DTE-DCE interface consists of the input/output circuitry in the interface, as well as the cables and connectors that link DCE and DTE.

The DTE-DCE interface has been mentioned several times as though it is something special. It is. The interface consists of the input/output circuitry in the DCE and in the DTE, and the connectors and cables that connect them. In most systems, this interface conforms to the RS-232 standard as published by the Electronics Industries Association (EIA) in the United States. (The RS-232 and other standard DTE-DCE interfaces will be discussed later in this book.) The RS-232 interface, and other serial interfaces that use some of the RS-232 specification but depart from it in some important way, are by far the most commonly used interfaces in data communications. The RS-232 standard specifies the rules by which data is moved across the interface between the DTE and the DCE and, therefore, ultimately from point A to point B. The word *serial* means that the bits cross the interface one at a time in series.

DTEs are a very important part of the process of moving data between points A and B. Not only are basic input and output capabilities important, but today's intelligent electronic terminals can perform many complex software-driven functions whose goal is to ensure better performance and accuracy of the data transfer. We'll look at these functions in several of the chapters to follow.

Similarly, while we devote a great deal of discussion to the interface between the DTE and the DCE, we spend less time on the interface between the DCE and the communications channel. This is because the latter interface is quite simple (either 2 wires or 4 wires, rather than 2 to 24 as in the RS-232 interface) and because there is not a problem with the sequencing of the electrical signals across this interface.

We won't spend a great deal of time discussing the transmission channel either, even though it is obviously crucial to the data communications system. The various electrical characteristics of the channel itself (such as its bandwidth, the relative delay at various frequencies, and other parameters) usually conform to published specifications, and these specifications are often contained in the tariffs published by the telephone companies or other carriers. We have very little control over the transmission channel itself (except to hang up and redial), and the equipment used for data communications is tolerant of a wide range of some of the problems, but unless the data transmission rate is at a very high speed, the communications channel usually does not cause any trouble.

So we really don't care much about how the channel works, as long as a standard voice-grade channel between points A and B is available. A standard voice-grade channel is a telephone line that normally would be used for voice communication, that is, a telephone conversation. Thus, a fundamental problem in data communications is that the transmission of digital data must be accomplished over facilities that were designed for voice (analog) communications. The modem, a type of DCE used to convert digital data to an analog form (such as speed or tones) for transmission over the telephone channel, is described later in this book.

What Have You Learned?

Now that the fundamental secrets of data communications have been revealed, let's briefly review the problem, the terms, and the parts of the system:

1. Problem: To encode information using some kind of standard code, convert it to a form that can be transmitted over the existing telephone network, transmit it between point A and point B without introducing errors, and reverse the process at the receiving end to recover the original information.

2. Channel: A transmission facility connecting points A and B. It's usually a voice-grade telephone channel provided by the telephone company. The channel can be established for the duration of a call (dial up) or from a permanent connection (leased line).

3. Data Terminal Equipment (DTE): At one end, the source of the data to be transmitted; at the other end, the sink that receives the transmitted data.

4. Data Circuit-Terminating (or Communications) Equipment (DCE): The conversion equipment between the DTE and the transmission channel. One type of DCE, the modem, converts the data into tones for transmission over the voice channel.

5. RS-232 Interface: The interface wiring and electronics between the DTE and the DCE equipment at either end of the system. Although there are other important interface standards, this is the most common.

6. Information: The data to be transmitted between A and B. It could be as simple as a command to turn on an indicator light, or as complex as the commands for drawing a multicolor illustration on a CRT display. In either case, the communications system itself is concerned only about moving the data between A and B without any error. The data communications system does not respond to, nor act on, the content of the data transmitted.

7. Internetworking: Hardware and software that enables information to flow between devices connected to different LANs and other computer systems.

8. Protocol: The rules for transmission of information between two points. They include rules for handling such questions as what to do if a transmission error occurs, or how to determine whether the receiver is ready to receive the transmission.

9. LAN and WAN: A local area network (LAN) interconnects devices within a building or campus, whereas a wide-area network (WAN) interconnects devices within a city or in different cities.

Quiz for Chapter 1

1. Which is not an example of data communications?

   a. A Teletype printing news bulletins.

   b. A computer transmitting files to another computer.

   c. An automatic teller machine checking account balances with the bank's computer.

   d. A salesman telephoning orders to the office.

2. Two-state (binary) communications systems are better because:

   a. They can interface directly with the analog telephone network.

   b. The components are simpler, less costly, and more reliable.

   c. People think better in binary.

   d. Interstate calls are less costly.

3. Which is not a positional notation system?

   a. Roman (MCMXXXVII).

   b. Binary (01111110).

   c. Decimal (1492).

   d. Hexadecimal (3A2B).

4. Codes are always:

   a. Eight bits per character.

   b. Either seven or eight bits per character.

   c. Agreed on in advance between sender and receiver.

   d. The same in all modern computers.

5. The Baudot code:

   a. Was invented by the Baudot brothers, Mark and Space.

   b. Requires the escape character to print numbers.

   c. Requires shift characters to provide sufficient combinations.

   d. Was invented by Emile's sister, Brigitte.

6. The standard ASCII:

   a. Is version II of the ASC standard.

   b. Has 128 characters, including 32 control characters.

   c. Is a subset of the 8-bit EBCDIC code.

   d. Is used only in the United States and Canada.

7. Extended ASCII:

   a. Adds extra digits to standard ASCII.

   b. Provides 128 additional character definitions beyond standard ASCII.

   c. Doubles the bit length of each ASCII character.

   d. Provides extra characters that you define.

8. Escape sequences:

   a. Use the ESC character to indicate the start of a special control sequence.

   b. Are used to switch (escape) between ASCII and EBCDIC codes.

   c. Are a popular daydream for inmates.

9. The principal difference between batch processing and online processing is that:

   a. Computer resources are used more efficiently for online processing.

   b. Teleprinters are used for batch processing; CRTs are used for online processing.

   c. Transactions are grouped for batch processing; transactions are processed as needed for online processing.

10. These are the key differences between current and emerging computer-based applications with respect to their communications requirements:

    a. Emerging applications will use graphics that require less transmission time.

    b. The use of voice will reduce the necessity to transmit text.

    c. Emerging applications will require additional data storage, which will result in additional transmission time.

    d. The integration of voice, video, and data will reduce transmission time.

11. DCE and DTE:

    a. Mean "digital communications equipment" and "digital termination and equipment."

    b. Are connected by either two or four wires.

    c. Refer to the modem and the computer or terminal, respectively.

12. The correctness and accuracy of the transmitted message content is:

    a. Verified by the modem.

    b. Determined by the sender and receiver, not by the communications system.

    c. Ensured by use of digital techniques.

Terminal Devices

About This Chapter

Having defined data communications in an overall sense, we now begin describing the various equipment and software that make up the system. We'll start with the part of the system that is most visible to the user—the terminal. Terminals are one of the most dynamic areas of the computer industry; they are associated with convenience, speed, and glamour. The great majority of data terminals used through the early- to mid-1980s fell into two categories: teleprinter terminals and CRT terminals. Growing additions to the latter category are small business computers and personal computers used as terminals. In fact, by the early 1990s, more personal computers were used as terminals than teleprinters and CRT terminals combined. We'll discuss both the older teleprinter terminals and the newer CRTs as well as the components of a personal computer that enable this device to function as a multipurpose communications terminal.

Teleprinters

The device that was invented to replace the Morse telegrapher was called the teleprinter. It was actually a form of specialized telegraph that used the five-bit character code. An early teleprinter is shown in Figure 2.1. The largest manufacturer of teleprinters in the United States was the Teletype Corporation, and thus the word *Teletype* has been commonly used to refer to any teletypewriter or teleprinter. This usage is improper, however, because Teletype is a trademark of Teletype Corporation.

FIGURE 2.1.

An early teleprinter.

The teleprinter, the next step in data communications after the Morse telegrapher, is a low-speed printer that has a serial communications interface.

A teleprinter can be defined as any device that combines a low-speed printer with a serial communications interface. Although a keyboard is an important component of most teleprinters, it is not required to fit this definition (which is used in the commercial marketplace). Thus, the common line printer qualifies if it has a serial interface.

Teleprinter Communications

Teleprinters use start-stop asynchronous transmission, which is the most widely used method of data communications for a serial interface. It is the simplest technique, but it's also the least efficient (the price paid for simplicity).

Teleprinters transmit at a speed much lower than the capacity of a telephone voice grade line. Common teleprinter speeds in North America are 75 and 110 bits per second (bps). Common speeds elsewhere in the world are 100 and 200 bps. The international teleprinter (telex) network and many European lines operate at 50 bps. Teleprinter signals are formed simply by switching an electrical current on and off or by reversing its direction of flow. The current is either 20 or 60 milliamperes, and the equipment is called current-loop equipment. (Most teleprinters today use RS-232 as the external interface, but current-loop circuitry still can be used internally.) The on and off pulses form a code that is interpreted by the receiving device. Single-current teleprinter signaling, also known as neutral or unipolar signaling, is common in the United States. Double-current signaling, also called polar or bipolar signaling, is more common in Europe. We'll discuss current-loop signaling more in Chapter 4, "Asynchronous Modems and Interfaces."

● Teleprinters transmit characters using a simple but slow asynchronous transmission method that either reverses current flow or turns it on and off.

Teleprinter Terminals

Two types of teleprinters are available: those with typewriter-style keyboards (called keyboard send-receive, or KSR), and those without keyboards (called receive-only, or RO). The typical teleprinter is capable of printing from 10 to 30 characters per second (cps) or from 100 to 300 words per minute (wpm), which is much faster than most typists. However, because much of the terminal's time might be devoted to printing output from a computer rather than entering data, it is usually desirable to have the fastest possible printing mechanism. Thus, teleprinters are available with printing speeds of up to 120 cps.

● The speed of the teleprinter's printing mechanism is very important in applications in which most of its time will be spent in receiving and printing incoming data.

In the usual operation of a teleprinter, a user enters inputs to the computer via the keyboard. The inputs are transmitted back (in what's called an echo) from the computer character-by-character to the printer and printed to verify receipt. Output originating in the computer or another source is printed as it is received. Thus, a "hard copy" of both the inputs and the outputs is available. Although many teleprinters are used in this way, some are strictly online printing devices and thus don't require a keyboard.

The classic and perhaps best application for teleprinter terminals is in interactive sessions with a computer, such as timesharing or bulletin boards. Here the comparative slowness of the teleprinter is not restrictive, and the printed copy is often quite useful. The slow speed of operation is not as noticeable as in other applications because much of the operator's time is spent in thinking, rather than in waiting for output. Another application for which teleprinters were popularly used during the 1960s through 1970s was in regional weather information networks. In this type of network, weather forecasts and related information were broadcast from a central computer to teleprinters connected to the computer via the installation of leased lines. Because the transmission of information was always from the computer to the teleprinter and no response was required nor sought, this was one of the primary applications for the use of RO teleprinters.

More modern teleprinters, such as the one illustrated in Figure 2.2, use various printing techniques and operate at many print speeds. They provide features such as programmable format control, adjustable forms control, upper- and lowercase printing, interchangeable character styles (fonts), bidirectional printing and paper feeding, selectable character and line spacing, status indicators, portability, and additional keys such as a numeric keypad.

FIGURE 2.2.

TI 820 KSR teleprinter.

Teleprinters that use microprocessors can be programmed for various applications. This has reduced their cost and extended the machine's life.

Manufacturers have incorporated the microprocessor into teleprinters to reduce design, development, and production costs while providing a variety of applications that can be implemented by either the vendor or the user. The microprocessor delays the time when a particular teleprinter design will become obsolete because future applications can be accommodated by reprogramming the microprocessor to perform other jobs. From the user's point of view, microprocessor technology also offers the major advantage of lower cost because the manufacturer's cost savings resulting from using microprocessors are passed on to the customer.

Compared to total terminal sales, few new teleprinter units are sold outside of the traditional record services markets (telex, twx, and private teleprinter network). Even most of these are specialized. An example is the portable printing terminal often used by a traveling businessperson whose needs are satisfied by a small, lightweight (three to eight pounds), hand-carried terminal. Such terminals are available from Texas Instruments and other vendors.

The rapid decrease in the price of portable computers means that they now can be used for applications that previously were reserved for portable terminals. Not only can portable personal computers communicate with large corporate computers, but these portables also enable the traveling businessperson to compose memorandums and letters and to analyze business decisions with spreadsheet programs. Although portable terminals communicating with corporate computers could perform such functions, the personal computer can complete these tasks in a local mode of operation, which eliminates many long-distance communication sessions.

Although many vendors call their personal computers portable, the word *transportable* might be more appropriate in certain cases. Personal computers that weigh between 20 and 30 pounds are best categorized as transportable, whereas truly lightweight (weighing under 12 pounds) personal computers can be considered portable, especially when you carry them through an airport.

Fortunately for the executive who travels, two new types of personal computers became available in the late 1980s: laptops and palmtops. Laptops, so named because they could literally be placed on a person's lap, normally weigh under 12 pounds, and many can fit into an attache case. Palmtops, so named because they can be lifted by closing one's hand around the device, usually weigh under 2 pounds. Both laptop and palmtop computers can perform most, if not all, computing functions associated with conventional personal computers while providing a high level of portability.

Both laptops and palmtops do have some drawbacks. The chief drawbacks of these portable computers include a compressed keyboard in which multiple key depressions might be required to generate some of the key functions for normal keyboards, and poor screen readability. The latter problem is now mainly associated with palmtops.

Figure 2.3 illustrates the interface of a Hewlett-Packard HP95XL palmtop computer to a U.S. Robotics Worldport fax/data modem. The HP95XL was one of the first palmtop computers to be sold. It included a copy of Lotus Development Corporation's popular 1-2-3 electronic spreadsheet program built into read-only memory (ROM). The Worldport fax/data modem enables an HP95XL user to transmit and receive text and fax messages at data rates up to 14,400 bits per second. By examining the size of the HP95XL, the modem, and the hands of the person holding both devices, you will note that the HP95XL and the Worldport modems both can easily fit into the palm of one's hand. Hence, both the computer and the modem are referred to as palmtop devices.

In the early 1990s, a new type of computer became available that has the potential to revolutionize the method by which we transmit and receive information. This device is commonly referred to as the Personal Digital Assistant, or PDA. Although similar in size to palmtops, PDAs are being marketed with integrated cellular communications capability to include data and fax modems designed to transmit and receive information via a cellular telephone connection. When acquired with this capability, the PDA enables a user to bypass the necessity to connect his device to a telephone to communicate. This can be a major benefit for travelers, because connecting a portable computer to a telephone-line jack can be difficult to impossible in many hotels, motels, and airports.

FIGURE 2.3.

*HP95XL palmtop
computer connected
to U.S. Robotics
Worldport palmtop
fax/data modem.
(Courtesy of U.S.
Robotics)*

Teleprinters Versus CRT Terminals

● A teleprinter's
disadvantages are
slower speed, little
or no variability in
format, and limited
reliability due to
mechanical wear.

The drawbacks to teleprinters involve speed, formatting, and reliability. Teleprinters are far slower in operation than CRT terminals; even their highest print speed doesn't compare to the 300 or 1200 characters per second on the CRT. Because teleprinters are designed primarily for message communications, they do not provide sophisticated capabilities for data editing or formatting. It is quite difficult to create a form on a teleprinter, and of course such attributes as blinking, highlighting, and similar enhancements that are available on a CRT terminal are impossible on a teleprinter. Although teleprinters are quite reliable, they nevertheless are electromechanical devices that are subject to wear and misalignment. CRT terminals, on the other hand, generally have higher reliability because of far fewer parts, most of which do not move.

Serial Printers

● Teleprinter terminal
serial printers,
either impact or
nonimpact, print
one character at a
time sequentially.

Teleprinter terminals use serial (or character) printers, so named because they print one character at a time. Such printers can be classified into two categories: impact printers, which mechanically strike the paper to produce a printed image, and nonimpact printers, which produce an image by some other means. Impact printers are further divided into two subcategories: those that produce a fully formed character, in which the character is created by impact from a single piece of type, and dot-matrix printers, in which the character image on the paper is formed by a matrix of dots. Nonimpact teleprinters form characters by the dot-matrix method only, using an electrothermal, an ink-jet, or a laser printing method.

IMPACT PRINTERS

Impact printing mechanisms include replaceable type-ball elements (as used on the IBM Selectric typewriters), daisy wheels (a flat disk with petal-like projections for the character elements), elements shaped like a cup with finger-like projections, moving type belts with the characters engraved on the belt, a rotating cylinder containing the characters, and a type block with characters embedded in the block. All of these mechanisms share the same advantages of fully formed characters in almost any style and shape, and the capability to make "carbon" copies. They also share the same disadvantages of low speed and mechanical complexity. No matter how the character is mounted or engraved on the type element, it must be positioned in front of the platen and then struck against an inked ribbon and paper to produce an image. This process limits the speed of the printer to a maximum of 120 cps (but it's usually much lower), and it creates a large amount of noise in the process.

● Impact printers are those that use mechanical action to strike a ribbon against the paper to print the desired character, either completely formed or in a dot matrix.

This speed limitation was an incentive for printer manufacturers to seek a different approach that would extend the upper limit of printing speed for serial impact printers. Their search led to the development of the dot-matrix printer. Dot-matrix printers are a compromise (and often a successful one) between decreased character quality and substantially higher print speeds of 180 cps or more. The printed image is formed from a rectangular matrix of dots, which was initially nine dots high by seven dots wide. Printing is performed by moving a print head containing a column of nine pins across the paper and selectively actuating the pins at seven successive intervals to form each character. Developments in dot-matrix printer technology increased the number of pins that could be placed on the print head, resulting in the availability of 18- and 24-pin print-head printers. Dot-matrix printers with these high-density print heads result in the printing of characters whose pin dots overlap to produce a nearly solid character format. This type of printing, which provides the appearance of an impact printer output, is referred to as near letter quality. Although dot-matrix printers contain comparatively few moving parts, they are subject to much wear and heat within the print head as a result of the succession of pin movements required to create each character.

Dot-matrix teleprinters are typically less expensive than similarly featured fully formed character teleprinters. With the improved print quality that's now available with high-resolution dot-matrix printing, most teleprinter users are satisfied with dot-matrix printers.

Another development that has improved speed in newer teleprinters is the bidirectional print head with logic-seeking control. The print head can print while moving in either direction (left to right or right to left). The logic-seeking control circuitry determines the shortest horizontal distance to move the print head to print the next line. Thus, on full pages of text, one line is printed left to right, the next is printed right to left, and so forth. This feature, available on both fully formed character printers and dot-matrix printers, eliminates the time required for a full carriage return to the left side for every line.

NONIMPACT PRINTERS

Nonimpact printers use electrothermal, ink-jet, or laser printing techniques. They are more reliable, quieter, and faster than impact printers.

The nonimpact types of teleprinters employ various electronic, optical, and chemical techniques to produce printed images. All nonimpact teleprinters currently on the market use dot-matrix character formation. Some of the printing techniques have been developed from xerography and facsimile communications techniques. Others were specifically developed for use in high-speed printing applications in which print speeds of more than 2000 lines (that's *lines,* not *characters*) per minute are not uncommon. Still others were designed to meet a specific goal, such as quiet operation.

The electrothermal printing technique is one nonimpact method. The print head applies heat through the matrix pins to chemically coated paper. The heat causes a chemical reaction, which produces a matrix of colored dots that forms the character. It is quiet and efficient, but some people object to having to supply special paper.

The ink-jet technique uses a stream of electrically charged ink droplets sprayed onto ordinary paper to produce the characters as shown in Figure 2.4. Dot placement is accomplished by electrostatic deflection plates that control the direction of the charged ink droplets, in much the same manner as electron beam position is controlled within a cathode ray tube. By electronic control of switching between reservoirs of different colored ink, instant color changes can be made as the printer operates. Ink-jet printers were originally very expensive, but prices have been reduced substantially in the past few years.

FIGURE 2.4.

Basic ink-jet printing technique.

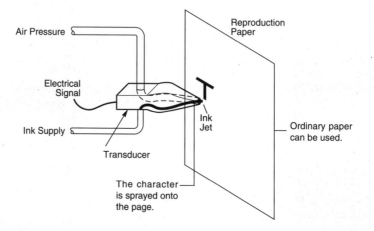

Air Pressure

Reproduction Paper

Electrical Signal

Ink Supply

Ink Jet

Ordinary paper can be used.

Transducer

The character is sprayed onto the page.

Laser printers create images of entire pages by "recording" on a rotating drum with a laser beam and imparting these images to paper. The laser beam focuses on a minute spot that continually scans along the length of the light-sensitive-coated drum. Turning the scanning beam off and on creates the pattern that is transferred to paper. The spot (or dot) resolution is as high as 600 by 600 per square inch.

Reliability of nonimpact printers is high compared to that of impact printers because they have few mechanical parts. Their incapability to produce more than one copy at a time (no carbon copies) might sometimes be a disadvantage, but their rapid, quiet, and reliable operation is certainly an advantage.

CRT Terminals

The cathode ray tube (CRT) terminal, also called a video display terminal (VDT), is a common interface between people and computers. The CRT terminal was originally developed as an alternative to teleprinter terminals. Its introduction in 1965 revolutionized the data communications environment, in which the teleprinter had been the only interface device. Although many companies entered the marketplace, prices remained high due to low-volume production and the cost (price and assembly labor) of discrete components. The advent of the integrated circuit, followed by large-scale integration, brought prices down, although they were still out of reach of the ordinary individual. Then came the microprocessor, which replaced much of the integrated circuit logic and drove prices still lower. The result is high-quality, high-performance, and relatively low-cost CRT terminals that even the hobbyist can afford. A CRT terminal designed for businesses is shown in Figure 2.5.

In many applications, the CRT terminal has replaced the teleprinter terminal as the interface between computers and people.

FIGURE 2.5.
TI 931 CRT terminal.

ASCII Terminals

A CRT terminal that can operate without a separate controller and can transmit and receive asynchronous data using the ASCII code is called an ASCII terminal.

In the computer industry, the term *ASCII display terminal* usually refers to a CRT terminal that operates without a separate controller, uses the ASCII code, and transmits and receives asynchronous data. This term originated with CRT terminals (the glass Teletype) designed to replace Teletype ASR 33/35 teleprinter terminals, and ASCII terminals are still described as being TTY- or Teletype compatible. ASCII terminals are available in a wide range, from low-end dumb units that do little more than emulate a teleprinter (or that emulate another CRT terminal, such as the ADM-3, which emulates a teleprinter), up to 132-column split-screen editing terminals with several pages of electronic memory storage.

CRT terminals have three capabilities in common:

- A keyboard that can generate a full alphanumeric character code set.
- A CRT monitor that can display the characters of that code set.
- The capability to send and receive data via communications lines to a remote host computer.

CRT terminals can be classed in one of three categories: dumb terminals, smart terminals, and user-programmable terminals.

CRT terminals fall into one of three categories: dumb, smart, and user-programmable. Of course, there is some overlap between categories, but we'll define them as shown here:

- Dumb terminals are Teletype-compatible and offer a limited number of functions—perhaps none beyond keyboarding and display. They are the lowest cost, but often the difference in price between them and the smart terminals is small compared to the difference in performance and features.
- Smart terminals offer extended functions, such as editing and formatted data entry. The user might be able to tailor the terminal to fit the application through limited programming, such as format creation, parameter definition, or input checking.
- User-programmable (or intelligent) terminals feature software support. The manufacturer provides an operating system (an assembler, a compiler, or an interpretive programming language), subroutines (I/O utilities; one or more protocol emulators), and one or two application programs, such as data entry and text editing. They provide some form of program storage and more memory for text.

DUMB VERSUS SMART TERMINALS

The description of the capabilities of teleprinters also describes the capability of the dumb CRT terminals except for print speed. These terminals essentially consist of a CRT, video (display), memory, and interface electronics. Few truly dumb terminals are still manufactured; virtually all CRT terminals currently manufactured are microprocessor controlled, making them smart terminals according to our definition. The microprocessor chips cost only a few dollars, which is less than the cost of the logic they replace.

The microprocessor programs (firmware) reside in read-only memory (ROM) or programmable ROM (PROM). ROM-resident programs control those features that are "permanent," whereas PROM-resident programs are typically produced in smaller quantities and implement customized or modifiable features. Either type can be replaced by a different type with a different program by simply removing the old chip and putting in a new one, although this feature is more talked about than actually used. In addition to controlling basic terminal functions, the microprocessor can provide protocol emulation, define the character code sets to be generated by the keyboard, implement special features, set control parameters, and so forth. Moreover, the microprocessor delays obsolescence, because future needs can be implemented via reprogramming.

In addition to the capability to simply display alphabetic and numeric characters, microprocessor control provides the capability to highlight characters by means of underscoring, reverse video, blinking, differing levels of brightness, and combinations of these attributes. One of the most impressive capabilities of these terminals is the capability to display a predefined form and let the operator "fill in the blanks" while checking the entries as they are made.

Many CRT terminals can display double-size characters, and most have a graphics character set for creating forms and formats. Some also support business graphics; for example, bar, column, and pie charts to graphically show sales, income and expense, inventory levels, and so forth. Interactive or engineering graphics, on the other hand, is a highly specialized area usually requiring a completely different, high-resolution graphics terminal.

> Microprocessor control has given CRT smart terminals the flexibility and capabilities to perform many operations beyond simple display and keyboarding.

USER-PROGRAMMABLE TERMINALS VERSUS PERSONAL COMPUTERS

Taken separately, the words *programmable* and *terminal* are precisely definable. But when combined to describe one class of equipment, their meanings become vague and difficult to define with precision. In 1979, a popular periodical defined a user-programmable terminal as a terminal that permits local file updating and accommodates user-written applications programs. At that time, this definition stirred up quite a bit of controversy because such a terminal would have to provide for the following features in addition to the basic terminal functions:

● The availability of, and the support and documentation of, at least one general-purpose programming language for development of programs by customer personnel.

● Entry of programs via the terminal keyboard.

> Because of the need for increased requirements, the emphasis has shifted to using microcomputers for terminal functions.

● The capability to access and retrieve programs stored in the host computer memory, and the capability to execute (use) those programs at the terminal.

Much of the value of user-programmable terminals is their off-line processing capability provided by the previously listed items. All user-programming terminals have built-in main memory that the user can employ to store and execute programs, but the capacity varies from as little as 1 kilobyte (usually written as 1K), which accommodates only a very small program, to as much as 512K (which accommodates a large program and much data). Most, although not all, user-programmable terminals also provide for local mass storage using floppy, hard, or cartridge disks, or cassette or cartridge magnetic tape.

With disks, tapes, memory, an operating system, and a programming language, the user-programmable terminal sounds a lot like a personal or professional computer, doesn't it? This is the revolution in the terminal market. Dumb terminals and low-end smart terminals are rapidly being squeezed aside by personal and professional computers and running terminal programs, which relegates terminals to specialized tasks. Many office workers now have a personal or professional computer on their desks, which can be either used stand-alone as a computer connected to a local area network or placed online to the large host computer. Files can be up- and down-loaded and processed wherever it makes the most sense to do so. All because of data communications and the microprocessor!

EMULATION

When the personal computer operates a communications program that enables the computer to duplicate the attributes of a terminal, the software is known as a terminal emulator program. Such programs permit the personal computer to communicate with mainframe application programs developed to work with predefined types of terminals.

Depending on the terminal emulation software marketed for the personal computer, you might be able to replace several types of terminals with one computer. For an example, consider the organization that has both Hewlett-Packard (HP) and Digital Equipment Corporation (DEC) mainframe computers. With HP 2645 and DEC VT100 terminal emulation software, one can use a personal computer to emulate common Hewlett-Packard and Digital Equipment Corporation terminal devices and thereby get full screen access to two different computer systems that are designed to operate with two specific types of terminals.

Non-ASCII Terminals

This section describes CRT terminals that do not fit the ASCII label, together with some specialized terminals that use other displays. Of these, the most important are the batch or cluster type.

BATCH TERMINALS

Communications between a terminal and its computer tends to fall into two basic categories, interactive and batch, which are distinguished by the types of functions to be performed. Terminals and software designed for interactive communications between the terminal and the host support conversational inquiry/response, interactive data entry, and other such applications. Batch communications, on the other hand, supports either remote job entry or remote batch data communications. Remote job entry (RJE), in which the terminal acts as a remote console for the central computer, allows local users to load and execute applications programs. For remote batch data communications, the terminal acts as a remote input/output device for an application program being performed in the host.

The reasons for these distinctions are efficiency and accuracy. An interactive terminal designed to communicate in asynchronous character-by-character mode is not very efficient for transmitting large blocks of data as required in the batch mode, nor is the error checking (if any) adequate to ensure correct transmission. On the other hand, it would be wasteful to tie up a complete remote batch terminal just to enable one user to use the keyboard to ask questions about particular data stored in the host computer with the answers sent back by the computer.

Although batch terminals were commonly used to access a remote computer during the 1960s and 1970s, the personal computer also affected the use of this type of terminal device. The widespread use of personal computers during the 1980s resulted in the development of hardware and software that enables many types of personal computers to function as remote job entry type terminals.

CLUSTERED TERMINALS

When a remote location generates a large amount of data via key entry, the use of a clustered system might be indicated. This is typical in large-scale data processing installations where it is common practice to control many peripheral units, such as CRT terminals and key-to-disk data input devices, at one location with a single control unit. Data entered through the keyboard devices are stored in a buffer for transmission or transfer to magnetic tape or disk. Then the output of many operators is transmitted in one block to the main computer at much higher speed than that used by teleprinters and ASCII CRT terminals. In addition to the key entry devices, storage, and controller, the cluster might include printers and mass storage. This type of architecture is fundamental to modern data processing. A widely used example is the IBM 3270 series.

●
Two different methods of terminal-computer communications, interactive and batch, effectively mesh user needs with the communications techniques.

●
Clustered terminals are generally used in remote, high-volume key-entry locations to facilitate the transfer of large quantities of data to a main computer.

IBM 3270 SERIES

The IBM 3270 is not a terminal per se but is a designation for a family of devices designed for use in clusters. The 3270 series has had a strong impact on the synchronous terminal market since its introduction in 1971. The first generation, which was discontinued in 1982, included the 3271/3272 control units, 3275 display station, 3277 display, and 3284/ 3286/3288 printers. In 1977, the product line was expanded and updated with the 3274 control unit, 3276 control/display, 3278 display, and 3287/3289 printers. In 1979, color displays and printers were added. In 1983, IBM made some long-awaited changes and enhancements to the 3270 product line. Added were the 3178 display station, a new 3274 control unit, the 3290 information panel (a gas plasma display), and the 3299 terminal multiplexer.

In 1986, a few years after the introduction of the new 3274, IBM announced its 3174 control unit. The device in some respects is similar to a personal computer because it can be customized through the addition of special adapter cards. Three of the key functions that can be added to a 3174 control unit are asynchronous ASCII terminal support in which the control unit performs protocol conversion and Ethernet and token-ring interfaces. The latter two interfaces permit devices on an Ethernet or token-ring LAN to access a mainframe via the 3174, which then functions as a gateway.

The 3299 multiplexer is normally used to reduce the amount of cable required to connect terminals to a control unit when the distance between the location of the terminals and the control unit exceeds a few hundred feet. Up to eight terminals can be connected to a 3299, with only one cable required to connect the 3299 to a control unit.

Newer terminals in the 3270 series include the 3179 color display station, the 3279G color graphics display station, the 3180 and 3191 monochrome display stations, and the 3192 and 3194 color display stations. The latter two are most notable for their design, which minimizes the desk space that they require compared to earlier terminals in the 3270 series.

In the area of personal computer connectivity to the 3270 series, IBM has introduced many products. The more significant products include a new control unit, as well as adapter cards that are installed into a system expansion slot of a computer in the IBM PC and PS/2 series. The adapter card permits direct connection of the personal computer to a control unit, which enables the PC to function as a 3270 terminal. With this configuration, personal computer users also can transfer files and do local processing, both of which are beyond the capability of conventional 3270 terminals. As previously mentioned, in 1986, IBM introduced the 3174 control unit, which features an optional Ethernet or token-ring gateway. This feature permits one member of the IBM PC series to be cabled to the 3174 as a gateway device on an Ethernet or token-ring local area network. Other personal computers are then connected to the gateway personal computer, enabling many personal computers on the network to get access via one personal computer.

In providing the PC interface, IBM finds itself in an interesting quandary. The 3270 line has been quite profitable over the years; now it faces competition from personal computers, especially those manufactured by IBM! As personal computing becomes the rule rather than the exception in most major corporations, the terminal industry is on the verge of the biggest change since the introduction of the CRT.

The many other firms that offer 3270-compatible products must likewise compete with personal computers. To remain competitive, these companies have traditionally offered some combination of lower prices, improved price performance, and shorter delivery times to penetrate the IBM "plug compatible" market. In addition to the 3270-compatible vendors, some ASCII terminal manufacturers have invaded the 3270 market through protocol conversion. On a 3270 network, synchronous terminals can be replaced with asynchronous terminals coupled with "black boxes" that convert the asynchronous data to synchronous form with the proper headers, check bits, and so forth. These devices allow an ASCII terminal to support the functional characteristics of the 3270 terminal. The advantage of this strategy is that ASCII terminals are considerably less expensive than their 3270 counterparts.

> ● The IBM 3270 family of clustered synchronous terminals is receiving strong competition from microcomputers.

Other Types of Terminals

Most terminals manufactured today employ a keyboard and a CRT. The popularity of this combination stems from its flexibility, high character capacity, and relatively low cost. Specialized needs, however, have led to the development of a broad range of other terminals, which include optical bar code readers, voice response units, portable terminals, and the ordinary tone dialing telephone. In addition, such things as supermarket cash registers, portable communicating terminals for inventory management, and a host of other types of equipment now employ data communications. By the DTE/DCE definition, all of these are terminals.

Parts of a Terminal

Having discussed the various types of terminals, let's now discuss the components of a typical CRT terminal. The ordinary user is concerned only with the components with which he or she interacts—the keyboard and the display. But first, let's talk about one of the current buzz words in the terminal business: ergonomics.

Ergonomics

ANSI standards define ergonomics as "a multidisciplinary activity dealing with the interactions between man and his total working environment, plus such traditional environmental aspects as atmosphere, heat, light, and sound, as well as the tools and equipment of the workplace."

Terminal manufacturers have become increasingly aware of the need to consider ergonomics in the design of their equipment. The trend toward making CRT terminals more "operator friendly" began in Europe, and most people agree that European manufacturers still lead in this area. Recent developments in terminals, such as sloped keyboards and green or amber displays, have come about because of ergonomic considerations.

Keyboards

Most display terminals now have keyboards that are detached or detachable. Most of these are connected to the console via a coiled cable, usually three to six feet long, which enables the operator to place the keyboard in a comfortable position while using the terminal. A more recent development is the "light-link" or cordless keyboard, in which an infrared transmitter/receiver replaces the cable to allow even more freedom of movement.

Another design factor is the slope and thickness of the keyboard. Most keyboards today are either sloped or stepped, with the angle being 5 to 15 degrees. Most recent terminals have sculptured key caps rather than flat key caps, which speeds data entry and improves operator comfort. Audible keyboard feedback might be provided by a beep or key click from a speaker, and tactile feedback might be provided by a unique "feel" when the stroke is registered. Like most other ergonomic considerations, the previous features are not, in themselves, the most important criteria for choosing one terminal over another; what they do indicate is the manufacturer's commitment to providing equipment that is up-to-date and easy to use.

KEYBOARD LAYOUT

Although terminal keyboards have been improved for user comfort and utility (ergonomics), little has been done to improve and standardize the keyboard layout.

The layout of the keyboard is a primary concern of ergonomics. The de facto standard typewriter key layout is that of the IBM Selectric typewriter illustrated in Figure 2.6. A keyboard that has this arrangement of the alphabetic keys is called a QWERTY (pronounced kwer-t) keyboard because these are the first six letters of the top row of alphabetic keys. The QWERTY is far from the best layout. In fact, the QWERTY keyboard layout was designed for early mechanical typewriters to arrange the key hammers to reduce key hang-ups. This arrangement also slowed the typist so that he or she could not key faster than the early typewriters could operate! In the 1890s, there were more than a hundred different typewriter keyboards because almost every company that made a typewriter used a different keyboard. These keyboard types included the Crandall (ZPRCHMI), the American (CJPFUBL), the Hall (KBFGNIA), and the Morris (XVGWSLZ).

Various attempts have been made to improve keyboard layout. Some had the letters of frequently used words close together. One proposed by Dr. August Dvorak put the five vowels under one hand and the five most common consonants under the other hand. There were circular keyboards, semicircular keyboards, keyboards with six rows, and keyboards with one long row. The idea of a shift key didn't come along until 1875; before that, upper- and lowercase letters were on different keys.

FIGURE 2.6.
IBM Selectric typewriter keyboard layout.

Despite numerous attempts to improve keyboard layouts, the QWERTY keyboard remains the industry standard. In fact, a comparison of the IBM Selectric typewriter keyboard, a product introduced in the 1950s and illustrated in Figure 2.6, with the keyboard of the IBM PC Convertible, a product introduced in the 1980s and illustrated in Figure 2.7, indicates the high degree of similarity between keyboard layouts. The basic QWERTY keyboard structure remains the same some 30 years later, with keyboard changes related to the incorporation of computer-operation-related keys on the PC Convertible keyboard. Those keys include the Alt, Ctrl, cursor position, function, Print Screen, and other specialized keys. Today, the primary difference between personal computer keyboards relates to the position of the function keys (across the top of the keyboard or located in two columns on the left), the inclusion or absence of a numeric keypad, and the placement of cursor-positioning keys.

PROGRAMMABLE KEYBOARDS

You might be thinking that the operator has no choice but to adapt because the keyboard is built-in and the key arrangement is fixed. Ten years ago that was true, but now it's not always true. Alternative keyboard arrangements (including the Dvorak) are available from some manufacturers, either as standard equipment or as add-on devices for several

●

The capability to program the keyboard provides the opportunity to rearrange the layout or key functions to suit personal taste.

FIGURE 2.7.

IBM PC Convertible portable computer keyboard layout. (Courtesy of IBM Corporation)

terminals and computers. More important, many keyboards are programmable. The processor in the terminal considers each key depression simply as a contact closure in a matrix of contacts. The matrix location represented by that row and column is used by the processor to look up the character in the corresponding location in a table in memory. Thus, the keyboard layout can be changed by simply reprogramming the table; that is, the C key could be defined in the table so that a *?* is printed rather than a *C*. This suggests that the terminal of the future might have several keyboards that can be changed by plugging in the new one and telling the program which table to use.

NUMERIC KEYPADS

Most terminals have some form of numeric keypad with the numerals 0 through 9 grouped like those on a 10-key adding machine to provide faster entry of numeric data. Other keys such as +, −, and . also might be included. The numeric keypad might be entirely separate from the main keyboard, or it might be implemented through an alternative definition of alphabetic keys (usually the "IOP" and "KL;" and "M,." groups). Using the main keyboard's number keys to enter numbers requires the use of both hands. Thus, number entry is faster with a numeric keypad because all the numerals are under the fingers of the right hand.

OTHER KEYS

In addition to the alphabetic and numeric keys, terminal keyboards offer various special keys that are unique to computer input. Unfortunately, there is no standard arrangement of these keys. These keys might include the Ctrl (control) key (which allows input of some or all of the ASCII control characters), Tab (usually programmable), Esc, arrow keys (which control cursor movement), and programmable F (function) keys.

For example, on the Wyse WY-50 terminal, the Line Delete key sends ESC R. Some keys send different codes in the shifted and unshifted positions. Thus, the unshifted Page key means scroll one page forward, and the shifted Page key means scroll one page backward. The eight function keys are capable of producing 16 code sequences when used with the Shift key. When power to the terminal is turned on, these keys are set to Ctrl+A@ through Ctrl+AO, but they can be changed by the computer program, which sends the terminal a series of escape sequences. For example, the sequence Esc z A DIR B: CR Del will reprogram the F2 key to send DIR B: followed by a carriage return. Each function key can be programmed with up to eight characters. Like most modern terminals, the WY-50 has the capability to display function key labels on the bottom line of the CRT screen.

Those users who think, "The more keys the merrier" should be very merry indeed because many terminals now have more than 100 keys. However, the keys sometimes are not laid out in the most useful way. For example, the cursor arrow keys might be in a row, rather than in a diamond pattern in which their direction can be felt. These additional keys might be packed close around the regular keyboard or arranged in logical groups and slightly separated from the main keyboard. When keys have unusual or unexpected placement, the operator is likely to press them by mistake. The result can be devastating.

● Special keys provide access to functions unique to computer input. No uniformity exists as to the positioning of these many keys on the keyboard.

OTHER INPUT DEVICES

Alternatives to keyboard input, which can make entry of specialized data easier, include light pens, touch-sensitive screens, graphic tablets, a "mouse" (a cursor-positioning device), and even speech input. Proponents of all of these devices, and more, suggest that they will eventually replace the keyboard for most input. Don't bet on it. Buy the most comfortable, best designed, easiest-to-use keyboard that you can find; it and the display are your window into the computer. The other devices can be quite useful (especially the mouse), but most input probably will be through the keyboard for a long time to come.

Display

There has been more discussion recently about CRT displays than about any other part of the terminal. Some researchers have noted eyestrain, headaches, dizziness, back pains, nausea, and nervous symptoms in workers whose jobs require that they operate CRT terminals for long periods. Eyestrain and fatigue are considerations that must be dealt with when designing a CRT display screen. Most CRTs are etched or contain a bonded faceplate to reduce glare; tilt and swivel adjustments are also popular for the same reason. The latter features also enable the operator to place the screen at the most comfortable viewing angle. The phosphor color and character size are important too. White, green, or amber phosphors are generally used in the United States, with green probably being the most popular.

The display provides the visualization of the terminal inputs and outputs. Most use dot-matrix character formation with 24 text lines having 80 characters per line.

Most display terminals use the dot-matrix technique to form characters. The more dots that are contained in the character cell, the better defined the character will appear on-screen. For years, 5 by 7 dot characters were standard, but today 7 by 7 and 7 by 9 as well as 9 by 11 dot characters are more common. Some manufacturers use high screen-refresh rates and noninterlaced scanning to reduce image flicker and improve legibility. The size of the characters generated depends on the size of the screen and the display format used. Characters are larger on 15-inch screens than on 12-inch screens; likewise, characters are larger in an 80-character-per-line format than in a 132-character-per-line format. Display enhancements such as double-height and double-width characters can make characters larger, but these are intended for highlighting important data, not for routine use.

Most CRT terminals display 24 text lines of 80 characters each. Many also provide a 25th line, which is used for labels, status, or other terminal- or program-related information. The status line sometimes is displayed in reverse video.

MEMORY-MAPPED DISPLAYS

When memory-mapped displays are used, the microcomputer can write into and read from the video memory just as from ordinary memory.

Most ASCII terminals use a technique called memory-mapped video. An advantage of the memory-mapped technique is that the microcomputer can write to and read from the video memory in the same way as ordinary memory because a portion of the ordinary memory is used for the video memory. The difference is that whatever characters are stored in video memory are displayed on the CRT when addressed by the microprocessor.

An 8-bit microprocessor uses two bytes (16 bits) for a memory address; thus, it can directly address 2^{16} or 65,536 memory locations. If each memory location can hold one character (which is the usual arrangement), and if the display size is 80 characters by 24 lines, then 1920 character locations are needed in video memory. If the program memory is restricted to addresses below 63,615, memory locations from 63,615 through 65,535 could be used for video memory to store an array of characters for the display.

Assume that the upper-left corner of the CRT display receives the character from the first location (63,615) in video memory, the next horizontal position on the CRT receives the character from the second location (63,616), and so forth. Thus, if the first video memory location contains *J*, the second *O*, the third *H*, and the fourth *N*, the upper-left corner of the CRT displays *JOHN*.

Memory-mapped displays are fast and inexpensive. Because the character set is translated into dots within the dot matrix using a table lookup technique, it is also possible to redefine the character set by changing the table entries (if the table is user-accessible). Line insertion and deletion, scrolling, and other effects are easily accomplished by moving data around in video memory, or even simpler, by changing starting addresses. The principal disadvantage of memory-mapped video of the type described is that it takes up space in the memory used to store programs and data. This usually is not a problem for terminals, but for computers, video memory is now usually separate. Also, computer video memory now is often "bit-mapped" rather than "character-mapped," as discussed in the preceding paragraphs. With bit-mapping, each dot on the screen has a separate memory location. This feature allows high-resolution graphic displays, but it requires much more video memory.

OTHER TYPES OF DISPLAYS

Although the CRT is the dominant display device today, there are other devices for displaying information. These include solid-state devices such as light-emitting diodes and liquid crystal displays, and plasma (gas discharge) matrices such as those used in the IBM 3290. These alternative types of displays provide extremely sharp images, but the dominance of the CRT remains unchallenged for now.

Features of a Typical Low-Cost Terminal

The Wyse WY-50 (Figure 2.8) is fairly typical of current terminal technology. Thus, an examination of its operating features will illustrate some of the previous points. When power is turned on, the WY-50 performs self-tests on the microprocessor, memory, communications and printer ports, keyboard, and display. The terminal halts all further operation if a fault is detected, and an error message pointing to the fault is displayed. The main display is 24 lines of 80 characters, plus a top line for local and host messages, and a bottom line for function-key labels. The main 24-by-80 display can be split horizontally into two screens. An escape sequence initiates this feature. For example, Esc x 1 + splits the screen horizontally, with the lower screen starting at line 12.

●

The Wyse WY-50 is an asynchronous terminal that also is capable of block-mode transmission. Special functions are available to display the dot-matrix characters.

Characters are formed by an 8-by-10 dot matrix in a 10-by-11 cell, which provides very good character definition. The terminal can display the 128 ASCII characters and various graphics characters. Normal and reverse video, underscore, dim, blink, and blank attributes can be assigned line-by-line in any combination. For example, Esc A1T creates a reverse video, half-intensity function-key labeling line. Actual labels are entered with another escape sequence; for example, Esc z 3 DEL CHAR enters DEL CHAR into the label field for the fourth function key (keys are numbered 0 through 7). Attributes and text are entered into the local and host message fields in a similar manner.

In addition to asynchronous character-by-character transmission, the WY-50 is capable of block-mode transmission. When in the block mode, the terminal performs editing and validation for data entered through the keyboard. This function requires a second page or screen of video memory. One 24-by-80 page is used as the date "form," and the second page is used to define the data-validation parameters. Local editing features include line insert and delete, character insert and delete, and automatic word wrapping.

FIGURE 2.8.

*Wyse WY-50 CRT
terminal.*

PC Terminals

The growth in the use of personal computers resulted in its adoption as a standard terminal device by many organizations. Some organizations, including several airlines, purchased tens of thousands of IBM PC and compatible personal computers for use with their online reservation systems during the 1980s. Other organizations use personal computers for both terminal emulation and local processing functions and have PCs coexisting with conventional terminals. Still other organizations connect personal computers to a local area network through the installation of an appropriate adapter card and the cabling of the adapter card to a network cable. This type of connection results in the personal computer becoming a workstation terminal device on the LAN. Regardless of the application or utilization, the processing capability of the personal computer can be used with appropriate hardware and software to provide terminal capabilities not available through the use of conventional terminals.

Figure 2.9 shows an IBM PS/2 Model 30 computer with keyboards and graphics monitor. This computer is similar to other members of the PS/2 family in that it contains a built-in serial port. The connector for this port, which is located at the rear of the computer, can be cabled to a modem. When appropriate communications software is loaded into the computer, it can then function as an asynchronous terminal.

FIGURE 2.9.
The IBM Personal System/2 Model 30 computer.

Through the addition of different types of adapter cards that are inserted into expansion slots within the system unit of a personal computer, you can alter the functionality and capability of the computer. For example, the addition of an internal fax/data modem enables the computer user to transmit and receive both text and fax messages. Figure 2.10 illustrates the GammaLink GammaFax CPi adapter card, which when inserted into a system expansion slot of an IBM PC or compatible personal computer, provides a fax/data transmission capability. This type of adapter card removes the necessity for a separate external fax/data modem. Because it uses the power of the computer and does not require a separate housing, it is usually less expensive than a stand-alone device. In addition, its use conserves space on the desktop. In some offices, desktop space is at a premium because the computer, telephone, and calendars compete for the fixed amount of space, and the addition of a stand-alone modem would further reduce the amount of space available for other use.

For synchronous transmission, IBM and third-party vendors manufacture various adapter cards that can be installed in system expansion slots in the system unit of that computer. Some adapter cards enable the PS/2 to be directly attached to IBM 3174 or 3274 control units. When terminal emulation software is loaded, the computer then functions as a 3278- or 3279-type terminal, providing the user with full screen access to mainframe computer applications. Other hardware adapter cards can be used to provide the PS/2 with batch terminal emulation capability to enable it to emulate various IBM and non-IBM remote job entry devices.

FIGURE 2.10.

*GammaLink
GammaFax CPi
adapter card.
(Courtesy of
GammaLink
Corporation)*

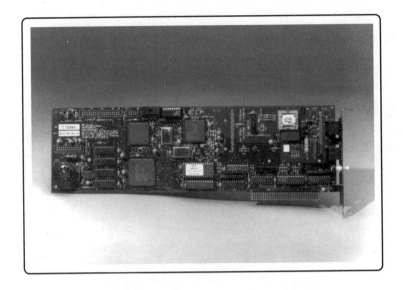

Perhaps the most popular type of communications adapter card used in a business envi-ronment is a LAN adapter card. Figure 2.11 illustrates the first LAN adapter card mar-keted by IBM for connecting personal computers to a broadband local area network in which transmission occurred by the radio frequency (rf) modulation of digital data. That is, the adapter card converted the binary ones and zeros of digital data into analog fre-quency tones for transmission on the network. The adapter card illustrated in Figure 2.11 represented an interim local area network used by IBM that was superseded by its token-ring network, which enables data to flow end-to-end in a digital format and whose opera-tion is described later in this book.

FIGURE 2.11.

*IBM broadband LAN
adapter card and
cable. (Courtesy of
IBM Corporation)*

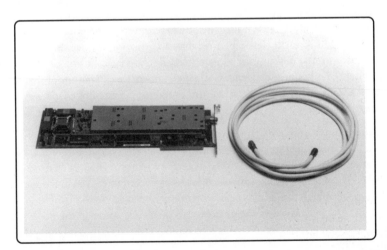

Although the type of adapter card inserted into the expansion slot of a personal computer governs its functionality and capability, note also that most PCs can support the installation and operation of multiple types of adapter cards. In fact, many modern operating environments, such as Microsoft Corporation's Windows and IBM's OS/2, enable you to switch easily between application programs that use different adapter cards. For example, you might first send a message to another user on the LAN through the use of an electronic mail program that communicates with the network by using a LAN adapter card. You then might switch to the use of a communications program that transmits data to a distant bulletin board through an internal modem card. Perhaps the most important thing to note concerning the use of communications adapter cards is that their use turns the personal computer into a multipurpose terminal. That is, with appropriate hardware and software, the PC can function as a LAN workstation, emulate a specific type of vendor terminal, function as a remote batch terminal, or perform another communications-related activity.

The use of a personal computer as a terminal enables hardware and software manufacturers to take advantage of the processing capability of the computer to provide additional capabilities. For example, by using a portion of the memory of the computer for temporary printer data storage, the personal computer can be programmed to accept a mixed data stream of video and printer destination data. This method enables the personal computer operator to maintain interactive transmission with a mainframe computer while a print job is routed to the PC, stored in memory, and dumped from memory to the printer.

A second advantage of the use of personal computers as terminals includes the expandability and upgradability of PCs. For example, additional memory can easily be added to most personal computers. Concerning upgradability, many personal computers get their display capability from the use of display adapters in a system expansion slot in the computer's system board. When a new video standard gains acceptance, most personal computers can have their existing video display adapters removed and a new adapter that supports the new standard installed. If video support was gotten from the use of a chip set installed on the system board, the installation of a video display adapter normally overrides the chip set, enabling the personal computer to support the new video standard.

Data Transmission

There are two methods by which data can be transmitted: serial and parallel.

Serial and Parallel Transmission

Data is commonly transferred between computers and terminals by changes in the current or voltage on a wire or channel. Such transfers are called parallel if a group of bits moves over several lines at the same time, or serial if the bits move one by one over a single line. Figure 2.12 illustrates parallel and serial data transmission.

FIGURE 2.12.

*Parallel and serial
data transfer.*

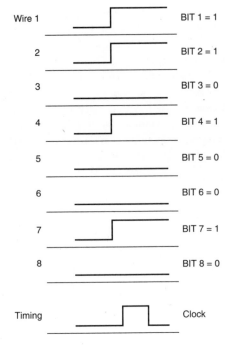

a. Parallel Transfer of ASCII "K", Even Parity

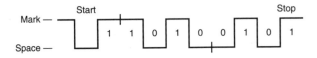

b. Serial Transfer of ASCII "K", Even Parity

In parallel data transmission, each bit of a character is sent over its own wire. In serial transmission, all bits travel over the same wire one after another.

In parallel transmission, each bit of a character travels on its own wire. A signal, called the strobe or clock, on an additional wire indicates to the receiver when all the bits are present on their respective wires so that the values can be sampled. Computers and other digital systems that are located near one another (within a few feet) normally use parallel transmission because it is much faster. As the distance between equipment increases, not only do the multiple wires become more costly, but also the difficulty of transmitting and receiving pulse signals on long wires increases.

Serial transmission is used for transmission over long distances. The conversion from parallel to serial and vice versa is accomplished with shift registers. Transmission of serial data is called synchronous if the exact sending or receiving time of each bit is determined before it is transmitted or received. It's called asynchronous if the timing of the bits in a character are not determined by the timing of a previous character.

Timing

Figure 2.13 illustrates a series of bits transmitted serially over a line. Note that although both the sender and the receiver use the same nominal clock rate, the receiver must somehow determine a more exact clock for decoding the data. This is one of the fundamental problems of data communications. In this case, the receiver retimes its clock on the negative-going edge of the transition (change) from one to zero of the start bit, then uses its new timing to find the middle of the start bit as shown in Figure 2.13a. Notice in Figure 2.13b that although the receiver clock is slightly fast, it doesn't cause an error because the sample strobe still occurs within each bit time.

● Bit timing is critical to the accurate transmission and reception of data.

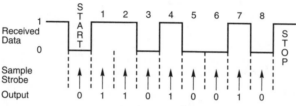

a. Ideal Sampling at Midpoint of Each Bit

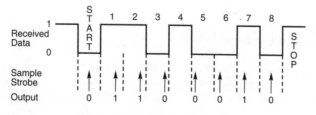

b. Sampling When Received Clock Is Slightly Fast

c. Sampling When Received Clock Is Too Slow

FIGURE 2.13.

Clocking asynchronous data.

Figure 2.13c shows a different situation. Here, the receive clock is so much slower than the transmit clock that the sample strobe does not sample bit 4 at all; thus, an error occurs in the output. The communications system must somehow ensure that the receive clock is timed so that errors do not occur. Although bit timing is very important, it alone isn't enough to complete the communications process.

Framing

The framing method used in asynchronous transmission defines a character by using start and stop bits to separate it from other characters.

Framing is the next step in timing after bit timing. In the example of Figure 2.13, it could be called character timing, because the start and stop bits frame one character for the receiver. This is the framing used in asynchronous data transmission, which is discussed in association with teleprinter operation in the next section. Synchronous data communications systems use different methods of framing, which will be discussed in later chapters.

Asynchronous Transmission

The first asynchronous communications systems used electric motors driving rotating contacts at each end. The rotation of the motors had to be synchronized.

Asynchronous communications systems evolved before electronic systems. Electromechanical systems therefore had to be used. The problem in those systems was the synchronization of the operation of two electromechanical devices (motors), one at each end of the line, whose speeds could not be easily adjusted. The timing and framing problem was solved by resuming each character using the edge of the start bit, which was required to be the first bit on the line. Nevertheless, if the difference in motor speeds was too great, the bit timing would drift with each successive bit until the sampling of the last received data bit in the character could be incorrect. Thus, five bits became the standard for the low-speed teleprinter code because the chance of error increased significantly if more bits were used.

Imagine an operator keying a teleprinter keyboard to produce characters for transmission. The framed character generated by each key depression begins with a start bit and ends with one or two stop bits. The stop condition is a mark or positive voltage on the line (negative voltage with double-current signaling). The positive voltage remains on the line until the next character starts because the line idle condition is internally defined as current flow or mark, rather than no current or space. When a space (start bit) is detected, the receiving device starts, and it will be in synchronization with the transmitting device.

ELECTROMECHANICAL METHOD

Current pulses, placed on the line by the sender's rotating armature, select the character to be printed through the synchronized receiver contacts.

The diagram in Figure 2.14 illustrates the operation of an electromechanical start-stop teleprinter machine. The sending device and the receiving device each have an armature, A, which rotates at a constant speed when a clutch connects it to an electric motor in the machine. Contacts on the armature connect an outer ring of contacts, B, to the transmission line. In the diagram, the armature is in its stop position. Current from the battery in the sender flows through the contact labeled stop, through the armature, and through the line to the receiver. This current causes the receive relay to remain energized, keeping the clutch disengaged, the armature stationary, and the teleprinter in the idle condition.

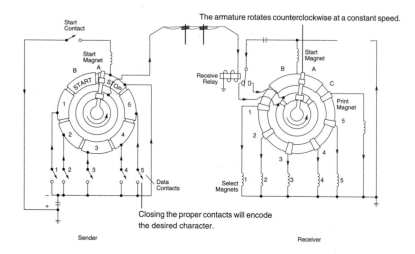

FIGURE 2.14.

Electromechanical start-stop coding and decoding.

Now suppose that an operator at the sending device presses the H key on the keyboard. In accordance with the five-bit code in Figure 1.4, data contacts 3 and 5 close to encode the H, and the start contact at the sending machine closes. This action energizes the start magnet to engage the clutch to turn the armature of the sending device counterclockwise. The armature connects the contacts on the outer ring to the line in sequence: start, 1, 2, 3, 4, 5, stop. Notice that the start contact and data contacts 1, 2, and 4 do not conduct current.

As soon as the armature of the sender travels to its start contact, the current through the line and the receive relay ceases. The receive relay is de-energized, and current flows through the other set of relay contacts and through the start magnet of the receiver. This action engages the clutch, and the receiver armature begins turning counterclockwise at approximately the same speed as that of the sender armature. When the sender armature is over data contact 3, current flows through the line and the receive relay. The receive relay is energized, and as the armature of the receiver passes over data contact 3 on the outer ring, current flows through select magnet 3.

Select magnet 5 is operated similarly. The operation of these two magnets causes the letter *H* to be selected on the type mechanism of the receiver. When the sender armature reaches its stop contact, the receiver armature passes over contact C, current flows to the print magnet, and the letter *H* is printed. Both armatures then come to rest in the position shown in the illustration, unless the sender is ready to transmit another character immediately.

Note that the start and stop elements have those exact functions; that is, they start and stop the armature rotation. As you can visualize, if there were much variation in the rotational speeds of the sending and receiving armatures, the armatures would not be in synchronization, and the character would be decoded incorrectly. As discussed previously, this is one reason that the Baudot code was limited to five symbols.

Bit timing within a character must be precise to prevent errors. However, the timing between characters is not of importance for accuracy.

With start-stop transmission, a new character can begin at any time after the stop bits of the preceding character have been received. The time between one character and the next is indeterminate, but within a character, the timing is precisely defined. For that reason, it might be better to call this technique "self-synchronized" or "internally synchronized," rather than asynchronous, meaning "not synchronized." (The lack of a continuous synchronous agreement between the transmitter and the receiver—specifically, the lack of a clocking signal within or accompanying the data channel—is the reason for the name "asynchronous.")

ELECTRONIC RECEIVING CIRCUIT

The electromechanical arrangements of the early teleprinters have been replaced with electronic circuits. Because these can be synchronized within closer tolerances, an eight-bit code can be used. An electronic circuit for receiving asynchronous serial data in an eight-bit code is shown in Figure 2.15. It utilizes a clock that runs at 16 times the symbol rate of the incoming data. This rapid rate is used to detect the 1 to 0 transition (when the start bit begins) as soon as possible after it occurs. The circuit that detects the 1 to 0 transition enables a spike detection circuit. Eight "ticks" of the 16X clock (one-half a bit time) are counted, and then the line is checked to see whether it is still in the 0 state. If it is not, it is assumed that the initial 1 to 0 transition was due to noise on the line, the spike detection circuit is reset, and no further action is taken.

FIGURE 2.15.

Asynchronous receiver.

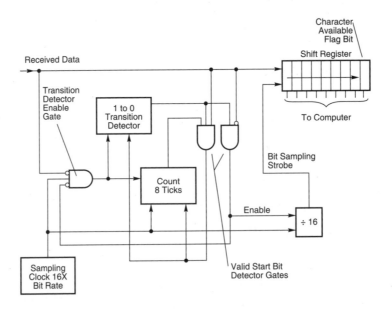

If the line is still at 0, a valid start signal has arrived. A counter is enabled that divides the 16X clock by 16 to produce a sampling clock that ticks once per bit time for the shift register. This tick occurs roughly at the center of the bit being sampled. The off-center error can be made smaller by sampling at 32 times the bit rate, and even further reduced by sampling at 64 times the bit rate. However, when higher sampling rates are used, the counter in the spike detection circuit and the counter in the bit sampler circuit must count proportionately higher.

The bit sampler circuit strobes the shift register eight times to sample the state of the line to get the eight bits into the serial-to-parallel shift register. Then a signal, called a flag, is sent to the computer or controller with which it is associated to announce that a character has been received. The computer then signals the shift register to transfer the eight bits in parallel into the processing circuits.

A problem with using only a shift register (called a single-buffered interface) is that when characters are arriving continuously, the computer has only the duration of the stop bit to read the received character before the next character begins entering the register. A simple improvement is to provide a holding register into which the received character can be parallel transferred as soon as the eighth bit has been sampled. A character-available flag is sent to the computer when the parallel transfer occurs, and the receiving register becomes available for the next character. This arrangement, called a double-buffered interface, is shown in Figure 2.16. In either case, the arrival of a character that cannot be handled because the preceding character has not been read is called a data overflow. If overflow occurs, most receiver circuits overwrite the old character with the new one (the old one is lost) and place an error signal on a separate lead to the computer.

●

A single-buffered interface requires the receiving computer to read each character as soon as it is received, with no break before the next one begins.

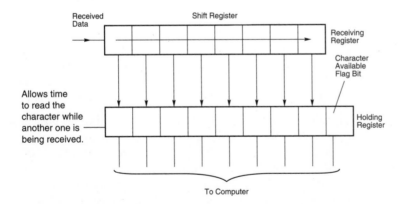

FIGURE 2.16.

Double-buffered interface.

STOP BITS AND TIMING ERRORS

With a double-buffered interface, the stop bit arrival time is no longer the only time available to the computer for reading the character, so there is time for circuitry to check the stop bit (sometimes called the ninth bit) to confirm that it is a 1. If it is not a 1, one of the following conditions exists: the communications channel path is broken, receiver timing is confused, or the transmitting station is sending a special signal. The existence of one of these conditions typically provides an error signal on a lead in the asynchronous receiver.

A double-buffered interface provides a holding register to hold the character for reading, and the next character received fills the receiving register.

Such an error occurs when the receiver has lost track of which zeros in the transmission are the start bits and which are just zeros in the data. If, for some reason, the receiver treats a data bit as a start bit, it assembles the next eight bits as a character. Because these eight bits are really parts of two characters (the end of one and the beginning of another), the ninth bit to arrive will not be the stop bit, but rather a data bit from the second character. If it is a zero, the error-checking circuit detects an error. Because framing is the process of deciding which groups of eight bits constitute characters, and this error is due to a failure in that process, it is called a framing error.

Failure in the framing process generally can be avoided. The idle line condition is a mark condition, and any amount of idle time more than a character time corrects this condition. Even if characters are sent continuously, the receiver eventually becomes realigned to the correct start elements, no matter which zero bit is chosen as the start bit. Of course, the characters received while the framing is not in alignment is decoded incorrectly.

THE UART

The electronic circuitry previously described has been reduced through the use of very large scale integrated circuitry onto a communications chip referred to as a UART (Universal Asynchronous Receiver Transmitter). A UART in its transmit mode converts the bits received in parallel, which represents a character within a computer, into a serial data stream and then transfers each bit onto the serial interface at an appropriate time. In addition, the UART frames the character to include the addition of start and stop bits and optionally add a parity bit before transmitting the bits in a serial sequence. When in its receive mode, the UART samples the line for incoming bits; forms a stream of bits into a character after removing the start, stop, and parity bits; and transfers the received character to the computer. The use of a parity bit for error detection is covered later in this book.

Through the use of UARTs that are no bigger than a thumbnail, it became possible to provide every type of personal computer, ranging in size from a desktop to a personal digital assistant, with a serial port. The UART normally is included on the motherboard of the computer and connected to the physical connector that represents the interface to the serial port. Although most readers are probably familiar with 15- and 25-pin connectors labeled "serial port" on many computers, the actual work in which parallel data inside the computer is converted into a serial bit sequence transmitted through the connector is performed by a UART inside the computer.

Other Types of Transmission

Asynchronous transmission is the most common in data communications simply because there are more low-speed terminals and small-computer applications in which it is used.

Large systems and networks usually use methods other than asynchronous. This is because of the large overhead penalty of 20 percent associated with start-stop codes; that is, 2 (the start and stop bits) out of the 10 bits transmitted are for control rather than for information. This is not a problem in conversational timesharing or many other types of interactive applications, in which more time is spent looking at the screen and transferring a file of 500,000 characters (4 million bits) at 9600 bps.

A second problem in such large transfers is error checking. The timesharing user originally had to check the input and output for errors by looking at the screen and rekeying or asking for retransmission of portions that contained errors. Such a procedure is clearly impractical for long file transfers that occur at fast rates and often without an operator present. Although transmission protocols have been developed to provide error-free asynchronous transmission, the use of this type of communications is oriented for relatively short transmission requirements. Applications requiring large-volume, high-speed data transfers necessitate a different method of data transfer. This method is called synchronous transmission.

In synchronous transmission, start and stop bits are not used. Characters are sent in groups, called blocks, with special synchronization characters placed at the beginning of the block and within it, to ensure that enough 0 to 1 or 1 to 0 transitions occur for the receiver clock to remain accurate. Error checking is performed automatically on the entire block. If any errors occur, the entire block is retransmitted. This technique also carries an overhead penalty (nothing is free), but the overhead is far less than the 20 percent for blocks of more than a few dozen characters. Figure 2.17 compares asynchronous and synchronous transmission of a sequence of characters.

● Large data communications systems normally do not use asynchronous transmission because the start-stop codes take too much time, and error detection and correction methods are impractical.

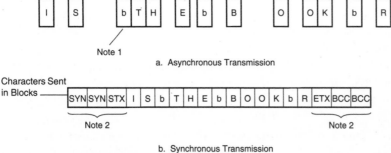

a. Asynchronous Transmission

Characters Sent in Blocks

b. Synchronous Transmission

NOTES:
1. b means blank (space character)
2. Transmission control characters

FIGURE 2.17.
Comparison of asynchronous and synchronous data transmission.

In addition to asynchronous and synchronous transmission methods to achieve receiver timing, there is now a third method called isochronous transmission. This technique is used in a few computer networks. It involves timing that is controlled by the network rather than the DCE or DTE, as is true for synchronous and asynchronous transmission. Synchronous and isochronous data transmission will be discussed later in this book.

What Have You Learned?

1. Compared to CRT terminals, teleprinters are much slower in printing, have limited formatting capability, don't have enhancements such as blinking and highlighting, and are less reliable in operation.

2. A serial or character printer prints one character at a time. The printer can be either an impact or a nonimpact printer. An impact printer can produce fully formed characters or characters formed by a dot matrix. A nonimpact printer usually uses a thermal, optical (laser), or ink-jet method.

3. CRT terminals can be classified as dumb, smart, and user-programmable. A dumb terminal is essentially the same as a teleprinter except for printing speed. A smart terminal has capabilities such as editing, formatting, highlighting, and blinking. A user-programmable terminal has a built-in programming language and the capability to store and execute programs.

4. As applied to terminals, ergonomics has to do with the color, character size, and nonglare surface of the display, and with the shape, position, and layout of the keys. It also is concerned with the physical position of both the display and the keyboard with respect to the operator.

5. The communications functionality and capability of a personal computer is altered through the addition of different types of adapter cards and the use of appropriate software.

6. In serial transmission, the bits are transmitted one at a time over a single wire. In parallel transmission, each bit of a group moves over its own wire, and all bits of the group move at the same time.

7. Both bit timing and framing are necessary to maintain synchronization for proper decoding in data communications. Bit timing usually is accomplished by clocking the bits. Framing usually is accomplished by inserting special bits or characters in the data stream just for that purpose.

8. In asynchronous transmission, each character is sent by itself and is framed by a start bit and stop bit. This is the transmission method used by teleprinters and ASCII terminals.

9. The UART receives data from a parallel format within a computer; frames the data by the addition of start, stop, and an optional parity bit; and transmits the data one bit at a time serially.

10. In synchronous transmission, many characters are sent together in groups called blocks. Each block is framed by special synchronization characters.

Quiz for Chapter 2

1. Teleprinters:

a. Are only for printing at remote locations, not for input.

b. Offer both high-speed operation and various formatting controls.

c. Have a printer for output and might have a keyboard for input.

2. Impact printers:

a. Strike a ribbon against the paper to produce character images.

b. Include ink-jet and thermal devices.

c. Are rapidly becoming obsolete.

3. Glass Teletypes:

a. Are among the most recent developments in CRT terminals.

b. Were so named because they had the same interface as teleprinters.

c. Are teleprinters designed to interface with fiber-optic transmission systems.

4. Electromechanical teleprinters:

a. Use a complex mechanical buffer to match speed between transmitting and receiving machines.

b. Use start/stop codes to synchronize sending and receiving equipment.

c. Are rarely used today.

5. ASCII terminals are generally defined as:

a. Terminals using synchronous transmission in EBCDIC.

b. Terminals using synchronous transmission in ASCII.

c. Terminals using asynchronous transmission in ASCII.

d. Any terminals having an American (dollar-sign) keyboard.

6. "3270" terminals refer to:

a. Asynchronous terminals made by IBM.

b. Any terminal that is painted blue.

c. Synchronous terminals that interface with an IBM-type cluster controller.

7. A multipurpose terminal refers to:

a. A terminal with a serial port.

b. A computer with both serial and parallel ports.

c. A terminal with a UART.

d. A computer to which communications functionality is added through the addition of hardware and software.

8. The difference between timing and framing is:

 a. Timing is concerned with the individual bits; framing is concerned with the boundaries between characters.

 b. Timing refers to serial transmission; framing refers to parallel.

 c. Timing is concerned primarily with asynchronous systems; framing is concerned with synchronous systems.

9. Escape codes are so called because:

 a. In effect, they provide a means to temporarily "escape" from the standard meanings of the character set.

 b. They initiate operation of the escapement mechanism in teleprinters.

 c. They cause the cursor to escape from the boundaries of the CRT screen and roam around in memory.

10. The QWERTY keyboard:

 a. Is still considered to be the layout allowing the greatest typing speed.

 b. Is the most popular keyboard, but not necessarily the best.

 c. Is a key layout that is rarely used.

11. Memory-mapped displays:

 a. Are associated with electromechanical teleprinters.

 b. Have the advantage that they do not take up memory space.

 c. Allow direct addressing of display locations by the processor.

12. The major differences between personal computer keyboards are:

 a. In the use of QWERTY versus other key layouts.

 b. In the use of the Shift key.

 c. In the position of function keys and the inclusion or omission of a numeric keypad.

 d. In the placement of the numeric keys on the keyboard.

13. Serial printers:

 a. Are used to transmit grain prices.

 b. Are faster than CRT terminals and offer more flexibility.

 c. Print one character at a time.

 d. Usually use serial interfaces.

14. Nonimpact printers:

 a. Are normally quieter than impact printers.

 b. Generate carbon copies easily.

 c. Produce fully formed characters.

15. CRT terminals:

 a. Are the most widely used hard-copy terminals.

 b. Offer high-speed display and formatting flexibility.

c. Do not normally use microprocessors.

16. User-programmable terminals:

    a. Are replacing personal and professional computers.

    b. Offer more flexibility at lower cost.

    c. Are being replaced by personal and professional computers.

17. Ergonomics:

    a. Involves the interface between people and machines, such as terminals.

    b. Is the application of ergo-economics to communications.

    c. Utilizes three-level ergo-coding for transmission over certain channels.

18. Serial and parallel transmission:

    a. Differ in how many bits are transferred per character.

    b. Are used in synchronous and asynchronous systems, respectively.

    c. Differ in whether the bits are on separate wires or all on one wire.

19. Memory-mapped displays:

    a. Are used for high-resolution graphics, such as maps.

    b. Use ordinary memory to store the display data in character form.

    c. Store the display data as individual bits.

20. Asynchronous transmission:

    a. Is less efficient than synchronous, but simpler.

    b. Is much faster than synchronous transmission.

    c. Is another name for isochronous transmission.

21. Single-buffering:

    a. Is more efficient than double-buffering.

    b. Is less efficient than no buffering.

    c. Provides very little time to unload the incoming character from the register.

22. Most terminal keyboards:

    a. Provide numerous additional specialized keys.

    b. Are strictly typewriter style, with few extra keys.

    c. Use the Dvorak layout.

Messages and Transmission Channels

About This Chapter

Useful communication requires four elements as shown in Figure 3.1: a message (information) to be communicated, a sender of the message, a medium or channel over which the message can be sent, and a receiver. Messages usually are information that is useful to people, but the sender and receiver might or might not be human. The medium must be one suitable to convey the type of message. In this chapter, we will examine in more detail the types of messages and the media that carry them.

FIGURE 3.1.

The elements of communication.

MESSAGE   RECEIVER

What Is Information?

A key to understanding the process of communications is the knowledge of what constitutes information, which is the topic of this section.

Information as a Quantity

The unit of information used in data communications is the bit, which has only two possible values, 1 and 0. Seven bits are needed to select any one of 128 different symbols in ASCII.

"Information," according to one definition, "is the communication or reception of knowledge or intelligence." Information is also "a numerical quantity that measures the uncertainty in the outcome of an experiment to be performed." This second definition has an application in the sending of messages. For example, suppose that we have a machine that can send only two symbols, A1 and A2. We can then say that the "experiment" is the accurate recognition of the two symbols (A1 and A2) being sent from one machine to another. As far as the receiving machine is concerned, it is just as likely to receive one symbol as the other. So we can say that the "numerical quantity" in this experiment is a unit of information that allows a selection between two equally likely choices. This quantity, or unit of information, is usually called a bit (a contraction of *binary digit*), and has two possible values, 0 and 1. If these two values are used to represent A1 and A2, then A1 could be represented by the bit value 0, and A2 by the bit value 1. The number of bits per symbol is 1, but we still need a way of selecting which symbol (bit) we want to use. A machine that needs only two symbols needs only a 1-bit select code (0 and 1).

A machine that uses only two symbols is not of much use for communication, but suppose that the machine used 128 symbols (like the standard ASCII character set). Then the number of equally likely choices to be handled is 128, and the number of bits (information) required to represent each of those 128 symbols is seven (refer to Table 1.1). You can see, then, that if the knowledge (or intelligence) to be communicated can be represented by a set of equally likely symbols, the amount of information required per symbol to communicate that knowledge is necessarily dependent on the total number of bits of information. The standard ASCII character set is particularly useful for selecting the information to be communicated because it can select one of 128 ASCII symbols with only one eight-bit byte, a common bit grouping in computers (the eighth bit is not used in this case). The extended ASCII character set that uses all eight bits per byte supports 256 symbols, doubling the number of ASCII symbols.

Information Content of Symbols

In many information systems, not every symbol is equally likely to be used in a given communication. The English language is a good example. In a message written in English, the letter *e* is 12 times more likely to occur than the letter *s*. This uneven distribution is also characteristic of particular groups of letters and of words. What this means, then, is that each of the 128 symbols in ASCII or 256 symbols in extended ASCII is not likely to occur an equal number of times in any given communication. For example, notice that the uses of the letters *e* and *g*, and the letter combinations *th* and *er*, are unequal in this paragraph.

In 1949, Claude Shannon published a book titled *The Mathematical Theory of Communication*. In this book, he discusses the uncertainty or amount of disorder of a system, which he called entropy. The entropy of a set of equally likely symbols (such as the digits 0–9 in a table of random numbers) is the logarithm to the base 2 of the number of symbols in the set. The entropy of the English alphabet, which contains 26 letters and a space, is then $\log_2(27) = 4.76$ bits per symbol. Because of the uneven use of letters in the English language, however, its entropy was estimated by Shannon as 1.3 bits per symbol. This means that the language is about 70 percent redundant and that it should be possible to reconstruct English text accurately if every other letter is lost or changed due to noise or distortion. Obviously, redundancy is desirable to raise the chances of receiving a good message when the medium is noisy. (The words *noise* and *noisy* in this book refer to electrical noise—that is, an electrical signal that is not supposed to be present.)

● Redundancy is the measurement of the probability of occurrence of any particular character in a character set.

Using Redundancy in Communications

Redundancy can be used to reconstruct a message even if part of the message is lost during transmission. It is very important in verifying data accuracy.

So, you wonder, what does all this have to do with the real world of data communications? Quite a bit, because almost every scheme in current use for sending data uses redundancy in an attempt to verify that the data has been received exactly as sent—that is, no errors have been introduced by the sending mechanism, the transmission medium, or the receiver. The redundant information might consist simply of a retransmission of the entire original message. Although simple to implement, retransmission is not efficient. Special techniques are therefore used to generate redundant information that is related to the message in a way that is known to both the sender and the receiver. The sender generates the redundant information during transmission and sends it with the message. The receiver regenerates and checks the redundant information when the message is received. This scheme is represented in Figure 3.2. Verification usually occurs at the end of each link in the chain making up the transmission path. The details of this process and various methods in current use are described in a later chapter.

FIGURE 3.2.

Error-checking points.

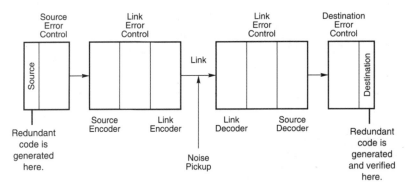

What Carries the Message?

Bounded data channels confine the signals within wires, coaxial cable, or optical-fiber cable. Unbounded channels permit the signal to radiate in all directions.

The physical channels (the media) that carry data are of two types: bounded and unbounded. In a bounded medium, the signals are confined to the medium and do not leave it (except for smaller leakage amounts). A pair of wires, coaxial cable, waveguide, and optical-fiber cable are examples of bounded media. The atmosphere, the ocean, and outer space are examples of unbounded media, in which electromagnetic signals originated by the source radiate freely into the medium and spread throughout the medium. The unbounded media are used by various radio frequency transmitting schemes to carry messages. The main feature of unbounded media is that when the signal is radiated from the transmitter, it radiates equally in all directions (unless restricted) and continues forever onward. As it moves farther from the source, the energy is spread over a larger area, so the level continually gets weaker at greater distances. As the wave moves through the medium, it is affected by natural disturbances, which can interfere with the signal.

Wire Pairs

The simplest type of bounded medium is a pair of wires providing a go and return path for electrical signals. Early telegraph systems used the earth itself rather than a wire for one of the paths, as shown in Figure 3.3a. Repeaters were inserted along the line to reduce the effects of noise and attenuation (loss of signal strength). However, this scheme did not work well because the earth is not always a good conductor and the path was susceptible to large noise currents induced by lightning. Losses were reduced by using two wires, as shown in Figure 3.3b, but because the line was still unbalanced to ground, it was subject to picking up noise from almost every noise-producing device. Finally, the balanced two-wire line shown in Figure 3.3c was used to greatly reduce noise pickup.

Wire pairs are the simplest type of bounded carrier. The two wires that provide the go and return signal path, when balanced to ground, provide the most protection from induced noise.

FIGURE 3.3.

Types of transmission circuits.

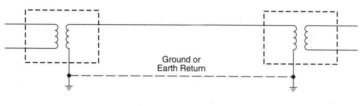

a. Single-Wire Unbalanced to Ground

b. Two-Wire Unbalanced to Ground

c. Two-Wire Balanced to Ground

The most common type of bounded medium consists of wire pairs twisted together and made into cables of from 4 to 3000 pairs. Because a wire acts as an antenna, several techniques are used to reduce electromagnetic interference (EMI). Most wires are shielded, and some wires are also twisted at 90-degree angles every so often. The twists serve to additionally suppress EMI. The size of the wire used varies from 16 AWG (American Wire Gauge) with a wire diameter of 0.05082 inch to 26 AWG with a diameter of 0.01594 inch. AWG wire sizes are inversely proportional to the diameter of the wire. That is, the lower the AWG, the thicker the wire, whereas a higher AWG indicates a thinner wire. In modern cables, each wire is insulated with a polyethylene or a polyvinyl chloride (PVC) jacket; however, a large quantity of older cable is still in use in which the insulation for each wire is paper.

Open-wire lines have low attenuation of voice frequencies due to the large size of the wire and the relatively large distance between the two wires when mounted on a crossarm of a utility pole. A typical value of attenuation for 104 mil (0.104 inch) diameter open wire lines is 0.07 decibel (dB) per mile, whereas 19-gauge (0.03589 inch diameter) twisted wire pairs in a multipair cable have a voice frequency attenuation of about 1 dB per mile.

> The size of the wires used and the distance between them affect the attenuation. Twisted wire pairs are limited to a maximum frequency of about 1 MHz.

The attenuation of twisted wire pairs rises rapidly with increasing frequency, and the amount of crosstalk between adjacent pairs also increases with frequency. The maximum usable frequency for wire pairs in cables is around 1 MHz without special treatment.

THE EFFECT OF INDUCTANCE

A concept that might not be obvious about paired wire circuits is that the addition of inductance in the line can help reduce attenuation at voice frequencies. The line impedance (AC resistance) is increased so that a given amount of power can be transmitted with less current but at a higher voltage. The result is a reduction in the series losses and an increase in the shunt losses. Because the series losses are usually the most severe, there is a net reduction in attenuation until the inductance rises to the point where series and shunt losses are equal.

> When a circuit is loaded with added inductance, attenuation can be reduced at higher frequencies so that the circuit response is relatively constant over the voiceband.

Adding inductance to wire pairs is called loading, and a circuit to which inductance has been added is called a loaded line or loaded circuit. The effect of loading is illustrated in Figure 3.4. The typical frequency-versus-attenuation performance is shown for a nonloaded 19-gauge cable pair and a 19-gauge cable pair loaded with 88 millihenrys of inductance every 6000 feet. (The standard notation for this is 19H-88 loaded pair.) Figure 3.4 shows that the attenuation of the loaded circuit is less than that of the unloaded one and that it changes very little with increasing frequency up to a certain point above 3 KHz. This point is called the cutoff point or cutoff frequency.

Loading was introduced around 1900 on long-distance open wire lines to reduce losses due to attenuation, because there were no amplifiers for the signals.

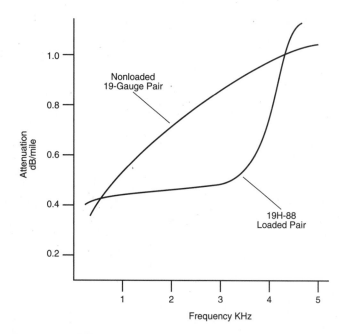

FIGURE 3.4.

Effect of inductance loading.

ELECTRONIC AMPLIFIERS

In 1883, Thomas Edison discovered the rectifying properties of the thermionic vacuum tube. A thermionic vacuum tube is one in which a stream of electrons is emitted by an incandescent substance. Edison's device was a two-element tube (called a diode) consisting of a cathode (the incandescent substance) and an anode.

The principle of thermionic vacuum tubes lay unused, however, until 1904. At that time, Sir John Ambrose Fleming, an English physicist and engineer, adapted the diode for use as a demodulator (detector) of radiotelegraph signals for the Marconi Wireless Telegraph Co. In 1906, Lee DeForest introduced a third element, called a control grid, to the diode and created the triode. By 1912, the triode and its associated circuits were developed for use as an amplifier.

When the use of the DeForest triode as an amplifier began in 1914, it was no longer necessary to load long-distance circuits, because the losses in the line could be compensated for by amplification. However, loading is still used on longer local loops (from the telephone office to the customer) because it is cheaper than adding active components for amplification. The presence of loading on local circuits has a considerable effect on their capability to carry high-frequency data signals, which causes problems for some new types of telephone service.

●
Electronic amplifiers eliminate the requirement to load long-distance circuits because amplification can compensate for the line losses.

Coaxial Cable

To make telephone service economical, a way had to be found to put more than one conversation onto a channel. Indeed, the invention of the telephone arose out of Alexander Bell's experiments on a "harmonic telegraph," an attempt to put more than one telegraph signal on a channel. Putting more conversations or more data on a single channel requires a larger bandwidth (capability to carry more frequencies), which, as a practical matter, means higher frequencies. Because the practical frequency limit for wire pairs is around 1 MHz, some other method had to be developed.

Some significant and interesting effects occur in the vicinity of a wire carrying an alternating current signal. One of these effects is that both an electric field and a magnetic field are created around the conductor. The magnetic field can induce the signal it is carrying into adjacent conductors. (In communications, the induced and unwanted signal is called crosstalk.) However, if one conductor of the pair is the ground side of the circuit and is made to surround the other conductor, both the radiated electric field and the magnetic field can be confined within the tube formed by the outer conductor, as illustrated in Figure 3.5.

FIGURE 3.5.

Structure of coaxial cable.

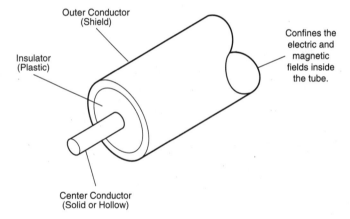

This medium is called a coaxial cable, because the two conductors have a common axis. The self-shielding works well at frequencies above about 100 KHz, but at lower frequencies, the "skin depth" of the current is comparable to the thickness of the outer conductor, and the shielding becomes ineffective. The resistive loss of coaxial cable increases in proportion to the square root of the frequency, making coaxial cable generally usable at frequencies of up to 2000 MHz, although some types can be used up to 10,000 MHz.

Waveguide

If the frequency of transmission is high enough, the electric and magnetic components of a signal can travel through free space, requiring no solid conductor. However, to avoid interference and losses due to signal spreading, and to be able to route the signal as desired, it is sometimes useful to confine these waves to another bounded medium called a waveguide.

Waveguides are commonly used at frequencies from 2000 MHz up to 110,000 MHz to connect microwave transmitters and receivers to their antennas. Waveguides are pressurized with dry air or nitrogen to drive out moisture from inside the waveguide because moisture attenuates the microwaves. Older waveguides were constructed with a rectangular cross section, but common practice today is to make the guides circular, as shown in Figure 3.6. Waveguides remain in use as a conductor of high-power, high-frequency signals, but optical-fiber cables are being used in newer systems.

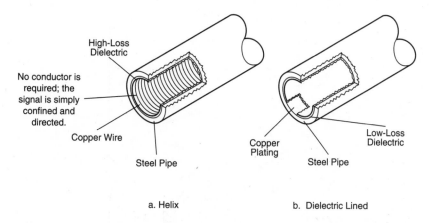

a. Helix

b. Dielectric Lined

FIGURE 3.6.

Circular waveguides.

Fiber-Optic Systems

The capacity of a transmission system is a direct function of the highest frequency it can carry. Progress in transmission technology has therefore been measured by the bandwidth of the media available to carry signals. Recent developments in the use of glass fibers to carry binary signals have shown these systems to be extremely well-suited to high-data-rate applications. Fiber-optic systems are attractive for several reasons:

● The low transmission loss, as compared with wire pairs or coaxial cable, allows much greater separation between repeaters. A fiber-optic system with no repeaters has been demonstrated that transmits 420 megabits per second (Mbps) over a span of 75 miles with an error rate several times lower than high-quality coaxial cable systems.

● Because the optical fibers carry light rays, the frequency of operation is that of light. The transmission wavelength used for current single-mode fibers is 1.2 micrometers, equivalent to a frequency of around 800 terahertz (800 trillion Hz).

●
Fiber-optic systems can handle high-capacity, high-frequency transmissions economically because they have low loss, are free of electromagnetic interference, are nonconductive, are noninductive, and do not radiate energy.

Such frequencies allow data transmission rates of 20,000 Mbps over short distances.

● Optical-fiber cables do not radiate energy, do not conduct electricity, and are noninductive. They are essentially free from crosstalk and the effects of lightning-induced interference, and they present no security problem from an inductively coupled "wire tap."

● Because optical-fiber cables transport light energy, they can be routed through most hazardous areas, such as oil refineries, grain elevators, and similar locations where the use of cables carrying electricity are either barred or represent a potential danger.

● Optical-fiber cables are smaller, lighter, and cheaper than metallic cables of the same capacity. It is economically feasible to provide several unused fibers in a cable for spares and for future growth. A cross section of a typical optical-fiber cable is shown in Figure 3.7.

FIGURE 3.7.

Typical optical five-fiber cable for direct burial.

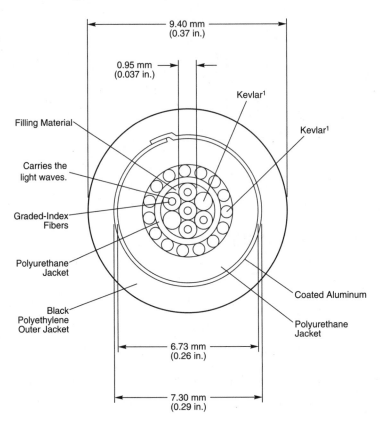

[1]Kevlar is a trademark of E.I. Du Pont de Nemours and Co.

One standard fiber-optic system currently in service is the AT&T FT3 lightwave system, which can carry 80,000 two-way voice conversations at the same time. The cable for this system is one-half inch in diameter and contains 144 fibers. Each fiber pair operates at 90 Mbps for a total data rate of about 6000 Mbps. The system provides one spare fiber for every operating one, and switchover to a spare is automatic on loss of signal in a fiber. A more detailed discussion of fiber-optic systems is given in Chapter 7, "Fiber-Optic and Satellite Communications."

High-Frequency Radiotelephone

By convention, radio transmission in the frequency band between 3 MHz and 30 MHz is called high-frequency (HF) radio. Frequency bands within the HF spectrum are allocated by international treaty for specific services, such as mobile (aeronautical, maritime, and land), broadcasting, radio navigation, amateur radio, space communications, and radio astronomy. HF radio has properties of propagation that make it less reliable than some other frequencies. HF radio does, however, allow communications over great distances with small amounts of radiated power.

HF radio waves transmitted from antennas on the earth follow two paths, as indicated in Figure 3.8, when they leave the antenna. The groundwave follows the earth's surface, and the skywave bounces back and forth between the earth's surface and various layers of the earth's ionosphere. The groundwave is useful for communications up to about 400 miles, and it works particularly well over water. The skywave propagates signals for up to 4000 miles with a path reliability of about 90 percent. Data signals are carried on HF radio systems as continuous wave (CW) radio telegraphy at about 15 bits per second (bps), and frequency shift keyed (FSK) single sideband signals are carried on HF at 75 bps. Higher data bit rates (up to 4800 bps) are converted to standard 3 KHz voice channel analog signals by modems, and these analog signals are transmitted on voice frequency (VF) carrier systems using HF radio.

●

High-frequency signals radiate from an antenna over two paths: a groundwave following the earth's surface and a skywave that bounces between the earth and the ionosphere.

FIGURE 3.8.

Paths of HF radio waves.

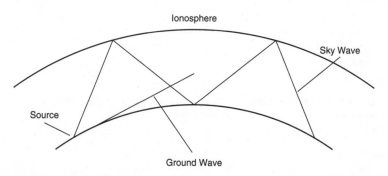

Microwave Radio

Microwave radio is used by line-of-sight carrier systems to carry large quantities of voice and data signals. It is affected adversely by atmospheric conditions and solid objects.

The tall towers with large horns or dish antennas that you see while driving through the countryside are the repeater stations for line-of-sight (LOS) microwave radio systems (sometimes called radiolink systems). Such systems can carry large quantities of voice and data traffic for several reasons:

- They require no right-of-way acquisition between towers.
- They can carry very large quantities of information per radio system, due to their high operating frequency.
- They require the purchase or lease of only a small area of ground for installation of each tower.
- Because the wavelength of the transmitted signal is short, an antenna of reasonable size can focus the transmitted signal into a beam. This provides a much greater signal strength at the receiver without increasing transmitter power.

Radiolink systems are subject to transmission impairments that limit the distance between repeater points and cause other problems. The microwave signals are

- Attenuated by solid objects (including the earth), and in addition, the higher frequencies are attenuated by rain, snow, and fog.
- Reflected from flat conductive surfaces (such as water and metal structures).
- Diffracted (split) around solid objects.
- Refracted (bent) by the atmosphere so that the beam can travel beyond the line-of-sight distance and be picked up by an antenna that is not supposed to receive it.

In spite of these possible problems, radiolink systems are highly successful and until the late 1980s carried a substantial part of all telephone, data, and television traffic in the United States. Beginning in the early 1980s, most long-distance communications carriers installed tens of thousands of miles of optical fiber. Since the late 1980s, most long-distance transmission has been moved off microwave systems to fiber-optic transmission systems. The microwave range of radio frequencies is allocated for various purposes by international treaty. Some of the frequency assignments for the United States are shown in Table 3.1.

Table 3.1. Frequency assignments for microwave radiolink systems.

Service	Frequency, GHz
Military	1.710–1.850
Operational Fixed	1.850–1.990
Studio Transmitter Link	1.990–2.110
Common Carrier	2.110–2.130

Service	Frequency, GHz
Operational Fixed	2.130–2.150
Common Carrier	2.160–2.180
Operational Fixed	2.180–2.200
Operational Fixed (TV)	2.500–2.690
Common Carrier and Satellite (downlink)	3.700–4.200
Military	4.400–4.990
Military	5.250–5.350
Common Carrier and Satellite (uplink)	5.925–6.425
Operational Fixed	6.575–6.875
Studio Transmitter Link	6.875–7.125
Common Carrier and Satellite (downlink)	7.250–7.750
Common Carrier and Satellite (uplink)	7.900–8.400
Common Carrier	10.7–11.7
Operational Fixed	12.2–12.7
CATV Studio Links	12.7–12.95
Studio Transmitter Link	12.95–13.2
Military	14.4–15.25
Common Carrier	17.7–19.3

Most common carrier radiolink systems carry analog signals, principally frequency modulation (FM). A few systems, however, carry digital signals. Two examples in extensive service in the United States are the AT&T 3A-RDS radio system, which operates in the 11 GHz band, and the AT&T DR-18 radio system, which operates in the 18 GHz band. The 3A-RDS system carries DS-3 digital signals at 44.736 Mbps, and the DR-18 system carries DS-4 digital signals at 274.176 Mbps. The DS-3 and DS-4 signals, which are made up of several lower bit-rate signals, are discussed in more detail later in this chapter.

Terrestrial radiolink systems are point-to-point; that is, the signal is transmitted in a beam from a source microwave antenna across the earth's surface to the antenna at which it is aimed. The width of the beam transmitted by a microwave antenna varies between 1 degree and 5 degrees as a function of the frequency of transmission and antenna size. As a result, the transmission is highly directional, which is desirable if the information is intended for only one destination (for example, a telephone conversation). For many applications, however, the information has multiple destinations (for example, TV broadcasts), which makes the satellite radiolink system more practical and desirable.

●
Although there are microwave systems that send data in digital form, most send data as analog signals.

Satellite Radiolink Systems

A satellite radiolink consists of an uplink transmitter signal to the satellite and a downlink retransmitted signal to receiving stations on earth.

Figure 3.9 is a simple model of a satellite radiolink system. The satellite contains several receiver/amplifier/transmitter sections, called transponders, each operating at a slightly different frequency. Each of the 12 transponders on each satellite has a bandwidth of 36 MHz. Individual transmitter sites, called uplink earth stations, send narrow beams of microwave signals to the satellite. The satellite acts as a relay station. A transponder receives the signal from a single transmitter, then amplifies it and retransmits it toward earth on a different frequency. Note that the transmitting earth station sends to only one transponder on a single satellite. The satellite, however, sends to all downlink receiving earth stations in its area of coverage, called its footprint.

FIGURE 3.9.

Satellite radiolink system.

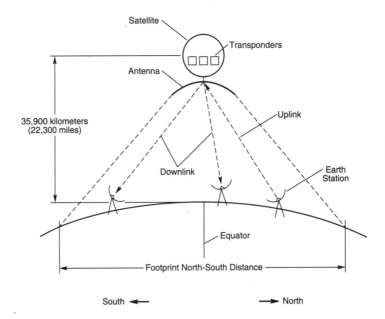

Commercial communications satellites are launched into geostationary orbit at an altitude of 35,900 kilometers (22,300 miles) above the equator. This means that the geostationary satellite is orbiting the earth at a constant speed and in the same direction as the earth's rotation about its axis. The orbiting speed is such that it causes the satellite to have a fixed location with respect to the earth. The earth station antennas, therefore, can be fixed in position and do not have to track a moving target in the sky. The angle of view for a geostationary satellite is almost 120 degrees wide. In principle, three such satellites equally spaced around the equator could cover the earth from 60 degrees north latitude to 60 degrees south latitude. In practice, the coverage angle is restricted to less than 110 degrees because the earth station's antenna must be elevated above the local horizon by more than 5 degrees.

Several types of signals are carried by satellite systems. For example, 6 MHz bandwidth standard TV programs, multiplexed 64 kilobits per second (Kbps) telephone channels, and high-speed data all can be carried simultaneously. One privately operated system, the Satellite Business System, which was merged with Hughes Network Systems, is all digital with each of the 10 transponders per satellite capable of carrying 43 Mbps of digital data.

Cellular Radio Systems

Americans have demonstrated an insatiable desire to communicate with each other anywhere, at any time. It seems that no location is too private, too noisy (audible noise), or too busy to exclude the installation of a telephone or a data terminal. Because Americans spend a lot of time in their cars, mobile telephones and data terminals are in great demand. Each telephone conversation requires a separate radio channel, and because only a limited number of such channels were available in the past, the demand for mobile telephone channels far outstripped the radio frequencies available to provide them. However, in 1982, a system allowing the reuse of channels within a metropolitan area, called the cellular radio system, began trial operation in Chicago. This system provides many more mobile telephone channels. It rapidly gained acceptance throughout the United States in the late 1980s.

●
The introduction of cellular radio systems effectively increased the number of radio channels available to mobile telephone systems.

A diagram of a simple cellular system is shown in Figure 3.10. A metropolitan area is divided into several cells, each of which is served by a low-powered transmitter and an associated receiver. The radio channels are suitable for data transmission up to 9.6 Kbps as well as voice. The number of radio channels assigned to each cell is sufficient for the predicted number of users in that cell at any one time. When a caller makes a call, his mobile unit automatically seizes a free channel in his current cell. When the caller moves out of the cell, the cell controller automatically switches control of the call from the cell being left to the one being entered. Even a different radio channel can be used, but the caller doesn't have to do anything and is never aware of anything happening. The call is linked from the cell controller to a central switching system. The central switching system can link the caller via radio to another mobile user or can access the public telephone network for connection to any fixed telephone.

The original cellular radio system was based on analog technology. It results in the dedication of a cell channel to one caller while that caller is located within the cell. This constraint limits the number of simultaneous conversations that an analog-based cellular radio system can support. In the late 1980s, research and development efforts resulted in a prototype digital-based cellular radio system in which several callers can share the use of a cell channel by time, a technique referred to as time division multiplexing. Due to the tremendous growth in the number of cellular telephone subscribers and their use of cellular radio systems, it is expected that digital-based systems will be in widespread use by the mid to late 1990s.

FIGURE 3.10.

Cellular radio system.

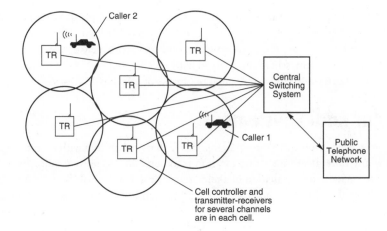

Caller 2

TR

TR

Central
Switching
System

TR

TR

TR

TR

Caller 1

Public
Telephone
Network

Cell controller and
transmitter-receivers
for several channels
are in each cell.

Effects of Bandwidth on a Transmission Channel

All transmission channels of any practical interest are of limited frequency bandwidth. The limitations arise from the physical properties of the channel or from deliberate limitations on the bandwidth to prevent interference from other sources. For primarily economic reasons, most data communications systems seek to maximize the amount of data that can be sent on a channel.

Theoretical Information-Handling Capacity of a Channel

Theoretically, a channel's data rate can be increased as desired as long as the signal-to-noise ratio increases. The practical maximum data rate limit was defined by Nyquist's theory to be two times the bandwidth.

Claude Shannon proved that the maximum capacity of an ideal channel whose only impairments are finite bandwidth and noise randomly distributed over that finite bandwidth is as shown here:

`C = W x Log₂[1 + (P/N)] bits per second`

In this formula,

P is the power in watts of the signal through the channel
N is the power in watts of the noise out of the channel
W is the bandwidth of the channel in hertz

Neglecting all other impairments, some typical values for a voice-grade analog circuit used for data are W = 3000 hertz, P = 0.0001 watts (–10 dBm), and N = 0.0000004 watts (–34 dBm). According to Shannon's Law, the value of C is as shown here:

`3000 x Log₂(1 + 250) = about 24,000 bits per second`

Shannon's value of C is normally not achievable because there are numerous impairments in every real channel besides those taken into account in Shannon's Law. Also, there are no ideal modems. However, Shannon's Law provides an upper theoretical limit to a binary channel. It is important to note that, due to the nature of the function Log_2, the value of C in the formula can be increased more readily by increasing W than by increasing (P/N).

Intersymbol Interference Reduces Capacity

One of the factors that tends to reduce the achievable capacity of a channel below the value of C in the formula is a problem called intersymbol (or interbit) interference. If a rectangular pulse like that shown in Figure 3.11 is input to a bandlimited channel, the bandwidth limitation of the channel rounds the "corners" of the pulse, as shown in the output waveform, and causes an undesired signal to appear. The "tail" or overshoot part of the new signal interferes with previous and subsequent pulses, adding uncertainty to the signal; that is, the signal might be incorrectly interpreted at the destination.

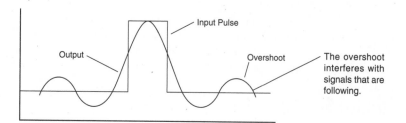

FIGURE 3.11.

Pulse response through a bandlimited channel.

Harry Nyquist analyzed the problem of intersymbol interference and developed an ideal rounded pulse shape for which that impairment is minimized. Nyquist also did much theoretical research dealing with sampling of analog signals for representation in binary form. Nyquist's Sampling Theorem says that if an analog signal is sampled 2f times per second, the samples can be used to perfectly reconstruct the original signal over a spectrum f hertz. For example, if a signal is sampled at the rate of 8000 times per second, those samples can be used to reconstruct the original signal with perfect accuracy over the range of 0–4000 hertz.

Bandwidth Requirements for Various Signals

The ratio at which information can be transmitted depends on the bandwidth of the transmission media.

Analog Signals

Transmission rates for data communications seem to follow a corollary of Parkinson's Law; that is, data rates increase to fill the bandwidth available. A good example is the introduction of low-cost modems operating at 9600 and 14,400 bps for personal computers, which are 32 and 48 times faster than the rate of 300 bps that was used for a long time. Large-scale integrated circuits made possible the remarkable increases in performance and decreases in price of these modems. In 1974, a 300 bps full-duplex modem cost $600 to $800. By 1988, a 1200 bps modem could be bought for under $100, whereas 2400 bps modems were then in the $175-to-$250 range. In 1988, 9600 bps modems designed for use on dial-up lines cost over $3000. By 1994, several vendors were selling such modems for under $125, whereas fax/data modems capable of operating at speeds up to 14,400 bps were readily available from numerous vendors for under $200.

As improved analog signal processing techniques continue to evolve, a given bandwidth can be used more efficiently.

The 300 bps full-duplex signals use two bands of frequencies, each occupying about 300 Hz. Thus, the total 600 Hz used out of the 3000 Hz available bandwidth is inefficient. The 1200 bps modems also are full-duplex and use most of the available bandwidth. Therefore, four times as much information can be sent in the same channel in a given time period. Modern 9600 bps modems use a sophisticated echo cancelling technique that enables both transmit and receive signals to flow on a common wire pair. Through sophisticated signal processing techniques, modems can even carry up to 24,400 bps using an analog signal over a voice channel.

Digital Signals

Transmission of signals in binary form can require considerably more bandwidth than an equivalent analog signal. For example, the transmission of 24 analog voice channels requires about 96 KHz (24×4 KHz). Transmission of these same 24 voice channels in digital form using the standard T1 time division multiplex format requires about 776 KHz, or about eight times as much bandwidth (776 / 96). However, the advantages gained by sending the signals as binary data more than offset the requirement for greater bandwidth. (For a discussion of the tradeoffs and advantages, refer to another book in this series, *Understanding Telephone Electronics*.)

Digital signals require a greater bandwidth than an equivalent analog signal. The advantages offered by transmitting signals in digital form more than offset this disadvantage.

Carrier Systems

In general, carrier systems are mechanisms that provide a means to send signals from more than one source over a single physical channel. The bandwidth available to carry signals in a particular medium can be allocated in two ways: by frequency or by time intervals.

Analog Carrier Systems

The frequency spectrum represented by the available bandwidth of a channel can be divided into smaller bandwidth portions, with each of several signal sources assigned to each portion. This is the principle of frequency division multiplexing (FDM). FDM is still used in some simple data communications systems, and at one time it formed the foundation for the long-haul part of the public telephone network. Since the 1980s, communications carriers have invested tens of billions of dollars in converting their infrastructure to digital technology, resulting in the replacement of essentially all carrier FDM systems by time division multiplexing (TDM) systems. Chapter 6, "Multiplexing Techniques," covers multiplexing technology to include the operation of FDM and TDM systems. One common example of a frequency division multiplexing system is a standard low-speed (300 bps) modem, which divides the spectrum available in a voice channel into two portions—one for transmit and one for receive (this concept of frequency division is discussed in more detail in a later chapter).

●
In FDM, the total available channel bandwidth is divided into smaller bandwidth portions (subchannels), each with its own signal source.

The electronic mechanisms that implemented FDM are called analog carrier systems. The carrier in an analog carrier system is a signal generated by the system, and the carrier is modulated by the signal containing the information to be transmitted. Table 3.2 shows the standard analog carrier systems in use in the public telephone network. However, as previously noted, most communications carriers have replaced their analog-based FDM equipment with digital-based TDM equipment.

Table 3.2. Analog carrier systems.

Multiplex Level	No. of Voice Circuits	Frequency Band, KHz
Voice Channel	1	0–4
Group	12	60–108
Supergroup	60	312–552
Mastergroup	600	564–3,084
Jumbogroup	3600	564–17,548

Digital Carrier Systems

The second method of dividing the capacity of a transmission channel among several separate signal sources is to allocate a very short period on the channel in a repeating pattern to each signal. This technique is called time division multiplexing (TDM). It is well suited to binary signals consisting of pulses representing a one or a zero. These pulses can be made of very short duration and still convey the desired information; therefore, many of them can be squeezed into the time available on a digital carrier channel.

●
TDM is used in digital carrier systems because many bits can be packed into the very narrow time blocks allotted to each of several signal sources.

The original signal can be an analog wave that is converted to binary form for transmitting, as in the case of speech signals in the telephone network, or the original signal can already be in binary form, as in the case of a business machine. The electronic systems that perform this TDM process are called digital carrier systems. As with the analog carrier systems, there is a standard hierarchy of digital carrier systems in the public telephone network, as shown in Table 3.3. Refer to Chapter 6, for specific information concerning time division multiplexing and the operation and utilization of a T1 multiplexer that can be used with a DS-1 digital carrier system.

Table 3.3. Digital carrier systems.

Digital Signal No.	No. Voice Circuits	Bit Rate, Mbps
DS-1	24	1.544
DS-2	96	6.312
DS-3	672	44.736
DS-4	4032	274.176

In examining the entries in Table 3.3, note that the lowest operating rate digital signal is indicated as DS-1, which consists of 24 voice circuits whose aggregate operating rate is 1.544 Mbps. Although the DS-1 digital signal is indeed the lowest operating rate signal in the digital carrier hierarchy, it is not the lowest operating rate digital transmission facility available for use. To understand why this is the case requires additional information about the DS-1 signal.

The DS-1 Digital Signal

In North America, the DS-1 is commonly referred to as a T1 line or circuit. That circuit was developed to relieve cable congestion in metropolitan areas by providing a transport mechanism for 24 digitized voice conversations to be simultaneously carried over one cable. To do so, each voice conversation is digitized using a technique referred to as pulse code modulation (PCM). Under PCM, an analog voice conversation is digitized at 64 Kbps. To provide information that enables one conversation to be distinguished from another and switched into and out of a group of conversations requires framing bits to be added to the T1 data flow. Those framing bits operate at 8000 bps and carry control information, error detection information, and a limited data link capability. Such capability, for example, enables two private branch exchanges (PBXs) to communicate with one another while transporting 24 voice conversations on a T1 circuit interconnecting the PBXs.

The 24 channels, each operating at 64 Kbps, results in an operating rate of 1.536 Mbps. When the 8 Kbps framing information is added to the T1 line, its operating rate becomes 1.544 Mbps.

Each voice channel in a DS-1 digital signal, referred to as a DS-0 or digital signal level zero channel, represents the lowest operating rate digital circuit marketed by communications carriers for direct connection to a channel on their T1 lines. Communications carriers also offer low-speed digital services operating at data rates from 2.4 Kbps up to 56 Kbps, using time division multiplexers to group multiple low-speed digital circuits onto a 64 Kbps circuit. The 64 Kbps circuit in turn is connected to a channel on a carrier's T1 line, which represents the basic backbone infrastructure used for transporting voice, data, and video across North America.

CARRIER DIGITAL OFFERINGS

The T1 circuit was originally limited to use by communications carriers to relieve the cable congestion in metropolitan areas. The successful use of this transmission facility resulted in AT&T and other communications carriers tariffing its use for commercial organizations and government agencies during the mid 1980s. Slower speed digital transmission services, such as AT&T's Dataphone Digital Service (DDS), actually preceded the public offering of T1 service because DDS was introduced during the mid 1970s.

DDS is a leased-line digital transmission service with operating rates of 2.4, 4.8, 9.6, 19.2, and 56 Kbps. A switched 56 Kbps offering is also available in certain cities.

The economics associated with the T1 tariff resulted in the monthly cost of a T1 line being 4 to 8 times the cost of one 56 Kbps DDS circuit. Because a T1 line has more than 24 times the capacity of a 56 Kbps DDS circuit, most organizations that required the use of multiple 56 Kbps DDS lines between common geographical locations soon replaced those circuits with T1 lines. In addition to the economics associated with the use of T1 lines, their additional data transport capacity enabled organizations to merge voice, data, and video applications onto a common circuit. In fact, by the early 1990s, the T1 circuit formed the backbone for most corporate and government networks.

The difference between the maximum data rate supported by DDS and the operating rate of a T1 circuit left many organizations unsatisfied with respect to the traffic-handling capacity of communications carrier circuits. Recognizing the requirements of those organizations for the use of a fraction of a T1 line's operating rate, communications carriers introduced fractional T1 (FT1) service in the early 1990s. Today, most communications carriers offer FT1 service in operating rates from 64 Kbps to 768 Kbps in increments of 64 Kbps. Although an organization contracts for a specific FT1 operating rate, the carrier normally installs a T1 line from the serving office to the customer's premises. The customer either installs equipment or gets equipment from the communications carrier, which places the customer's data into a group of DS-0s that represents the contracted FT1 service.

To illustrate the economics associated with the use of FT1, Table 3.4 lists AT&T's monthly Interoffice Channel Charges in effect in early 1994 for that carrier's Accunet Spectrum of Digital Services, that vendor's name for FT1 service. To put those monthly charges in perspective, readers should note that AT&T's 56 Kbps DDS service has monthly per-mile charges ranging from $5.88 to $1.34 based on the length of the circuit. In comparison, AT&T's T1 circuit, which provides a 1.544 Mbps operating rate, has a monthly mile charge of $3.50 regardless of the length of the circuit. Table 3.5 lists AT&T's 56 Kbps DDS and T1 circuit mileage charges in effect in early 1994. In comparing the costs listed in Table 3.5 to the costs listed in Table 3.4, it is reasonable to conclude that most DDS usage will be replaced by FT1 service, whereas organizations that require slightly more than half the bandwidth of a T1 circuit will more than likely order a full T1 line.

Table 3.4. AT&T Accunet Spectrum of Digital Services Interoffice Channel Charges.

Channel Operating Rate	Monthly Charge Per Mile
64 Kbps	$0.32
128 Kbps	$0.57
192 Kbps	$0.83
256 Kbps	$1.08
320 Kbps	$1.31
384 Kbps	$1.53
448 Kbps	$1.73
512 Kbps	$1.92
576 Kbps	$2.02
640 Kbps	$2.25
704 Kbps	$2.39
768 Kbps	$2.52

Table 3.5. AT&T 56 Kbps DDS and T1 monthly circuit charges.

Circuit Miles	56 Kbps DDS	T1 (1.544 Mbps)
1–50	$5.88	$3.50
51–100	$3.78	$3.50
101–500	$2.38	$3.50
500+	$1.34	$3.50

What Have You Learned?

1. Information is a numerical quantity that measures the randomness of a system.

2. Symbols such as letters have an information content. Not every symbol is equally likely to occur.

3. The redundancy of a system measures how likely symbols are to be repeated.

4. Data communications systems use redundancy to detect and correct errors in transmission.

5. Signals can travel through guided and unguided transmission media.

6. Adding inductance to pairs of wires is called loading. Loading is used to reduce high-frequency attenuation over the wire pair.

7. Fiber-optic transmission systems send data signals as light rays. These systems have much higher bandwidth and have immunity from most external interference.

8. Transmission rates over channels are limited by the bandwidth of the channel, the signal-to-noise ratio, and the amount of intersymbol interference in the transmitted waveform.

9. The use of different types of digital transmission systems is based on bandwidth availability and economics.

Quiz for Chapter 3

1. The amount of uncertainty in a system of symbols is also called:

    a. Bandwidth.

    b. Loss.

    c. Entropy.

    d. Quantum.

2. The twists in twisted wire pairs:

    a. Reduce electromagnetic interference.

    b. Occur at a 30-degree angle.

    c. Eliminate loading.

    d. Were removed due to cost.

3. Redundancy measures:

    a. Transmission rate of a system.

    b. How likely symbols are to be repeated.

    c. Time between failure.

    d. System cost.

4. An example of a bounded medium is:

    a. Coaxial cable.

    b. Waveguide.

    c. Fiber-optic cable.

    d. All the above.

5. Loading refers to the addition of:

    a. Resistors.

    b. Capacitors.

    c. Bullets.

    d. Inductance.

6. Coaxial cable has conductors with:

    a. The same diameter.

    b. A common axis.

    c. Equal resistance.

    d. None of the above.

7. Fiber-optic cable is suitable for:

    a. Routing through conduits.

    b. Use in most hazardous areas.

    c. Pulling connectors.

    d. Mobile video applications.

8. Fiber-optic cables operate at frequencies near:

    a. 20 MHz.

    b. 200 MHz.

    c. 2 GHz.

    d. 800 THz.

9. HF radio waves follow how many basic paths on leaving the transmitter?

    a. Two.

    b. Four.

    c. One.

    d. Many.

10. Digital cellular radio systems:
    a. Expand the number of cells.
    b. Allow multiple subscribers to share the use of cells.
    c. Allow multiple subscribers to share the use of a common channel within a cell.
    d. Extend the transmission distance of subscribers within a cell.

11. The area of coverage of a satellite radio beam is called its:
    a. Beamwidth.
    b. Circular polarization.
    c. Footprint.
    d. Identity.

12. Transmission of binary signals requires:
    a. Less bandwidth than analog.
    b. More bandwidth than analog.
    c. The same bandwidth as analog.
    d. A license from the FAA.

13. The standard first-level digital multiplex system in the United States operates at:
    a. 2.048 Mbps.
    b. 44.736 Mbps.
    c. 1.544 Mbps.
    d. 9600 bps.

14. The use of Dataphone Digital Services:
    a. Can be expected to increase.
    b. Provides a higher operating rate than FT1 service.
    c. Can be expected to be replaced by FT1 service due to the lower cost of that service.
    d. Provides a higher operating rate than T1.

Asynchronous Modems and Interfaces

About This Chapter

Having laid the groundwork by describing the form of the data (codes), the source of the data to be transmitted (terminals), and the transmission media, we now can discuss how the data is transmitted. This chapter explains how modems work in terms of frequency, bandwidth, and modulation, and it describes the data terminal equipment/data communications equipment (DTE/DCE) interface. Due to the role of the microprocessor in adding intelligence to modems, this chapter also covers smart-modem features. Features described and discussed in this chapter include command sets, error detection and correction, data compression, protocol spoofing, and the Microcom MNP protocol.

Why Data Can't Be Transmitted Directly

Although it might not have been obvious at the time, the reasons that modems are necessary were discussed in Chapter 3, "Messages and Transmission Channels." Remember that the switched telephone network uses various transmission methods from wire pairs to microwave, but only in the local area (primarily within

● Digital information cannot be transmitted directly over the switched telephone network because the portion of the network beyond the central office cannot carry direct current.

the area served by a Central Office) does an actual metallic path (wire) exist from one telephone to another. This means that we cannot transmit data in its original form as a series of pulses much farther than from our telephone to the Central Office (CO). Actually, if loading coils are used in the local loop, we can't even transmit it that far. As discussed in Chapter 3, the bandwidth (the passband) of the telephone channel beyond the CO after it has been filtered and amplified is approximately 300 to 3400 Hz, as shown in Figure 4.1. Because direct current (zero Hz) is below 300 Hz, it is not within the passband. Thus, data in its original pulsed DC or "baseband" form cannot be transmitted over this channel.

FIGURE 4.1.

Telephone channel bandwidth.

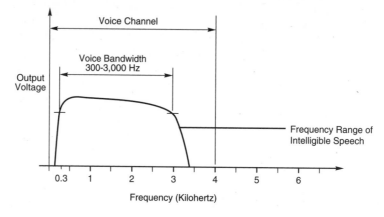

Solving the Problem with Modems

● A transmitting modem changes the digital signals produced by computers to an analog signal with a frequency bandwidth that can be transmitted over the telephone network.

● A receiving modem converts the analog signal back to its original digital form so that the receiving computer can use the data.

Because we are interested in transmitting data beyond the CO using the existing telephone network, we need to change the data pulses to another form that can be transmitted over the telephone channel. Because the telephone network is designed and optimized for transmission of analog signals in the voiceband, why not make the data look like these analog signals for transmission? This is exactly the function of a modem. The ones and zeros of the data stream from the DTE are converted to tones (or analog waveforms resembling tones) having frequencies within the 300 to 3400 Hz range. Thus, the modem is nothing more than a rather complex interface device.

At the transmitting end, incoming pulses from the DTE are converted to tones and transmitted over the telephone channel; at the receiving end, the tones are converted back to pulses, which are passed to the DTE. In other words, the transmitting modem modulates an analog signal, called a carrier, with the data (more about modulation in the next section) and uses the analog signal to carry to the other end of the telephone circuit. The receiving modem demodulates the analog signal to recover the data in its original pulse form and passes it to the receiving DTE. In fact, the name "modem" is a contraction of the words *modulator-demodulator*. One important fact to remember is this: A modem does not operate on the content of the data; it merely changes the form for transmission. The data compression capability of modern smart modems is discussed later in this chapter.

In actuality, software in the form of instructions burned into read-only memory (ROM) and referred to as firmware controls a microprocessor in the modem that operates on data before its modulation. Although many articles and books note that modems operate on data, technically it is the microprocessor in the modem that does so. The modem's internal circuitry merely changes the form of the data for transmission.

Telephone Channel Restrictions on Modems

In addition to the bandwidth limits, another restriction of the telephone channel that affects modem design is inherent in any analog transmission facility; that is, the transmission is best at frequencies near the center of the passband and poorer for frequencies toward the upper and lower limits of the passband. High-speed modems use almost all the voiceband for one channel. Therefore, most high-speed modems in North America use a carrier frequency of 1700 to 1800 Hz because these frequencies are very near the middle of the voiceband. Low-speed modems, because of their narrower bandwidth requirements, can use more than one carrier frequency within the voiceband and still operate in the "good" portion of the band.

Still another restriction of the telephone channel is that certain frequencies cannot be used. The telephone network uses the transmission channel for passing information and control signals between the switching offices. This process, called in-band or in-channel interoffice signaling, uses tones at frequencies within the voiceband. A modem cannot use these same frequencies because the network might interpret them as control tones, with disastrous results to the call.

●
Modems cannot use the frequencies in the transmission channels that are used for telephone network signaling.

Modem Interfaces

A modem has an interface to the telephone network and an interface to the DTE. The one to the telephone network is the simpler because that interface consists of only two wires, called the "tip" and "ring." As long as the modem adheres to the voltage, current, power, and frequency rules of the telephone company, the telephone channel is really just a pipe to move analog tones from one place to another.

The interface wiring between the modem and the DTE is more complex and is governed by standards discussed later in this chapter. This interface also requires that certain procedures (called a protocol) be observed in establishing communications between the two ends. First, the DTE and the modem at the transmitting end must establish communication with one another. The DTE indicates to the modem that it wants to transmit, and this modem signals to the modem at the other end of the circuit to see whether it is ready to receive. Because, in general, modems do not store data, the receiving modem must contact its DTE to see whether it is ready to receive. (This communication between the equipment often is referred to as "handshaking.") After the transmitting modem knows that the receiving modem and DTE are listening on the line, it notifies the transmitting DTE,

●
A protocol establishes the procedures used by the transmitting and receiving equipment in establishing and maintaining communications. "Handshaking" ensures that the equipment is ready to go.

which then begins passing data to the transmitting modem for modulation and transmission. On the receiving end, the receiving modem demodulates the incoming signal and passes the received data to the receiving DTE.

In half-duplex transmission (only one direction at a time), when the transmitter is finished and wants a reply from the other end, the channel must be "turned around." To do this, much of the handshaking must be done again to establish transmission in the opposite direction, and this turnaround handshaking must occur each time the direction is changed. In full-duplex transmission (both directions simultaneously), the transmission uses two different carrier frequencies. Thus, the handshaking is necessary only for the initial setup.

Analog Modulation

Modulation is the process of using some medium as a carrier to carry information between two points. For example, we could send Morse code by turning a flashlight on and off to modulate the light beam. Reflection on this process reveals that we are changing some property of the carrier to represent the data—in this instance, it is the intensity of the beam. (This might be more easily understood if we imagine using a bright light for a mark and a dim light for a space. In this case, we are modulating the brightness or "amplitude" of the light beam to send data.)

A sine wave that might be used as a carrier in a modem is illustrated in Figure 4.2. Sine waves not only are mathematical functions, but they also are fundamental phenomena of the physical universe. Sine waves are generated by devices such as electromechanical generators and electronic oscillators.

A man named Fourier discovered that any series of pulses, sounds, voltages, or similar waves can be broken down into a series of sine waves of varying frequencies and amplitudes. This means that human speech, in the air or on a telephone wire, can be analyzed in terms of the sine waves it contains. That is not to say that the human larynx creates speech by combining sound waves at different frequencies; it simply means that Fourier analysis is a fundamental and useful tool for analyzing the characteristics of any transmission channel or device, whether it be a modem or the speakers of a high-fidelity sound system.

As illustrated in Figure 4.2a, a sine wave can be defined by its frequency and amplitude. Frequency is measured in cycles per second with the unit of measurement termed the Hertz (Hz). That is, one cycle per second equals one hertz. Amplitude can be measured in units of volts peak-to-peak, volts peak, and volts root mean square (rms), as indicated in the illustration.

Another parameter of a sine wave is the phase of the wave, but it has meaning only in reference to another wave of the same frequency. Two different sine waves having the same frequency can be compared by the amount by which one leads or lags the other. Because

A sine wave signal often is used as the carrier in an analog modulation process. A sine wave can be easily generated by electromechanical generators and electronic oscillators.

Frequency, amplitude, and phase are the characteristics of a sine wave that can be varied to achieve modulation.

one complete cycle of a sine wave occurs in 360 degrees, we can consider the difference between the two waves in terms of degrees, as indicated in Figure 4.2b. The amplitudes of the two waves so compared do not have to be the same, but the frequencies must be exactly the same.

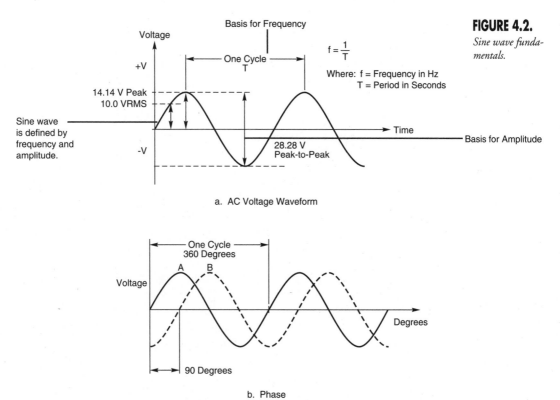

FIGURE 4.2.

Sine wave fundamentals.

Because the frequency, amplitude, and phase completely characterize a sine wave, these are the only parameters of the carrier sine wave that can be changed to modulate the carrier for transmitting information from one modem to another. All modems, therefore, use amplitude, frequency, or phase modulation, or some combination of these parameters.

Figure 4.3 illustrates amplitude, frequency, and phase modulation. Notice that the same sequence of ones and zeros of the data stream affect the carrier in different ways. After modulation, the pulses are represented by an AC signal having frequencies within the voiceband. Thus, the information can be transmitted over telephone channels. Actually, simple amplitude modulation is not used for data communications because it is very susceptible to electrical noise interference, which can cause errors in the received data. Low-speed modems use frequency modulation, higher speed modems use phase modulation, and the very highest speed modems for voiceband transmission use a combination of phase and amplitude modulation.

The modem converts the ones and zeros of the data stream into an analog signal that is within the telephone voiceband so that data can be transmitted over the telephone network.

FIGURE 4.3.
*Types of analog
modulation.*

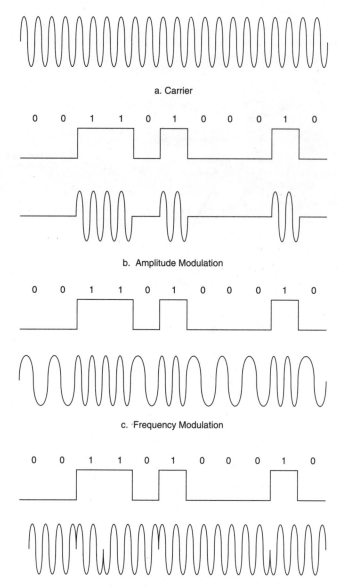

a. Carrier

0   0   1   1   0   1   0   0   0   1   0

b. Amplitude Modulation

0   0   1   1   0   1   0   0   0   1   0

c. Frequency Modulation

0   0   1   1   0   1   0   0   0   1   0

d. Phase Modulation

By separating
channel bandwidths,
modems can
transmit and receive
data simultaneously.
The calling modem
is set to the originate
mode, and the
answering modem is
set to the answer
mode.

Low-Speed Modem Operation

With this background, we can describe how a standard 0–300-baud low-speed modem
works. Figure 4.4 shows the voiceband divided into two subbands for transmission in both
directions simultaneously. Recall that such two-way transmission is called full-duplex,
meaning that the same bandwidth is available in both directions at the same time.

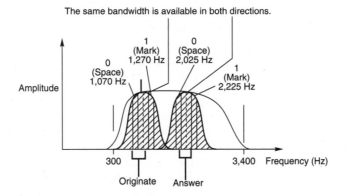

FIGURE 4.4.

Frequencies used for 300-baud full-duplex transmission.

For some people, the process of transmitting data over one channel in two directions at the same time might be hard to visualize. One could think of it as being similar to two people talking on the same local call simultaneously. Both people can talk and hear at the same time, although they might have trouble understanding each other because the entire bandwidth of the channel is available to both parties in both directions. However, the modems completely separate the data into the two bands shown, one for each direction, so that each can understand the other.

The separation is accomplished when one modem is set to the originate mode and the other is set to the answer mode, by a switch on each modem or through the issuance of commands to each modem from attached DTEs. The terms *originate* and *answer* come from the use of low-speed modems in dial-up computer applications in which a user calls a computer. The calling modem is usually in the originate mode, and the called modem is in the answer mode (makes sense, doesn't it?). By doing things this way, the marking tone of the answer modem (the high-pitched "whistle" heard when it answers) also disables any echo suppressors (which interfere with data transmission) that might be in the circuit.

In Figure 4.4, notice that the originate modem transmits zeros (spaces) at 1070 Hz and ones (marks) at 1270 Hz. The answer modem also transmits spaces and marks, but at 2025 and 2225 Hz, respectively. This type of modulation is called frequency-shift keying (FSK). (The term *keying* means turning a transmitter on and off.) The appropriate mark or space frequency is simply turned on and off by the transmitting modem as it wants to send a one or zero. If you listen on a telephone line that is carrying low-speed FSK modem transmissions, you might hear a warbling sound as the frequencies shift back and forth.

If the originating modem transmits zeros at 1070 Hz and ones at 1270 Hz, at what frequency does it receive zeros and ones? For compatibility with the answer modem that transmits zeros and ones at 2025 and 2225 Hz, the originating modem receives zeros and ones at those frequencies. Similarly, the answer modem receives zeros and ones at 1070 Hz and 1270 Hz, to maintain transmission compatibility with the originating modem.

●

FSK is a simple, economical modulation technique used in low-speed modems. The mark and space each are assigned a particular frequency, then transmitted simply by switching the appropriate frequency on and off.

The FSK modem just described is more commonly known as a Bell System 113–type device. Originally, the Bell System supplied all modems that could be attached to the switched telephone network. By the time other vendors were permitted to sell modems for use on the switched network, the Bell System's monopoly had created a large base of telephone company devices, which encouraged vendors to manufacture modems compatible with Bell System products.

In Europe, the Consultative Committee for International Telephone and Telegraph (CCITT) developed a standard for an FSK operating modem known as V.21. The V.21 standard uses different originate and answer frequencies for marks and spaces in comparison with the Bell System 113–type device, due to the requirement to avoid control frequencies used on European telephone networks. The CCITT V.21 modem uses 980 Hz for a mark and 1180 Hz for a space in its originate mode, whereas it is designed to receive a mark and space at 1650 and 1850 Hz, respectively. Due to the differences in operating frequencies, a Bell System 113 and CCITT V.21 modem are incompatible with one another.

High-speed modems use phase modulation because it requires less bandwidth for the same data rate.

FSK is a straightforward and economical modulation method that works well over telephone channels, so the logical question is this: "Why not use it for higher speed modems?" The answer is "between the lines" (no pun intended) of Figure 4.4. Higher data rates require more bandwidth. Thus, if we wanted to transmit at higher speeds, the mark and space frequencies for each subband would have to be farther apart, and the two subbands would have to be separated further to provide enough bandwidth. Soon we would be outside of the telephone channel; in other words, we would require more bandwidth than is available. Therefore, higher speed modems use some form of phase modulation, because phase modulation requires the least bandwidth of the three analog modulation methods.

Bell System 212A and V.22 Modems

Until the mid 1980s, the Bell System 212A modem was the most popular upgrade for Bell System 113–type modem users. The 212A modem can be considered two modems in one because it employs FSK modulation using the Bell System 113 frequency assignments at 300 bps. At its higher 1200 bps rate, it uses dibit phase shift keyed (DPSK) modulation. Under DPSK modulation, two bits at a time are encoded into one phase shift or signal change. Thus, the modem's signal rate (commonly known as its baud rate) is 600, or one-half of its 1200 bps data rate. The phase shift encoding of the 212A-type modem is illustrated in Table 4.1.

Table 4.1. 212A-type modem phase shift.

Dibit	Phase Shift (Degrees)
00	90
01	0
10	180
11	270

When a 212A modem operates at 1200 bps, it can transmit data either asynchronously or synchronously. One key advantage to using 212A-type modems is that when connected to a computer, they can receive transmission from terminal devices operating at either 300 or 1200 bps.

The CCITT V.22 standard is similar to the 212A at 1200 bps. However, at the 212A's lower data rate, the two modems are incompatible. The V.22 modem's second data rate is 600 bps compared with the 212A's lower data rate of 300 bps. A second major difference between the lower speeds of the two modems is in the method of modulation used. The 212A uses FSK modulation at 300 bps, whereas the V.22 uses two-phase PSK at 600 bps. Fortunately, the V.22 modem is used primarily in Europe, whereas the 212A-type modem is used primarily in North America.

V.22bis

The CCITT V.22bis (*bis* meaning "second" in Latin) has received widespread acceptance throughout the United States and Europe during the past few years and represents one of the few modems that can be used for worldwide communications. The V.22bis recommendation governs modems designed for asynchronous data transmission at 2400 bps over the switched telephone network, with a V.22 fallback method of operation. When the V.22bis modem operates in its fallback mode, incompatibility problems can arise because of the different methods used to manufacture this modem.

In the United States, most if not all V.22bis modems follow the Bell System 212A specifications for fallback operations—DPSK at 1200 bps and FSK at 300 bps. In Europe, most V.22bis modems follow the CCITT V.22 specifications for fallback operations, which include two-phase PSK at 600 bps. Thus, at their lowest fallback rate, V.22bis modems manufactured for use in North America are incompatible with those manufactured for use in Europe.

Nonstandard Modems

The requirements of personal computer users for higher transmission rates for file transfer and interactive full-screen display operations resulted in several vendors designing proprietary operating modems to achieve data rates that would have been beyond belief several years ago. To achieve data rates up to 19.2 Kbps over the switched telephone network, some modems incorporate data compression and decompression algorithms, whereas others attempt to transmit data on up to 512 distinct frequencies over the communications link bandwidth.

Modems incorporating compression really operate at variable data rates because throughput depends on the susceptibility of the data to the compression algorithms in the modem. As an example of how a modem can compress data, consider the sequence ACCOUNT*bbbbbbb*AMOUNT, in which *b* indicates a blank or space character. This sequence could represent the column headings of a report; it's similar to most accounting reports that contain columns of data with each column separated by spaces from the next column. If the modem uses a special character denoted as S_c to show space compression, the sequence is transmitted as ACCOUNT S_c7 AMOUNT between modems. At the receiving modem, the character S_c indicates the occurrence of space compression, and the number 7 indicates the number of space characters compressed. This information provides the receiving modem with the capability to decompress the data into its original form.

To prevent the natural occurrence in the data stream of a character indicating space compression and thus falsely affecting the modem at the opposite end of the data link, the originating modem is programmed to stuff an extra space-compression-indicating character into the transmission sequence. Thus, if the data stream into the modem is XYZS$_c$ABC, the modem transmits the sequence XYZS$_c$S$_c$ABC. At the receiving modem, the occurrence of the first S_c character causes the modem to examine the next character. When the receiving modem finds a second S_c character following the first, it disregards the second S_c character, restoring the data stream to its original form while preventing a false decompression of the data.

Until 1990, most compression modems used a mixture of compression algorithms. Although the actual throughput is variable, the net effect of compression is roughly double the data transfer rate of the device. In 1990, the CCITT promulgated its V.42bis recommendation. V.42bis defines a modified Lempel-Ziv compression algorithm for use in modems. This data compression technique was adopted by more than 20 modem vendors by the beginning of 1991 and by 1994 was incorporated into most intelligent modems.

Two competitive data compression methods are MNP Class 5 and Class 7. Microcom Corporation licensed MNP Class 5 compression to more than 50 modem vendors during the 1980s. Later, Microcom licensed its enhanced data compression incorporated into MNP Class 7 to other modem manufacturers. Due to the large base of MNP-compatible modems that were manufactured before the development of the V.42bis compression standard, most modem manufacturers incorporate support for both MNP and V.42bis. This dual compression support enables modern modems to have compression compatibility with older modems that support only MNP compression as well as newer modems that either support both MNP and V.42bis or support only V.42bis compression. The MNP modem protocol is discussed later in this chapter.

For further information covering data compression techniques and applications, refer to the book *Data Compression, 3rd Edition,* by Gilbert Held. Published by John Wiley & Sons in 1991, this book explains 11 compression algorithms and contains BASIC language programs that can be used to compress and decompress data.

Error Detection and Correction

When a modem compresses data before its modulation, the effect of a single bit error can be far more pronounced than when no compression occurs. To illustrate this effect, assume that the data sequence AAAAAAAA occurred. Assume that the modem is programmed to replace a string of more than three repeated characters by a special compression-indicating character followed by the number of characters that were compressed and the character that was compressed. Further assume that the special compression-indicating character is represented by the bit sequence 11111111 and that the character A is represented by the bit sequence 01000001.

> The effect of a bit error on compressed data is more pronounced than the effect on noncompressed data.

Figure 4.5 illustrates the potential effect of a bit error on a compressed sequence of bits. In Figure 4.5a, the original repeated character sequence of eight A's is shown. In Figure 4.5b, that sequence is compressed into the character sequence S_c8A, in which S_c is the previously discussed compression-indicating character. Figure 4.5c indicates the compressed binary sequence. That sequence of 24 bits in effect represents 40 bits, because the three-compressed-character sequence represents eight noncompressed characters.

a. Repeated character sequence: AAAAAAAA

b. Compressed character sequence: S_c 8   A

c. Compressed binary sequence: 11111111 00001000 01000001

d. Occurrence of bit error: 11111111 00001000 01000011

e. Received compressed character sequence: S_c 8   C

f. Decompressed character sequence: CCCCCCCC

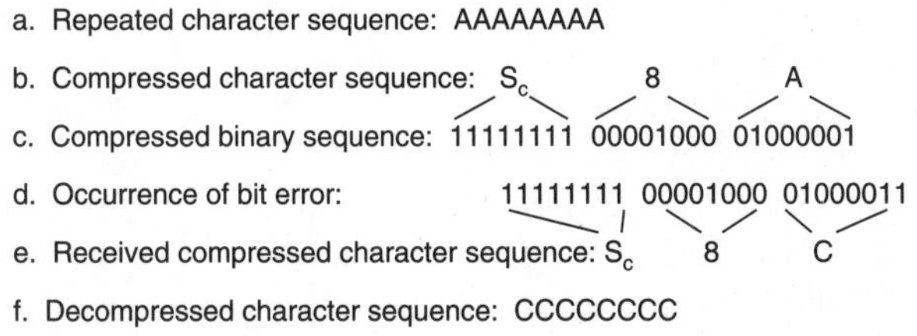

FIGURE 4.5.

Potential effect of a bit error on compressed data.

In Figure 4.5d, it was assumed that a bit error occurred that changed the next-to-last bit in the 24-bit sequence. The effect of that bit error is to change the binary value of the third character in the compressed character sequence from decimal 65 to decimal 67. This results in the character being changed from an A to a C, as indicated in Figure 4.5e, which when decompressed results in a string of eight C's replacing the original noncompressed sequence of eight A's.

If the bit error occurred in the repeat character indicator position, the number of characters decompressed would be in error. If the bit error corrupted the compression-indicating character, the receiving modem would not recognize that compression occurred. In this situation, the compression-indicating character would be received as some other character, and the modem's decompression algorithm would not know it was supposed to operate on the two following characters. Thus, the original string of eight A's would be received as the three-character sequence X8C, in which X would represent the character resulting from a bit error corrupting the compression-indicating character.

As indicated by the preceding examples, the effect of a bit error on compressed data can be significantly more pronounced in comparison to the effect of a bit error on noncompressed data. This is the rationale for the inclusion of an error detection and correction feature built into every modem that has the capability to perform data compression.

Although a modem's error detection and correction feature can be set to operate on noncompressed data, it is automatically placed into operation whenever the modem is set to perform compression. This ensures that the integrity of compressed data is maintained.

In an error detection and correction mode of operation, the originating modem first groups data to be transmitted into blocks of characters. A mathematical algorithm is performed on each block that results in the generation of one or more check characters that are appended to each block. For example, the modem might treat each data block as one long binary number and divide that number by a fixed polynomial, resulting in a quotient and remainder, with the remainder used as a check character. The modem then transmits each block to include its check character or characters. The receiving modem performs a similar operation on each received data block. That is, the receiving modem might treat the block as one long binary number and divide that number by the same fixed polynomial used to generate the checksum.

When the division process is completed, the receiving modem would use the remainder as a locally generated checksum and compare that checksum to the checksum appended to the received data block. If the two checksums match, the data is assumed to be received without error, and the receiving modem transmits an acknowledgment to the transmitting modem. The acknowledgment informs the transmitting modem that it can discard the previously transmitted block as it was received without error. If the two checksums do not match, the receiving modem assumes that one or more bit errors occurred that altered the composition of the data block. The receiving modem discards the block and transmits a negative acknowledgment to the transmitting modem, which serves as a request for that modem to retransmit the preceding block. Thus, error correction is performed by retransmission.

Because modems performing error detection and correction must store a previously transmitted block until a receiving modem indicates that it was accepted, modems with this feature must have buffer storage. The actual amount of storage required is based on the method used to perform error detection and correction. Currently, the most popular method of error detection and correction used by modems is MNP Class 4. With the development of V.42bis data compression, the CCITT promulgated the V.42 error detection and correction standard.

The V.42 error detection and correction standard actually defines two methods of error detection and correction: LAPB and MNP Class 4. LAPB, an acronym for link access protocol balanced, represents the error detection and correction method used by the Higher Level Data Link Control (HDLC) protocol used at the network layer. LAPB is the primary method of modem error detection and correction specified by the V.42 standard; MNP Class 4 represents a secondary or alternative method. Due to the large base of MNP-compatible modems, many V.42-compatible modem users typically set the modem's error detection and correction mode to MNP Class 4. Later in this chapter, we will discuss how such modem features as data compression and error detection and correction are enabled and disabled.

Packetized Ensemble Protocol Modem

A second type of nonstandard modem gaining widespread acceptance is known formally as a Packetized Ensemble Protocol Modem. This modem incorporates a high-speed microprocessor and roughly 70,000 lines of instructions built into read-only memory (ROM) chips to achieve a revolutionary advance in modem technology.

Under the Packetized Ensemble Protocol mode of operation, the originating modem simultaneously transmits 512 tones onto the line. The receiving modem determines which tones are usable and reports back to the originating device the usable frequencies over which data can be transmitted. The originating modem then selects a transmission format most suitable to each tone, forms a group of bits into a packet for transmission on each tone, and adds an error-checking group of bits that covers the data to be transmitted before actually transmitting the data over the full bandwidth. The receiving modem performs a check based on the same algorithm used by the first modem to develop the error-checking group of bits. If the transmitted and locally generated check group of bits do not match, the receiving modem requests the transmitting modem to retransmit the data, which results in error corrections by retransmission that is transparent to the modem user.

One of the prime advantages of a Packetized Ensemble Protocol Modem is its capability of adjusting automatically to the usable frequencies on a line. This capability enables the modem to lower its fallback data rate in small increments to correspond to the loss of a few tones at one time.

Figure 4.6 illustrates the transmission rate of a Packetized Ensemble Protocol Modem compared with a conventional modem as the noise level on a circuit increases. The Packetized Ensemble Protocol Modem loses its capability to transmit on one or a few tones as the noise level increases, resulting in a gradual decrease in the data rate of that modem. In comparison, most conventional modems, such as a 9600 bps device, are designed to fall back to a predefined fraction of their main data rate, such as 7200 or 4800 bps.

FIGURE 4.6.

Transmission rate versus noise level.

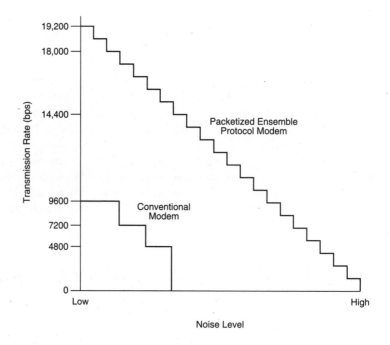

The original Packetized Ensemble Protocol Modem was developed by Telebit Corporation and is marketed as the Trailblazer. Other vendors, including Racal-Vadic, have entered into various marketing agreements with Telebit that enable them to market this modem.

Interface and Signaling Standards

There are many "standards" and "recommended practices" used to define data communications interfaces and signaling. In fact, the entire problem of data communications can be looked at as the task of passing information through a series of interfaces and transmission channels without loss of meaning.

Correct interfacing between equipment is of utmost importance to achieve error-free data communications. The most common interface standard is RS-232.

The interface that is of the greatest interest is the one between the equipment that originates and/or receives the data, the Data Terminal Equipment (DTE), and the equipment that handles the problem of transmitting them from place to place, the Data Communications Equipment (DCE). Computers are called Data Terminal Equipment (whether or not they look or act like a CRT or another terminal). Modems are called Data Communications Equipment (also called data circuit-terminating equipment or data sets) because their function is to communicate the data rather than consider, compute, or change them in any way.

Terms such as RS-232, V.24, RS-422, RS-423, RS-449, X.21, X.25, current loop, and several others are the designations of the various standards and recommendations designed to make the task of connecting computers, terminals, modems, and networks easier. As we'll see, manufacturers have in many cases used the standardized interfaces for functions that were never intended. This method helps by not increasing the number of interfaces, but it adds to the confusion of the user.

In terms of the present computer and communications world, the Electronic Industries Association (EIA) RS-232 is the standard. We'll therefore describe it and use it as a way to explain interfaces in general. We'll consider some of the limitations of RS-232, and we'll discuss some of the newer developments that eventually might replace RS-232.

The RS-232 and V.24 Interface

The proper name of RS-232 is "Interface Between Data Terminal Equipment and Data Communication Equipment Employing Serial Binary Data Interchange." Currently, the most popular version of RS-232 is revision C, which is formally referred to as RS-232C. In the late 1980s, revision D was introduced, which was followed by revision E in the early 1990s. The latest version will eventually supersede RS-232C and RS-232D. All three versions of the RS-232 standard have a large core of common functions and operating features that will collectively be referred to as RS-232. We will designate an appropriate revision to describe specific functions associated with each version of RS-232. What is written here also applies to CCITT Recommendation V.24, which is almost identical to RS-232, but the electrical signal characteristics are specified separately in CCITT Recommendation V.28.

● The RS-232 standard covers the mechanical and signal interface between data terminal equipment and data communications equipment employing serial binary data interchange.

In addition to explanatory notes and a short glossary, the RS-232 standard covers four areas:

● The mechanical characteristics of the interface (which has some surprises)
● The electrical signals across the interface
● The function of each signal
● Subsets of signals for certain applications

MECHANICAL INTERFACE

As with any standard, the purpose of RS-232 is primarily as a reference for designers of equipment; therefore, it is not a tutorial, and not particularly easy reading. (Perhaps that explains why it seems that many people who write about RS-232 have never read it.) Almost anyone in the computer or communications field, including authors, will tell you that the DB-25 connector is defined in the standard. That is simply not true when referencing RS-232C. It wasn't until reference D was introduced that the 25-pin interface

● Connector shape and pin arrangement are not covered in the standard, but the assignment of signals to connector pins, the connector gender, and cable length and capacity are covered.

connector was formally specified. Until RS-232D, all that the mechanical section covered was the assignment of signals to the connector pins (discussed in the next section), which piece of equipment has the female connector (the DCE), the recommended maximum cable length (50 feet), and the maximum cable capacitance (2500 picofarads).

Because the DB-25 connector became almost universally associated with RS-232C, its pin arrangement is shown in Figure 4.7. However, it was not defined in the standard until revision D, and some manufacturers (notably IBM) use a different connector on some of their equipment. That connector is referred to as a DB-9, which, as its nomenclature indicates, defines a nine-pin connector. This connector is normally used as a serial port interface on notebook and laptop computers as well as on many desktop computers that combine serial and parallel ports onto a single adapter card. The DB-9 connector requires less mounting space on the rear of a computer and provides manufacturers with a mechanism to reduce the size of a computer while still providing a built-in serial port connection. A later portion of this chapter describes the RS-232 circuits carried within a DB-9 connector and their relationship to the circuits carried within a DB-25 connector. RS-232D additions and changes to RS-232C are indicated in parentheses in Figure 4.7.

FIGURE 4.7.

Typical RS-232 female connector.

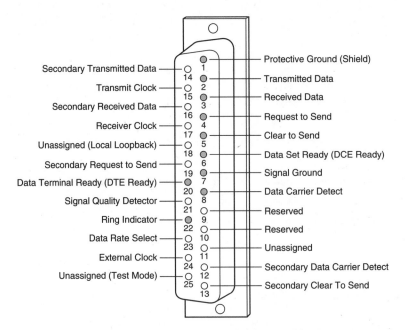

RS-232D Additions/Changes to RS-232C Indicated in Parentheses

ELECTRICAL AND FUNCTIONAL INTERFACES

Although it doesn't make much sense to say that one part of a standard is more important than another, the heart of RS-232 is certainly the electrical and functional sections. The electrical portion covers the all-important voltage and current specifications for each pin, along with such features as the requirement that the equipment not be damaged if any two pins are shorted together (which is not to say that the equipment would still work, but it's not supposed to burn up). The functional portion, perhaps the most important of all, defines the sequencing of the signals and the action taken by the DTE and DCE in response.

The standard covers the specifications for current and voltage, special electrical considerations, and the sequencing of signals across the interface.

Although the RS-232 standard defines the procedures for automatic answering by the modem and for reversing the transmission direction in half-duplex communications, it does not define automatic dialing. This is covered in EIA Standard RS-366. As you will see later, many newer modems incorporate automatic dialing in ways that the authors of RS-232 and RS-366 did not imagine.

A Pin-by-Pin Tour of RS-232

In Figure 4.8, the signals are numbered and named according to three standard systems, plus a fourth that isn't a standard but that many people use. The first is by pin number, which is the way that people who deal regularly with the interface think of the signals: pin 2, pin 3, pin 5, and so forth. The second is the EIA designation: BA, BB, CB, and so forth. The third is the CCITT designation: 103, 104, 106, and so on. The fourth is an abbreviation of the signal description: TD for Transmitted Data, RD for Received Data, CTS for Clear To Send, and so forth. A given signal often has more than one of these abbreviations because they aren't standard. Now we'll take a pin-by-pin tour and look at the signals by category and function.

PINS 1 AND 7, PROTECTIVE GROUND (GND) AND SIGNAL GROUND (SG)

If provided, Pin 1 is connected to the chassis of the equipment and is intended to connect one end of the shield if shielded cable is used. Shielded cable can be used to minimize interference in high-noise environments. Never connect the shield at both ends of the cable. Pin 7 is the common reference for all signals, including data, timing, and control signals. Pin 7 must be connected at both ends for the DTE and DCE to work properly across the serial interface. Under RS-232D, pin 1's use is modified to provide shielding, and this conductor is referred to as the shield.

Two grounds are provided: chassis (frame) ground (pin 1) for the system, and a reference signal ground (pin 7) for the signals on all the other pins.

Pin 7 is the reference signal ground for all the other pins and thus is very important. The interface will not work without it because none of the signal circuits would be completed. One difficulty of RS-232 is the use of two separate grounding wires; grounding of distributed analog systems is often difficult, and having two ground paths doesn't help any. For example, suppose that there is an RS-232 cable between two pieces of equipment where the Protective Ground is open (or not connected) but where the Signal Ground is connected to the power outlet ground at both ends. However, due to problems in the building's ground circuit, the two ends are at different ground potentials. This causes a current to flow through the Signal Ground Wire, and the resistance in the wire causes a difference in potential to develop between pin 7 at one end and pin 7 at the other end. If this potential is large enough, it could cause the data to be received incorrectly.

FIGURE 4.8.

RS-232 pin designations.

PIN NO.	EIA CKT.	CCITT CKT.	Signal Description	Common Abbrev.	From DCE	To DCE
1	AA	101	Protective Chassis Ground (Shield)	GND		
2	BA	103	Transmitted Data	TD		X
3	BB	104	Received Data	RD	X	
4	CA	105	Request to Send	RTS		X
5	CB	106	Clear to Send	CTS	X	
6	CC	107	Data Set Ready (DCE Ready)	DSR	X	
7	AB	102	Signal Ground/Common Return	SG	X	X
8	CF	109	Received Line Signal Detector	DCD	X	
9			Reserved			
10			Reserved			
11			Unassigned			
12	SCF	122	Secondary Received Line Signal Detector		X	
13	SCB	121	Secondary Clear to Send		X	
14	SBA	118	Secondary Transmitted Data			X
15	DB	114	Transmitter Signal Element Timing (DCE)		X	
16	SBB	119	Secondary Received Data		X	
17	DD	115	Receiver Signal Element Timing		X	
18			Unassigned (Local Loopback)			X
19	SCA	120	Secondary Request to Send			X
20	CD	108/2	Data Terminal Ready (DTE Ready)	DTR		X
21	CG	110	Signal Quality Detector	SQ	X	
22	CE	125	Ring Indicator	RI	X	
23	CH	111	Data Signal Rate Selector (DTE)			X
23	CI	112	Data Signal Rate Selector (DCE)		X	
24	DA	113	Transmitter Signal Element Timing (DTE)			X
25			Unassigned (Test Mode)		X	

RS-232D Additions/Changes to RS-232C Indicated in Parentheses

PINS 2 AND 3, TRANSMITTED DATA (TD) AND RECEIVED DATA (RD)

The voltage polarities transmitted and received on the data lines (pins 2 and 3) range from 5 to 25 volts for logic 0 and 1, and are reversed on the control lines.

At last we're getting down to the nitty-gritty. These are the pins that count; if it weren't for the data that passes through them, all the rest would be unnecessary. One important point to remember is that all signal names in the RS-232 standard are as viewed from the DTE. Thus, the DTE transmits on pin 2 and receives on pin 3, but the DCE transmits on pin 3 and receives on pin 2. If you imagine yourself as a computer (easier than imagining yourself as a modem), the names are easier to understand.

For people accustomed to more modern electronic interfaces, RS-232 signal levels might be a bit surprising because they are not TTL levels. In RS-232C, a positive voltage between 5 and 15 volts on pin 2 or 3 with respect to pin 7 represents a logic 0 level, and a negative voltage between –5 and –15 volts on either pin represents a logic 1. These are levels for data; the voltage polarities are reversed for logic 0 and 1 on the control lines. Under RS-232D and RS-232E, the ON and OFF voltage ranges were extended to +25 V and –25 V, respectively.

PINS 4 AND 5, REQUEST TO SEND (RTS) AND CLEAR TO SEND (CTS)

Terminals cannot transmit until Clear to Send (CTS) is received from the DCE. For private-line transmission, CTS is usually linked to Request to Send (RTS). In such cases, the DTE can use RTS to turn on the modem transmission carrier if the modem is so optioned. In this type of application, the relationship between RTS and CTS is usually a simple count-down timer that is optioned when the DCE is installed. The time delay will be set to such a value as to allow time for the carrier to turn on and become stable before CTS is returned to the DTE. If the DCE is optioned for constant carrier (without regard to RTS), the RTS/CTS delay is usually set to zero.

The signals on pins 4, 5, 6, and 20 are the handshaking signals that establish the communications link.

PINS 6 AND 20, DATA SET READY (DSR) AND DATA TERMINAL READY (DTR)

Data Set Ready (DSR)—that is, Modem Ready—is used to indicate that the modem is powered on and is not in test mode. In dial-data applications, Data Terminal Ready (DTR) is used to create the equivalent of an off-hook condition. When the modem is in auto-answer mode, DTR can be asserted in response to the ring indicator to tell the modem to answer the incoming call. Under RS-232D, the signal on pin 6 was renamed DCE Ready, and the signal on pin 20 was renamed DTE Ready.

PIN 8, RECEIVED LINE SIGNAL DETECTOR (DCD OR CD)

The Received Line Signal Detector signal is usually called Data Carrier Detect (DCD) or Carrier Detect (CD). The term CD should be avoided, however, because it can be confused with the EIA designation of CD for pin 20. The modem asserts DCD whenever it receives a signal on the telephone line that meets its internal criteria for amount of energy at the carrier frequency. Many DTEs require this signal before they will transmit or accept data. For this reason, in applications in which no modem is present, pin 8 usually is tied to pin 20, which in most cases is asserted whenever the DTE is turned on.

The Received Line Signal Detector is asserted when the modem receives a carrier of sufficient strength for reliable communications.

PIN 22, RING INDICATOR (RI)

When the DCE detects a ringing signal on pin 22, it tells the DTE that the phone is ringing. The DTE tells the modem to answer the phone by asserting pin 20.

The Ring Indicator (RI) signal is the means by which the DCE tells the DTE that the phone is ringing. Virtually all modems that are designed to be directly connected (via an FCC-approved modular plug) to the telephone network are equipped for auto answer. This means that the modem can recognize the standard ringing voltage, indicate the ringing to the DTE, and answer (take the line off-hook) when told to do so by the DTE. Pin 22 is asserted by the DCE in time with the cadence of the ringing signal on the line. Thus, when the ringing voltage is present, RI is true (on); between rings, RI is not true (off). The DTE tells the modem to answer the phone by asserting pin 20, DTR.

The 10 pins and signals in the foregoing descriptions are by far the most often used of those defined in RS-232 and V.24. It is very unlikely that equipment or cables for the small-computer market will be equipped with any other proper RS-232 signals, although sometimes (unfortunately) other pins are used in nonstandard ways that can cause problems when equipment is interconnected. We will now quickly cover the functions of the remaining pins in the specification.

PINS 15, 17, 21, AND 24

Pins 15, 17, and 24 are used by synchronous modems to control bit timing. Pin 21 indicates that the quality of the received carrier is satisfactory.

Synchronous modems use the signals on pins 15, 17, 21, and 24. Because the transmitting modem must send something (a 1 or 0) at each bit time, the modem controls the timing of the bits from the DTE. Similarly, the receiving modem must output a bit and associated timing whenever received. Pin 15 (Transmitter Signal Element Timing—DCE source) and pin 17 (Receiver Signal Element Timing—DCE source) are used for these purposes. In instances in which the transmitter timing comes from a source other than the transmitting modem (such as another modem in a multiplexing situation), pin 24 (Transmitter Signal Element Timing—DTE source) is used. Pin 21 (Signal Quality Detector) indicates that the received carrier meets some predetermined criterion for quality.

PIN 23, DATA SIGNAL RATE SELECTOR

Pin 23 looks for two pins in the chart of Figure 4.7, but actually it is either Data Signaling Rate Selector (DTE source) or Data Signaling Rate Selector (DCE source). Some modems, called dual-rate or "gearshift" modems, allow switching between two transmission speeds. Sometimes the speed is selected automatically by the modem during the training (initializing) sequence, or it might be selected by the transmitting DTE. The signal on pin 23 controls whether the modem uses the high or low speed. Usually the modem at the calling end sets the speed for the connection and informs its DTE. The calling modem signals the speed to the answering modem, which informs the called DTE by asserting Data Signaling Rate Selector (DCE source).

SECONDARY CHANNELS: PINS 12, 13, 14, 16, AND 19

Some modems are equipped with both primary and secondary channels. The five secondary signals—Secondary Transmitted Data, Secondary Received Data, Secondary Request to Send, Secondary Clear to Send, and Secondary Received Line Signal Detector—allow control of the secondary channel in the same way as described for the primary channel. In these modems, the primary transmission channel usually has the higher data rate, and the secondary channel transmits in the reverse direction with a much lower data rate (for example, 75 bps).

● In modems equipped with primary and secondary channels, the secondary channels carry signals in the reverse direction and at a much lower data rate.

Some Examples of RS-232 Connections

Now that you understand the functions of the various signals, we'll look at some examples of RS-232 interfaces. We'll begin with a simple example in which the interface is used in the proper way. Later, we'll discuss how the interface is used in ways for which it was not intended.

● Not all the RS-232 pins are used in every application, but the minimum DTE-DCE interface connections are transmitted data, received data, signal ground, and frame ground.

Computer to Modem Interface

When you call from your home computer to another computer over telephone lines, you are using the Universal Seven-Part Data Circuit that was defined in Chapter 1, "An Overview of Data Communications," and illustrated in Figure 1.9. Your computer is connected to a modem through an RS-232 interface, and the modem is connected to the telephone network. At the far end, whether it is a local or long-distance call, the other computer is similarly connected to a modem through an RS-232 interface. Figure 4.9a shows an absolutely minimum RS-232 interface for the "normal" DTE-DCE connection.

Asynchronous Modem Control

The major problem with the four-conductor interface illustrated in Figure 4.9a is the lack of control circuits routed between the modem and the terminal. For example, after you establish a connection to a distant modem, you likely would want a method to alert you to the fact that your communications connection with the distant modem was broken. This would require your terminal to monitor pin 8, which provides a carrier detect signal. As previously noted, intelligent modems include built-in buffer memory to hold data blocks until a distant modem acknowledges the correct receipt of the block. Because buffer memory is finite, the modem must have a method to inform the terminal device to suspend transmission to the modem until its buffer is emptied to the point where the modem can again receive data. This process, known as flow control, can be implemented in several ways to include a toggling of the Clear to Send signal by the modem. Later in this chapter, flow control is described in detail.

FIGURE 4.9.

Minimum RS-232 interface.

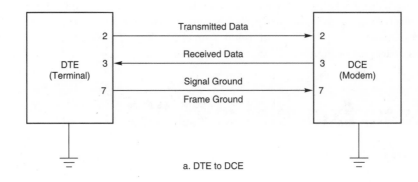

a. DTE to DCE

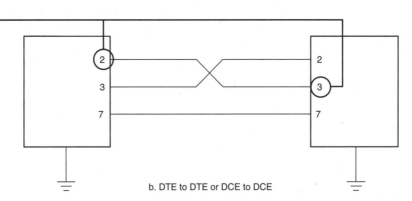

Pins 2 and 3 must be interchanged if both computer and VDT are set up as DTE.

b. DTE to DTE or DCE to DCE

Another control circuit missing from Figure 4.9a is Ring Indicator (RI) on pin 22. Its omission precludes the automatic answering operations.

To enable a terminal to inform an attached modem that it is operational and ready to receive data requires the inclusion of the Data Terminal Ready signal on pin 20. Similarly, for the modem to provide an indication to the terminal that it is powered on requires the inclusion of the Data Set Ready circuit on pin 6. Last but not least, for the terminal device to inform the modem that it has data to transmit requires the inclusion of the Request to Send circuit on pin 4.

The inclusion of the preceding control circuits results in a core set of 10 circuits required for an asynchronous intelligent modem. Because it is common practice to strap frame ground to signal ground, this reduces the number of RS-232 circuits required for asynchronous intelligent modem operations to 9 and explains why computer manufacturers incorporated DB-9 connectors as the interface to serial ports on many desktop computers and almost all laptop and notebook computers.

Table 4.2 compares the DB-9 and DB-25 pins with respect to the DB-9 connector. In examining the entries in Table 4.2, it becomes obvious that a special type of cable is required to connect the serial port of a computer with a DB-9 connector to the DB-25P (P for plug) connector that will be plugged into a DB-25S (S for socket) connector built into almost all modems. That cable must cross pin 1 at the DB-9 connector to pin 8 at the DB-25 connector end of the cable. Similarly, pin 2 at the DB-9 connector end of the cable must be crossed to pin 3 at the DB-25 connector end of the cable, and so on.

Table 4.2. DB-9 to DB-25 pin correspondence.

DB-9	Conductor Circuit	DB-25
1	Carrier Detect	8
2	Receive Data	3
3	Transmitted Data	2
4	Data Terminal Ready	20
5	Signal Ground	7
6	Data Set Ready	6
7	Request to Send	4
8	Clear to Send	5
9	Ring Indicator	22

Computer to Video Display Terminal Interface

The video display terminal (VDT) uses the simplest possible interface, as Figure 4.9 shows. If both the computer and the VDT are set up as DTE, pins 2 and 3 must be interchanged at the VDT end of the cable, as Figure 4.9b shows. Otherwise, each would expect to transmit data on the same wire.

This interchange usually is done at one of the cable connectors. However, an adapter with the wiring interchange done between its back-to-back connectors can be inserted between one end of a standard cable and the equipment. This adapter, often called a modem eliminator or null modem, permits the standard cable wiring to be left as is. These adapters are available in any combination of connector gender, that is, male-to-male, male-to-female, and female-to-female.

Computer to Serial Printer Interface

The label on the box for your new printer says, "Serial interface connects directly to the RS-232 port of your computer." When you open the box, you see a connector on the back of the printer that looks just like the RS-232 connector on your modem. (The manufacturer also charges you quite a bit extra for the absolutely essential printer cable, but that's another story.) So it appears that the RS-232 interface on your computer does double duty: it can connect to a modem or to a printer.

●

When an RS-232 cable is used to connect peripheral equipment to a computer, it might have to be modified.

But the RS-232 was never intended for connecting peripheral devices such as printers to DTEs such as computers. It's not that it won't work; the problem comes in the confusion of identities. The computer is almost always (when talking about RS-232, it always pays to say "almost always") internally wired as a DTE, and modems are always wired as DCEs (yes, always, because the role of the modem is defined precisely in the standard), but what about the poor printer? Is it DTE or DCE, fish or fowl? Does it use the same signals (and pins) that the modem uses, or are some different? Can you get by without buying that expensive special printer cable—can you use your modem cable, which, after all, looks just like the printer cable and even has the same connectors?

NONSTANDARD USE OF A STANDARD

You probably have already guessed that the answer is bad news, or you wouldn't be reading about it. The RS-232 and other standards are intended to define the interface between DTEs and DCEs for communications over networks, usually telephone facilities. They don't address the idea of using the interface as a general serial input/output port. The wiring and control of a peripheral device in the same room, such as a printer (or another computer), is simply not considered in the standard. This means that the manufacturers are presented with a useful solution to the interfacing problem but have few guidelines (and no hard-and-fast rules) on how to apply it. The result is a certain amount of confusion in the marketplace. The purpose of this section is to help clarify what happens across the interface to aid in solving the problem if necessary.

●

Modified RS-232 cables often have pins that are not connected, or they are interchanged or jumpered to adapt the cable for the desired interface connections.

One source of the confusion is that printers and similar peripherals simply don't do the same things that modems do, and they therefore don't need the same control signals. The printer doesn't need to send and receive some of the signals that the modem needs, and it needs some signals that the modem doesn't. One question is whether pin 2 or pin 3 of the RS-232 connector will be used for data transfer. In the sense of the standard, both the computer and the printer are DTE, and when a DTE is connected directly to another DTE, most of the signals defined in RS-232 are unnecessary. Although the manufacturer's special printer cable looks like an RS-232 cable, some of the pins aren't connected at all, and some of the pin connections are interchanged or jumpered together to adapt the interface on both ends. So the printer manufacturer's claim that its product is "RS-232 compatible" really means that the equipment accepts and generates only a small fraction of the RS-232 signals and (probably) doesn't violate any other parts of the standard.

Flow Control

Imagine that we decide to write our own software (called a printer driver) to pass data through the RS-232 port to the printer. We've bought the manufacturer's cable, and we've checked things such as bit rate, parity, number of stop bits, and character code. Suppose that the printer is set up for ASCII seven-bit characters, odd parity, and one stop bit. The printer manual says it can operate at 9600 bits per second, and because that's the fastest our computer can output serial data, we'll use that speed. Now we send a page of text to the printer, using our driver program. What happened? After the first line or two, there were more missing characters than were printed. It looks as though they never made it to the printer! There doesn't seem to be any rhyme or reason, but every time we try to print using our program, data is lost. Why?

Let's compare data rates. Asynchronous ASCII uses 7 bits for the character code, 1 for the parity bit, 1 for the stop bit, and 1 for the start bit, for a total of 10 bits per character. Because the computer is transmitting 9600 bits per second to the printer, the character rate must be 960 characters per second.

Digging out the printer manual one more time, we see that the printer's maximum rate is 80 characters per second. That means we are sending 12 times as much data as the printer can accept. No wonder the data was getting lost. The printer buffer would fill up, then data would be lost until buffer space became available again. What we need is a simple handshake mechanism to stop the computer from sending data when the buffer fills up and to turn it on again when the buffer empties. This is called flow control, and RS-232 is bound to have it, right? Wrong! RS-232 was designed for communicating between computers over telephone channels; the assumption is that any flow control mechanism needed is built into the software at either end. As you'll see next, various schemes have been used for flow control with varying degrees of success.

> ●
> The RS-232 assumes that the flow control needed by modems would be furnished by the software at either end of the communications network.

METHODS USED FOR FLOW CONTROL

From the previous discussion about RTS and CTS (pins 4 and 5), it would seem that these signals could be used for flow control. Although they often are used in this way, they shouldn't be, for many reasons. The problem is that the DCE is not allowed to drop Clear to Send until the DTE drops Request to Send. RTS and CTS are indeed handshake lines; the problem is that they indicate something besides that the DCE is ready to accept data. The RTS and CTS signals are intended to allow the terminal to request control of the communications link from the modem. The terminal assumes that it will keep the link as long as it needs it, and the DCE cannot arbitrarily drop Clear to Send whenever it wants to do so. This means that CTS cannot properly be used by the DCE as a flow control indicator; the DCE (or equipment such as a printer posing as DCE) can't raise and lower

> ●
> The RTS and CTS lines should not be used for flow control because it is very likely that data will be lost.

Clear to Send to tell the DTE to pause or restart transmission. Put another way, the DTE and the communications link are handshaking, not the DTE and the DCE. The handshake is for the purpose of establishing message transmission, not character-by-character or line-by-line acknowledgment for a printer.

Suppose that we decide to use RTS and CTS for flow control anyway (as some manufacturers who should know better have done). If the printer drops Clear to Send in the middle of a character transmission, what does that mean? If the transmitter stops immediately in the middle of the character, that character is sure to be garbled because timing is important in serial communications. If the transmitter waits until the character is transmitted and then stops, there might be no room in the printer's buffer for the last character. Because this possibility is not considered in the standard, the success of RTS-CTS as a flow control mechanism cannot be predicted without studying the manuals for both of the devices involved. Even taking that action is no guarantee of success, but the odds are better.

Some manufacturers avoid the conflict by using the Data Terminal Ready or Data Set Ready (DTR or DSR) pins, depending on whether their printer thinks it is DTE or DCE. For example, if pin 6 (DSR) is used to provide flow control, the printer turns off pin 6 when it can accept no more data and turns it on again when its buffer is nearly empty. Still, there is no assurance that the device on the other end of the cable will recognize the signal or interpret it correctly because these lines were not intended to be used for flow control.

●

A way to achieve flow control is for the peripheral equipment to send special characters to the computer, which uses software to recognize the characters.

Another method for flow control is for the printer to send special characters for pause and return over the data line (pin 3, RD) to the computer. The software driver recognizes the special characters and controls the terminal output according to the character received. ASCII codes DC1 and DC3 (device controls 1 and 3) are often used, but they usually are called XON and XOFF. On the standard keyboard, these characters correspond to Control+Q (resume) and Control+S (pause). The printer logic transmits Control+S when its buffer is approximately 80 percent full and Control+Q when the buffer is below 20 percent full.

Some printer manufacturers use both the DSR line and the RD line (XON/XOFF). However, problems might occur with either method. In instances in which the printer is connected to a modem (perhaps a short-haul modem on another floor of the building), there is no connection between the DSR circuits at the opposite ends (nor between RTS/CTS), so use of other pins is impossible. XON/XOFF should work fine in this instance, provided that the software recognizes it, and provided that the printer logic anticipates buffer overflow in time. Problems also can occur if several terminals are multiplexed together because the reverse characters are stored for a short time in the multiplexer.

●

In summary, RS-232 is not very reliable for flow control because it was not designed for this application.

Of course, these problems occur because RS-232 was never intended for flow control or for DTE-to-DTE connections. We should not be surprised when individually arranged flow-control methods don't always work; they simply are not part of the standard. In spite of the most intelligent modem, manufacturers support the use of RTS and CTS control signals as a mechanism for enabling flow control from the DTE to the modem and the modem to the DTE. Fortunately, most of those modems also support XON/XOFF flow control and might also support other characters that can be used as a flow control mechanism.

Limitations of RS-232

It would seem that the lack of a flow control mechanism is the major drawback of RS-232, but actually that isn't the case. Flow control is handled much better through software than through hardware, and that is the direction in which new systems are moving. Small-computer peripherals just haven't gotten there yet. RS-232 does have some limitations that restrict its use, however. After discussing these limitations, we'll look at some standards that don't have these limitations and offer other advantages as well.

Distance Limitations

The principal problem with RS-232 is its distance limitation of 50 feet. With all but the highest data rates, much longer cable runs can be successful, but they never seem quite long enough, and there's always a risk of losing data. The distance restriction is not a serious disadvantage when the modem is close to the computer or terminal and the long-haul transmission to a remote computer takes place over telephone lines. In local applications, however, RS-232 cables often are used to connect terminals directly to computers because it is convenient to use the same terminal and computer interface whether or not a modem connection is used. (Also, the RS-232 connector is probably the only one provided.) For these connections, the 50-foot limit becomes restrictive.

> ●
> The RS-232 standard of 2500 picofarads for stray capacitance can be restrictive in direct computer-to-terminal connections.

An RS-232 transmitter generates a voltage between +5 and +25 volts for one of the two possible signal states (space), and a voltage between –5 and –25 volts for the opposite state (mark). Unfortunately, these voltage levels are not the same as those inside the computer and terminal, which use standard TTL and MOS logic. This means an additional power supply (usually ±12 volts) is required for the RS-232 levels. As Figure 4.10 shows, an RS-232 receiver circuit recognizes voltages above +3 V as spaces and voltages below –3 V as marks. When a signal changes from one condition to the other, the specification limits the amount of time in the undefined region to 5 percent of a bit period. This requirement determines the maximum amount of stray capacitance allowable in the cable because capacitance limits the rise time (or transition time) of the signal. RS-232 specifies that the capacitance must not exceed 2500 picofarads (pF). Because the cables generally used for RS-232 have a capacitance of 40 to 50 picofarads per foot, RS-232 limits cables to 50 feet (2500/50 = 50).

FIGURE 4.10.

RS-232 data signal levels at the receiver.

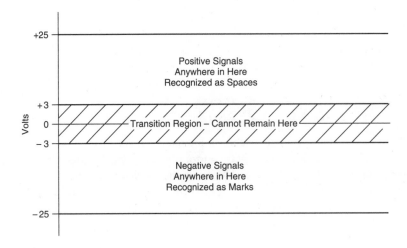

Speed Limitations

A second limitation is the maximum transmission speed of 20,000 bps, although this is not usually a disadvantage in applications between computers and terminals. The data rate between a computer and a terminal is usually less than or equal to 19,200 bps at best, and it is difficult (and might be expensive, in terms of modem costs) to transmit data even at this rate over the switched telephone network.

Ground Limitations

Improper grounding of control and data signal grounds can cause signals to be misinterpreted.

The third disadvantage of RS-232 is, as discussed previously, its grounding method. The problem is not so much with the protective (chassis) ground as with the control and data signals; all are referenced against the same signal ground wire (pin 7). This method, called unbalanced transmission, works satisfactorily most of the time. However, if there is a difference in ground potential between the two ends of the cable (quite likely for long runs), the transition region between a space and mark is narrowed. When this situation occurs, the possibility exists that a signal will be misinterpreted, as Figure 4.11 shows. Just as the various parts of the standard work together (speeds within the standard usually work fine over cables that are also within the standard), so the various restrictions interact. If you try to drive cables that are too long at speeds that are too high, all these problems tend to bite you at once.

Other Interfaces

Although RS-232 is the most commonly used interface, several additional interfaces are frequently used to connect data terminal equipment to data communications equipment. Those interfaces include RS-444A, RS-422A, and RS-449.

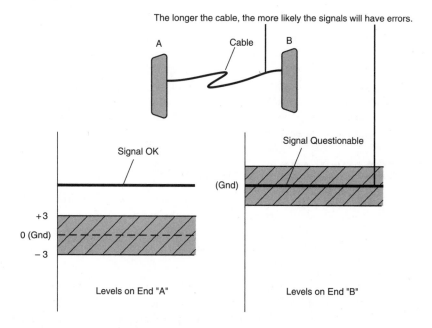

The longer the cable, the more likely the signals will have errors.

FIGURE 4.11.
Problems because of differing ground potentials in RS-232.

An Old Standby: The Current Loop

RS-232, for all its faults, at least defines connector pins and signal levels. No such standards exist for teleprinters. The serial transmission format is defined, with start and stop bits, data bits, and parity bits, but the electrical interface varies with the manufacturer, and control signals are unknown. In teleprinters, the signal interface is called the current loop. Rather than positive and negative voltages representing logic ones and zeros, the current loop uses presence or absence of current. Presence can be either 20 or 60 milliamperes, depending on the teleprinter model and manufacturer. No standard connector or standard pinouts exist for current-loop operation.

The idea of the current loop is to switch a current on and off. The active side of the transmission line generates the current, and the passive side switches or detects it. Because either the receiver or transmitter can be active, there are four possibilities: active receiver, active transmitter, passive receiver, and passive transmitter. Because of the convenience of locating the power supply at just one end of the link (usually at the computer), all four of these signals are found in a single computer-to-terminal connection.

Despite the lack of standards, designers of serial devices for computers like to include current-loop interface capability. It's a useful interface because teleprinters are still a cost-effective solution as a combination printer and terminal, and many devices other than teleprinters use it. Where RS-232 is limited to a 50-foot cable, a current loop can be up to 1500 feet long and handle data rates of up to 9600 bps without a special power supply. Unfortunately, the current-loop interface is completely incompatible with RS-232 and

●
When the serial data transmission format is defined by the presence or absence of current, the signal interface is called a current loop.

●
Data rates up to 9600 bps can be handled using current loops, even when cable lengths are longer than those allowed for RS-232 interfaces.

requires either hardware that has both interfaces built-in or interface boxes. The interface boxes can be built to adapt to any of the four possible interfaces. For example, if two microcomputers that are to be connected both contain the active interface, an active-to-active converter is required to directly connect them. Similarly, to connect a passive terminal directly to another passive terminal, a passive-to-passive converter is required. Fortunately, the converters can be easily constructed using an optoisolator. The active-to-active converter does not even need a power supply, although the passive-to-passive must have one to generate the current.

RS-422A, RS-423A, and RS-449

Useful though the current loop might be in some cases, most of the world is not moving away from RS-232 back to teleprinters. Instead, the movement is toward three types of interfaces. Two are similar to RS-232, but with some of the warts removed; the other is quite different, with hardware functions replaced by software. We'll examine the ones more like RS-232 first.

In the early 1970s, the EIA introduced the RS-422A, RS-423A, and RS-449 standards to overcome the defects of RS-232 while at the same time incorporating and improving on the advantages of the current-loop interface. A major change was to unbundle the electrical, mechanical, and functional specifications of RS-232 into separate documents. RS-422A and RS-423A cover only electrical specifications; RS-449 covers control functions.

RS-422A

By using balanced transmission based on the RS-422A standard, greater speed in data transmission is achieved, and ground potential problems are eliminated.

To allow transmission at high data rates, RS-422A uses two separate wires for each signal. This technique, called balanced transmission, doubles the number of wires in the cable but permits very high data rates and minimizes the problem of varying ground potential. Because ground is not used as a voltage reference, RS-422A grounding requirements are much less critical than those of RS-232, and the use of the Signal Ground wire is optional with RS-422A.

Another major difference between RS-422A and RS-232 is the transition region between mark and space states. With the elimination of the ground potential problem, the transition region can be much narrower. In RS-422A, the difference between the voltages on the two wires determines whether a mark or a space is sent. This difference is only 0.4 V in RS-422A, whereas it is 6 V (+3 V and –3 V) in RS-232. If the difference signal between the two wires is positive and more than 0.2 V, the receiver reads a mark; if it is negative and more than –0.2 V, the receiver reads a space. These voltage values allow suitable transmitters and receivers to be implemented with the ±5 V power supply commonly available in computers.

RS-423A

RS-423A transmits at lower speeds and uses one wire as a common return path for all signals in a given direction (unbalanced transmission like RS-232, but with two return wires). The RS-423A standard operates in both RS-232 and RS-422A environments. It provides users of existing RS-232 interfaced equipment with a way to move to the new RS-422A regime, including a defined RS-232 to RS-422A adapter connector.

Because of the much smaller transition region, RS-422A transmitters do not drive RS-232 receivers correctly. RS-423A equipment, on the other hand, interfaces with RS-232 signals. Each direction of transmission uses a common return path that is connected to ground only at the transmitter end. The receiver determines whether a mark or a space is present by examining whether the signal wire is negative or positive with respect to the common return. Because this return path does not connect to ground in the receiver, the problem of ground currents does not arise.

In an RS-423A transmitter, the voltage difference between the signal line and the common return must be at least 4 V—positive for a space and negative for a mark. This gives an 8 V transition region, which is compatible with RS-232 receiver circuitry but which presents the same power supply problem that occurs with RS-232. Because the RS-423A receiver must properly respond to the same 0.4 V transition region as an RS-422A receiver, an RS-422A transmitter can be used with RS-423A receivers.

> ●
> The RS-423A standard defines an adapter for use between RS-232C and RS-422A that enables RS-232C equipment to interface with RS-422A equipment.

RS-449

RS-449 is the intended successor to the functional portion of RS-232, including the mechanical specification of the plugs and sockets. Apart from its improved speed and distance specifications, RS-449 offers some minor functional enhancements over RS-232 in automatic modem testing and provision for a standby channel, but it still does not incorporate outward dialing. The acceptance of RS-449 in the marketplace seems questionable at this time.

Figure 4.12 shows the RS-449 signals with the corresponding RS-232 and V.24 signals. Notice the similarity between the new and old standards. The major differences are in the grounding arrangements (Send Common and Receive Common) and testing facilities. Apart from these, only a few miscellaneous signals have been added. All signals use the RS-423A transmission standard except those that can optionally use the RS-422A for higher speed links. (Two wires are specified for each of these.) The signals are divided between a 37-pin and a 9-pin connector, and the ground and common signals are handled separately for each cable. Many applications will not need the smaller cable because it contains only signals relevant to the secondary channel.

> ●
> The RS-449 standard, which uses two connectors rather than one, is intended to replace the functional portion of RS-232. Even so, it has no provision for automatic dialing.

FIGURE 4.12.

Comparing RS-449 with RS-232 signals.

RS-449		RS-232*		CCITT Recommendation V.24	
SG	Signal Ground	AB	Signal Ground (Shield)	102	Signal Ground
SC	Send Common			102a	DTE Common
RC	Receive Common			102b	DCE Common
IS	Terminal in Service				
IC	Incoming Call	CE	Ring Indicator	125	Calling Indicator
TR	Terminal Ready	DC	Data Terminal Ready (DTE Ready)	108/2	Data Terminal Ready
DM	Data Mode	CC	Data Set Ready (DCE Ready)	07	Data Set Ready
SD	Send Data	BA	Transmitted Data	103	Transmitted Data
RD	Receive Data	BB	Received Data	104	Received Data
TT	Terminal Timing	DA	Transmitter Signal Element Timing (DTE Source)	113	Transmitter Signal Element Timing (DTE Source)
ST	Send Timing	DB	Transmitter Signal Element Timing (DCE Source)	114	Transmitter Signal Element Timing (DCE Source)
RT	Receive Timing	DD	Receive Signal Element Timing	115	Receiver Signal Element Timing (DCE Source)
RS	Request to Send	CA	Request to Send	105	Request to Send
CS	Clear to Send	CB	Clear to Send	106	Ready for Sending
RR	Receiver Ready	CF	Received Line Signal Detector	109	Data Channel Received Line Signal Detector
SQ	Signal Quality	CG	Signal Quality Detector	110	Data Signal Quality Detector
NS	New Signal				
SF	Select Frequency			126	Select Transmit Frequency
SR	Signaling Rate Selector	CH	Data Signaling Rate Selector (DTE Source)	111	Data Signaling Rate Selector (DTE Source)
SI	Signaling Rate Indicator	CI	Data Signaling Rate Selector (DCE Source)	112	Data Signaling Rate Selector (DCE Source)
SSD	Secondary Send Data	SBA	Secondary Transmitted Data	118	Transmitted Backward Channel Data
SRD	Secondary Receive Data	SBB	Secondary Received Data	119	Received Backward Channel Data
SRS	Secondary Request to Send	SCA	Secondary Request to Send	120	Transmit Backward Channel Line Signal
SCS	Secondary Clear to Send	SCB	Secondary Clear to Send	121	Backward Channel Ready
SRR	Secondary Receiver Ready	SCF	Secondary Received Line Signal Detector	122	Backward Channel Received Line Signal Detector
LL	Local Loopback	(LL)	(Local Loopback)	141	Local Loopback
RL	Remote Loopback			140	Remote Loopback
TM	Test Mode	(TM)	(Test Mode)	142	Test Indicator
SS	Select Standby			116	Select Standby
SB	Standby Indicator			117	Standby Indicator

*RS-232D Additions/Changes to RS-232C Indicated in Parentheses

One of the major problems that prevented more than a token acceptance of the RS-449 standard is its use of two connectors, with each connector differing in size and conductor connection from the RS-232 connector used with tens of millions of DTEs and DCEs. Recognizing that RS-449 would probably not fulfill its intended role, the EIA announced the RS-530 standard in the late 1980s as the successor to RS-449. Both RS-442 and RS-423 standards will continue to exist, and both are referenced by the RS-530 standard.

RS-530

RS-530 is similar to RS-449 in that it provides equipment with the capability to transmit data above the RS-232 limit of 20 Kbps. Like RS-232, RS-530 uses the nearly universal 25-pin D-shaped interface connector.

The RS-530 standard gets its capability to transmit data above 20 Kbps by the use of balanced signals in place of several RS-232 secondary signals and the Ring Indicator signal. This balanced signalling technique is accomplished by the use of two wires with opposite polarities for each signal to minimize distortion.

Table 4.3 summarizes the RS-530 interchange circuits based on their pin assignments. Although no equipment conforming to this new standard was marketed at the time this book revision was prepared, its elimination of the Ring Indicator signal suggests that its use will be reserved for non-PSTN applications.

Table 4.3. RS-530 interchange circuits.

Pin Number	Circuit	Description
1		Shield
2	BA	Transmitted data
3	BB	Received data
4	CA	Request to send
5	CB	Clear to send
6	CC	DCE ready
7	AB	Signal ground
8	CF	Received line signal detector
9	DD	Received signal element timing (DCE source)
10	CF	Received line signal detector
11	DA	Transmit signal element timing (DTE source)
12	DB	Transmit signal element timing (DCE source)
13	CB	Clear to send
14	BA	Transmitted data
15	DB	Transmitter signal element timing (DCE source)
16	BB	Received data
17	DD	Receiver signal element timing (DCE source)

continues

Table 4.3. continued

Pin Number	Circuit	Description
18	LL	Local loopback
19	CA	Request to send
20	CD	DTE ready
21	RL	Remote loopback
22	CC	DCE ready
23	DC	DTE ready
24	DA	Transmit signal element timing (DTE source)
25	TM	Test mode

RS-366

The RS-366 standard is different because it deals with automatic dialing under computer control.

None of the RS-standards discussed provides for automatic dialing of calls by a computer. RS-232 and RS-449 provide specifications for answering calls, but not for dialing. A different standard, RS-366, covers automatic calling units. The reason is that until the late 1980s, equipment for placing calls under computer control was expensive because the actions required in making a telephone call can be quite complicated. The dialing equipment must be able to determine whether the line is free, take the phone off hook (in effect), wait for and recognize a dial tone, dial the number, and understand and respond to the various call progress tones (such as the busy signal) the telephone system provides to indicate the status of a call.

The principal use of RS-366 automatic dialing equipment in data communications is for dial backup for private-line data circuits, and for automatic dialing of remote terminals to allow them to transmit data. For example, a company's central computer could be programmed to automatically dial the computer in each branch office each evening and to cause (via software) the day's transactions to be transmitted to the main office.

The growth in availability of low-cost intelligent modems that respond to commands generated by DTEs has considerably reduced the use of RS-366–based automatic dialing equipment. Although RS-366 is still used to control the operation of synchronous modems, the use of RS-366 is expected to further decline because many modem manufacturers now are incorporating a synchronous dial control capability into their products.

CCITT X.21

The CCITT has charted a course different from the RS-standards, a course that was predicated on the eventual availability of direct digital connection to a digital telephone network. Then all data transmission will be synchronous, and the communications equipment will provide bit and byte timing signals. The CCITT X.21 recommendation, introduced in 1976, includes the protocol for placing and receiving calls and for sending and receiving data using full-duplex synchronous transmission. Byte-timing signals are an option, but one that nearly all digital telephone exchanges will almost certainly provide. In sharp contrast to RS-232, RS-449, and RS-530, X.21 uses only six signals. The electrical specifications are contained in recommendations X.26 (corresponding to EIA RS-422A) and X.27 (corresponding to EIA RS-423A).

> The CCITT standards are aimed toward direct digital data communications. CCITT X.21 covers both automatic dialing and answering, and it uses full-duplex synchronous transmission.

The eventual maximum line speed under X.21 is likely to be 64,000 bps, the data rate now used to encode voice in digital form in the telephone network. In Europe, British Telecom offers X.21 customer data rate access to its Kilostream digital service at 2.4, 4.8, 9.6, 48, and 64 Kbps. Customer data rates up to 9.6 Kbps are converted to a line rate of 12.8 Kbps, whereas data rates of 48 and 64 Kbps both use a line rate of 64 Kbps for transmitting through the Kilostream network.

The circuits used in X.21 are given in Table 4.4. The first two circuits listed provided the voltage reference and ground connections. The computer sends data to the modem on the transmit line, and the modem returns data on the Receive line. The Control and Indication circuits provide control channels in two directions. The Signal Element Timing line carries the bit timing, and the Byte Timing line carries the byte timing. Although the Control and Indication lines are control lines, most of the controlling information uses the Transmit and Receive lines. The computer changes the state of Control when it wants to place a call, just as you lift the handset when you want to dial. To end the call, the computer changes Control back to the idle state. Similarly, the modem changes the state of Indication when the remote telephone is answered and changes it back if it shuts down. All the dialing information travels on the Transmit line in coded form, and all the information about tones comes back on the Receive line.

Table 4.4. CCITT X.21 signals.

Interchange Circuit	Name	To DCE	From DCE
G	Signal Ground or Common Return	(Note)	
Ga	DTE Common Return	X	
T	Transmit	X	
R	Receive		X

continues

Table 4.4. continued

Interchange Circuit	Name	To DCE	From DCE
C	Control	X	
I	Indication		X
S	Signal Element Timing		X
B	Byte Timing		X

Note: See Recommendation X.24.

The major advantage of X.21 over RS-232, RS-449, and RS-530 is that the X.21 signals are encoded in serial digital form. For example, when a dial tone is received, a continuous sequence of ASCII "+" characters is sent to the computer on the Receive wire. In effect, this is a digital dial tone. The computer dials the number by transmitting it as a series of ASCII characters on the Transmit line, one bit at a time. After dialing the call, the computer receives call progress signals from the modem on the Receive wire. These signals indicate such things as number busy, access disallowed, and network congestion.

By using serial digital coding rather than dedicated wires for special functions, X.21 establishes a basis for providing special services in computer communication. A short-code-dialing or repeat-last-call facility would be extremely useful, for example, to reconnect a call every time you complete a line of typing at the terminal. (Some European nations are trying this approach to networking right now.) If the line could be disconnected while you are typing, long-distance calls would be much cheaper. Of course, this would also depend on the tariff policies of the telecommunication carriers. Using X.21 could allow many of the advantages of telecommunications by the packet-switching technique without the associated complexity.

> X.21, with its signal encoded in serial digital form, permits a few signal lines to accomplish all functions.

Although X.21 is defined as the lowest (or "physical") level of the international X.25 packet-switching protocol, it is far ahead of its time because direct digital connection to public telephone networks is hardly possible now. For this reason, CCITT offers the X.21bis recommendation as an interim measure to connect existing computer equipment to packet communication services. X.21bis is virtually identical to CCITT V.24 and RS-232. (Packet switching and CCITT protocols are discussed more in a later chapter.)

Types of Modems

Next, we'll cover the types of modems available, including the asynchronous (300 or 300/1200 baud) auto-answer modem, the full-duplex asynchronous private line modem, the half-duplex asynchronous private line modem, and smart modems.

Asynchronous (300 or 300/1200 Baud) Auto-Answer Modem

Asynchronous 300- or 300/1200-baud modems are usually used with personal computers. The signals needed are Protective Ground, Signal Ground, Transmitted Data, Received Data, Request To Send, Clear To Send, Data Terminal Ready, Ring Indicator, Received Line Signal Detector, and possibly Data Set Ready. Pin 20 (DTR) indicates that the computer is ready to receive calls, and Pin 22 (RI) indicates that the modem is receiving the telephone ringing signal, going high and low as the ringing current goes off and on. (This is the way a modem can count how many rings to wait before answering.) If the computer leaves pin 20 (DTR) on all the time, the modem answers incoming calls without delay. If DTR is off, the computer turns it on in response to receiving an RI signal to tell the modem to answer the call. At the completion of the call, the computer turns off pin 20 (DTR) to cause the modem to disconnect the line (go on hook).

● The asynchronous 300 or 300/1200-baud auto-answer modem is normally used with unattended personal computers that are connected to dial-up circuits.

The following sequence of events is one possible set that can happen when a computer receives a call from another computer via a low-speed asynchronous modem and manual modem operations are employed. When the modem detects ringing, it turns on pin 22 (RI), the DTE responds by asserting pin 20 (DTR), and the modem goes off hook to answer the phone. The answering DTE asserts pin 4 (RTS), which commands the modem to turn on its transmitter. After the RTS-CTS delay, the modem responds by asserting CTS. At the other end of the line, the computer operator hears the carrier signal and either pushes the data button or puts the telephone handset into the acoustic coupler. Now the calling modem's transmitter turns on, producing its own carrier tone. When the modem at the receiving computer hears this carrier, it turns on pin 8 (DCD). On receiving this signal, the receiving computer begins transmitting data to tell the sending computer to log on, and so forth. Some operating systems wait for the caller to transmit a special character to begin the log-on process.

At the end of the session, the caller logs off, causing the receiving computer to terminate the call. It turns off pin 4 (RTS), which causes the receiving modem to turn off its carrier signal. The receiving computer then drops pin 20 (DTR), causing the modem to go on hook to "hang up" the telephone line. At the calling end, pin 8 (DCD) goes off, the operator replaces the handset, and the action is complete.

When modems with an automatic answering capability are used, the previously described operations occur automatically and without operator intervention. If you can envision a typical data center or even a modern bulletin board system, you can get an appreciation for the use of automatic answering modems. Without this capability, one or more operators would be required to be on duty to place receiving modems into their data mode in response to incoming calls generating ringing signals. In fact, data centers during the late 1950s and early 1960s relied on the use of operators to place modems into their data mode in response to incoming calls. Fortunately for operators whose level of job satisfaction in those days was probably equivalent to watching paint dry, the development of automatic answering modems enabled computers to be programmed to answer incoming calls automatically. This formed the basis for the emergence of unattended bulletin board systems, which began to appear during the late 1970s and early 1980s and which today number in the tens of thousands.

Full-Duplex Asynchronous Private Line Modem

A private line modem does not have the capability for automatic answering because it's not needed; the modem is always online.

The full-duplex asynchronous modem could be used on switched lines as well. It is called a private line modem because it is not equipped for automatic answer. The signals used are Protective Ground, Signal Ground, Transmitted Data, Received Data, Received Line Signal Detector (pin 8), and Data Set Ready (pin 6). Pin 8 (DCD) says, in effect, "I hear something like a modem talking to me"—in other words, that another modem is trying to make contact on the line. Pin 6 (DSR) usually is not used in asynchronous modems, but it could indicate that the modem is ready and not in voice or test mode.

Half-Duplex Asynchronous Private Line Modem

The signals used in the half-duplex asynchronous modem are Protective Ground, Signal Ground, Transmitted Data, Received Data, Request To Send, Clear To Send, Received Line Signal Detector, and possibly Data Set Ready. Pins 4 and 5 (RTS and CTS) control the transmission direction in the half-duplex operation. The computer asserts pin 4 (RTS) when it wants to transmit. The modem responds by turning on pin 5 (CTS) to indicate that it is ready to receive characters to be transmitted. There is a built-in delay (typically 200 milliseconds) between the Request To Send and the Clear To Send response because the modem must generate the carrier waveform and allow it to stabilize. When transmission is completed in that direction, the computer drops pin 4 (RTS), causing the modem to turn off the transmitter and to drop CTS. The process of determining who transmits when, and how to tell when the other end is finished, is the responsibility of the software protocol, which is outside the modem and the RS-232 interface.

Smart Modems

By combining a microprocessor with a modem, both data communications and automatic dialing can be realized in one unit—a "smart modem."

The so-called "smart" or "intelligent" modem combines a standard modem and a microprocessor to provide both data communications and automatic dialing in one unit. (One of the first intelligent modems to be marketed is the Smartmodem 1200 made by Hayes Microcomputer Products, Inc.) A smart modem accepts commands in ASCII form over the same RS-232 interface used for data transmission and can respond over the same interface with either status codes or sentences. For example, the computer operator would turn the modem on and load the terminal software, then type a code such as AT DT1-800-772-5942. This code tells the modem to take the phone line off hook, wait for a dial tone, then tone dial (using DTMF tones) the number 1-800-772-5942. The modem will attempt to do this. If the number is busy, the modem's response, "number busy," would appear on the computer's screen. Modems of this type usually can redial the last number entered, and many of these modems automatically keep trying a number at preset intervals if they encounter a busy signal. Some modems can store a list of frequently called numbers (such as the preceding one) that the user can select by entering only a two- or three-digit code.

The smart modem contradicts our previous statement that modems don't look at the data that passes through them, because it does examine some of the information coming over the RS-232 interface for its commands. Smart modems are being used increasingly by business and individual computer users, and a number of software products support these modems. Virtually all the numerous developed communications software products support the basic Hayes modem command set, which has become a de facto standard. Thus, if you are considering the purchase of a smart modem, it would be wise to consider one that is compatible with the Hayes commands.

The Hayes command set consists of a basic set of commands and command extensions. The basic commands, such as placing the modem off hook and dialing a number, are applicable only to modems designed to transmit and receive data at that speed.

Commands in the Hayes command set are initiated by transmitting an attention code to the modem, followed by an appropriate command or set of commands. The attention code is the character sequence AT, which must be input by the user or sent to the modem by a software program in all uppercase or all lowercase letters. The requirement to prefix all command lines with the code AT has led many modem manufacturers to denote their modems as Hayes AT compatible or simply AT compatible.

A Hayes Smartmodem can hold up to 40 characters in its command buffer, permitting a sequence of commands to be transmitted to the modem on one command line. This 40-character limit does not include the attention code, nor does it include spaces placed in a command line to make it more readable. Table 4.5 lists the major commands included in the basic Hayes command set. Other modems, such as the Telebit Trailblazer, employ a command set that is a superset of the Hayes command set.

Table 4.5. Major commands of the basic Hayes command set.

Command	Description
A	Answer call
A/	Repeat last command
C	Turn modem's carrier on or off
D	Dial a telephone number
E	Enable or inhibit echo of characters to the screen
H	Hang up telephone (on hook) or pick up telephone (off hook)

continues

Table 4.5. continued

Command	Description
I	Request identification code or request checksum
M	Turn speaker off or on
O	Place modem online
P	Pulse dial
Q	Request modem to send or inhibit sending of result code
R	Change modem mode to "originate-only"
S	Set modem register values
T	Touch-Tone dial
V	Send result codes as digits or words
X	Use basic or extended result code set
Z	Reset the modem

Although communications software that supports the basic Hayes command set operates with this modem, such software might not be capable of supporting many of the advanced features incorporated into the Telebit modem. In fact, communications software that supports only the basic Hayes command set might not be sufficient to use most of the advanced features incorporated into both Hayes and other vendor modem products developed over the past five years. Those features, such as error detection and correction, data compression, fax/data mode selection, and operating rates above 2400 bps, are usually enabled through the use of extended command codes or settings in predefined modem S registers. This explains why it is no trivial exercise to develop a communications program that supports the features of a large number of modems developed by different vendors. A later section in this chapter examines a few of the extended commands used to enable different features built into several popular modems.

This is the basic format required to transmit commands to a Hayes-compatible modem:

```
AT Command[Parameter(s)]Command[Parameter(s)]..Return
```

Each command line includes the prefix AT, followed by the appropriate command and the command's parameters. The command parameters are usually the digits 0 or 1, which serve to define a specific command state. As an example, C1 is the command that tells the modem to turn on its carrier signal, whereas C0 is the command that causes the modem to turn off its carrier signal. Up to 40 characters can be entered into a command line, and each command line must be terminated by a carriage return character.

To illustrate the use of the Hayes command set, suppose that you want to automatically dial information for New York City. The number is 212-555-1212. First, you tell the modem to go off hook, which is similar to picking up a telephone handset. Then, you tell the modem the type of telephone system you are using—pulse or touch-tone—and the telephone number to dial. If you have a terminal or personal computer connected to a Hayes-compatible modem, the following commands would be sent to the modem:

```
AT H1
AT DT9,1,212-555-1212
```

In the first command, the 1 parameter used with the H command places the modem off hook. In the second command, DT tells the modem to dial a telephone number using touch-tone (T) dialing. The digits 9 and 1 are included in the telephone number because it is assumed that you had to dial 9 to gain access to an outside line through your company's switchboard and 1 for long distance. The commas between the outside line (9), long-distance access number (1), and the area code (212) cause the modem to pause for two seconds before dialing the area code. Usually, two seconds is long enough for you to hear the outside line and long-distance dial tones before the modem dials the next number.

Because a smart modem automatically goes off hook when dialing a number, the first command line is not required and is normally used for receiving calls. In the second command line, the type of dialing does not have to be specified if a previous call was made because the modem automatically uses the last type specified. Although users with only pulse dialing availability must specify P in the dialing command when using a Hayes Smartmodem, other vendors offer modems that can determine automatically the type of dialing facility that the modem is connected to, then use the appropriate dialing method without requiring the user to specify the type of calling.

The MNP Protocol

Among the first modems to offer an error detection and correction feature were products manufactured by Microcom, Inc. This company created a revolution in modem technology by developing a modem protocol known as MNP, an acronym for Microcom Networking Protocol.

MNP is a communications protocol built into MNP-compatible modems that supports interactive and file transfer applications. In developing MNP, Microcom recognized that the first implementation of the protocol would not necessarily be the last and structured it to accommodate changes in its implementation. To accomplish this, the major functions of the protocol are divided into classes. When an MNP modem communicates with another MNP modem, the two devices negotiate with each other to operate at the highest mutually supported class of MNP service.

Table 4.6 summarizes the features associated with available MNP classes. Until 1990, Microcom licensed MNP only through Class 5 to other modem manufacturers. In that year, Microcom began to offer full MNP licenses. Thus, an MNP-compatible modem, although compatible with all other MNP modems, might be compatible with only a sub-set of available MNP classes unless a third-party vendor got a full license and incorporated all MNP classes into the product.

Table 4.6. MNP classes.

Class	Description of Functions Performed
Class 1	Uses asynchronous byte-oriented half-duplex transmission that provides an efficiency of approximately 70 percent. A 2400 bps modem using MNP Class 1 gets a throughput of 1690 bps.
Class 2	Uses asynchronous byte-oriented full-duplex data transmission that provides an efficiency of approximately 84 percent. A 2400 bps modem using MNP Class 2 gets a throughput of approximately 2000 bps.
Class 3	Strips start and stop bits from asynchronous data, enabling synchronous bit-oriented full-duplex transmission between modems. This provides an efficiency of about 108 percent, enabling a 2400 bps modem to get a throughput of approximately 2600 bps.
Class 4	Adds adaptive packet assembly in which packet sizes are dynamically adjusted based on the number of retransmission requests. Also adds Data Phase Optimization, which provides a mechanism to reduce protocol overhead. The efficiency of Class 4 is approximately 120 percent, enabling a 2400 bps modem to get a throughput of 2900 bps.
Class 5	Adds data compression to Class 4 service, which provides an average compression ratio of 1.6 to 1, meaning that every 16 characters are compressed into 10 characters for transmission. This increases the protocol efficiency of Class 5 to approximately 200 percent, enabling a 2400 bps modem to get a throughput of about 4800 bps.
Class 6	Adds Universal Link Negotiation and Statistical Duplexing to Class 5. Universal Link Negotiation enables MNP modems to begin operation at a common low-speed modulation method and negotiate the use of an alternative higher speed modulation method. At the end of a successful link negotiation for Class 6 operation, the two modems operate at 9600 bps using V.29 technology. Statistical Duplexing results in the monitoring of user traffic patterns to enable the dynamic allocation of V.29 half-duplex transmission to resemble full-duplex transmission. Under Class 6 9600 bps operations, MNP provides an average throughput approaching 19,200 bps.

Class	Description of Functions Performed
Class 7	Adds an enhanced data compression capability to MNP based on a Huffman statistical encoding technique. Under Class 7, a compression ratio between 2.0 and 3.0 is achievable, which increases throughput from two to three times the modem's operating rate.
Class 8	Is no longer marketed.
Class 9	Adds support of V.32 modulation to Class 7, providing a throughput up to three times the 9600 bps full-duplex operating rate of a V.32 modem.

In examining the entries in Table 4.6, you will note the inclusion of such terms as V.29 and V.32. Both reference CCITT modulation standards, with V.29 originally developed as a half-duplex 9600 bps modulation technique for use on leased lines. Microcom, as well as other vendors, modified that technology to work on the PSTN. In addition, using the intelligence of a microprocessor to monitor the direction of transmission, it became possible to quickly turn off the transmitter of one modem and turn on its receiver, enabling the half-duplex transmission mode to resemble full-duplex transmission. In comparison, a V.32 modem uses echo cancellation technology to enable transmission and reception of data to occur simultaneously on the PSTN, and it provides an inherent full-duplex transmission capability. Both V.29 and V.32 modulation are described in Chapter 5, "Synchronous Modems, Digital Transmission, and Service Units."

V.42 Recommendation

Although MNP error detection and correction is included in more than one million modems manufactured by Microcom and by more than a hundred third-party vendors, as previously discussed in this chapter, it is not the primary method of error detection and correction recommended for use in modems by the CCITT. In 1990, the CCITT promulgated its V.42 recommendation.

Unlike other CCITT V series recommendations that govern modern modulation techniques, the V.42 recommendation defines a protocol in which modems block data for transmission and generate and add a cyclic redundancy check (CRC) to each block for error detection. In recognition of the large installed base of MNP modems, MNP error detection and correction is supported as a secondary standard. That is, a V.42-compatible modem first attempts to communicate in its error-free mode using LAPB. If the distant modem does not support the V.42 protocol, the V.42 modem next attempts to communicate using MNP error control.

Data Compression

Although the CCITT V.42 recommendation supports MNP error control, the V.42bis recommendation, which is a data compression scheme that requires the use of the V.42 protocol, does not support a secondary method of compression. This theoretically means that for your V.42bis modem to operate in a compressed mode, it must communicate with another V.42bis-compatible modem. Fortunately, most V.42bis modems also include MNP support through Class 5, enabling you to communicate in both a data compressed mode and an error control mode with another MNP modem.

The key difference between V.42bis and MNP Class 5 or Class 7 is in their method of data compression. V.42bis uses a technique known as Lempel-Ziv, which can operate on single characters as well as on strings. In comparison, MNP compression primarily operates on single characters and is slightly less efficient. When using a V.42bis modem that incorporates V.32 modulation, the 9600 bps operating rate of the modem can achieve a throughput of up to 28,400 bps when data is very susceptible to compression.

Interface Versus Operating Rate

To effectively use data compression requires you to set your modem's interface data rate to exceed its operating rate. To understand why this is required, consider Figure 4.13, which illustrates the relationship between the interface speed and the operating rate of a modem.

FIGURE 4.13.

The relationship between interface speed and modem operating rate.

If the interface speed equals the operating rate, data compression will not increase the throughput of the modem. To increase the modem's throughput, you must set the interface rate to at least twice the modem's operating rate. For example, if the modem operates at 2400 bps, you should set the interface rate to at least 4800 bps. This setting allows more bits in the form of characters to enter the modem per unit of time than can be transmitted. Then, data compression can attempt to reduce the bits entering the modem so that they can be transmitted at the modem's operating rate, increasing the modem's throughput.

Flow Control

A second consideration you must take into account when using error control either by itself or with data compression is flow control. To see why flow control is necessary, consider Figure 4.13. Assume that the interface speed is set to 4800 bps and that the operating rate is 2400 bps. If the modem cannot effectively compress data, perhaps due to the composition of the data, the rate at which data enters the modem will exceed the rate at which it is placed onto the line. Although the modem has a buffer, eventually it will overflow, and data will be lost. Hence, a method is required to regulate the flow of data into the modem. This method is called flow control.

Most modems support at least two methods of flow control, referred to as XON/XOFF and CTS/RTS. The XON/XOFF method of flow control results in the modem transmitting an XOFF character to your computer to disable transmission, and an XON character to enable transmission to resume. Because your computer might require a capability to regulate data from the modem if you are printing received data or performing another mechanical-related operation, you can also use XON and XOFF from your computer to the modem to enable and disable transmission from the modem to your computer.

The CTS/RTS method of flow control references the use of the Clear to Send (CTS) and Request to Send (RTS) control signals at the interface between the computer and the modem. When the modem regulates flow control, it drops the CTS signal to inform the computer to stop transmission and raises the CTS signal to inform the computer to resume transmission. When the computer regulates the flow of data from the modem, it toggles the RTS signal lead.

In setting flow control, you must ensure that your computer and modem are set to use the same method. Concerning which method to select, if you expect to transfer files that might contain control characters, including an XOFF, you should use the CTS/RTS method of flow control. Otherwise, the reception of an XOFF would inadvertently turn off your computer's capability to transmit data.

Extended Command Sets

Although the basic Hayes command set was sufficient for supporting most intelligent-modem operations during the early 1980s, by the late 1980s, many modem vendors were introducing advanced features that were not supported by the basic Hayes command set. Although Hayes Microcomputer Products introduced a series of extended commands to govern the operation of advanced features incorporated into that vendor's product line, other vendors did not wait for Hayes and introduced features into their modems that were controlled by extended commands they developed. The result of this action was the development of a series of extended command sets whose operation is applicable to only one or a few modems. To illustrate this fact, Table 4.7 lists the first 11 extended commands supported by two popular fax/data modems capable of transmitting at rates up to 14,400 bps, the Practical Peripherals 14400 FXMT and the U.S. Robotics Sportster 14400 FAX. Because extended commands are prefixed with the ampersand, another term used to reference those commands is ampersand commands.

Table 4.7. Comparing extended command operations.

Extended Command	Modem Function	
	Practical Peripherals 14400 FXMT	U.S. Robotics Sportster 14400 FAX
&A	Connect when autoanswering	ARQ results code
&B	V.32 automatic retrain	Data rate terminal to modem
&C	DSD signal operation	DCD signal operation
&D	DTE signal operation	DTE signal operation
&F	Undefined	Load factory settings
&G	Guard tone operation	Guard tone operation
&H	Undefined	Transmit data flow control
&I	Undefined	Received data software flow control
&K	Flow control	Data compression
&L	Dial/leased line mode	Undefined
&M	Synchronous mode selection	Error control

In examining the entries in Table 4.7, note that the general modem function controlled by the extended command is listed for each modem. In many cases, there are several extended commands based on a numeric value following the sequence *ampersand, letter*. For example, &B0 would disable V.32 automatic retraining on a Practical Peripherals 14400 FXMT modem, whereas &B1 would enable that feature.

In comparing the functions controlled by each extended command listed in Table 4.7, you will note that software developed to control one modem cannot issue the same extended commands to control features on the other modem.

This limitation explains why it is important to verify that a communications program you intend to purchase supports a particular modem that you have or that you anticipate purchasing. Otherwise, you might have to either manually enter appropriate commands to take advantage of many of the features built into the modem or forego using those features.

It is important to verify that a communications program supports the extended commands recognized by the modem you use.

What Have You Learned?

1. A modem (modulator-demodulator) changes data pulses to analog tones that the telephone channel will pass.

2. Frequency-shift keying is the type of modulation used by most low-speed modems. Phase modulation or a combination of phase and amplitude modulation is used in high-speed modems.

3. Data terminal equipment (DTE) is the equipment that originates or receives the data in digital form.

4. Data communications equipment (DCE) is the equipment that converts the data from the DTE to the form required for the transmission channel. A modem is DCE.

5. The signal levels, signal identification, and wiring between the DTE and the DCE are governed by standards.

6. The RS-232 and CCITT V.24 standards for the DTE-DCE interface are the ones used most in the present computer and communications world.

7. RS-422A, RS-423A, and RS-449 are relatively new standards that overcome the defects of RS-232. The widespread adoption of RS-449, however, will probably be superseded by the RS-530 standard.

8. A communications program that is limited to supporting basic Hayes commands might not be capable of using the advanced features built into most modern modems.

9. Without an appropriate method of flow control, a modem can lose data when its interface speed is set to a higher value than its operating rate.

Quiz for Chapter 4

1. Flow control is:

    a. What is done by people who open and close floodgates on dams.

    b. The process whereby the modem matches the rate of the receiver.

    c. The process of starting and stopping the terminal output to avoid loss of characters by the receiving device.

2. Buffering is:

    a. The process of temporarily storing data to allow for small variations in device speeds.

    b. A method of reducing the severity of communications headaches.

    c. Storage of data within the transmitting modem until the receiver is ready to receive.

3. Direct machine-to-machine transmission over long distances without modems is not practical because:

    a. Copper wire does not transmit DC efficiently.

    b. A DC path that will handle data in pulse form does not exist.

   c. Data comes from the computer in the form of tones, not pulses.

4. Modulation is the:

   a. Varying of some parameter of a carrier, such as its amplitude, to transmit information.

   b. Utilization of a single transmission channel to carry multiple signals.

   c. Transmission of pulses in DC form over a copper wire.

5. RS-232, RS-449, RS-530, V.24, and X.21 are examples of:

   a. Standards for various types of transmission channels.

   b. Standards for interfaces between terminals and modems.

   c. Standards for interfaces between modems and transmission facilities.

   d. Standards for end-to-end performance of data communications systems.

6. V.42 defines:

   a. Compatibility with MNP Class 5 data compression.

   b. A method of data storage.

   c. Two methods of error detection and correction.

   d. Compatibility with MNP Class 7 enhanced data compression.

7. The cable connecting a DB-9 connector at one end to a DB-25 connector at the other end must

cross-connect pin 8 at the DB-9 side to which pin at the DB-25 side:

   a. 4.

   b. 22.

   c. 5.

   d. 2.

8. A smart modem can:

   a. Detect transmission errors and correct them automatically.

   b. Correctly answer multiple-choice quizzes.

   c. Accept commands from the terminal via the RS-232 interface.

9. RTS/CTS:

   a. Is the way the modem indicates ringing, and the way the terminal indicates that it is ready for the call to be answered.

   b. Is the way the DTE indicates that it is ready to transmit data, and the way the DCE indicates that it is ready to accept data.

   c. Are the pins that represent received transmissions and carrier transmissions.

10. Pin 7, the Signal Ground:

   a. Completes the circuit for control and data signals.

   b. Indicates a failure in the ground side of the transmission line.

   c. Completes the circuit for control signals but not data signals.

11. Pin 22, the Ring Indicator:

    a. Must be present on all modems connected to the switched network.

    b. Is used on acoustic-coupled modems but not on direct-connect types.

    c. Is asserted when ringing voltage is present on the line.

12. The reason that many cables have "RS-232" connectors with some wires crossed or connected to each other is:

    a. There are various RS-232 standards.

    b. Many computers and peripherals use RS-232 serial interfaces, but not as DTE-to-DCE.

    c. Asynchronous modems reverse the direction of transmitted and received data from the standard.

13. Extended command sets supported by modern modems:

    a. Are standardized.

    b. Are prefixed with the letter *E*.

    c. Use different commands to control many advanced modem features.

    d. Can be counted on to provide a high-speed data transfer capability without requiring flow control.

Synchronous Modems, Digital Transmission, and Service Units

About This Chapter

In this chapter, you will be introduced to the signaling methods used by synchronous modems, the American and International standards that apply to synchronous data modems, and the concepts used in higher speed (above 19,200 bits per second) wideband devices. This will be followed by an examination of the techniques of direct transmission of binary signals without modems, called digital transmission. Because the transmission of binary signals over long distances without modems requires the use of devices known as service units, the operation and utilization of those devices will also be covered in this chapter.

Synchronous Signaling and Standards

Synchronous signaling permits data to be transmitted without gaps between characters, enabling higher data transfer rates to be achieved.

A Search for Higher Data Rates

Like the Olympic athlete whose motto is *alitus, cititus, fortitus,* the aims of the data communications systems designer in the development of high-technology products are to pack more data per channel, deliver it at a faster speed, and deliver it at a lower cost. The transmission of a larger quantity of data through a channel of a given bandwidth with smaller and cheaper devices is a natural target. Because in many cases the channel available is a standard voice-grade line, and the cost of the channel dominates the cost of the system, a large amount of design effort has gone into the production of devices that will send the largest number of bits per unit time through standard (voice-grade) channels. One result has been synchronous signaling.

Sending the Clock with the Data

Binary signals have two basic parameters: amplitude and duration. As the number of information bits sent per unit of time increases, the bit duration decreases.

Binary signals sent over a channel represent the quantization of data in two dimensions: amplitude (voltage of the electrical wave) and time (the duration of each signaling element). As the number of signaling elements per unit time (the "baud rate") increases, the duration of each element must decrease, as illustrated in Figure 5.1. If, as is the case with the asynchronous modems, the time base for the transmitter and receiver are independent, small differences between the two clocks become increasingly likely to cause errors due to the sampling of the data at the wrong time. This problem is overcome in synchronous modems by deriving the timing information from the received data.

FIGURE 5.1.

Baud rate versus element duration.

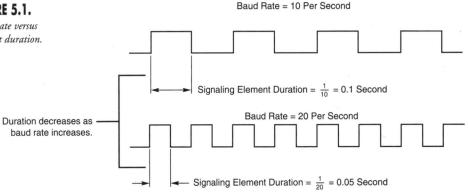

More Bits per Baud

The data rate is limited by the bandwidth of the voice-baud channel to about 2400 baud. One way to increase the data is to pack two or more bits in a baud.

Recall that in a previous chapter, it was stated that for a channel of given bandwidth, the maximum signaling rate is fixed by the channel bandwidth and the signal-to-noise ratio (Shannon's formula). Because voice-grade channels have a fixed bandwidth (about 3000 Hz), they have a fixed maximum baud rate (about 2400 baud). The solution to this dilemma is to pack more than one bit into one signaling element—that is, two or more bits per baud.

Typical Synchronous Components

The greater complexity and cost of synchronous modems over asynchronous units is due to the circuitry necessary to derive the timing from the incoming data and to pack more than one bit into one baud. Synchronous modems typically consist of four components, as shown in Figure 5.2: transmitter, receiver, terminal control, and power supply. We will look at the first three of these items in some detail.

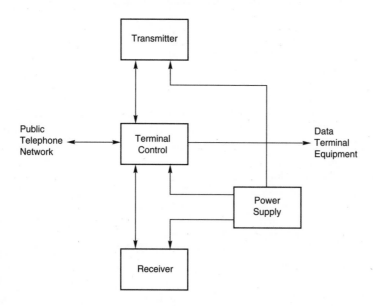

FIGURE 5.2.

Synchronous modem block diagram.

Transmitter

As shown in Figure 5.3, the transmitter section of a synchronous modem typically consists of timing (clock), scrambler, modulator, digital-to-analog converter, and equalizer circuits.

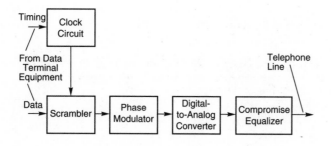

FIGURE 5.3.

Modem transmitter block diagram.

TIMING CIRCUIT

● The internal clock of the transmitting modem is phase-locked with the external clock source when the DTE or another modem provides the timing.

The timing circuit provides the basic clocking information for both the modem and the data terminal equipment (DTE) that is providing the data to be transmitted. Certain data circuit arrangements require that the clocking for the transmitted data be supplied by the DTE (which can be another modem). In these cases, an option is usually provided in the modem to phase-lock the internal clock to an external clock source, input through the DTE interface. The internal timing is usually controlled by a crystal oscillator to within about 0.05 percent of the nominal value.

SCRAMBLER

● Enough 0 to 1 to 0 changes must exist in the data stream to keep the receiving modem's clock synchronized. The scrambler ensures that the changes occur by modifying the data stream in a controlled way.

Because the receiver clock is derived from the received data, those data must contain enough changes from 0 to 1 (and vice versa) to ensure that the timing recovery circuit will stay in synchronization. In principle, the data stream provided by the associated terminal or business machine can consist of any arbitrary bit pattern. If the pattern contains long strings of the same value, the data will not provide the receiver with enough transitions for synchronization. The transmitter must prevent this condition by changing the input bit stream in a controlled way. The part of the transmitter circuitry that does this is called the scrambler.

Scramblers are usually implemented as feedback shift registers, which can be cascaded (connected in series) as shown in Figure 5.4. Input bit No. 1 is modified by adding the state of selected bits of the seven-bit register to the incoming bit. Input bits 2, 3, and so forth are modified by the preceding bits, as indicated in the illustration. The scramblers are designed to ensure that each possible value of phase angle is equally likely to occur, to provide the receiver demodulator with enough phase shifts to recover the clocking signal. Although sampling is necessary for the reasons cited previously, it increases the error rate, because an error in one bit is likely (and in some cases is certain) to cause an error in subsequent bits. To counteract this problem, some modems encode the input to the scrambler into the Gray code so that the most likely error in demodulation (picking an adjacent phase state) will cause only a one-bit error when decoded at the receiver. As shown in Table 5.1, the Gray code has the property that between any two successive binary numbers (tribit numbers in this case), only one bit changes state.

Table 5.1. Binary and Gray code equivalence for three-bit code.

Decimal	Binary	Gray Code
0	000	000
1	001	001
2	010	011
3	011	010

Decimal	Binary	Gray Code
4	100	110
5	101	111
6	110	101
7	111	100

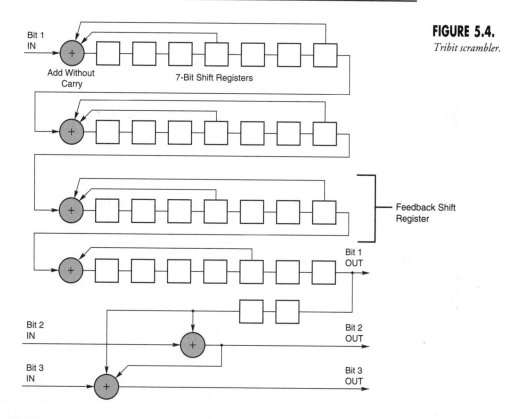

FIGURE 5.4.

Tribit scrambler.

MODULATOR

The modulator section of the transmitter converts the bit patterns produced by the scrambling process into an analog signal representing the desired phase and amplitude of the carrier signal. The carrier frequency, baud rate, and number of bits represented by each baud is different for modems of different data rates. The modulator collects the correct number of bits and translates them into a number giving the amplitude of the electrical signal that is correct for the carrier frequency and phase of the carrier at that instant. Modulation techniques differ for modems of different speed and from different manufacturers. Some of the more common ones are discussed later in this chapter.

●

Specific modulator characteristics such as the baud rate, number of bits per baud, and modulation techniques vary for modems of different rates and from different manufacturers.

DIGITAL-TO-ANALOG CONVERTER

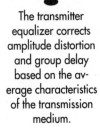

The digital-to-analog converter changes the binary encoded signal from the modulator into the required analog voltage.

The binary encoded signal from the modulator is fed to a digital-to-analog converter, which produces the actual analog voltage required. This in turn goes through a low-pass filter to remove frequencies outside of the voice baud, then through a circuit called an equalizer, which compensates for transmission impairments on the line.

EQUALIZER

The transmitter equalizer corrects amplitude distortion and group delay based on the average characteristics of the transmission medium.

The transmission equalizer is called a compromise or statistical equalizer because it is set to compensate for the nominal or average characteristics of the transmission medium. The equalizer compensates for amplitude distortion in the medium and for the problem called group delay. Group delay measures the amount by which a signal of one frequency travels faster in the transmission medium than a signal of a different frequency. Group delay usually is expressed in microseconds (μs) at a given frequency. Nominal values of delay variation versus frequency for some commonly available voice-grade channels are given in Table 5.2.

Table 5.2. Group delay variation versus frequency for conditioned transmission lines.

Conditioning Applied to Voice Grade Channel	Frequency Range (Hz)	Delay Variation (μs)
Basic (none)	800–2600	1750
C1	800–2600	1750
C2	600–2600	1500
C3	600–2600	260–300
C4	800–2800	500
C5	600–2600	300

Receiver

As shown in Figure 5.5, the receiver section of a synchronous modem typically consists of an equalizer, timing (clock) recovery, a demodulator, a descrambler, and a DTE interface.

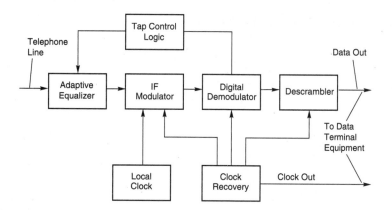

FIGURE 5.5.

Modem receiver block diagram.

EQUALIZER

The equalizer section of the transmitter is relatively simple because it can compensate only for the average of expected errors on the output channel. The receiver equalizer, however, must compensate for the actual errors introduced in the transmission path. This is done by using an adaptive equalizer, which measures errors observed in the received signal and adjusts some parameter of the circuit (usually the receiver clock frequency) to track slowly varying changes in the condition of the transmission line.

Delay distortion has the greatest effect on transmission of an analog signal. As mentioned previously, analog signals of different frequencies travel at different rates through a transmission medium. Because each signaling element contains many frequencies, the signaling elements arrive at the receiver over a period of time rather than all at once. The frequencies that travel faster (leading frequencies) arrive earlier, and those traveling slower (lagging frequencies) arrive later. The leading and lagging frequencies not only fail to make their proper contribution to the proper signaling element, but also cause interference with signaling elements behind and ahead of the proper element. The equalizer must get the parts of each element back together and cancel their effects on other elements.

The adaptive equalizer does this by use of a tapped delay line that stores the analog signal for a period. This time period includes the main signaling element to be corrected at the center, and several element times before and after the center, as shown in Figure 5.6. The taps in the delay line allow the analog voltage representing the signal to be picked off at specific time intervals before and after the element of interest. The time interval between each tap is the reciprocal of the baud rate. The voltage from each tap is amplified by a variable-gain amplifier whose gain is controlled by an amount determined by the correction calculator circuit.

In response to a phase error signal developed by the demodulator circuit, the correction calculator determines the amplitude and polarity of the signal needed from each tape amplifier. What makes the equalizer adaptive is that the error signal is continuously

The receiving equalizer must deal with actual errors in the received signal. The errors are measured and corrected by adjusting specific circuit parameters.

The adaptive equalizer compensates for delay distortion by temporarily storing the analog signal in a tapped delay line. The signals from each tap, amplified by a different amount as determined by the amount of error detected, are summed to form the corrected signal.

derived from the difference between the phase of the received signal and a nominal phase value determined by the demodulator.

FIGURE 5.6.

Adaptive equalizer.

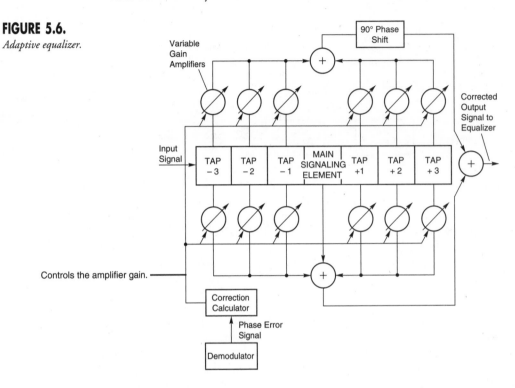

The circuit adapts itself fairly slowly to changing line conditions because of all the delays. This can be a disadvantage for half-duplex operation, or at start-up on a one-way link, so a start-up or training sequence of bits usually is sent first to allow the receiver to adapt more rapidly than it would on random data. This is called training. The amount of time required by the modem to retrain after changing the direction of transmission must be less than the turnaround time or request-to-send, clear-to-send (RTS-CTS) delay. This delay effectively reduces the data transmission rate on the circuit. Contemporary 4800 bps modems have RTS-CTS delays in the 10 to 20 millisecond (ms) range (about 50 to 100 bit times).

The equalizer section of some modern modems attempts to minimize the amount of line time lost in turnaround by a dual-speed or "gearshift" technique. This technique causes the modem pair to start at a lower data rate (say 2400 bps) at which training is very fast, and to transmit data at that rate while the adaptive equalizer goes through its training cycle. The modems then "shifts gears" to run at the full data rate, as shown in Figure 5.7. Because for short messages the RTS-CTS delay is the controlling factor in throughput, and for long messages the transmission speed is dominant, the speed-changing technique minimizes the delay while still providing the higher speed.

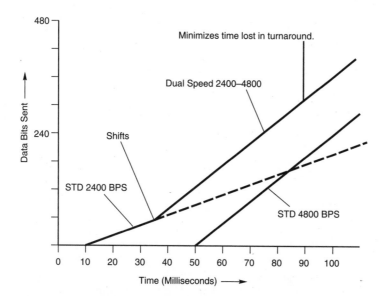

FIGURE 5.7.

Dual-speed modem performance.

The incorporation of microprocessors into modems enabled their processing capability to be used to control numerous functions, including automatic equalization. When a pair of modems performs automatic equalization, each modem periodically transmits a training signal to the modem located at the opposite end of the circuit. The receiving modem knows the expected composition of the training signal and automatically adjusts its equalization to enable the best reception of the signal. In fact, you can probably think of automatic equalization as being similar to fine-tuning on your television. After it's set, it operates without requiring operator intervention. Today, almost all synchronous modems include an automatic equalization feature that compensates for both amplitude distortion and group delay.

To illustrate the operation of automatic equalization, consider Figure 5.8, which indicates how a modem compensates for the amplitude distortion of a signal by a technique referred to as attenuation equalization. Because high frequencies attenuate more rapidly than low frequencies, the modem measures circuit attenuation similar to the inverted U-shaped curve over the pass band of the channel. The modem then sets its equalization circuitry to generate a level of attenuation inverse to that occurring from the circuit as indicated by the upper U-shaped curve. The result of the attenuation equalization process is to produce a near-uniform or level amount of attenuation across the pass band of the circuit. In addition to simplifying procedures required for automatic equalization, the use of fast microprocessors has also reduced the training time required for equalization. Because no data can be transmitted during the training process, decreasing training time results in an increase in modem throughput.

FIGURE 5.8.

*Attenuation
equalization.*

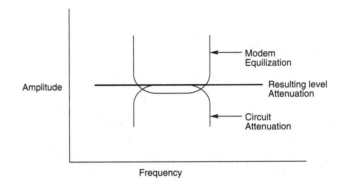

TIMING RECOVERY

At the receiver, the incoming signal from the line is modulated or frequency translated using an internal clock. The resulting intermediate frequency is processed to produce a clock signal at the rate at which the data is actually being received. This signal is applied as the reference to a phase-locked loop oscillator. The output of this oscillator is a stable signal locked to the incoming line frequency in both phase and frequency.

DESCRAMBLER

The descrambler section of the receiver performs an operation that is the inverse of the scrambler described in the section on the transmitter. If the data have been Gray coded by the transmitter before scrambling, they are converted back to straight binary, then applied to the DCE interface circuit.

Terminal Control Section

Each of the terminal control interface points requires different control and response signals.

The control section of synchronous modems must deal with two external interfaces: the telephone line at one end and the business machine at the other. If the modem is to be used on the public dial telephone network, it must be able to perform the following tasks:

- Sense the ringing signal.
- Provide line supervision (connecting and disconnecting the modem and the telephone line).
- In some cases, provide a busy indication to the incoming line without tying up telephone central office equipment.

At the other end, the control section must connect to the associated business machine or data terminal equipment (DTE). The DTE interface for most modems conforms to one of two standards: the Electronic Industries Association (EIA) RS-232, or the International

Telephone and Telegraph Consultative Committee (CCITT) Recommendation V.24. These standards were covered in Chapter 4, "Asynchronous Modems and Interfaces."

INTERFACE CIRCUITS

Most synchronous modems support the set of interface circuits shown in Table 5.3. The backward-channel circuits (CCITT circuit numbers 118 through 122) are required only in modems that provide a reverse or backward channel for control information in the opposite direction to normal data flow. The Data Terminal Ready circuit (CCITT circuit No. 108.2) is required only for modems used on the dial-up connections.

Table 5.3. Synchronous modem DTE interface circuits.

Circuit Number		Designation
EIA	**CCITT**	
AA	101	Equipment Ground
AB	102	Signal Ground
BA	103	Transmitted Data
BB	104	Received Data
CA	105	Request to Send
CB	106	Clear to Send
CC	107	Modem Ready
CD	108.2	Data Terminal Ready
CE	125	Ring Indicator
CF	109	Received Line Signal Detector (Carrier)
CG	110	Signal Quality Detector
CH	111	Data Signal Rate Detector (DTE Source)
CI	112	Data Signal Rate Detector (DCE Source)
DA	113	Transmitted Signal Element Timing DTE Source)
DB	114	Transmitted Signal Element Timing DCE Source)
DD	115	Received Signal Element Timing (DCE Source)
SBA	118	Secondary (Backward Channel) Transmitted Data
SBB	119	Secondary Received Data
SCA	120	Secondary Request to Send
SCB	121	Secondary Clear to Send
SCF	122	Secondary Received Line Signal Detected (Carrier)

The Clear-to-Send signal is returned to the DTE in response to assertion of the Request-to-Send signal. It is delayed by the modem, however, by the amount of time necessary for the modem to "turn the line around"—that is, to send the required training pattern to the distant end.

EXTERNAL TIMING

Systems that have terminals remote from the terminating modem on the main channel require the remote modem be synchronized to the originating modem.

Many standard 9600 bps and higher-speed modems designed for leased-line operations usually contain internal time division multiplexers, which allow more than one terminal to operate simultaneously over a single channel. In many cases, one or more channels are carried to terminals remote from the first modem, terminating the circuit as shown in Figure 5.9. In such cases, which apply only to full-duplex operation, the clock signal for all the modems in the path must be synchronized to only one of the modems. The external clock input (EIA circuit DA) for the extension modem circuit is fed from the receive clock from the primary modem (EIA circuit DD), causing the clocks in all the modems to be slaved to the single modem at the originating end. Refer to Chapter 6, "Multiplexing Techniques," for information concerning the operation and utilization of time division multiplexers.

FIGURE 5.9.

A multiple-modem circuit requiring external clocking.

Modems B , C, and D use the same timing as Modem A.

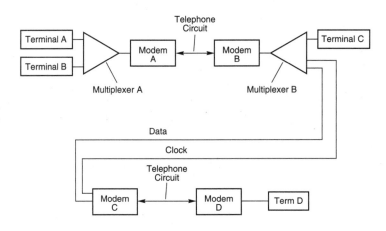

Modem C must be supplied an external clock from multiplexer B, which must use the received data clock from Modem B.

Standard Modems

We'll now examine the implementation of some currently available modems, as well as evolving modems that can be expected to be readily available by the time you read this book. The types of modems that will be examined include these:

- 2400 bps half-duplex and full-duplex
- 4800 bps half-duplex and full-duplex

- 9600 bps half-duplex and full-duplex
- 9600 bps full-duplex modems that operate over two-wire dial-up circuits
- 14,400 bps full-duplex modems that operate over two-wire dial-up circuits
- 14,400 bps full-duplex modems that operate over four-wire leased lines
- 19,200 bps full-duplex modems that operate over two-wire dial-up circuits
- 24,400 bps full-duplex modems that operate over two-wire dial-up circuits

2400 bps Half-Duplex Two-Wire or Full-Duplex Four-Wire (DPSK)

Two common 2400 bps modems are the Western Electric 201 and the CCITT V.26.

WESTERN ELECTRIC 201

A good example of the basic synchronous modem is the Western Electric (WE) 201 diagrammed in Figure 5.10. It operates at 1200 bauds with a carrier frequency of 1800 Hz. This modem uses a kind of phase shift modulation called the differential phase shift keying (DPSK) technique and encodes two bits (called a dibit) into one signaling element (two bits per baud). Phase shift keying encodes the binary values as changes of the phase of the carrier signal, as discussed in a previous chapter. Differential phased shift means that the reference point from which the phase angle is measured at any signaling interval is the phase angle of the immediately preceding interval. The WE 201 shifts the phase by multiples of 45 degrees according to Table 5.4.

The Western Electric 201 is representative of standard 2400 bps synchronous modems. This modem encodes two bits per baud using differential phase shift keying (DPSK).

Table 5.4. WE 201 phase coding.

Dibit	Phase Change in Degrees
00	45
10	135
11	225
01	315

With this technique, the signal is self-referenced; that is, no separate absolute phase information needs to be transmitted, and the most likely error (picking an adjacent phase value) causes only a one-bit error. The WE 201 contains a local clock that is phase-locked to the detected phase of the incoming signal. Differences between the nominal phase values given in Table 5.4 and the detected phase of the incoming signal referenced to the phase of the local clock are used to measure the quality of the incoming line signal. Because the phase

DPSK requires no absolute phase information to be transmitted. It has its own clock that is phase-locked to the phase of the received signal.

of the received signal changes for each signaling interval, there is always sufficient energy at the 1200-baud rate to recover the baud clock.

FIGURE 5.10.

WE 201 modem block diagram.

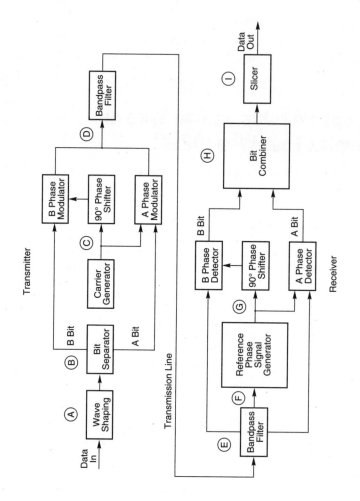

A. At the transmitter input, pulses are generated according to the data input, then filtered to shape them for modulation.

B. Alternate bits in the stream become A bits, and the others become B bits.

C. The two bit streams phase modulate a sine wave carrier. The carrier for the B bit stream is phase shifted by 90 degrees with respect to the A carrier.

D. The outputs of the modulators are combined, and the bandpass filter eliminates unwanted signals before transmission.

E. At the receiver, another bandpass filter removes noise and other unwanted signals.

F. The input signal is used to synchronize a sine wave reference phase signal.

G. The reference signal is applied directly to the A phase detector but is phase shifted 90 degrees before application to the B phase detector.

H. The A and B bit streams from the detectors are combined into a single bit stream.

I. The slicer output consists of clean rectangular pulses that convey the same data as the transmitter input.

CCITT V.26

The CCITT has published a recommendation for a standard 2400 bps modem with the designation "Recommendation V.26—2400 bits per second modem standardized for use on leased telephone-type circuits." It specifies a full-duplex, 1200-baud DPSK modem with a modulation rate of up to 75 baud in each direction on an optional "backward channel." In Europe, V.26 modems are commonly built into television receivers to provide a transmission capability for accessing Videotex systems. When the modem is used in this manner, pressing buttons on a TV remote control results in the transmission of "page" selection numbers to a Videotex system. The Videotex system in turn transmits the requested "page," which is displayed on the TV set. Because a small quantity of data flows from the TV set to the Videotex system in the form of page number requests, the use of the V.26 modem is reversed. That is, the 75-baud "backward channel" is used to transmit page number requests while Videotex information flows on the primary channel to the TV set.

The V.26 recommendations are generally similar to the specifications for the WE 201 (largely because the WE 201 had by 1968 become a de facto standard). One interesting difference is that the assignment of dibits to phase change values is allowed alternative sets of values. Alternative A is given in Table 5.5, and alternative B is the same as that given in Table 5.4 for the WE 201. Use of alternative A leads to the problem of no phase change at all for long strings of 00 dibits. Thus, the energy content in the transmitted stream at the 1200-baud rate is greatly reduced, making baud clock recovery uncertain.

> ●
> The CCITT V.26 2400 bps modem is similar to the WE 201, but one significant difference is the alternative set of phase codes.

Table 5.5. V.26 alternative A phase coding.

Dibit	Phase Change in Degrees
00	0
01	90
11	180
10	270

Recommendation V.26 specifies the form of the synchronizing signal between two modems to be continuous transmission of dibit 11 (giving continuous 180-degree phase shifts) during the RTS-CTS sequence. It also specifies incoming signal levels of –26 dBm or higher for the modem to assert the Carrier Detect (Circuit 109) and –31 dBm or lower for it to negate Carrier Detect. It is recommended that the modem be designed so that the operator cannot control the send level or receive sensitivity.

4800 bps Half-Duplex Two-Wire or Full-Duplex Four-Wire Modems (DPSK)

Modems representative of 4800 bps devices include the CCITT V.27 and Western Electric 208 modems.

CCITT V.27

The CCITT Recommendation V.27 specifies a 4800 bps modem for use on leased telephone-type circuits. The modem has the following features:

- Can operate in either half- or full-duplex.
- Uses differential phase shift keying with eight phases.
- Provides an optional 75 bps backward channel in both directions for supervisory signaling.
- Has a manually adjustable equalizer.

● Although the manual equalizers mentioned in CCITT V.27 are no longer used, most of the standard is still used as the basis for many modems today, particularly in Europe.

This recommendation was promulgated in 1972, and the state of the modem art has progressed far beyond the manually adjustable equalizer. However, the remainder of the recommendation is the basis for many current modems, particularly for the European market. The carrier frequency is 1800 Hz, the modulation rate is 1600 baud, and the basic phase shift interval is 45 degrees. To signal at 4800 bps with 1600 baud requires that each baud represent three bits (tribits). The tribit to phase-change amount for V.27 is given in Table 5.6.

Table 5.6. V.27 phase coding.

Tribit Value	Phase Change in Degrees
001	0
000	45
010	90
011	135
111	180
110	225
100	270
101	315

The synchronization pattern for the V.27 modem is composed of continuous ones in tribits for at least 9 ms to train the demodulator, plus continuous ones at the input to the transmit scrambler until the CTS lead (circuit 106) is asserted by the transmitting modem to synchronize the scramblers. The general operation of a scrambler was described earlier in the chapter, but the details of the V.27 scrambler follow.

The transmitter scrambler divides the message polynomial, of which the input data bits are the coefficients in descending order, by a generating polynomial, which for V.27 is equal to $1 + X^{-6} + X^{-7}$. This division is continuously performed as each bit enters the scrambler, and the result is taken as the transmitted data pattern. The transmitted pattern is then searched continuously over 45 bits for repeating patterns of 1, 2, 3, 4, 6, 9, and 12 bits, which are eliminated. The result is sent as the scrambled data pattern. Figure 5.11 shows a feedback shift register that implements the polynomial division process.

> The scrambler implements dividing the message polynomial by a generating polynomial by means of a feedback shift register.

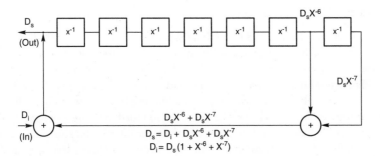

FIGURE 5.11.
CCITT V.27 scrambler.

WESTERN ELECTRIC 208

The WE 208 modem is another 4800 bps modem that at one time was widely used in the United States. It had been supplied by AT&T and the Bell Operating Companies when they were part of the Bell System. It is a DPSK unit, using eight phase angles to represent eight different groups of three bits. The coding pattern (after Gray-coding the binary input) for the WE 208 is given in Table 5.7.

Table 5.7. WE 208 phase coding.

Tribit	Relative Phrase in Degrees
001	22.5
000	67.5
010	112.5
011	157.5
111	202.5

continues

Table 5.7. continued

Tribit	Relative Phrase in Degrees
110	247.5
100	292.5
101	337.5

The carrier frequency for the WE 208 is 1800 Hz, and the baud rate is 1600 baud. The WE 208 is not equipped with an internal multiplexer because the 1600-baud rate of the modem is not a standard data rate for any other modem or business machine. The design of the WE 208 was covered in the previous section on typical synchronous modem components, including the scrambler implementation as four 7-bit feedback shift registers to randomize the first bit of each tribit.

The demodulator in the WE 208 multiplies the carrier frequency by eight, then measures the interval between the 1600-baud clock transition and the first positive value of the current carrier cycle. This measurement is done digitally, and successive values of the count are compared to determine the phase shift that occurred during the preceding signaling interval. The measured phase shift, with any errors that might be present due to line noise, demodulator errors, baud clock errors, and such, is rounded to the nearest permitted value (22.5 degrees, 67.5 degrees, and so forth), and the transmitted tribit sequence is extracted and decoded from Gray code to binary. An error feedback signal is developed as the difference between the actual phase of the signal, as demodulated, and the nominal value. This error signal is monitored, and it causes the modem to retrain if it becomes too large.

The WE 208 modem normally operates with a basic retraining time of 50 ms, but it can be changed with internal strapping (jumper wires) to 150 ms for operation on long circuits (more than 2000 miles). Even this delay probably is still too short for operation on satellite links, due to the very long (about 650 ms) round-trip propagation delay.

> The WE 208 uses DPSK to encode tribits to transmit 4800 bps at 1600 bauds. Its design and operation are similar to the typical standard synchronous modem.

9600 bps Half-Duplex Two-Wire or Half/Full-Duplex Four-Wire

Although the Western Electric 209 modem was one of the first devices to operate at 9600 bps, the CCITT V.29 currently dominates the market for 9600 bps operations.

MODULATION TYPES

To increase the data rate of a synchronous modem over 4800 bps, it is necessary to either increase the baud rate or increase the number of bits per baud. Standard 9600 bps modems do both. The baud rate is increased to 2400 bauds, and the input data is taken four bits at a time (quadbits) for controlling the output of the modulator. Two modulation schemes are commonly used to read these extreme data rates: vestigial sideband modulation (VSB) and quaternary amplitude modulation (QAM).

The choice between modems using one of the two modulation schemes is less a matter of performance than of economics. Some VSB modems require little or no line conditioning, whereas a few QAM unit manufacturers generally recommend at least C2 conditioned circuits. The VSB units are less complex internally, which usually allows a price advantage over QAM units.

> The data rate of the standard 9600 bps modem is increased by increasing its baud rate to 2400 bauds and increasing the number of bits per baud to four.

VESTIGIAL SIDEBAND MODULATION

Because it is possible to transmit a double-sideband frequency-modulated (FM) signal (with a WE 202 type modem) at 1800 bps, one would think that it should be possible to send at 3600 bps using only one sideband because the entire bandwidth would be available for the one sideband. This is not possible, however, with an FM signal (the signal can't be recovered), but it is possible to use an amplitude-modulated (AM) single-sideband signal to transmit at 4800 bauds. Four different carrier amplitudes are used to represent the four different values of bits taken two at a time; thus, each baud represents two bits, which gives an effective rate of 9600 bps.

> The VSB transmitter modulator takes two bits at a time and constructs a four-level signal that modulates the carrier to transmit 9600 bps.

A VSB transmitter has a scrambler and Gray coder similar to those of 4800 bps modems. The modulator, however, takes the bits two at a time to form a four-level signal, which modulates a 2853 Hz carrier. The carrier and upper sideband are suppressed, and a 2853 Hz pilot signal is added back to what remains, but 90 degrees out of phase. A signal that is 90 degrees out of phase is called a quadrature signal because "in quadrature" means at right angles to the original carrier. The quadrature signal does not interfere with the modulated single-sideband signal, but it is necessary for the receiver to recover the exact frequency and phase of the original carrier so that it can recover the data.

The receiver's local 2853 Hz oscillator is locked to the phase and frequency of the pilot signal recovered from the received signal. This adjusted clock is used to demodulate the received single-sideband signal into the four-level 4800-baud baseband signal. The signal is processed by a 60-tap adaptive equalizer to remove intersymbol interference, then is put through a decision circuit to recover the dibits, which are then unscrambled.

Training a 60-tap equalizer is a lengthy process that reduces the cost effectiveness of using 9600 bps modems on half-duplex circuits. A four-segment training sequence must be sent to perform the following tasks:

- Set the automatic gain control circuits.
- Acquire the phase of the carrier tone.
- Set the equalizer tap coefficients.
- Synchronize the scrambler.

In the CCITT Recommendation V.29 for a 9600 bps modem, the total four-segment sequence takes about 250 ms.

QUADRATURE AMPLITUDE MODULATION

Modems using quadrature amplitude modulation achieve a data rate of 9600 bps by encoding four bits per baud and by using a baud rate of 2400.

QAM modems use some combination of differential phase shifts and amplitudes totaling 16 states of encoded four bits per baud. This combined with a baud rate of 2400 gives the desired 9600 bps. The CCITT Recommendation V.29 specifies 8 phases, with two possible signal amplitudes at each phase change. The WE 209 modem uses 12 phases and three amplitudes, but some combinations of phase and amplitude are not allowed. Constellation patterns are shown in Figure 5.12. The choice of the number of phases and level spacing represents the modem manufacturer's best guess at the type and severity of various transmission-line errors the modem is likely to experience. It can be argued, however, that the V.29 recommendation resulted in a more optimal selection than the WE 209 due to the near-universal use of V.29 modems.

FIGURE 5.12.

QAM modem constellation patterns.

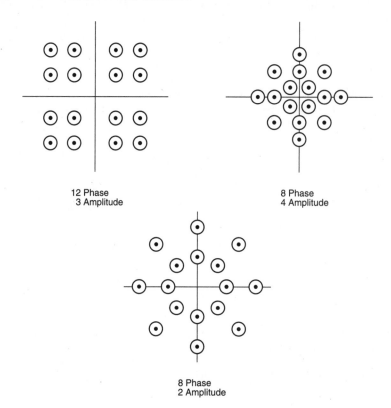

12 Phase
3 Amplitude

8 Phase
4 Amplitude

8 Phase
2 Amplitude

CCITT RECOMMENDATION V.29—9600 BPS MODEM

The carrier frequency for the CCITT V. 29 modem is 1700 Hz, and it operates at 2400 bauds. This modem is specified to operate at 9600 bps with fallback rates of 7200 and 4800 bps. It has an automatic adaptive equalizer and can optionally contain a multiplexer for carrying up to four separate data streams whose aggregate (combined) rate does not exceed 9600 bps. The combined data stream to be transmitted is scrambled, then divided into sets of four bits (quadbits). The first bit (in time) of each quadbit determines the amplitude of the transmitted signal, as illustrated in Figure 5.13, and the remaining three bits determine the phase shift to be applied, as shown in Figure 5.14. The resultant "constellation pattern" resembles Figure 5.15.

● The CCITT V.29 modem's maximum data rate is 9600 bps, but it has automatic fallback to 7200 and 4800 bps if the error rate is too high.

Absolute Phase	Q1	Relative Signal Element Amplitude
0°, 90°, 180°, 270°	0	3
	1	5
45°, 135°, 225°, 315°	0	$\sqrt{2}$
	1	$3\sqrt{2}$

FIGURE 5.13.

Bit Q1 determines amplitude.

Q2	Q3	Q4	Phase Change*
0	0	1	0°
0	0	0	45°
0	1	0	90°
0	1	1	135°
1	1	1	180°
1	1	0	225°
1	0	0	270°
1	0	1	315°

FIGURE 5.14.

Bits Q2, Q3, and Q4 determine phase shift.

*Note—The phase change is the actual online phase shift in the transition region from the center of one signaling element to the center of the following signaling element.

At the fallback rate of 7200 bps, only three bits per baud are encoded, and there is no amplitude change. At the 4800 bps fallback rate, two bits per baud are encoded and they specify only four phase shifts.

Except for the WE 209-type modem, most 9.6 Kbps modems manufactured throughout the world adhere to the V.29 standard. This makes a V.29 modem popular for use on international leased lines because the selection of the modem to be placed on either end of the line might be restricted to one or a few models due to some countries' government restrictions. By using V.29, the modems' compatibility among different vendor products is ensured, which enables data transmission compatibility on international leased lines.

Although the V.29 modulation method provides compatibility with respect to modulation, many modems employing this standard are not compatible with one another. This lack of compatibility is attributable to the fact that several vendors designed proprietary modems to provide a pseudo full-duplex transmission capability over the two-wire public-switched telephone network. To accomplish this, modem designers added a microprocessor and memory to a V.29 data pump and developed several proprietary schemes to get a pseudo full-duplex transmission capability. One scheme involves adding a slow-speed reverse channel to a V.29 data pump to provide transmission at 300 bps in one direction and at 9600 bps in the other direction. Each modem monitors the flow of data in both directions and changes the assignment of the primary and reverse channels to correspond to the quantity of data flow in each direction.

FIGURE 5.15.

Signal space diagram at 9600 bps.

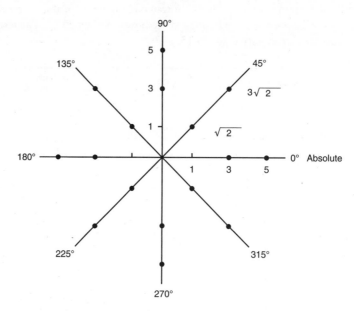

Although data can flow in both directions simultaneously, each direction operates at a different speed. Thus, the modem is asymmetrical and provides users with the impression that it operates as a true full-duplex device. Asymmetrical transmission was incorporated by several modem manufacturers to support the communications requirements of personal computers. Included in an asymmetrical modem is an asynchronous-to-synchronous converter, which enables the asynchronous data flow of personal computers to be used with a modified V.29 pump that operates synchronously.

When asymmetrical modems reached the marketplace in the late 1980s, they were considered as potential successors to the V.22bis modem discussed in Chapter 4, "Asynchronous Modems and Interfaces," due to the high price of V.32 modems. Unfortunately for asymmetrical modem manufacturers, the lack of standards governing the asymmetrical transmission technique, as well as a significant reduction in the cost of V.32 modems (discussed in the next section in this chapter), inhibited the asymmetrical modems' widespread acceptance. Today, most persons requiring high-speed data transmission on the PSTN use V.32 or V.32bis modems. The one exception to this is the U.S. Robotics HST and HST Dual series of modems.

In the late 1980s, U.S. Robotics developed an asymmetrical 9600 bps modem that was marketed as the HST, an acronym for high-speed transmission. The company, among the first to recognize the growing popularity of bulletin board systems, provided bulletin board system operators with an attractive discount to enable them to purchase HST modems. This action resulted in a large number of individual personal computer users purchasing HST modems to get a high-speed transmission file transfer capability when accessing bulletin board systems.

Although reductions in the cost of V.32 modems have significantly increased their popularity, there is a large base of HST modems used with bulletin board systems. To provide compatibility with those modems, U.S. Robotics continues to manufacture HST modems as well as HST Dual modems, the latter a term used to indicate that the modem supports two major modulation methods. Today, U.S. Robotics offers HST Dual modems that support V.32 and HST, V.32bis and HST, and the emerging V.32 turbo and V.32 fast techniques, as well as HST.

CCITT V.32

A CCITT recommendation promulgated in the late 1980s and whose modulation technique forms the foundation for a series of higher speed modems used with personal computers is the V.32 standard. This standard is based on a modified quadrature amplitude modulation technique and is designed to permit full-duplex 9.6 Kbps transmission over the switched telephone network. The key to the operation of a V.32 modem is a built-in echo cancelling technique that enables transmitted and received signals to occupy the same bandwidth.

When the V.32 modem connects to another V.32 modem, two high-speed channels in opposite directions are established, as illustrated in Figure 5.16. Each of these channels occupies roughly the same bandwidth as the other channel. Intelligence built into the receiver in each modem permits the modem to cancel the effects of its transmitted signal, which enables each device to distinguish its sending signal from the signal being received.

Early V.32 modems required sophisticated circuitry to carry out echo cancelling. The circuitry made the cost of V.32 modems two to three times the cost of V.29 modems, which provide the same data transmission rate on leased lines and was one of the contributing factors for the development of asymmetrical modems. Because firms manufacturing semiconductors developed chip sets to implement echo cancelling, the cost of V.32 modems significantly decreased during 1990. By 1991, the cost of V.32 modems had declined to under $1000 per unit, and by early 1994, their cost had fallen below $300 per unit, resulting in their widespread use in both home and office.

FIGURE 5.16.

CCITT V.32 channel derivation.

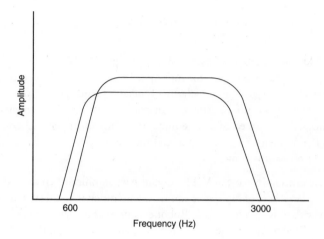

The V.32 modem uses a carrier frequency of 1800 Hz and a modulation rate of 2400 baud. Under the V.32 standard, two methods of data coding are defined—nonredundant coding and Trellis coding. Under nonredundant coding, the data stream generated by the DTE is first divided into groups of four consecutive data bits. The first two bits in time, which are designated $Q1_n$ and $Q2_n$ in each four-bit sequence, are differentially encoded into $Y1_n$ and $Y2_n$, according to Table 5.8. Bits $Y1_n$, $Y2_n$, $Q3_n$, and $Q4_n$ are then mapped into the constellation pattern illustrated in Figure 5.17. This results in a 16-point signal constellation pattern when nonredundant coding is used at 9600 bps.

Table 5.8. V.32 differential quadrant coding for 4800 bps and for nonredundant coding at 9600 bps.

Inputs		Previous Outputs		Phase Quadrant Change	Outputs		Signal State For 4800 bps
$Q1_n$	$Q2_n$	$Y1_n\text{-}1$	$Y2_n\text{-}1$		$Y1_n$	$Y2_n$	
0	0	0	0	+90°	0	1	B
0	0	0	1		1	1	C
0	0	1	0		0	0	A
0	0	1	1		1	0	D
0	1	0	0	0°	0	0	A
0	1	0	1		0	1	B
0	1	1	0		1	0	D
0	1	1	1		1	1	C
1	0	0	0	+180°	1	1	C

Inputs		Previous Outputs		Phase Quadrant Change	Outputs		Signal State For 4800 bps
$Q1_n$	$Q2_n$	$Y1_n-1$	$Y2_n-1$		$Y1_n$	$Y2_n$	
1	0	0	1		1	0	D
1	0	1	0		0	1	B
1	0	1	1		0	0	A
1	1	0	0	+270°	1	0	D
1	1	0	1		0	0	A
1	1	1	0		1	1	C
1	1	1	1		0	1	B

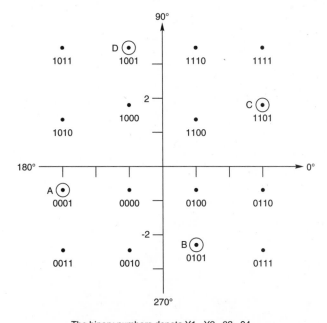

The binary numbers denote $Y1_n$ $Y2_n$ 03_n 04_n

16-point signal structure with nonredundant coding for 9600 bps and subset A B C D of states used at 4800 bps for training.

FIGURE 5.17.

V.32 nonredundant coding signal constellation pattern.

Similar to nonredundant coding, under Trellis coding, the data stream generated by the DTE is subdivided into groups of four consecutive data bits. The first two bits in time, $Q1_n$ and $Q2_n$ in each group, are first differentially encoded into the outputs $Y1_n$ and $Y2_n$ according to Table 5.9. The two differentially encoded bits, $Y1_n$ and $Y2_n$, are then used as input to a convolutional encoder that generates a redundant bit, $Y0_n$. That bit and the four information-carrying bits ($Y1_n$, $Y2_n$, $Q3_n$, and $Q4_n$) are then mapped into one of two sets of coordinates of the signal element to be transmitted. One set of coordinates is used with nonredundant coding, whereas the second set of coordinates is used with Trellis coding. Table 5.10 lists the two alternative V.32 signal state mappings for 9600 bps operations. When you plot each of the possible Trellis coding points listed in Table 5.10, you get a 32-point signal constellation. Figure 5.18 illustrates the 32-point signal constellation when Trellis coding is used by a V.32 modem, as well as the four states used at 4800 bps and for modem training.

Table 5.9. V.32 differential encoding for use with Trellis coded alternative at 9600 bps.

Inputs		Previous Outputs		Outputs	
$Q1_n$	$Q2_n$	$Y1_n\text{-}1$	$Y2_n\text{-}1$	$Y1_n$	$Y2_n$
0	0	0	0	0	0
0	0	0	1	0	1
0	0	1	0	1	0
0	0	1	1	1	1
0	1	0	0	0	1
0	1	0	1	0	0
0	1	1	0	1	1
0	1	1	1	1	0
1	0	0	0	1	0
1	0	0	1	1	1
1	0	1	0	0	1
1	0	1	1	0	0
1	1	0	0	1	1
1	1	0	1	1	0
1	1	1	0	0	0
1	1	1	1	0	1

Table 5.10. Alternative signal-state mappings for 9600 bps operations.

(Y0)	Y1	Y2	Q3	Q4	Nonredundant Coding		Trellis Coding	
		Coded Inputs			Re	Im	Re	Im
0	0	0	0	0	-1	-1	-4	1
	0	0	0	1	-3	-1	0	-3
	0	0	1	0	-1	-3	0	1
	0	0	1	1	-3	-3	4	1
	0	1	0	0	1	-1	4	-1
	0	1	0	1	1	-3	0	3
	0	1	1	0	3	-1	0	-1
	0	1	1	1	3	-3	-4	-1
	1	0	0	0	-1	1	-2	3
	1	0	0	1	-1	3	-2	-1
	1	0	1	0	-3	1	2	3
	1	0	1	1	-3	3	2	-1
	1	1	0	0	1	1	2	-3
	1	1	0	1	3	1	2	1
	1	1	1	0	1	3	-2	-3
	1	1	1	1	3	3	-2	1
1	0	0	0	0			-3	-2
	0	0	0	1			1	-2
	0	0	1	0			-3	2
	0	0	1	1			1	2
	0	1	0	0			3	2
	0	1	0	1			-1	2
	0	1	1	0			3	-2
	0	1	1	1			-1	-2
	1	0	0	0			1	4
	1	0	0	1			-3	0
	1	0	1	0			1	0
	1	0	1	1			1	-4

continues

Table 5.10. continued

					Nonredundant Coding		Trellis Coding	
(Y0)	Y1	Y2	Q3	Q4	Re	Im	Re	Im
	1	1	0	0			-1	-4
	1	1	0	1			3	0
	1	1	1	0			-1	0
	1	1	1	1			-1	4

FIGURE 5.18.

A 32-point signal structure with trellis coding for 9600 bps (states A B C D used at 4800 bps and for training).

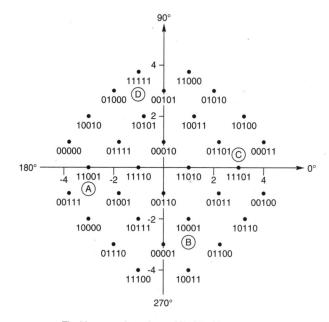

The binary numbers denote $Y0_n$ $Y1_n$ $Y2_n$ 03_n 04_n

● A Trellis coded modem has an error rate up to an order of magnitude less than another modem without this coding capability.

The extra bit generated by Trellis coding permits interdependencies between signal points to be noted, in effect permitting the receiving modem to recognize misplaced signal points in the signal constellation and to correct most errors. This results in a modem using Trellis coding having an error rate up to an order of magnitude less than another modem without this coding capability. Thus, almost all V.32 modems are operated using their Trellis coding capability rather than their nonredundant coding capability.

In addition to operating at 9600 and 4800 bps, a V.32 modem is V.22bis compatible. This compatibility enables the V.32 modem to communicate at 2400 bps with the large base of V.22bis modems that have been installed worldwide.

CCITT V.32bis

The V.32bis standard was ratified by the CCITT in February 1991. It provides a mechanism for achieving data rates up to 14,400 bps over the switched telephone network. Like the V.32 standard, V.32bis uses echo cancellation to get full-duplex transmission on the two-wire switched telephone network. It also uses Trellis coding to reduce the probability of errors occurring at the receiving modem due to the modem mistaking one constellation point for an adjacent point. The key difference between the V.32bis and V.32 modems concerns the former's method of getting a 14,400 bps operation. To do so, the V.32bis modem operates on six bits at a time and adds a redundant bit for Trellis coding. This method results in a signal constellation pattern of 127 or 128 points and an operating rate of 6 bits per baud times the 2400 (modem) baud rate, providing a data rate of 14,400 bps.

Most V.32bis modems support V.42 compression. This combination provides a potential throughput of 57.6 Kbps because that compression technique typically provides an average compression ratio of 4:1. In comparison, a V.32 modem with V.42 compression enabled provides a maximum throughput of 38.4 Kbps based on a compression ratio of 4:1.

In addition to a high-speed operating rate of 14,400 bps, a V.32bis modem supports an operating rate of 12,000 bps, as well as downward compatibility with the V.32 modem. Because the latter is compatible with the V.22bis modem, the V.32bis modem is compatible with both the V.32 and the V.22bis modems.

CCITT V.33

The CCITT V.33 modem standard was promulgated in 1988. It formed the basis for the V.32bis standard, which followed a few years later.

Developed to provide 14,400 bps full-duplex operations on leased lines, the V.33 modem does not use echo cancellation. This is because the four-wire leased line provides two signal paths, which removes the necessity for using that technique.

Similar to the V.32bis modem, which actually followed the V.33, the V.33 modem operates at 14,400 bps by packing six data bits into a baud and using a 2400-baud rate. At that data rate, the V.33 modem adds a redundant bit, which results in the generation of a 127- or 128-point signal constellation pattern. Like the V.32bis modem, the V.33 has a secondary signaling rate of 12,000 bps. However, the V.33 modem, unlike the V.32bis, has no additional downward compatibility because it was developed for use on leased lines.

One additional difference between the V.33 modem and its switched network V.32bis equivalent concerns a multiplexing option specified by the V.33 standard. Under the V.33 standard, a multiplexer option can be included that enables the combination of 2400, 4800, 7200, 9600, and 12,000 bps data sources to produce a single aggregate bit stream at either 12,000 or 14,400 bps for transmission. The multiplexer is a time division multiplexer (discussed in Chapter 6) that enables multiple data sources to share the use of a leased line. Because it is very difficult to get people to agree to access the same switched telephone number at the same time, multiplexers are not incorporated into dial modems. In comparison, leased lines are used to permanently provide a connection between two fixed locations. Leased lines provide an opportunity for economic savings by sharing the use of the line among two or more users.

CCITT V.34

Previously referred to as V.fast, the V.34 standard represents several years of effort by modem manufacturers to develop a product that can support data rates up to 28.8 Kbps using multidimensional Trellis codes and an advanced equalization technique known as precoding. Under the proposed V.34 standard, which is expected to be completed by the latter part of 1994, three-dimensional Trellis coding will provide a significantly greater level of performance in comparison to V.32 and V.32bis modems. This increase in performance results not only from the higher data transfer rate of V.34 modems, but also from their lower error rate due to the use of three-dimensional Trellis coding. The lower error rate reduces the need for retransmission, which improves modem performance.

To provide compatibility with previously developed modems, the V.34 modem is downward compatible with V.32bis and V.32 modems. Because the V.32 modem provides compatibility with V.22bis and most modem vendors add V.23, V.21, and Bell System 212 compatibility, a V.34 modem can provide the capability to support seven distinct modulation methods.

One of the problems V.34 users can expect to encounter concerns the capability to use the modem effectively when it is set to perform compression and is communicating with another V.34 modem. The reason is that when compression is enabled, the modem becomes capable of receiving data from an attached DTE at 115.2 Kbps to support an operating rate of 28.8 Kbps and a compression ratio of 4:1. Unfortunately, the UART built into the serial port of many modern computers and almost all previously manufactured computers are 8250 or 16450. This nomenclature references part numbers of National Semiconductor chips, although the actual chips are available from many vendors.

The 8250 UART, which was used in all IBM PC, PC XT, and compatible computers, starts to lose characters at data rates beyond 19.2 Kbps. The 16450, which was originally used with the PC AT and compatible computers as well as most 80386 systems, can result in lost data at operating rates above 57.6 Kbps, limiting its use to V.32bis modems. To effectively support data transfer rates at 115.2 Kbps requires the use of the 16550 UART. This means that you might have to replace an existing UART to effectively use a V.34 modem. As an alternative to the replacement of a UART, several vendors anticipate marketing V.34 modems that can be cabled to the parallel port of a personal computer because that port can support a sustained data transfer rate of over 150 Kbps. Because most communications programs are limited to supporting the use of serial ports, users might be restricted to employing a modem-manufacturer-supplied program to use a V.34 modem connected to a parallel port.

Although the CCITT has yet to promulgate recommendations covering higher speed leased-line modems, several vendors have introduced 19.2 Kbps TCM-based devices. In 1986, Codex Corporation became the first to introduce an "Eight-State Trellis Coded Modulation" modem, but Paradyne, NEC, and Fujitsu followed shortly with their own versions. Although the initial cost of 19.2 Kbps modems exceeded $10,000 per unit, by mid 1994, several vendors were offering them for under $1,000, a price that encourages their widespread use.

Digital Transmission

In transmission systems that are not restricted by the bandwidth limitations of the voice-grade channel, it is advantageous to transmit the binary information from the source as binary data without conversion to analog form. The reasons for this were explained in Chapter 3, "Messages and Transmission Channels." For end-user applications, the devices that connect between the business machine (DTE) and the channel usually are called service units, digital modems, wireline modems, or channel interface units; most persons and organizations now use the term service unit. Although data is transmitted end-to-end in digital form, the line coding used on digital transmission facilities differs from the digital coding used by computers and at the familiar RS-232 interface between DTEs and DCEs.

It is advantageous to transmit data in binary form, rather than converting it to analog form. However, digital transmission must be restricted to channels with greater bandwidth than the voiceband.

When digital transmission facilities were first made available for commercial use, two types of service units were required to be gotten by customers who used this service: Data Service Units (DSUs) and Channel Service Units (CSUs). Because a discussion of the operation and utilization of DSUs and CSUs requires basic knowledge of digital line coding and code violations, we will first discuss those topics before focusing on the two types of service units used with digital transmission facilities.

The most obvious difference between voiceband modems and direct digital transmission units is the increased bandwidth required by the latter. Recall from Chapter 3 that this increase is about a factor of eight. Thus, digital transmission is restricted to channels with bandwidths greater than the 3 KHz voiceband.

Line Coding

There are several techniques that can be used to code data. To help you understand the advantages and disadvantages of different methods, we'll examine the operation of several coding techniques.

UNIPOLAR CODE

The NRZ code works well for the shielded and short travel paths within a machine, but it is not suited for long-distance use because residual DC shifts the "zero" level.

The waveform of binary signals normally used in computers and terminals is called unipolar; that is, the voltage representing the bits varies between 0 V and +5 V, as shown in Figure 5.19a. (The code shown is called NRZ, Non-Return to Zero, because the voltage does not return to zero between adjacent 1 bits.) This representation works well inside machines where the transmission paths are short and well shielded, but it is unsuitable for long paths because of the presence of residual DC levels and the potential absence of enough signal transitions to allow reliable recovery of a clocking signal. Signal conditioning devices (the previously mentioned channel interface units) are used to convert the unipolar waveform to one of several different patterns that meet the goals of no long-term DC residual in the signal and strong timing content. Several of these signal patterns are shown in Figure 5.19b through 5.19e.

FIGURE 5.19.

Line coding of binary pulses.

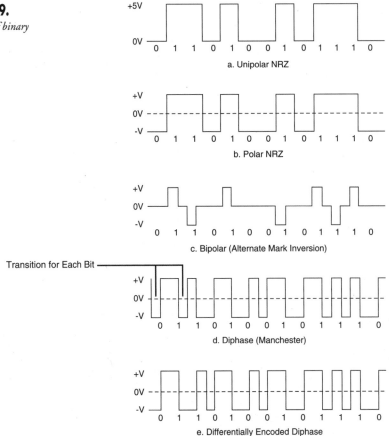

a. Unipolar NRZ

b. Polar NRZ

c. Bipolar (Alternate Mark Inversion)

d. Diphase (Manchester)

e. Differentially Encoded Diphase

POLAR NRZ CODE

The simplest pattern that eliminates some of the residual DC problem is called a polar NRZ line code. It is shown in Figure 5.19b. This coding merely shifts the signal reference level to the midpoint of the signal amplitude. This shift has the effect of reducing the power required to transmit the signal by one-half compared with unipolar but has the disadvantage of having most of the energy in the signal concentrated around zero frequency, as illustrated in Figure 5.20.

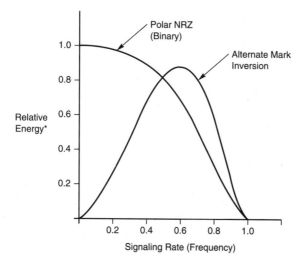

*With equally likely 1's and 0's

FIGURE 5.20.

Energy distribution of encoded pulses.

A more satisfactory coding scheme is that used in the so-called T1 digital transmission system. This scheme, called bipolar or alternate mark inversion (AMI), is illustrated in Figure 5.19c. This format has no residual DC component and has zero power in the spectrum at zero frequency, as Figure 5.20 shows. It achieves these goals by transmitting pulses with a 50 percent duty cycle (only half as wide as the pulse interval allows) and by inverting the polarity of alternate 1 bits that are transmitted. Note that the bipolar format is really a three-state signal (+V, 0 V, –V). This increase in the code space of the signal adds redundancy without increasing the bandwidth of the signal and makes performance monitoring easier. Ensuring that long strings of zero bits do not occur (with an accompanying lack of timing information) is left to the transmitting terminal or channel interface.

The block diagram of a circuit to receive the bipolar signal and decode it into straight binary is shown in Figure 5.21. Note that the AMI pulse format is rectified into polar pulses inside the receiver, where suppressing the DC component of the signal is no longer critical.

●

The bipolar (alternate mark inversion) coding scheme eliminates residual DC and has zero power in the spectrum at zero frequency. The polarity of every other 1 bit is inverted.

FIGURE 5.21.

Bipolar decoder.

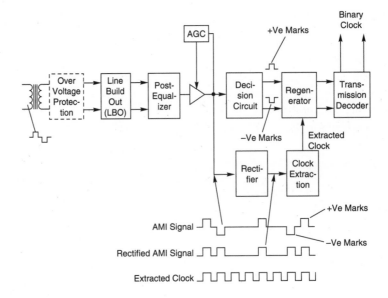

DIPHASE CODE

In diphase coding, strong timing information is provided by having a transition for every bit, and residual DC is eliminated by having both polarities for every bit.

Another technique that has received considerable acceptance is called digital biphase, diphase, or Manchester coding. It is illustrated in Figure 5.19d. The diphase code provides strong timing information by supplying a transition for every bit, whether it be a one or a zero. If the diphase signal is differently encoded, as Figure 5.19e shows, it is even possible to determine the absolute phase of the signal because only a zero has a transition at the beginning of an interval. It also eliminates the residual DC problem by providing both a positive and a negative polarity for every bit.

All these desirable characteristics are gained, however, at the expense of requiring twice the bandwidth of a bipolar signal. Thus, diphase coding is not used by communications carriers, for whom bandwidth is a precious commodity. Instead, diphase coding has found considerable use in providing digital signaling on several types of local area networks because the bandwidth of the LAN cable does not have to be used to support the communications requirements of different organizations. The diphase scheme is used on the Ethernet local area network developed by the Xerox Corporation, Digital Equipment Corporation, and Intel Corporation. A modified diphase coding technique, referred to as differential Manchester coding, is used on the token-ring local area network.

Repeaters

Because it is not possible to separate the noise from an analog signal after the two are mixed on a transmission path, both the noise and the desired signal are amplified in repeaters. The signal-to-noise ratio gets progressively worse as the path length increases.

This effect does not occur when digital signals are used, because a different kind of repeater, called a regenerative repeater (Figure 5.22), can be used. This repeater doesn't just amplify the pulses; it regenerates them to restore the shape of the binary signal exactly as it was when it left the originating transmitter. This is a major advantage of the digital transmission technique because it is possible in principle, and to a large extent in practice, to reduce the error rate of the signal to as low a value as desired merely by putting the repeaters closer together.

The regenerative repeater used in digital transmission doesn't just amplify the input signal; it actually regenerates the binary signal so that it is just like the original signal.

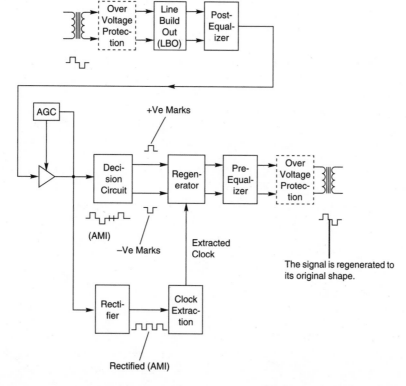

FIGURE 5.22.

Regenerative repeater.

The regenerative repeater, like the sending line terminal circuit, has some of the same functions as a modem. For example, it does certain electrical transformations on the input waveform to make it suitable for the transmission path. Both the sending and the receiving ends of these operations can be studied by referring to Figure 5.22. On the input end, the line build-out (LBO) circuit matches the post-equalizer circuit with the length of the transmission cable on the input end. The post-equalizer circuit compensates for the frequency and phase nonlinearities of a standard length of input circuit, which is represented by the output of the LBO. The equalized input signal is amplified by an amplifier controlled by an automatic gain control (AGC) circuit; then the stabilized and normalized

●

The regenerative repeater has phase and frequency correction circuits to compensate for nonlinearities in the transmission path.

input goes to a clock-extraction circuit and a decision circuit/regenerator. The clock-extraction circuit, which is driven by the received data transitions, clocks the regenerator so that the original signal is regenerated exactly.

Bipolar Violations

Bipolar transmission requires that each data pulse representing a logical one is transmitted with alternating polarity. A violation of this rule is defined as two successive pulses that have the same polarity and are separated by a zero level.

A bipolar violation indicates that a bit is missing or miscoded. Some bipolar violations are intentional and are included to replace a long string of zeros that could cause a loss of timing and receiver synchronization or to transmit control information. Figure 5.23 illustrates one example of a bipolar violation. The top of that figure shows the correct encoding to the bit sequence 01101010, using bipolar return-to-zero signaling. In the lower portion of Figure 5.23, the third one bit is encoded as a negative pulse. It represents a violation of the bipolar return-to-zero signaling technique, in which ones are alternately encoded as positive and negative voltages for defined periods.

FIGURE 5.23.

Bipolar violations.

A. Bipolar Coding of Data

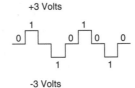

+3 Volts

-3 Volts

B. Bipolar Violation

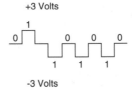

+3 Volts

-3 Volts

Two successive negative or positive pulses
represent a bipolar violation of a bipolar return
to zero signaling technique.

On DDS transmission facilities, a maximum of five consecutive zeros is permitted. This means that a bipolar violation must be employed to maintain synchronization whenever a string of six or more zeros is encountered. Otherwise, repeaters on the line connecting the carrier office and the customer, as well as service units at the line interface, might not be able to get clocking as a result of an absence of ones from the signal. This could result in a loss of synchronization with the signal.

To ensure a minimum ones density at 2.4, 4.8, 9.6, and 19.2 Kbps, any sequence of six consecutive zeros is encoded as 000X0V, in which

> 0 denotes zero voltage transmitted (binary zero),
>
> X denotes a zero or + or –A volts, with the polarity determined by conventional bipolar coding, and
>
> V denotes a + or –A volts, with the polarity in violation of bipolar rule.

Figure 5.24 illustrates the zero suppression sequence used to suppress a string of six consecutive zeros. For transmission at 56 Kbps, any sequence of seven consecutive zeros is encoded as 0000X0V.

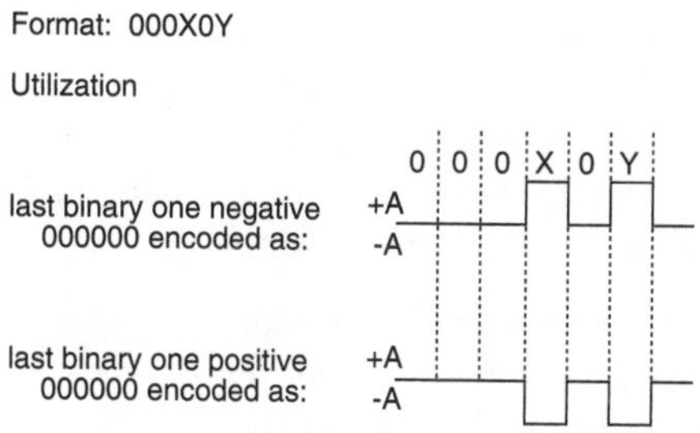

Format: 000X0Y

Utilization

last binary one negative
000000 encoded as:

last binary one positive
000000 encoded as:

FIGURE 5.24.

DDS zero suppression sequence.

In addition to providing a mechanism to suppress a string of binary zeros, bipolar violations can also be used to transmit network codes that affect the operation of digital circuit terminating equipment, such as DSUs and CSUs. For example, when a DTE does not have data to transmit, the absence of a signal would result in the loss of clocking by repeaters on the line between the customer and the carrier's office. In this situation, the DSU/CSU transmits a bipolar violation sequence that enables repeaters to maintain clocking but that is recognized as an idle sequence and ignored by equipment at the carrier's office. Another example of the use of an intentional bipolar violation would be a sequence of bits that forms a loop-back code. The loop-back code would be recognized by the line-terminating equipment as a request to interconnect transmit and receive wire pairs on a four-wire circuit, enabling the circuit to be tested without human intervention.

For T1 circuits, AT&T publication G2411 sets the ones density requirement to be n ones in each window of $8 \times (n+1)$ bits, in which n varies from 1 to 23. This means that a T1 carrier cannot have more than 15 consecutive zeros ($n=1$) and that there must be approximately three ones in every 24 consecutive bits ($n=2$ to 23). Several methods are used to provide this minimum ones density on T1 circuits, including Binary 7 Zero Code Suppression and Binary 8 Zero Substitution (B8ZS). The latter, which represents the use of intentional bipolar violations, is discussed in Chapter 6, "Multiplexing Techniques."

Service Units

There are two distinct types of service units whose utilization can be categorized by the type of transmission facility they are used with. Those two digital transmission facilities are AT&T's Dataphone Digital Service (DDS) and equivalent offerings by other carriers, and T1 transmission lines.

Data Service Unit

Data Service Units are used at data rates from 2.4 Kbps through 56 Kbps for transmission on DDS. DSUs can also be used at 64 Kbps to get access to a fractional T1 line operating at that data rate. In actuality, transmission on DDS and on a 64 Kbps fractional T1 facility requires the use of a DSU and a Channel Service Unit. The CSU, which is located between the DSU and the digital line, physically terminates the line while providing signal amplification and initiating remote loop-back operations in response to special codes received over the line. The DSU is located between the user's terminal equipment and the CSU. The DSU converts unipolar digital signals from terminal devices into a bipolar digital format for transmission over the digital network. In addition, the DSU provides timing recovery, control signaling, and synchronous sampling.

Before deregulation, the CSU was provided by the communications carrier, whereas the DSU could be gotten from the carrier or from third-party sources. This resulted in an end-user connection to the DDS network similar to that illustrated in the top portion of Figure 5.25, in which the CSU terminated the carrier's four-wire loop and the DSU was cabled to the CSU. In this configuration, the CSU terminates the carrier's circuit. In addition, a separate CSU was designed to perform signal regeneration, monitor incoming signals to detect bipolar violations, and perform remote loop-back testing.

FIGURE 5.25.

The DSU/CSU connections.

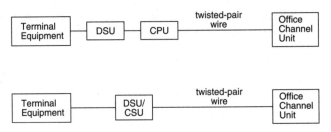

Most manufacturers combine the functions of a DSU and CSU into a single device for use on low speed digital transmission facilities.

Since deregulation, most communications vendors have manufactured combined DSU/CSU devices, integrating the functions of both devices into a common housing that is powered by a common power supply. The lower portion of Figure 5.25 illustrates the connection of end-user terminal equipment to DDS using a combined DSU/CSU unit.

Channel Service Unit

Unlike transmission on DDS and equivalent carrier facilities in which the DSU originated as a separate device, these functions are built into most types of data terminal equipment (DTE) designed for operation on T1 lines. Thus, a CSU designed for 1.544 Mbps operation was developed as a separate entity to both interface a T1 line and provide a mechanism for the built-in DSU of most DTEs to be connected to the digital transmission facility.

In addition to performing a line termination function, a CSU used on a T1 facility provides signal amplification and initiates remote loopbacks similar to the functions performed by the CSU portion of a combined DSU/CSU used on DDS transmission facilities. Two additional functions performed by the CSUs connected to T1 transmission facilities include frame formatting and the computation of performance measurement statistics. Frame formatting is the process of encoding every 193rd bit to provide synchronization framing and, in some instances, to generate and store performance measurement data. Concerning the latter, industry standards require CSUs to both compute various performance statistics and store those statistics for transmission when predefined codes embedded in the T1 framing are received. Readers are referred to Chapter 6, "Multiplexing Techniques," for specific information concerning frame formatting and performance measurement statistics associated with T1 lines.

What Have You Learned?

1. The bandwidth of a channel sets a limit on the modulation or baud rate of the channel.

2. The data rate through a channel can be increased by sending more than one bit per baud.

3. Synchronous modems modulate a carrier wave in phase or amplitude, or both, to send more than one bit per baud.

4. Synchronous modems send the clock signal along with the data. They are more expensive than asynchronous modems because of the additional circuitry necessary to recover the clock from the data.

5. Usually, only phase modulation is used in 2400 bps modems, but both phase and amplitude modulation are used in 4800 and 9600 bps modems.

6. The most important transmission impairment that synchronous modems must deal with is differential delay distortion. Such modems have adaptive equalizers to correct for this distortion.

7. Accurate recovery of the signal in both synchronous modems and digital transmission of binary signals depends on having a sufficient number of one bits transmitted.

8. Asymmetrical transmission involves the assignment of different transmission operating rates for each direction.

9. The use of a high-speed modem with its data compression facility enabled might require the replacement of your computer's UART to support the modem's effective data transfer capability.

10. Digital transmission uses regenerative repeaters rather than amplifiers to correct the line signal.

11. Intentional bipolar violations can be used to maintain synchronization or to transmit control information on digital circuits.

Quiz for Chapter 5

1. What is one principal difference between synchronous and asynchronous transmission?
   a. The bandwidth required is different.
   b. The pulse heights are different.
   c. The clocking is mixed with the data in asynchronous transmission.
   d. The clocking is derived from the data in synchronous transmission.

2. Synchronous modems cost more than asynchronous modems because:
   a. They are larger.
   b. They must contain clock recovery circuits.
   c. The production volume is larger.
   d. They must operate on a larger bandwidth.

3. The scrambler in a synchronous modem is in the:
   a. Control section.
   b. Receiver section.
   c. Transmitter section.
   d. Terminal section.

4. Binary codes are sometimes transformed in modems into:
   a. Hexadecimal.
   b. Huffman codes.
   c. Gray code.
   d. Complementary codes.

5. The digital-to-analog converter in a synchronous modem sends signals to the:
   a. Modulator.
   b. Transmission line.
   c. Terminal.
   d. Equalizer.

6. The receive equalizer in a synchronous modem is called:
   a. A compromise equalizer.
   b. A statistical equalizer.
   c. An adaptive equalizer.
   d. An impairment equalizer.

7. The receive equalizer reduces delay distortion using a:

    a. Tapped delay line.

    b. Difference engine.

    c. Descrambler.

    d. "Gearshift."

8. A Western Electric 201 modem operates with a carrier frequency of:

    a. 1000 Hz.

    b. 1200 Hz.

    c. 1800 Hz.

    d. 600 bauds.

9. The CCITT V.26 modem has a modulation rate of:

    a. 1200 Hz.

    b. 1200 bauds.

    c. 1560 cps.

    d. None of the above.

10. The transmission signal coding method for a T1 carrier is called:

    a. Binary.

    b. NRZ.

    c. Bipolar.

    d. Manchester.

11. If a modem packs six bits into each signal change and operates at 2400 baud, its operating rate is:

    a. 2400 bps.

    b. 4800 bps.

    c. 9600 bps.

    d. 14,400 bps.

12. The use of V.42 compression with a V.32bis modem operating at 14,400 bps can result in a maximum throughput of:

    a. 14,400 bps.

    b. 19,200 bps.

    c. 38,400 bps.

    d. 57,600 bps.

13. A bipolar violation:

    a. Represents a zero bit followed by a one bit.

    b. Occurs when two successive pulses have the same polarity and are separated by a zero level.

    c. Occurs when two successive pulses have the same polarity and are separated by a one level.

    d. Represents a one bit followed by a zero bit.

14. On a digital circuit, the absence of a transmitted signal:

    a. Has no effect on equipment.

    b. Occurs when a DTE has no data to transmit.

    c. Is compensated for by the transmission of intentional bipolar violations to maintain equipment clocking.

    d. Occurs only after 9 p.m.

Multiplexing Techniques

About This Chapter

Until now, we have primarily focused on communications between individual devices, such as a personal-computer user transmitting information to a mainframe computer or an individual using a telephone to place a long-distance call. Whenever there is a requirement for the use of two or more transmission paths that are partially or completely routed in parallel, there also exists an opportunity to economize on transmission cost through multiplexing.

In this chapter, we will focus on the multiplexing techniques used by communications carriers and business organizations to share transmission facilities. After examining communications carrier multiplexing techniques, including frequency division multiplexing (FDM) and time division multiplexing (TDM), we will conclude with a discussion of the applicability of those techniques to business organizations, as well as the use of statistical time division multiplexers (STDM) by those organizations.

Multiplexing

Multiplexing provides a mechanism to share the use of a common channel or circuit by two or more users. As such, its original development was based on economics.

UNDERSTANDING

Sharing a Channel

Just as modulation can be understood using the idea of sending code with a flashlight, so multiplexing has a simple analogy. Imagine that you have several letters to take to the post office. You could get into the car and take one letter, mail it, come back home and get the second letter, take it to the post office and mail it, come back to get the third…silly, right? Why not take all the letters in the same trip, because they're all going to the post office?

This is what multiplexing amounts to: using a resource (in this case, the car going to the post office) to carry more than one message at a time. In the systems we are concerned with, a microwave system is a transmission facility (like the car), and a telephone call is the message (like the letter). The transmission facility is divided in either of two ways in order to share it: by frequency or by time.

Frequency Division Multiplexing

FDM translates the frequencies within each of several voice-band channels to different frequency channels that are combined and transmitted together.

Figure 6.1 shows the use of frequency division multiplexing (FDM) to carry more than one telephone conversation over a transmission channel. In effect, the frequencies in each call are changed so that they can be placed side-by-side in a wideband channel and transmitted as a group. At the other end, the frequencies in each call are changed back to the original frequencies. FDM was the mainstay of telephone transmission for many years; it is more efficient in terms of bandwidth than digital systems. The problem is that noise is amplified along with the voice. This fact, and the great decrease in cost of digital electronics, has led to the widespread replacement of FDM systems with time division multiplexing (TDM) systems.

FIGURE 6.1.

Frequency division multiplexing.

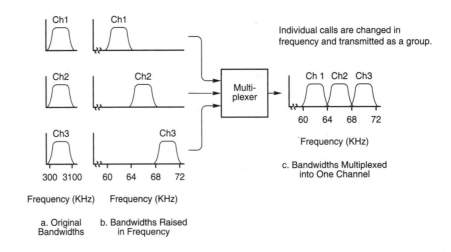

A second and perhaps more important reason for the tremendous reduction in the use of FDM during the past two decades was the conversion of most long-distance communications carrier transmission facilities from analog to digital. This conversion resulted in voice conversations being digitized at a carrier central office and carried in digital format to another central office. At the distant central office, the digitized conversation was converted back into its analog form and was routed to the destination telephone connected to that central office. By 1990, U.S. Sprint had converted all of its long-distance circuits to digital, and AT&T and MCI had converted more than 90 percent of their long-distance transmission facilities. A few years later, all long-distance communications in the United States were being transported over digital circuits, and most European communications carriers were well along on similar conversion efforts. To get an appreciation for the method by which analog voice is converted into a digital format, we'll examine digital modulation, which forms the basis for the use of TDMs by communications carriers.

Digital Modulation

Sine waves are all we have to work with in transmitting over the analog telephone channel because it doesn't transmit pulses. Digital transmission systems will transmit pulses, and with them we can encode either analog or digital information by modulating pulses.

Figure 6.2 shows three ways to modulate a series of pulses to carry data. When the amplitude of the pulses is varied to represent analog information, the method is called pulse amplitude modulation (PAM). This method is very susceptible to electrical noise interference. In the second method, called pulse width modulation (PWM), the information is represented by varying the width of the pulses. Both of these techniques are used in telephone switching equipment, such as a private branch exchange (PBX). The third technique, which varies the position of pulses within a group of pulses (called the frame) to represent information, is called pulse position modulation (PPM).

●
Digital modulation
methods include
PAM, PWM, PPM,
and PCM.

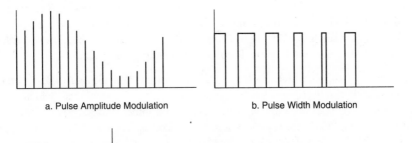

a. Pulse Amplitude Modulation

b. Pulse Width Modulation

c. Pulse Position Modulation

FIGURE 6.2.
Pulse modulation.

Figure 6.3 shows the process of sampling an analog signal as in PAM, but the amplitudes of the samples are encoded into binary numbers represented by constant amplitude pulses that are transmitted. This process, called pulse code modulation (PCM), overcomes the noise interference problem of PAM. Most long-distance telephone calls are transmitted by PCM.

FIGURE 6.3.

*Pulse code modula-
tion.*

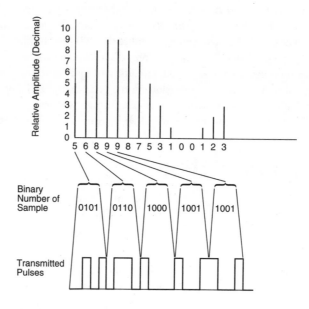

PCM

●
PCM involves a
three-step process:
sampling, quantiza-
tion, and coding.

The PCM system used by communications carriers employs a three-step process: sampling, quantization, and coding. During the sampling process, the analog signal is sampled 8000 times per second. This sampling rate is based on the Nyquist theorem, which states that to faithfully reconstruct an analog signal, the number of sample points must equal twice the maximum frequency of the signal. Because each voice channel has a bandwidth of 4 kilohertz (KHz), the sampling rate becomes 8000 samples per second.

The resulting samples, which are illustrated in the top portion of Figure 6.3, represent an infinite number of voltages. Thus, the second step in the PCM process, which is called quantization, reduces the PAM signal to a limited number of discrete amplitudes. The third step in the PCM process, which is known as coding, reduces the number of unique values of the PAM signal so that they can be coded through the use of an eight-bit byte. For simplicity, the lower portion of Figure 6.3 uses four bits to represent each PAM signal sample; in actuality, however, eight bits are used.

One of the earliest uses of PCM systems was to relieve cable congestion in urban areas during the 1960s. At that time, communications carriers installed equipment called channel banks in their central offices. Each channel bank contained a codec, time division multiplexer, and line driver. The codec (coder-decoder) accepts and samples 24 analog voice signals. It produces a series of PAM signals that are quantized and coded into eight-bit bytes. The TDM combines the digitized bit stream from each of the 24 inputs into one high-speed serial bit stream, and the line driver converts the electrical characteristics of the bit stream for transmission on the circuit-linking channel banks. Figure 6.4 illustrates a channel bank system that was the forerunner of what is now commonly known as a T-carrier transmission system.

> ●
> Early PCM systems were used to relieve cable congestion in urban areas.

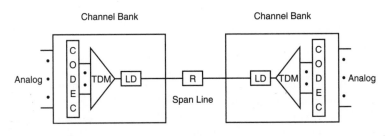

FIGURE 6.4.

Channel bank system.

Legend
CODEC - Coder - Decoder
R   - Repeater
LD   - Line Driver

The repeater illustrated in Figure 6.4 actually represents a series of devices installed approximately 6000 feet from one another on the span line. Each repeater examines the digital pulses transmitted on the span line connecting a pair of channel banks and regenerates each pulse. Because the repeater "throws away" the old pulse and generates a new pulse, it removes any prior distortion. In comparison, amplifiers used with analog transmission boost the strength of an analog signal, including increasing any prior distortion to the signal. This explains why, in general, digital transmission provides a higher level of signal quality and lower error rate than analog transmission.

> ●
> Repeaters on a span line regenerate the digital pulses, removing any prior distortion to the pulses.

Framing

To provide a method of synchronization of transmission, a framing format was developed for use with channel banks. Currently, the most popular framing format is called D4; however, a new framing format called ESF is gaining in use.

Under the D4 framing format, which is illustrated in Figure 6.5a, a frame bit is used to prefix each group of 24 eight-bit bytes, with each byte representing a digitized voice sample for each of 24 voice channels. Thus, a D4 frame contains 1 + 24 × 8, or 193 bits. The framing bits of 12 frames are used to develop a framing pattern that enables a receiving channel bank to synchronize itself to the transmission of data from a channel bank at the opposite end of a span line.

> ●
> Under D4 framing, the frame bit of 12 frames is used to provide a synchronization pattern.

FIGURE 6.5.

*D4 framing structure
and framing pattern.*

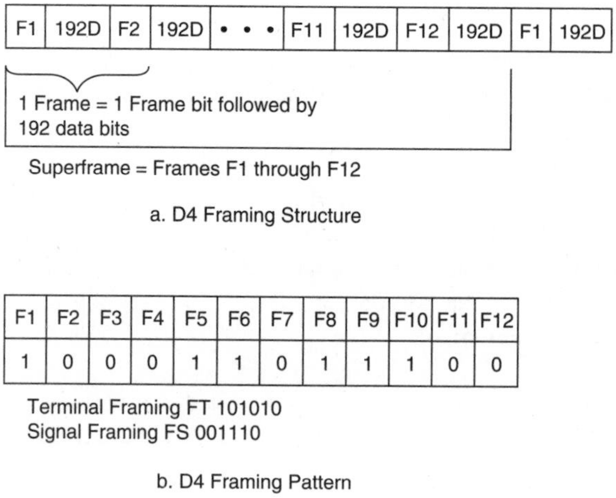

F1	192D	F2	192D	• • •	F11	192D	F12	192D	F1	192D

1 Frame = 1 Frame bit followed by
192 data bits

Superframe = Frames F1 through F12

a. D4 Framing Structure

F1	F2	F3	F4	F5	F6	F7	F8	F9	F10	F11	F12
1	0	0	0	1	1	0	1	1	1	0	0

Terminal Framing FT 101010
Signal Framing FS 001110

b. D4 Framing Pattern

The framing bits in a D4 superframe are alternately designated as terminal framing bits (Ft) or signal framing bits (Fs). The terminal framing bits consist of the odd framing bits, as illustrated in the lower portion of Figure 6.5. Under D4 framing, the Ft bits form an alternating pattern of ones and zeros, enabling one frame to be distinguished from another. Thus, the sequence of terminal framing bits is also referred to as a Frame Alignment Signal.

The signal framing bits that represent the repeating pattern "001110" are the even frame bits. These bits are used to define multiframe boundaries and enable the extraction of signaling bits from frames. Signaling bits are used to carry such mechanical signaling information as on-hook, off-hook, dialed digits, and call progress information. The method used to provide signaling bits, called bit robbing, is beyond the scope of this book. Readers are referred to the book *Digital Networking and T-Carrier Multiplexing,* authored by Gilbert Held and published by John Wiley & Sons, Inc., of New York, for detailed information concerning digital transmission systems, including the bit-robbing process.

ESF extends D4 framing to 24 consecutive frames, enabling synchronization patterns as well as performance measurement information to be transmitted.

A second framing format, known as extended superframe or ESF, extends D4 framing to 24 consecutive frames. Unlike D4 framing, which contains a specific repeating pattern, ESF framing contains both fixed and variable patterns. Out of the 24 frame bits in an extended superframe, only 6 are used for a framing pattern for synchronization.

The remaining frame bits are used to transmit error performance and network monitoring information. Although only 30 percent of channel banks currently support ESF framing, this percentage is expected to increase due to the performance measurement data it provides.

The T-Carrier

The span line illustrated in Figure 6.4 is now commonly referred to as a T-carrier. This circuit originally provided communications carriers with the capability to multiplex 24 voice conversations on one high-speed digital circuit.

Because each voice conversation is sampled 8000 times per second and each sample is encoded into 8 bits, the digitization rate per channel is 8000 samples/second × 8 bits/sample, or 64 Kbps. The aggregate of 24 channels represents a data rate of 64 Kbps × 24, or 1.536 Mbps. Because the framing rate is 8000 bits per second, the operating rate of the T-carrier is 1.536 Mbps + 8 Kbps, or 1.544 Mbps.

Until the early 1980s, the use of T-carrier transmission facilities was limited to communications carriers. Since then, the use of the T-carrier has been made available to commercial organizations. In the digital transmission hierarchy of carrier facilities, the 1.544 Mbps transmission rate represents the first level in the hierarchy and is commonly referred to as a T1 transmission facility. As a result of the commercial availability of this transmission facility, a large number of independent companies began to manufacture T1 multiplexers. Through the use of this type of multiplexer, companies could integrate the transmission of voice, data, and video between locations, routing this mixture of data onto a common high-speed transmission line operating at 1.544 Mbps.

Figure 6.6 illustrates one example of an organization's use of a T1 multiplexer that enables the integration of voice, data, and video transmission. In the example shown, the T1 multiplexer contains PCM cards that enable analog voice conversations routed from a Private Branch Exchange (PBX) to be digitized before being multiplexed. If a digital PBX was installed, data could be directly multiplexed without the use of PCM cards.

● The T-carrier provides a transmission path for multiplexing up to 24 voice conversations.

● Through the use of a T1 multiplexer, organizations can transmit voice, data, and video information on a common circuit operating at 1.544 Mbps.

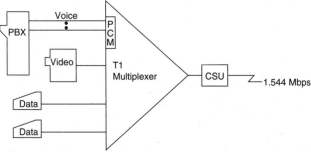

FIGURE 6.6.

Typical T1 multiplexer application.

Legend:

PCM - Pulse Code Modulation cards that sample, quantize, and encode each
         analog voice signal into a 64 Kbps digital data stream.
CSU - Channel Service Unit

Digital data is manipulated within a T1 multiplexer in a unipolar NRZ format, as previously indicated in Figure 5.19a. Although this data representation format is commonly used by the computer systems, electronic equipment, and the data terminal equipment (DTE) to data communications equipment (DCE) interface, it is unsuitable for transmission on a T1 transmission facility.

When span lines were first routed between channel banks, communications carriers desired a method that would allow them to transmit both a digital signal and power on the same circuit, separating the signal from the power through the use of a transformer at each channel bank location. To get this capability, a signaling method that resulted in no residual DC voltage was required, which would enable the use of transformers to separate the signal from the power carried on the line. The resulting line coding method that provided this capability is the bipolar alternate mark inversion (AMI) coding format previously illustrated in Figure 5.19c.

> ●
> Bipolar coding enables a signal and power to be carried on a common line and separated by the use of a transformer.

Most T1 multiplexers convert unipolar RTZ signals into bipolar AMI signals for transmission. However, prior to actual transmission on the T1 line, the digital signal must be framed according to the line code supported by the communications carrier—D4 or ESF. The framing function is but one of several operations performed by the channel service unit (CSU). Other functions performed by CSUs include storing performance data when an ESF framing format is used, recognizing and responding to network codes transmitted by the communications carrier and equipment connected to the T1 line, and transmitting a minimum number of binary ones, referred to as "ones density."

Ones Density

> ●
> A minimum number of marks, referred to as "ones density," must flow on a digital transmission facility to enable repeaters to get timing from the data.

The requirement for a ones density level on T1 circuits resulted from the need of repeaters to maintain timing. If a long string of binary zeros was transmitted, the repeaters on a span line could conceivably lose timing. Thus, the CSU must be capable of ensuring that a binary one or mark pulse occurs every so often, which enables repeaters to get timing from the pulse.

Specifically, carrier requirements are such that the number of consecutive zeros must be less than 15, and each eight-bit byte must include at least one "1" bit. To support carrier ones density requirements, several techniques are used, including binary 7 (B7) zero code suppression and binary 8 zero substitution, among others.

Under B7 zero code suppression, a 1 bit is substituted in bit position 7 of an all-zero byte. Although this technique ensures that the carrier's ones density requirements are met, it also restricts data to seven usable bits rather than eight. This means that each 64 Kbps voice channel multiplexed on a T1 line is restricted to 64 Kbps $\times$ 7/8, or 56 Kbps, when used for data transmission.

To understand why bit position 7 was selected for substitution, consider a worst-case scenario, as illustrated in Figure 6.7. In this example, the 8-bit byte representing the 24th channel contains a mark in bit position 1 followed by the remainder of the byte's bit positions set to zero. If the framing bit following the 24th channel has a value of zero and is followed by an all-zero byte, 16 bit positions would be between marks if bit position 8 had its value altered to 1. Normally, this would be more desirable because it represents the least significant position in a byte and would minimize its effect on a digitized voice signal. However, selecting bit position 8 would then violate the carrier's ones density requirements, which resulted in the selection of bit position 7 for substitution.

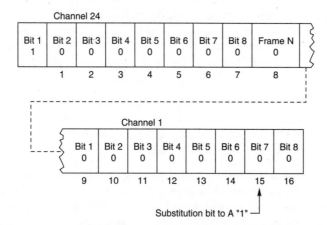

FIGURE 6.7.

B7 zero code suppression worst-case scenario.

Binary 8 Zero Substitution (B8ZS), developed by Bell Laboratories, represents a considerable improvement over B7 Zero Suppression because it enables data to be transmitted at 64 Kbps on a voice channel. This capability, in which a minimum ones density is gotten without corrupting data, provides what is known as a clear channel. Under B8ZS coding, each byte of eight consecutive zeros is replaced by a code that includes an intentional bipolar violation. Figure 6.8 illustrates the B8ZS coding process.

●

B8ZS provides a clear channel capability, enabling data transmission to occur at 64 Kbps on a voice channel.

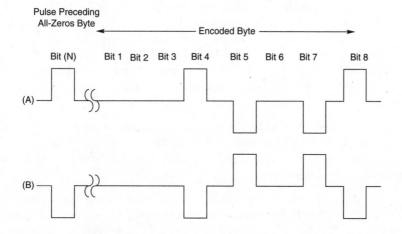

FIGURE 6.8.

B8ZS coding.

On examination of Figure 6.8, the coding used becomes more meaningful if we review how bipolar coding normally functions. That is, under bipolar coding, marks or binary ones are encoded using alternating polarities, and spaces are encoded as a zero voltage level. Thus, the encoded byte, when the pulse preceding an all-zeros byte was positive, commences with bit position 4 high, which represents a bipolar violation. This is illustrated at A in Figure 6.8. Next, bit positions 5 and 7 are both encoded as negative marks, which represents another bipolar violation. Because bits 4 and 8 are positive pulses while bits 5 and 7 are negative pulses, the encoded byte does not result in any DC voltage buildup, although it violates bipolar coding rules. At the receiving CSU, the encoded byte is recognized as defining the occurrence of an all-zeros byte, and the CSU then replaces the B8ZS code with eight binary zeros. Similarly, if the pulse preceding an all-zeros byte was negative, the all-zeros byte is encoded in the opposite manner, as illustrated at B in Figure 6.8.

> B8ZS coding uses intentional bipolar violations to maintain a minimum ones density.

Note that the state of bit position 4 represents a bipolar violation with respect to the pulse preceding the all-zeros byte, whereas bit positions 5 and 7 represent a bipolar violation with respect to each bit position's polarity. Also note that there are an equal number of positive and negative pulses to prevent DC voltage buildup.

The bipolar violations contained in the B8ZS coding represent intentional bipolar violations. Other examples of intentional bipolar violations are loopback codes that when recognized by a CSU place it in a loopback mode of operation. Intentional bipolar violations do not represent coding errors. In comparison, unintentional bipolar violations do represent coding errors resulting from line impairments whose measurement over a period provides an indication of the quality of a digital circuit.

Time Division Multiplexing

The T1 multiplexer that evolved from channel banks represents one of the earliest types of TDMs. Until T1 lines were made available for use by commercial organizations, most TDMs were manufactured for use with analog leased lines or low-speed Dataphone Digital Service (DDS) digital transmission facilities. When used with analog leased lines, the aggregate data rate of the TDM is normally limited to 19.2 Kbps, whereas its use with DDS limited its aggregate data rate to 56 Kbps. The 19.2 Kbps operating-rate limitation on analog leased lines is a constraint resulting from the operating rate of leased-line modems. In comparison, the 56 Kbps DDS operating-rate limitation is a service offering constraint.

> When multiplexing is used by commercial organizations, the rationale for multiplexing is the same as for communications carriers—economics.

Most communications networks used by organizations include several TDM systems that are used primarily because of economics. When one circuit and a pair of multiplexers replace two or more data circuits, the savings that accrue from the elimination of data lines usually can pay for the required equipment in less than a year.

To understand the rationale for using multiplexers, consider an example in which eight terminals located in San Francisco must communicate with a mainframe computer located in Chicago. If each terminal requires four hours of computer access per day and the cost of one hour of communications on the switched telephone network is $30, conventional dialing by each terminal operator to Chicago costs the organization $960 per day. If a month has 22 business days, the monthly cost for accessing the Chicago computer would slightly exceed $21,000, exclusive of the cost of the modems.

When terminal devices at one location require access to a computer at a second location, multiplexing should be considered. Figure 6.9 illustrates a network configuration that could be used to satisfy the San Francisco to Chicago communications requirements of the organization.

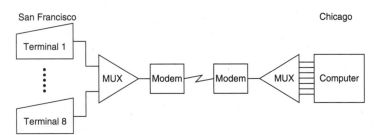

FIGURE 6.9.

Using multiplexers to reduce communications costs.

Assuming that the cost of each multiplexer is $3,000 and the leased line costs $1,000 monthly, during the first year, the multiplexing method would cost $18,000, exclusive of modems. In the second year of operation, the cost of multiplexing would be reduced to $12,000 because we assume that the equipment was purchased the first year. Thus, in this example, the two-year cost of multiplexing is $30,000, resulting in a substantial savings.

A second reason for the use of multiplexers is the relative fixed cost associated with their use. Multiplexer systems are connected to one another by leased lines with rates that can increase slightly from year to year because of tariff changes. The cost of the multiplexer system is rather stable and predictable because the cost of the line is billed monthly based on the distance between locations and is not dependent on usage. In comparison, the cost of using the switched telephone network depends on many factors, including the duration of the call, the distance between calling and called parties, the day and time the call was originated, and whether operator assistance was required. If only a few terminal users increase their connect time 15 minutes per day, the monthly cost of communications could substantially increase.

Operation

A TDM, as its name implies, uses time as a reference for multiplexing data. To understand the operation of a TDM as well as the limitations associated with this technology, we'll examine how data from a few terminals or personal computers are multiplexed and demultiplexed. Figure 6.10 illustrates the multiplexing of data from three terminal devices at a remote location to a mainframe computer at another location. For simplicity of illustration, it was assumed that terminal 1 transmitted the character sequence "BA," terminal 2 transmitted "DC," and terminal 3 transmitted "FE." The TDM at the remote location scans each port connected to a terminal for data, recognizing "A," "C," and "E" as input to ports 1, 2, and 3 of the multiplexer during the first scan. The TDM accepts data from each port and builds a multiplexing frame that represents the data from each port during the scan. Thus, frame 1 contains the character sequence "ECA," and frame 2 contains "FDB." In actuality, each TDM frame will also contain synchronization characters prefixing data as well as data from one or more scans.

FIGURE 6.10.

The multiplexing process.

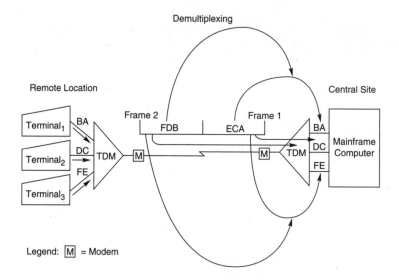

At the receiving TDM, the position of data in each frame is used to ensure the correct demultiplexing of data. As indicated in Figure 6.10, "A" is the first position of frame 1, which tells the TDM that that byte of information should be output onto port 1 of the multiplexer. Similarly, in frame 1 the character "C," which is located in the second position, and "E," which is located in the third position, inform the multiplexer at the central site to output those characters onto ports 2 and 3, respectively. Next, the data in frame 2 is examined by the central site multiplexer. Because "B" is in position 1, it is output onto port 1. Next, "D" and "F," which are located in positions 2 and 3 of frame 2, are output onto ports 2 and 3. Thus, the TDM demultiplexing process depends on the position of data within each frame.

The position of data within a TDM frame is used to ensure that data is demultiplexed correctly.

To understand the limitation of the TDM process, consider the actual operation of terminal devices. Some terminal operators might be reading a manual, attempting to determine how to correct a programming error or how to respond to a message requesting a specific type of data entry. Other terminal operators might be diligently entering data or receiving information, while some operators might be on a coffee break or simply thinking about the response they should enter to an application program they are accessing. Thus, at any instant, it is highly probable that there is no data transmission activity from or destined to one or more terminal devices. Because a TDM demultiplexes by the position of data in each frame, the absence of activity could result in the misinterpretation of data. To prevent this problem from happening, a TDM inserts null characters in each frame whenever there is no activity when input from a port is sampled by the TDM scanning process.

At the receiving multiplexer, the null characters maintain the positioning within the frame required for demultiplexing to occur correctly. They are "stripped," however, by the receiving multiplexer and are not output to devices attached to the TDM.

Although the use of null characters ensures that demultiplexing occurs correctly, it also indicates that the multiplexing process is not as efficient as it could be. For example, when several terminal users are on a break, thinking, or even entering data at a normal typing rate, most frames flowing between multiplexers contain a large percentage of null characters. Thus, for most periods, data transmission between TDMs is highly inefficient. Although a T1 multiplexer has the same inefficiency, its 1.544 Mbps operating rate enables the transmission of up to hundreds of devices to be carried on one very high-speed line. In comparison, TDMs connected to analog or DDS circuits operating at much lower data rates are limited to supporting a much smaller population of devices. Thus, the inefficiency of TDMs is much more pronounced when used with analog or DDS transmission facilities. This inefficiency resulted in the development of a different type of multiplexer for use on those transmission facilities. This type of multiplexer, referred to as a statistical time division multiplexer (STDM), provides a much higher level of line utilization efficiency than TDMs and has essentially replaced the use of TDMs by many organizations.

STDMs

In comparison to TDMs, which use fixed frames with data positioned in each frame, STDMs use variable-length frames. To understand the operation of STDMs, we'll examine how variable frames are created. In doing so, we will discuss one of several methods used to create variable positional information within a multiplexing frame.

To understand the operation of STDMs, assume that eight terminal devices are connected to a multiplexer as illustrated in Figure 6.11a. Further assume that during one scan operation, terminals 1, 2, 3, and 6 were active and transmitted the characters X, Y, Z, and Q, respectively. If the STDM employs a bit map character to denote the activity of each port during a scan, the multiplexer sets the bit position that corresponds to a port to a 1 if there is activity. Otherwise, a bit map position setting of 0 indicates that no activity occurred on a port during the scan.

●
Null characters are inserted into TDM frames to enable demultiplexing to occur based on the position of data within a frame.

●
STDMs create variable-length frames.

FIGURE 6.11.

STDM operation.

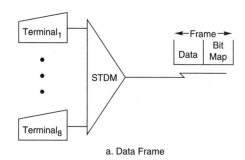

a. Data Frame

Terminal	Terminal Activity	Frame	
1	X	00100111	Bit Map
2	Y	X	Frame
3	Z	Y	Data
4	No Activity	Z	
5	No Activity	Q	
6	Q		
7	No Activity		
8	No Activity		

b. Frame Construction

The frame construction example illustrated in Figure 6.11b indicates how the use of a bit map can reduce the size of a frame when some ports connected to the STDM are inactive. In this example, terminals 1, 2, 3, and 6 were active; hence, bit map positions 1, 2, 3, and 6 were set to ones. Therefore, the character from each terminal can be added after the bit map to form a variable-length frame without requiring the use of null characters, because the bit map indicates the actual position of each character in the frame.

In general, an STDM can double to quadruple the number of asynchronous data sources serviced by a conventional TDM. This additional servicing capability is known as the multiplexer's service ratio. In addition to taking advantage of idle times, the STDM strips start, stop, and parity bits from each asynchronous character before transmission and "rebuilds" the character when it is demultiplexed. Some STDMs add data compression to a list of functions they perform, further increasing their service ratio.

Service Ratio

To understand the concept of an STDM's service ratio, first consider Figure 6.12a, which illustrates the use of a conventional TDM connected to a modem operating at 9600 bps. When a conventional TDM is used to multiplex data, the aggregate input data rate cannot exceed the output data rate. Hence, up to eight terminals operating at 1200 bps could be serviced by the TDM, resulting in a total input of 8 × 1200, or 9600 bps, being equal to the line operating rate.

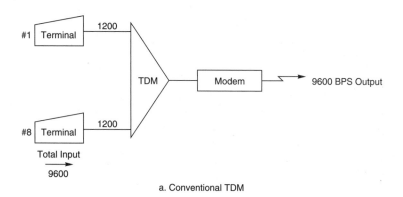

FIGURE 6.12.

STDM service ratio.

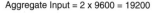

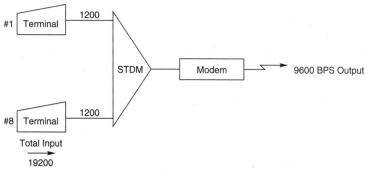

If the STDM's service ratio is 2, on the average it can service an aggregate input twice the line operating rate, or 19,200 bps. The term "on the average" is used because during a long period, some terminals are powered off and unused, some terminal operators are thinking about what to do next, and other terminal operators are entering data or receiving responses to their queries. Due to the previously explained STDM functions, over a prolonged period, the multiplexer can accept an input data rate of twice its output rate.

Consider a worst-case scenario, however, in which each terminal is a personal computer and every terminal operator attempts to transmit a large file at the same time. In this situation, the total input to the STDM becomes 19,200 bps, and the multiplexer cannot take advantage of idle times because each terminal is transmitting a continuous sequence of data. Even after stripping start, stop, and parity bits, the aggregate input data rate will exceed the line operating rate. Although the STDM contains a buffer area, as each terminal continues to transmit data, the buffer area would eventually fill and overflow, resulting in a loss of data. To prevent the loss of data, the STDM initiates flow control to turn off one

●

A service ratio of a multiplexer indicates the average data input to an STDM based on its line operating rate.

or more devices whenever its buffer reaches a certain level of occupancy. Then, as data from its buffer is transmitted onto the line and the level of buffer occupancy decreases to a certain level, the STDM turns off flow control, allowing devices connected to the multiplexer to resume transmission.

The capability of STDMs to service, on average, two to four times the aggregate data rate of the line connecting multiplexers resulted in their wide acceptance by most organizations. By 1990, almost 80 percent of all TDMs incorporated a statistical multiplexing process. Today, conventional TDMs are primarily used in which delays from the use of flow control cannot be tolerated—such as in T1 multiplexers, in which a delay in voice would be most annoying.

Low-Speed Voice/Data Multiplexers

Combining the operational capability of TDM and statistical time division multiplexers resulted in a new type of multiplexer for use by organizations requiring the transport of both voice and data. Known as a low-speed voice/data multiplexer, this device was developed for organizations that required the use of a few voice and data circuits between two locations. As such, this device fills a rapidly expanding market for organizations with small branch offices that require both voice and data communications capability to a regional office of company headquarters. Because the key to the operation of this multiplexer is its capability to digitize voice at data rates significantly below the PCM operating rate of 64 Kbps, we will first focus on a few of the methods used by this class of communications equipment to digitize voice conversations through voice compression.

Adaptive Differential Pulse-Code Modulation

ADPCM predicts the next voice sample based on the level of the previously sampled signal. This method halves the digitization rate to 32 Kbps.

Adaptive Differential Pulse-Code Modulation (ADPCM) is a voice digitization and compression technique that reduces PCM eight-bit samples to four-bit words, with each four-bit word representing 16 quantization levels. Those levels, which represent sample amplitudes under PCM, now represent the difference between successive samples under ADPCM. They permit a digitization data rate of 32 Kbps rather than the 64 Kbps operating rate required by PCM.

The key to the operation of ADPCM is the fact that the amplitude of voice does not rapidly change when sampled 8000 times per second. This fact enabled engineers to design adaptive predictor circuitry into ADPCM equipment that anticipates the value of the next sample based on the level of the previously sampled signal. A feedback loop used by the predictor minimizes the possibility of deviations between samples. Because this technique results in a very accurate prediction value, the difference between the predicted and the actual signal is relatively small, enabling it to be encoded through the use of four bits. If successive samples increase in their value difference, the adaptive predictor adapts to this change by increasing the range represented by the four bits. This adaption process decreases the signal-to-noise ratio, however, and reduces the accuracy of the decoded signal.

For normal voice conversations, ADPCM provides a voice quality that is most difficult to differentiate from a PCM-digitized voice conversation.

The key difference between ADPCM and PCM is in the area of modem transmission support. PCM can support modems operating at data rates up to 24 Kbps. In comparison, due to the use of an adaptive predictor, ADPCM is limited to supporting modem rates up to 4.8 Kbps. At higher operating rates, the modem signal changes too fast to be accurately predicted by ADPCM, resulting in an increase in transmission errors as the modem operating rate increases. Thus, ADPCM is primarily used in private networks that can restrict the use of voice channels to ADPCM-digitized voice and other channels to data. In comparison, communications carriers normally cannot restrict the use of the switched telephone network to modems that operate at or below 4.8 Kbps, which explains why most carriers use PCM equipment to digitize voice communications for transportation over the switched telephone network.

> ●
> The key limitation of ADPCM is in its incapability to reliably pass modem signals at data rates above 4800 bps.

Continuously Variable Slope Data Modulation

Continuously Variable Slope Data Modulation (CVSD) is a voice digitization technique originally developed for military use. This digitization technique has gained acceptance in the commercial market as a mechanism to digitize voice at a low data rate.

The key to the operation of CVSD is the fact that the higher the rate at which an analog signal is sampled, the smaller the resulting difference between sampled amplitudes. This means that at a high enough sampling rate, the difference between sampled amplitudes can be represented by a single bit.

That bit represents the change in the slope of the analog voice conversation. The bit is set to 1 to represent an increase in the slope between two samples, 0 to represent a decrease in the slope. Figure 6.13 illustrates the operation of CVSD.

> ●
> By sampling at a high rate, CVSD encodes the difference between sampled amplitudes in a single bit, which represents the change in the slope of the voice amplitude from the previous sample.

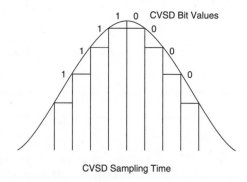

FIGURE 6.13.

CVSD operation.

Under CVSD, an increase in the slope of the sampled conversation is represented by a '1', and a decrease in the slope is represented by a '0'.

CVSD commonly operates at 32K and 16K samples per second, resulting in digitization rates of 32 Kbps and 16 Kbps. At 16 Kbps, CVSD is four times as efficient with respect to its data rate than PCM and twice as efficient as ADPCM. However, due to its use of a single bit to represent a change in slope, CVSD is not recommended for use by modems transmitting data.

Although CVSD is not to be used for transporting modulated data, its capability to represent a voice conversation at a low data rate resulted in the use of this technique as well as ADPCM as a mechanism to transport digitized voice by low-speed voice/data multiplexers.

As previously noted, a low-speed voice/data multiplexer can be considered as a combination TDM and statistical time division multiplexer. The TDM portion of the device is used exclusively for multiplexing two or more digitized voice conversations onto a fixed portion of the operating rate of the high-speed line that the multiplexer is connected to. Although the term *high-speed line* is used, the operating rate of the composite channel of the voice/data multiplexer is typically 56 or 64 Kbps—relatively low in comparison to a T1 multiplexer. This explains why this voice/data multiplexer is commonly referred to as a low-speed voice/data multiplexer. For example, a low-speed voice/data multiplexer connected to a 64 Kbps digital leased line might multiplex three voice conversations using CVSD onto 48 Kbps of the 64 Kbps leased line. The statistical time division multiplexer would then contend with one or more data sources for the remaining 16 Kbps operating rate of the leased line.

Figure 6.14 illustrates the bandwidth allocation of a 64 Kbps digital leased line based on the previously mentioned scenario. In this example, each voice conversation is digitized and is always placed into a fixed slot of 16 Kbps. In comparison, data sources contend for the remaining 16 Kbps. This technique ensures that each voice digitized signal is always carried by the multiplexer and eliminates potential delays from the statistical multiplexing process that could cause havoc to a reconstructed voice conversation.

> Because each CVSD-encoded bit represents a change in the slope of an analog signal, this technique is ill-suited for carrying modem-modulated data.

FIGURE 6.14.

Potential voice/data multiplexer bandwidth allocation.

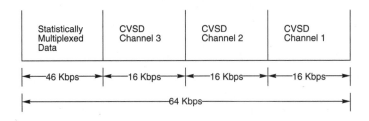

To illustrate the potential use of low-speed voice/data multiplexers in an organizational environment, assume that a branch office and a regional office each have a PBX. Also assume that branch office employees regularly converse with persons at a regional office and have between one and three simultaneous calls between offices during normal business hours. Also assume that 10 low-speed (2400 bps) terminals in the regional office require access to a computer located in the regional office.

Figure 6.15 illustrates as a network diagram schematic the use of a pair of low-speed voice/ data multiplexers between branch and regional offices to consolidate both voice and data communications requirements between the two locations onto one 64 Kbps digital circuit. In this example, each PBX has three lines routed into a data/voice multiplexer installed at each office. Through the use of CVSD adapter cards installed in both multiplexers, each voice conversation will be digitized into a fixed 16 Kbps time slot, as previously illustrated in Figure 6.14.

The ten 2400 bps terminals illustrated in the lower-left portion of Figure 6.15 would be statistically multiplexed into a fixed 16 Kbps time slot, as previously illustrated in Figure 6.14. If all ten terminals were transmitting files to the computer in the regional office, the aggregate terminal data rate of 24 Kbps would exceed the capacity of the fixed 16 Kbps time slot. If this situation occurs or another situation occurs in which enough terminals become active that their aggregate transmission exceeds the fixed 16 Kbps time slot, the multiplexer issues flow control to inhibit one or more data sources from transmitting.

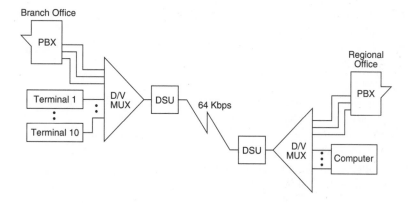

FIGURE 6.15.

Using low-speed voice/ data multiplexers.

Although flow control affects only the throughput of data, its use on voice traffic would result in random voice delays that would be entirely unacceptable for conducting a conversation. Thus, a voice/data multiplexer uses TDM for multiplexing voice conversations and STDM onto a fixed time slot for multiplexing data.

From an economic perspective, a voice/data multiplexer can pay for itself in as little time as one or two months. Of course, the actual payback period depends on the distance between locations, current and anticipated switched-telephone-network usage, the number of voice and data sources to be multiplexed, and the cost of voice/data multiplexers.

●

A voice/data
multiplexer uses flow
control only to
inhibit data traffic.

What Have You Learned?

1. Multiplexing is the process of sharing the use of a transmission facility by time or by frequency.

2. The conversion of most long-distance communications carrier transmission facilities from analog to digital resulted in a large replacement of FDM by TDM systems.

3. To faithfully reproduce an analog signal, it must be sampled at a rate equal to twice the bandwidth it occupies.

4. Repeaters regenerate digital pulses, removing any prior distortion. In comparison, amplifiers boost the strength of analog signals, including increasing any prior distortion.

5. Framing is used to provide a method of synchronization between channel banks.

6. D4 framing is restricted to providing synchronization data, whereas ESF framing enables the flow of performance measurement information as well as synchronization data.

7. Bipolar transmission allows a digital signal and power to be carried on the same line and separated from one another by the use of transformers.

8. A minimum number of binary ones, known as "ones density," must occur on a digital transmission line to enable repeaters to get timing from data.

9. Intentional bipolar violations, which occur when two successive marks have the same polarity, can be used to convey information or maintain a minimum ones density on a digital transmission facility.

10. When no activity occurs on a TDM input port, the multiplexer inserts a null character into the frame it builds. This character maintains the correct positioning of data from all ports, enabling demultiplexing to occur by position of data within a frame.

11. ADPCM and CVSD enable voice conversations to be digitized at data rates one-half to one-fourth that of PCM.

12. A voice/data multiplexer uses time division multiplexing to support multiple voice conversations and uses statistical time division multiplexing to support multiple data sources.

Quiz for Chapter 6

1. Multiplexing is:
    a. The process of increasing bandwidth on a channel.
    b. A technique that enables more than one data source to share the use of a common line.
    c. Mailing letters at the Post Office.
    d. The capability to share frequency by time.

2. One of the reasons frequency division multiplexing has essentially been replaced by time division multiplexing is because:
    a. There is more time than frequency.

b. It is difficult to place channels side by side.

c. Noise is amplified with voice when an FDM system is used.

d. Most available frequencies have been used.

3. When the amplitude of pulses is varied to represent analog information, the method is called:

a. PCM.

b. PWM.

c. PAM.

d. PPM.

4. The PCM sampling rate is 8000 samples per second because:

a. That represents the maximum rate that technology supports.

b. This rate allows unique values.

c. This rate allows the faithful reconstruction of an analog signal.

d. This rate is easily produced by a sampling chip.

5. In general, digital transmission provides a higher level of signal quality than analog transmission because:

a. Repeaters regenerate digital pulses and remove distortion, whereas amplifiers increase an analog signal, including any prior distortion to the signal.

b. Digital signals are smaller than analog signals and cannot be easily distorted.

c. Analog signals are continuous and are not easily distorted.

d. Digital signals are easier to sample than analog signals.

6. The D4 framing pattern contains a sequence of:

a. 24 bits.

b. 4 terminal and 8 framing bits.

c. 8 terminal and 4 framing bits.

d. 12 bits.

7. Bipolar signaling is used in place of unipolar signaling on T1 lines because:

a. Bipolar signaling produces twice as many marks as a unipolar signal.

b. It allows transmission at polar locations.

c. Bipolar signaling reduces residual DC voltage buildup, allowing a digital signal to be separated from power through the use of a transformer.

d. It allows transformers to be spaced far from one another, which reduces the cost of transmission.

8. B7 Zero Code Suppression is a technique that:

a. Allows data to flow on a digital line.

b. Ensures that each byte has at least one mark bit.

c. Is the latest clear channel encoding technique developed by Bell Laboratories.

d. Provides a clear channel transmission capability, allowing 64 Kbps data transmission on a voice channel.

9. Intentional bipolar violations:

a. Represent coding errors caused by line impairments.

b. Are used to convey information or maintain a minimum number of ones on a digital line.

c. Result in successive marks having opposite polarities.

d. Occur only in the laboratory.

10. Demultiplexing by a time division multiplexer occurs based on:

a. The position of data within a frame.

b. The position of a frame within a group of frames.

c. The activity of a connected device.

d. The priority assigned to a connected device.

11. The key to the operation of ADPCM is:

a. Fast sampling.

b. High amplitude.

c. Adaptive predictor.

d. Digitization.

12. The maximum modem operating rate that can be transported by ADPCM is:

a. 300 bps.

b. 1200 bps.

c. 4800 bps.

d. 9600 bps.

13. The higher the rate an analog signal is sampled:

a. The smaller the difference between sampled amplitudes.

b. The larger the difference between sampled amplitudes.

c. The greater the noise level.

d. The more bits required to represent the sample.

14. Common CVSD digitization rates are:

a. 8 and 64 Kbps.

b. 64 and 128 Kbps.

c. 4 and 8 Kbps.

d. 32 and 16 Kbps.

15. A voice/data multiplexer will not flow control:

a. Voice.

b. Data.

c. Time slots.

d. Odd channels.

Fiber-Optic and Satellite Communications

About This Chapter

This chapter is about transmission of data using light as a carrier. This chapter details some of the history of the development of this form of communications and explains why the technique has generated so much excitement in the communications world. We will discuss why fiber-optic systems work and will cover some of the terms used in describing their operation. Some current terrestrial and undersea fiber-optic systems will be described. We will discuss the application of fiber optics to local area data networks. Finally, we will look at some of the techniques and considerations in transmitting data via geostationary satellites.

UNDERSTANDING

Introduction and Historical Perspective

Alexander Graham Bell was a very curious and inventive man. In 1880, four years after the invention of the telephone, he patented an "Apparatus for signaling and communicating, called Photophone." This device, illustrated in Figure 7.1, transmitted a voice signal over a distance of 2000 meters using a beam of sunlight as the carrier. As the speech into the speaking trumpet vibrated the mirror, the light energy that reflected onto the photovoltaic cell was varied. The electric current produced by the cell varied in accordance with the varying light energy.

FIGURE 7.1.

Alexander Bell's Photophone.

Demonstrates basic principles of optical transmission.

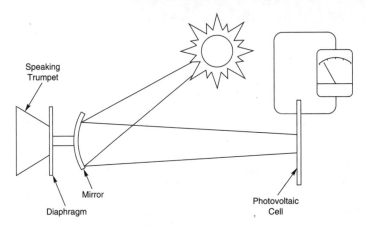

The device demonstrated the basic principle of optical communications as it is practiced today. The two requirements for commercial success, however, were almost a hundred years away. These requirements were a powerful and reliable light source, and a reliable and low-cost medium for transmission.

The use of light as a commercially feasible communications system had to wait until the development of the laser as a powerful, reliable light source, and the clad glass fiber as an inexpensive, reliable medium.

In 1960, the laser was recognized as the long-sought light source, and systems were tried using both the atmosphere and beam waveguides as the transmission medium. The application of a glass fiber with a cladding was proposed in 1966, and by 1970, fibers with losses of only 20 decibels per kilometer (dB/km) were demonstrated. Since then, progress in the invention and application of fiber optics has been startling. Fibers with losses of less than 0.2 dB/km have been demonstrated in the laboratory (in 1979), as have systems that can transmit at data rates in excess of 400 million bits per second (Mbps) for distances in excess of 100 km without repeaters or amplifiers. Advances in fiber optics threaten to obsolete satellite systems for some kinds of communications (point-to-point where large bandwidths are required, such as transoceanic telephone systems) only 15 years after the satellite systems were commercially employed as the communications systems of the future.

Optical-fiber transmission has come of age as a major innovation in telecommunications. Such systems offer extremely high bandwidth, freedom from external interference, immunity from interception by external means, and cheap raw materials (silicon, the most abundant material on earth).

Fundamentals of Fiber-Optic Systems

Optical fibers guide light rays within the fiber material. They can do this because light rays bend or change direction when they pass from one medium to another. They bend because the speed of propagation of light in each medium is different. This phenomenon is called refraction. One common example of refraction occurs when you stand at the edge of a pool and look at an object at the bottom of the pool. Unless you are directly over the object, as shown in Figure 7.2a, it will appear to be farther away than it really is, as indicated in Figure 7.2b. This effect occurs because the speed of the light rays from the object increases as the light rays pass from the water to the air. This causes them to bend, changing the angle at which you perceive the object.

Light rays are guided within the optical fiber by the phenomenon of light refraction. Refraction is the change in direction of light rays caused by the change in speed of propagation when they pass from one medium to another.

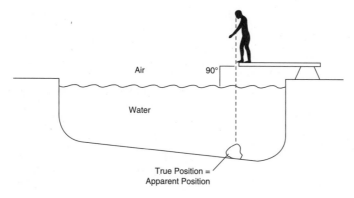

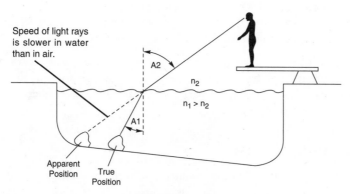

FIGURE 7.2.
Bending of light rays.

Snell's Law

How optical fibers work can be explained by Snell's Law, which states that the ratio of the sine of the angle of incidence to the sine of the angle of refraction is equal to the ratio of the propagation velocities of the wave in the two respective media. This is equal to a constant that is the ratio of the refractive index of the second medium to that of the first. Written as an equation, Snell's Law looks like this:

$$\frac{\sin A_1}{\sin A_2} = \frac{V_1}{V_2} = K = \frac{n_2}{n_1}$$

In this equation,

> A_1 and A_2 are the angles of incidence and refraction, respectively,
>
> V_1 and V_2 are the velocities of propagation of the wave in the two media, and
>
> n_1 and n_2 are the indices of refraction of the two media.

Using Snell's Law, the light rays will be totally contained within the fiber-optic material when the angle of incidence is greater than the critical angle.

The parameters are demonstrated graphically in Figure 7.3. In each case, A_1 is the angle of incidence, and A_2 is the angle of refraction. The index of refraction of material 1, n_1, is greater than the index of refraction of material 2, n_2. This means that the velocity of propagation of light is greater in material 2 than in material 1.

FIGURE 7.3.

Index of refraction.

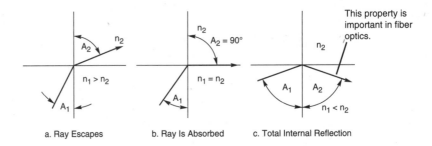

a. Ray Escapes   b. Ray Is Absorbed   c. Total Internal Reflection

Figure 7.3a demonstrates how a light ray passing from material 1 to material 2 is refracted in material 2 when A_1 is less than the critical angle. Figure 7.3b demonstrates the condition that exists when A_1 is at the critical angle and the angle A_2 is at 90 degrees. The light ray is directed along the boundary between the two materials.

As shown in Figure 7.3c, any light rays that are incident at angles greater than A_1 of Figure 7.3b will be reflected back into material 1 with angle A_2 equal to angle A_1. The condition in Figure 7.3c is the one of particular interest for optical fibers, and it will be discussed further in following sections.

Fiber Composition

An optical fiber is a dielectric (nonconductor of electricity) waveguide made of glass or plastic. As shown in Figure 7.4, it consists of three distinct regions: a core, the cladding, and a sheath or jacket. The index of refraction of the assembly varies across the radius of the cable, with the core having a constant or smoothly varying index of refraction called n_c, and the cladding region having another constant index of refraction called n. The core possesses a high refractive index, whereas the cladding is constructed to have a lower refractive index. The result of the difference in the refractive indexes is to keep light flowing through the core after it gets into the core, even if the fiber is bent or tied into a knot. For a fiber designed to carry light in several modes of propagation (called a multimode fiber), the diameter of the core is several times the wavelength of the light to be carried, which is a measure of the distance between two cycles of the same wave measured in nanometers (nm) or billionths of a meter, and the cladding thickness will be greater than the radius of the core. Following are some typical values for a multimode fiber:

Optical fibers are constructed with three separate regions: the fiber core, the cladding around the core, and the protective outer sheath.

- An operating light wavelength of 0.8 micrometers (μm).
- A core index of refraction n_c of 1.5.
- A cladding index of refraction n of 1.485 (=0.99 × n_c).
- A core diameter of 50 μm.
- A cladding thickness of 37.5 μm.

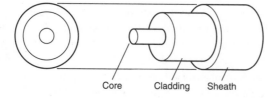

Core   Cladding   Sheath

FIGURE 7.4.
Optical-fiber construction.

The clad fiber would have a diameter of 125 μm, and light would propagate as shown in Figure 7.5.

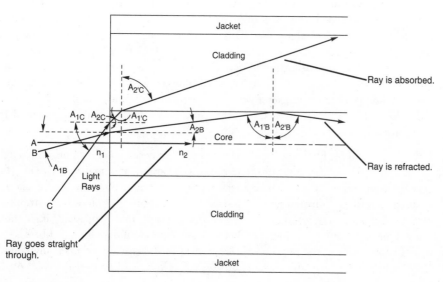

FIGURE 7.5.
Light ray paths in multimode fiber.

The angle at which light rays enter an optical fiber determines how the rays will propagate in the fiber— parallel to the fiber axis, in a zigzag path, or not at all.

A light source emits light at many angles relative to the center of the fiber. In Figure 7.5, light ray A enters the fiber perpendicular to the face of the core and parallel to the axis. Its angle of incidence A_1 is zero; therefore, it is not refracted, and it travels parallel to the axis. Light ray B enters the fiber core from air ($n_1 = 1$) at an angle of incidence of A_{1B} and is refracted at an angle A_{2B} because n_2 is greater than n_1. When light ray B strikes the boundary between the core and the cladding, its angle of incidence, $A_{1'B}$, is greater than the critical angle. Therefore, the angle of refraction, $A_{2'B}$, is equal to $A_{1'B}$, and the light ray is refracted back into the core. The ray propagates in this zigzag fashion down the core until it reaches the other end.

If the angle of incidence, A_{1C}, is too large, as it is for light ray C, the light ray strikes the boundary between the core and the cladding with an angle of incidence, $A_{1'C}$, less than the critical angle. The ray enters into the cladding and propagates in, or is absorbed in, the cladding and jacket (which is opaque to light).

Multimode and Single-Mode Propagation

> The angle at which light enters an optical fiber is called its mode of propagation. When a fiber carries more than one mode, it is a multimode fiber.

For optical fibers in which the diameter of the core is many times the wavelength of the light transmitted, the light beam travels along the fiber by bouncing back and forth at the interface between the core and the cladding. Rays entering the fiber at differing angles are refracted varying numbers of times as they move from one end to the other and consequently do not arrive at the distant end with the same phase relationship as when they started. The differing angles of entry are called modes of propagation (or just modes), and a fiber carrying several modes is called a multimode fiber. Multimode propagation causes the rays leaving the fiber to interfere both constructively and destructively as they leave the end of the fiber. This effect is called modal delay spreading.

Because most optical communications systems transmit information in digital form consisting of pulses of light, the effect of modal delay spreading limits the capability of the fiber to transport recognizable pulses. This is because modal delay spreading broadens the pulses in the time domain, as illustrated in Figure 7.6. The effect of pulse spreading is to make it difficult or impossible for an optical receiver to differentiate one pulse from another after a given transmission distance. Thus, after a predefined transmission distance, a multimode fiber either causes a very high error rate or precludes the capability of the pulse to be recognized and terminates the capability of the cable to be used for communications.

> Much of the power in a single-mode fiber, which does not have a core diameter large enough to transmit more than one mode, is propagated in the cladding.

If the diameter of the fiber core is only a few times the wavelength of the transmitted light (say a factor of 3), only one ray or mode will be propagated, and no destructive interference between rays will occur. These fibers, called single-mode fibers, are the media that are used in most transmission systems. Figure 7.7a and Figure 7.7b show the distribution of the index of refraction across, and typical diameters of, multimode and single-mode fibers. One of the principal differences between single-mode and multimode fibers is that most of the power in the multimode fiber travels in the core, whereas in single-mode fibers, a large fraction of the power is propagated in the cladding near the core. At the point where the light wavelength becomes long enough to cause single-mode propagation, about 20 percent of the power is carried in the cladding, but if the light wavelength is doubled, more than 50 percent of the power travels in the cladding.

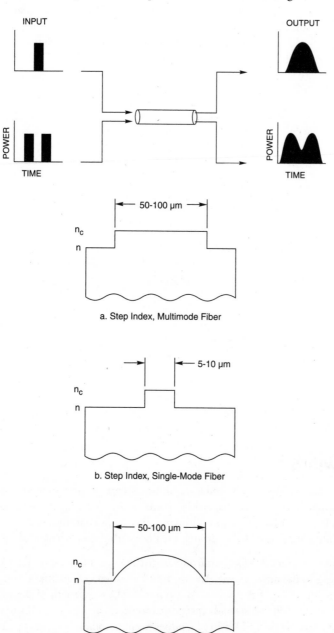

FIGURE 7.6.
Pulse spreading.

a. Step Index, Multimode Fiber

b. Step Index, Single-Mode Fiber

c. Graded Index, Multimode Fiber

FIGURE 7.7.
Refractive index profiles.

Graded-index multimode fibers have fairly equal propagation delays due to a reduction in inter-modal dispersion.

Figure 7.7c shows the distribution of another kind of multimode fiber, called a graded-index fiber. The index of refraction varies smoothly across the diameter of the core but remains constant in the cladding. This treatment reduces the inter-modal dispersion by the fiber, because rays traveling along a graded-index fiber have nearly equal delays. Other refractive-index profiles have been devised to solve various problems, such as reduction of chromatic dispersion. Some of these profiles are shown in Figure 7.8; the step and graded profiles are repeated for comparison.

FIGURE 7.8.

Different refractive index profiles for optical fibers.

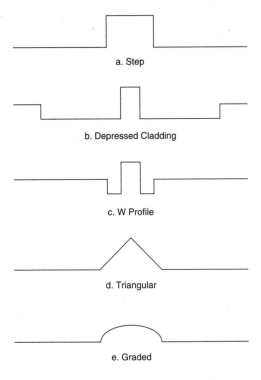

a. Step

b. Depressed Cladding

c. W Profile

d. Triangular

e. Graded

Bandwidth

Material dispersion is the spreading of pulses that occurs when the light source sends light through the optical fiber at more than one wavelength.

The limitations on bandwidth in fiber-optic systems arise from two main sources: modal delay spreading and material dispersion. Modal delay spreading, which was previously described, is evident primarily in multimode fibers. Material dispersion arises from the variation in the velocity of light through the fiber with the wavelength of the light.

If the light source, such as a light-emitting diode (LED), emits pulses of light at more than one wavelength, the different wavelengths travel at different velocities through the fiber. This causes spreading of the pulses. At a typical LED wavelength of 0.8 μm, the delay variation is about 100 picoseconds (ps) per nanometer (nm) per km. If the width of the spectrum emitted by the LED is 50 nm, pulses from the source are spread by 5 nanoseconds (ns) per km. This limits the modulation bandwidth product to about 50 to 100 MHz/km.

Fortunately, at certain wavelengths (near 1.3 and 1.5 μm for some types of fibers), there is a null in the material dispersion curve, giving much better modulation bandwidth performance. Figure 7.9 shows the relationship of loss in doped silicon glass fibers versus light wavelength. Most current development work is aimed at making fibers, light sources, and detectors that work well at the loss nulls at 1.3 and 1.5 μm.

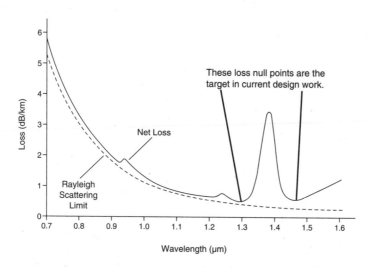

FIGURE 7.9.

Net spectral loss curve for a glass core.

Attenuation

The loss in signal power as the light travels down the fiber is called attenuation. Attenuation in the fibers is controlled mainly by four factors: radiation of the propagated light, called scattering; conversion of the light energy to heat, called absorption; connection losses at splices and joints in the fiber; and losses at bends in the fiber.

●

Signal power loss (attenuation) is a function of four factors: scattering, absorption, connections, and fiber bending.

SCATTERING LOSSES

Scattering arises due to microscopic imperfections in the fiber, such as the inclusion of water in the glass. The effect of impurities in the transmission medium is evident when we look up at the sky and see a blue color. In fact, deep space has no color (appears as black), but due to the scattering of sunlight by the dust in the atmosphere, the sky appears bright blue.

There is a limit below which scattering cannot be reduced, no matter how perfectly the glass fiber is made, because of irregularities in the molecular structure of glass. This limit, called the Rayleigh scattering limit, has a strong wavelength dependence $(1/\lambda^4)$. Thus, as the wavelength of the light source increases, the effect of Rayleigh scattering on optical loss is reduced. This effect is shown graphically in Figure 7.9. For light with a wavelength of 0.8 μm, it is about 2.9 dB/km. At a wavelength of 1.3 μm, the value is about

●

Scattering occurs because of microscopic imperfections in the fiber.

0.3 dB/km, and at 1.55 μm wavelength, the limit is about 0.15 dB/km. Commercially available glass fibers exhibit losses of about 3.5 dB/km at 0.8 μm, and 0.7 to 1.5 dB/km at 1.3 and 1.5 μm. There is less attenuation through 6 meters (about 20 feet) of good quality optical-fiber glass than through an ordinary clean windowpane.

ABSORPTION LOSSES

● Opaque imperfections also cause signal power loss because when a light beam strikes them, some of the light's energy is converted into heat.

Absorption refers to the conversion of the power in the light beam to heat in some material or imperfection that is partially or completely opaque. This property is useful, as in the jacket of the fiber, to keep the light from escaping the cable, but it is a problem when it occurs as inclusions or imperfections in the fiber. Current fiber-optic systems are designed to minimize intrinsic absorption by transmitting at 0.8, 1.3, and 1.5 μm, where there are reductions in the absorption curve for light.

CONNECTION LOSSES

● A relatively large amount of signal power is lost at every connection point, particularly at repair splices.

Connection losses are inevitable. They represent a large source of loss in commercial fiber-optic systems. In addition to the installation connections, repair connections will be required because experience has shown that a typical line will be broken accidentally two or three times per kilometer over a 30-year period. The alignment of optical fibers required at each connection is a considerable mechanical feat. The full effect of the connection is not gotten unless the parts are aligned correctly. The ends of the fibers must be parallel to within one degree or less, and the core must be concentric with the cladding to within 0.5 μm. Production techniques have been developed to splice single-mode fibers whose total diameter is less than 10 μm by using a mounting fixture and small electric heater.

The heater is usually an electric arc that softens two butted fiber ends and allows the fibers to be fused together. Due to the cost of an electric arc and the time required to let the heated ends cool, other methods to connect broken fibers, such as mechanical splices and couplers, are more commonly used. Mechanical splicing is based on the use of a mechanical clamp to permanently splice together two fibers. This task is accomplished through the use of a portable workstation that is used to prepare each fiber end. That preparation includes stripping a thin layer of plastic coating from the fiber core before its splicing. The typical mechanical splice loss is approximately .15dB. In comparison, the use of a connector enables fibers to be glued to the device through a special epoxy after each fiber is stripped to its proper dimension. The connector provides a splice that joins the two fibers to enable light to pass from one fiber to the other. Although connector loss can range from .25 to 1.5dB, use of connectors is preferred for many labor-intensive applications because the process is relatively quick and can usually be accomplished in 30 minutes or less with a minimal amount of equipment.

BENDING LOSSES

Bending an optical fiber is akin to playing crack-the-whip with the light rays. As light travels around the bend, the light on the outside of the bend must travel faster to maintain a constant phase across the wave. As the radius of the bend is decreased, a point is reached where part of the wave would have to travel faster than the local speed of light—an obvious impossibility. At that point, the light is lost from the waveguide. For commercial single-mode fiber-optic cables operating at 1.3 and 1.5 μm, the bending occurring in fabrication (the cables are made with the fibers wound spirally around a center) and installation does not cause a noticeable increase in attenuation.

● Bending the fibers also can cause signal loss because the light rays on the outside of a sharp bend cannot travel fast enough to keep up with the other rays, and they are lost.

Numerical Aperture and Acceptance Angle

The numerical aperture of the optical fiber is a measure of its light-gathering capability (much like the maximum f-stop of a camera lens). The numerical aperture is defined as the maximum angle of incidence of a ray that is totally reflected at the core/cladding interface. Mathematically, the numerical aperture, NA, is expressed in this way:

$$NA = \sqrt{n^2_{core} - n^2_{cladding}}$$

The optical power accepted by the fiber varies as the square of the numerical aperture, but unlike the camera lens f-stop, the numerical aperture does not depend on any physical dimension of the optical fiber.

The acceptance angle is the maximum angle that an entering light ray can have relative to the axis of the fiber and still propagate down the fiber. A large acceptance angle makes the end alignment less critical when fibers are being spliced and connected.

● The numerical aperture is the measure of a fiber's capability to gather light. The acceptance angle is the largest angle at which a light ray can enter and still propagate down the fiber.

Fiber-Optic Subsystems and Components

There are several components that provide the foundation for the construction of fiber-optic systems and subsystems. Those components are discussed in the following five sections of this chapter.

Fiber Production

Optical fibers are fabricated in several ways, depending on the vendor and the purpose of the system. The core and cladding regions of the fiber are doped to alter their refractive indices. This doping is carried out by heating vapors of various substances such as germanium, phosphorus, and fluorine, and depositing the particles of resulting oxidized vapor or "soot" on high-quality fused-silica glass mandrels, called preforms. The preforms are a large-scale version of the core and cladding that is then heated to a taffy-like consistency and drawn down into the actual fiber. The core and cladding dimensions have essentially the same relationship in the final fiber as in the preform. Deposition of the dopants is done in one of three standard ways: outside, inside, and axial vapor deposition.

Light Sources

Light sources for fiber-optic systems must convert electrical energy from the computer or terminal circuits feeding them to optical energy (photons) in a way that allows the light to be coupled effectively to the fiber. Two such sources currently in production are the surface light-emitting diode (LED) and the injection laser diode (ILD).

LIGHT-EMITTING DIODES

To convert the electrical energy of a computer or terminal to light energy for use by an optical-fiber system, LEDs or ILDs are used.

A cross section of a surface LED is shown in Figure 7.10. It emits light over a relatively broad spectrum, and it disperses the emitted light over a rather large angle. This causes the LED to couple much less power into a fiber with a given acceptance angle than does the ILD. Currently, LEDs are able to couple about 100 microwatts (μW) of power into a fiber with a numerical aperture of 0.2 or more with a coupling efficiency of about 2 percent. The principal advantages of LEDs are low cost and high reliability.

FIGURE 7.10.

Construction of light-emitting diode of 1.3 μm operation.

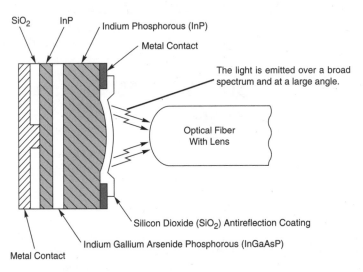

INJECTION LASER DIODES

A cross section of a typical ILD is shown in Figure 7.11. Because of its narrow spectrum of emission and its capability to couple output efficiently into the fiber lightguide, the

ILD supplies power levels of 5 to 7 milliwatts (mW). At present, ILDs are considerably more expensive than LEDs, and their service life is generally less by a factor of about 10. Other disadvantages of laser diodes are that they must be supplied with automatic level control circuits, the laser power output must be controlled, and the device must be protected from power supply transients.

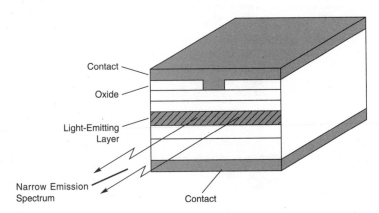

FIGURE 7.11.
Construction of injection laser diode.

Contact

Oxide

Light-Emitting Layer

Narrow Emission Spectrum

Contact

Light Detectors

At the receiving end of the optical communications system, the receiver must have very high sensitivity and low noise. To meet these requirements, there is a choice of two types of devices to detect the light beam, amplify it, and convert it back into an electrical signal: the integrated p-i-n field-effect transistor (FET) assembly and the avalanche photodiode (APD).

In the p-i-n FET device, a photodiode with unity gain (the p-i-n device) is coupled with a high-impedance front-end amplifier. This device combines operation at low voltage with low sensitivity to operating temperature, high reliability, and ease of manufacture.

The avalanche photodiode produces a gain of 100 or more; however, it also produces noise that might limit the receiver sensitivity. The APD devices require high voltage bias that varies with temperature. Receivers using APDs are so sensitive that they require as few as 200 phototons to be detected at the receiver per bit transmitted at data rates of 200 to 400 Mbps.

Wavelength Multiplexing

A combination of single-mode fiber (low dispersion by the transmission medium), narrow output spectrum (power concentration at a single frequency), and narrow dispersion angle (good power coupling) from ILDs makes possible the extreme bandwidth-distance characteristics given for systems at the beginning of this chapter. The narrow ILD emission spectrum also makes it possible to send several signals from different sources down

●
Light detectors are used at the receiving end of the optical fiber to detect, amplify, and convert the light signal back into its original electrical form.

●
Wavelength multiplexing, a technique similar to frequency division multiplexing, is used to send light signals from several sources down the same fiber.

the same fiber by a technique called wavelength multiplexing. The capability to multiplex several analog signals in the frequency domain (FDM) has been described in detail in Chapter 6, "Multiplexing Techniques." As illustrated in Figure 7.12, wavelength multiplexing at optical frequencies is the equivalent of FDM at lower frequencies. Light at two or more discrete wavelengths is coupled into the fiber with each wavelength carrying a channel at whatever modulation rate is used by the transmission equipment driving the light source. Thus, the information capacity of each fiber is doubled or tripled.

FIGURE 7.12.

Wavelength multiplexing.

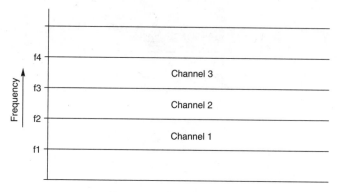

a. Frequency Division Multiplexing

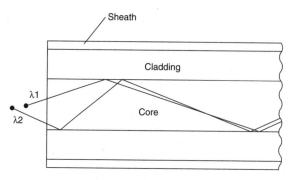

b. Wavelength Division Multiplexing

Transmission Systems

During the past decade, most carrier transmission systems have moved from the use of copper wire to optical fiber. In fact, by mid 1994, almost 100 percent of long-distance communications was carried over optical transmission systems.

Local and Intercity Systems—The FT3C System

An AT&T study in 1978 noted a striking advantage of installing a digital transmission system over comparable analog systems: $900 per circuit termination when interconnecting a number of digital switching machines. The savings came from the difference in requirement for terminal multiplexing equipment. The AT&T FT3C lightwave system was devised to provide the most economical digital transmission system possible with the current state of the fiber-optic art. It used wavelength multiplexing techniques to send three 90 Mbps signals over the same fiber, giving more than 240,000 digital channels at 64,000 bps in a cable containing 144 optical fibers. The first application of the system was in the Northeast Corridor project by AT&T, between Boston and Washington, and in the North/South Lightwave Project on the West coast of the United States by Pacific Telesis, between San Francisco and San Diego. Figure 7.13a is a map of the Northeast Corridor system, which contains 78,000 fiber-kilometers of lightwave circuits. Figure 7.13b is a map of the North/South Lightwave Project. The two systems were placed in service in 1983 and have been considerably expanded since then.

The significant advantages associated with the use of fiber-optic transmission systems resulted in tens of thousands of miles of fiber being installed during the 1980s. By early 1991, U.S. Sprint had converted 100 percent of its intercity transmission facilities from microwave to fiber, and AT&T and MCI Communications were working toward completing the conversion of their systems to fiber, whose conversions were completed within the next few years.

●

Studies by AT&T of a digital lightwave transmission system indicated that it would cost less than traditional systems because of differences in terminal multiplexing equipment requirements and cost.

SONET

Advances in the use of fiber-optic transmission systems resulted in a requirement for standards to enable interoperability between interexchange carriers and telephone companies. In addition, a considerable growth in communications from companies and government agencies resulted in a requirement to define the interface of commercial communications equipment to an evolving optical network. The resulting standard, known as the Synchronous Optical Network (SONET), represents a transport vehicle capable of supporting data rates in the gigabit range, optical interfaces, network management, and diagnostic testing methods.

Until SONET standards were developed, there was a void in compatibility between fiber terminal equipment operating at rates above the DS3 transmission rate of 44.736 Mbps. That operating rate is formed by a communications carrier using a device known as an M13 multiplexer to combine 28 DS1 channels into a DS3 signal. The resulting DS3 signal is asynchronous because each DS1 signal is independently timed. Although each DS1 signal includes 8000 bits per second for framing, the resulting multiplexed DS3 signal includes three intermixed framing signals, which makes it almost impossible to locate an individual DS0 signal within the DS3 signal. Thus, to remove one PCM digitized voice signal in a carrier's DS3 transmission hierarchy typically required the carrier to first

●

SONET is an optical standard that enables the fiber-optic transmission systems of interexchange carriers and telephone companies to be interoperable.

demultiplex the DS3 signal, requiring additional equipment and adding to the cost of the carrier's infrastructure. Recognizing this problem, the developers of the SONET standard developed a frame structure that enables lower speed channels within a higher speed signal to be easily removed or added to the signal, a process known as drop (removal of the signal on a channel) and insert (addition of a signal on a channel).

FIGURE 7.13.

Fiber-optic networks.

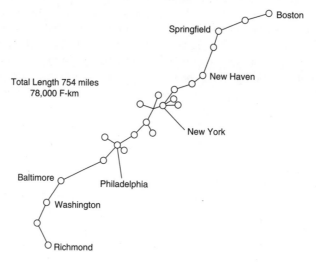

a. Fiber-Optic Network for Northeast Corridor

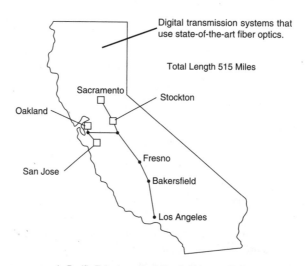

b. Pacific Telephone North/South Lightwave Project

Figure 7.14 illustrates the SONET frame structure. As indicated, the basic SONET frame consists of nine rows of bytes with 90 bytes per row, with 8000 of these frames transmitted each second. This arrangement results in a composite data rate of 51.84 Mbps. Because 27 bytes of each 810-byte frame represent overhead, the payload of the basic SONET frame is limited to 50.112 Mbps, with 2.3 Mbps representing overhead. That overhead includes positioning information that enables a single DS0 channel to be identified and data easily extracted or inserted into the channel position.

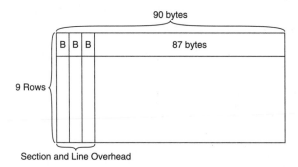

FIGURE 7.14.
SONET frame structure.

This also means that a DS3 signal representing 28 DS1 signals can be carried within the basic SONET frame, and each of the 672 DS0 channels within the 28 DS1 signals can have data easily removed (dropped) or added (inserted).

The basic SONET frame illustrated in Figure 7.14 that occurs 8000 times per second is referred to as a Synchronous Transport Signal-Level 1, or STS-1. SONET is called synchronous because the frame is synchronized with respect to each input DS0 channel through the use of pointers in the 27 bytes of overhead per frame, which results in a synchronous multiplexing format. In addition to pointers, a significant portion of the overhead bytes in the STS-1 frame are reserved for management data, enabling network management functions to include loopback, bit error rate testing, and collection and reporting of performance statistics to be carried within the SONET frame.

THE OPTICAL INTERFACE

One of the major elements included in the SONET standard is its set of defined optical interfaces. Until the development of SONET, each manufacturer designed its fiber terminal device to its own optical signal interface. This "do it yourself" approach precluded terminal devices from different vendors from being able to be interconnected to a common fiber backbone. Under SONET, 256 OC (optical carrier) optical interfaces are defined, although the current standard explicitly calls for the use of 8 interfaces. Those interfaces, listed in Table 7.1, define the SONET digital signal hierarchy. Note that the OC-1 level represents an STS-1 signal, whereas higher levels represent multiplexed STS-1 signals.

Table 7.1. SONET signal hierarchy.

Level	Line Rate	DS3 Channels
OC-1	51.84 Mbps	1
OC-3	155.52 Mbps	3
OC-9	466.56 Mbps	9
0C-12	622.08 Mbps	12
OC-18	933.12 Mbps	18
OC-24	1.244 Gbps	24
OC-36	1.866 Gbps	36
OC-48	2.488 Gbps	48

The pointers within a SONET frame enable data to be directly added or removed from individual DS0 channels without first requiring the demultiplexing of the composite signal.

Although SONET primarily represents a standard for optical interoperability among public network transmission providers, it also provides the capability for large organizations and government agencies to provide an STS-1 signal to the central office of a public network provider through the use of an optical multiplexer connected to a fiber routed from the customer premise to the carrier's central office. Figure 7.15 illustrates the use of an STS-1 signal to the public network. Note that due to the pointers imbedded into the SONET frame, the carrier can easily break out previously multiplexed signals originating at the customer's optical multiplexer without having to demultiplex and remultiplex the data stream as would be required when a DS3 signal is used. Eventually, SONET should reduce the cost of transmission for large network users as well as increase network reliability due to the use of fiber directly to the customer premises.

FIGURE 7.15.

Using SONET to connect public and private networks.

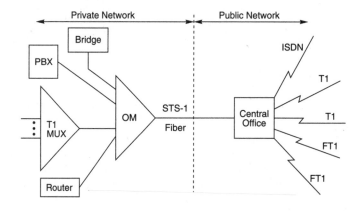

Legend OM optical multiplexer
PBX private branch exchange

International Systems—The SL Underwater Cable

The advent of optical-fiber technology for undersea cables provides point-to-point channel capacity equal to satellite systems at reduced cost and without long transmission delays, unstable environmental interference, induced noise, and broadcast of potentially sensitive information to half the world.

Undersea cable systems have some understandably difficult environmental requirements. The environment includes pressures of 10,000 pounds per square inch (psi) at depths of 7300 meters, salt water, and the possibility of mechanical damage from anchors and earth movement in shallow waters. An important requirement for these systems is that the regenerator spacing be as wide as possible to cut down on the system failure probability and the power requirements, because power must be fed from the ends of the cable.

A schematic of the SL Undersea Lightguide System is shown in Figure 7.16. It is composed of a high-voltage power supply, a supervisory terminal, a multiplexer with inputs for several types of information, the cable light source, the cable itself, and the repeaters. The cable is made of a central core and a surrounding support, as shown in Figure 7.17. The core has an outside diameter of 2.6 mm and consists of 12 optical fibers wound helically around a central copper-clad steel wire called a kingwire, all embedded in an elastomeric substance and covered with a nylon sheath. This assembly is in turn covered with steel strands, a continuously welded copper tube, and an insulation of low-density polyethylene for electrical insulation and abrasion resistance. The outside diameter of the completed cable is 21 mm (about 0.8 in.).

●

Undersea optical-fiber cables can provide a data communications channel with a carrying capacity equal to satellite systems, but with greater security, less interference, less noise, and lower cost.

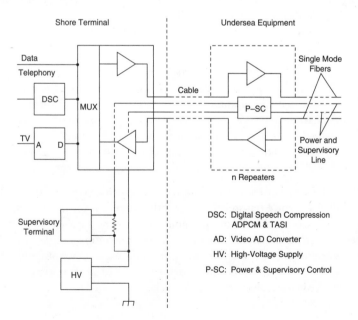

FIGURE 7.16.

The SL Undersea Lightguide System.

FIGURE 7.17.

Embedded fiber core cable.

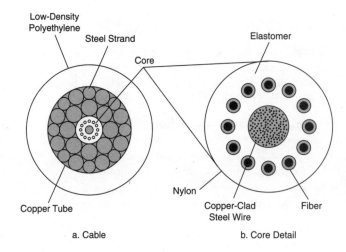

a. Cable   b. Core Detail

The fibers are single-mode optical lightguides operating at 1.312 μm. The data rate on each fiber pair is 280 Mbps, and repeaters are spaced every 35 km. The total capacity of the system is more than 35,000 two-way voice channels. Inputs from binary data sources are multiplexed directly into the stream. Analog channels are first converted to binary by the adaptive delta modulation technique, then processed by a type of digital circuit (Digital TASI) that interleaves inputs from a number of input speech channels onto a smaller number of output channels. The light sources for the systems are ILDs operating near 1.3 μm with an average output power of 1 mW (0 dBm). Light detectors are indium-gallium-arsenide (InGaAs) p-i-n diode receivers followed by silicon bipolar transimpedance amplifiers. Three spare laser diodes, which can be switched in remotely if a failure occurs, are provided per circuit.

By the late 1980s, several fiber-optic undersea cables were laid across the Atlantic, linking New York to England, France, and Spain via light transmission. The successful operation of those systems resulted in communications carriers expanding their plans for fiber-optic undersea cables. At the time this book revision was written, several trans-Pacific and trans-Mediterranean fiber-optic cables were in the process of being installed. By the mid-1990s, most voice, data, and video transmissions between the United States and Europe, Japan, and Australia will be routed via fiber-optic cable between continents.

As the use of fiber-optic cable has increased, a corresponding decrease has resulted in the use of satellites for voice transmission. The primary reason for the wide acceptance of fiber-optic cable over satellites is the immunity of the fiber-optic cable to electromagnetic interference as well as the elimination of one-half second or longer delays associated with the use of satellites due to the signal having to traverse a distance of more than 50,000 miles during transmission. Today, most satellites are used for television and data transmissions that are insensitive to transmission delays.

Fiber to the Home

One of the most publicized terms in the field of communications is the so-called "digital highway." First promoted by Vice President Gore as a term to represent the interconnections of computer research centers via high-speed optical transmission, the term has been applied to all types of high-capacity communications to include fiber cables routed to the home.

By early 1994, several field tests of fiber to the home were being conducted in California and Florida. Each test was similar in that the large bandwidth capacity of an optical fiber enabled the simultaneous transmission of up to hundreds of television signals along with voice conversations and interactive data channels. Where each test differed was in the scope of interactivity offered to the home consumer and the ability of the consumer to request different functions interactively. Some tests enabled the consumer to order films to be displayed at a predefined time, a feature known as video-on-demand. Other tests primarily focused on providing consumers with online banking, grocery ordering, and catalog shopping. A new term used to define the provider of integrated voice, data, and video is multimedia, although the range of services offered by different multimedia vendors currently varies considerably from vendor to vendor.

Today, the home multimedia effort is in its infancy, probably equivalent to where the personal computer industry was during the 1970s. Although it's difficult to predict the outcome of current field trials as well as the range of services that will be offered to consumers, one thing is certain. Regardless of the resulting suite of services offered to the consumer under the labels "video-on-demand," "multimedia," or another term, those services will be transported through the use of fiber-optic cable to the home.

Satellite Transmission Systems

Satellite transmission systems provide users with the ability to bypass conventional communications carrier offices, as well as to broadcast information to multiple locations for a nominal cost.

Basic Satellite Technology

Satellite communications systems are basically line-of-sight microwave systems with a single repeater. As stated in Chapter 3, "Messages and Transmission Channels," the satellite is said to be in geostationary orbit. It is called a geostationary satellite because the speed of the satellite is matched to the rotation of the earth at the equator. Because of the great distance of the satellite from the earth (about 22,300 miles) and antenna size limitations that limit focusing capability, the cone of coverage for a single satellite transmitter can be as large as the entire continental United States.

●
Broad focus of the downlink signal and propagation delay caused by the great distance between earth and satellite can present problems in two-way satellite communications.

For those transmission services that originate at a single point and flow to many points in one direction, such as television and radio signals, the large area of coverage is ideal. The relatively long delay between the instant a signal is sent and when it returns to earth (about 240 milliseconds (ms)) has no undesirable effect when the signal is going only one way. However, for signals such as data communications sessions and telephone conversations, which go in both directions and are intended to be received at only one other point, the large area of coverage and the delay can cause problems.

Data and telephone conversations usually proceed as a series of messages in one direction that are answered or acknowledged by messages in the other direction. When the delay between the message being sent and the reply or acknowledgment is long, the transmission rate of information slows down. In the case of voice messages, long delays between utterance and reply make the speaker think he or she has not been heard or understood. This leads to requests for repeating (the equivalent of negative acknowledgment in the data world) and increased frustration. There is also a serious privacy issue with communications that are intended for only one destination but are broadcast so that an entire continent can receive them. One of the factors causing the rush to all-digital transmission is the ease of encrypting information in digital form so that when the inevitable interception of broadcast signals occurs, the information intercepted is at least somewhat difficult to decipher.

A satellite transmission system consists of one or more earth stations and a geostationary satellite that can be seen by the stations. Separate frequencies are assigned for sending to the satellite (the uplink) and receiving from the satellite (the downlink). The current frequency assignments for satellite systems are shown in Table 7.2.

Table 7.2. Frequency assignments for satellite systems.

Uplink Frequencies	Downlink Frequencies
5.925–6.425 GHz	3.700–4.200 GHz
7.900–8.400 GHz	7.250–7.750 GHz
14.00–14.50 GHz	11.70–12.20 GHz
27.50–30.00 GHz	17.70–20.20 GHz

The main components of a satellite system are the earth sending and receiving stations and a geosynchronous satellite equipped with transponders.

Satellites are equipped with multiple repeater units called transponders. Many systems have 10 or 12 transponders, but a new series of international satellites, called INTELSAT VI, has 46 transponders. Transponders are assigned different uses, but in the case of those used for voice or voice-equivalent data communications channels (nominal 4 KHz bandwidth), the transponder capacity can be as large as 3000 channels.

The INTELSAT VI satellite provides a total bandwidth, using frequency reuse techniques, of 3460 MHz.

Multiple Access Systems

Telephone switching systems and data multiplexers are designed based on the fact that not every telephone or terminal that can send information will do so at the same time; or alternatively, the telephone or terminal user does not need or want to pay for the entire capacity of a channel. These conditions are also true for the users of satellite systems. Several methods have been devised to allow sharing of the satellite and earth station resources among several users so that it appears that the transmission channel is dedicated to each user.

FREQUENCY DIVISION MULTIPLE ACCESS

Frequency Division Multiple Access (FDMA) is simply another example of the familiar data and voice transmission technique called frequency division multiplexing (FDM). This technique is used to allocate small portions of a large bandwidth (500 MHz for satellite transponders) to individual users. For instance, a telecommunications common carrier in a particular country, say Brazil, might want 132 voice-grade channels for sending voice- and analog-coded data to various other countries. The bandwidth required on the current international satellite systems for this many channels is 10 MHz. Because one transponder has a bandwidth of 500 MHz, it could accommodate 50 users, each requiring 132 channels. The Brazilian user might be allocated the frequency band between 5990 and 6000 MHz for the uplink to the satellite, and the corresponding downlink frequencies would be 3765 to 3775 MHz. Other users might be assigned similar portions of the bandwidth in the same transponder. For example, a Portuguese user might be allocated the 6220 to 6230 MHz uplink band and the 3995 to 4005 MHz downlink band. A Canadian user might operate on the 5930 to 5940 MHz uplink band and the 3705 to 3715 MHz downlink band. Figure 7.18 illustrates how the three users each have one uplink, all into a single transponder, but all users can receive all three downlinks. This arrangement makes possible simultaneous two-way transmissions between any of the three sites using only a part of one satellite transponder.

● Satellites using FDMA have the available bandwidth of a transponder divided into smaller segments.

FIGURE 7.18.

Multiuser satellite system.

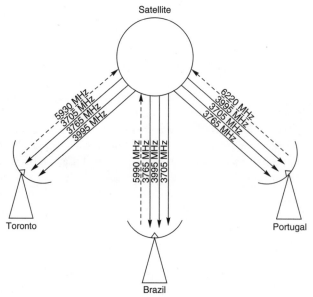

Each user has a permanently assigned channel.

TIME DIVISION MULTIPLE ACCESS

In TDMA, access to a satellite transponder is divided into discrete time frames.

Time Division Multiple Access (TDMA) is the equivalent of FDMA, but in the time domain rather than the frequency domain. TDMA works just like time division multiplexing (TDM) for land-based data and voice transmissions, with each satellite transponder having a data rate capacity of between 10 and 100 Mbps. While a station is sending on the uplink, it has available the entire data rate capacity of the transponder, but then it must stop sending for a short time to allow another station access to the transponder. The information flows to the satellite in frames, each frame containing one burst of information from each earth station allowed access to the single transponder. A typical format for a frame is shown in Figure 7.19. The sum of the durations of the individual bursts do not quite equal the frame time in order to give some guard time between bursts.

Timing for keeping the station bursts apart is a major problem, and it is complicated by two facts. First, the satellites are not perfectly stationary in orbit (each appears to travel in a small figure-eight pattern). Also, the times of travel of the signal between different earth stations and the same satellite are different because of different slant range distances. TDMA techniques allow the satellite transmitter to be operated at higher power levels than FDMA. This method is permissible because only one carrier at a time occupies the transponder, reducing the amount of intermodulation distortion generated.

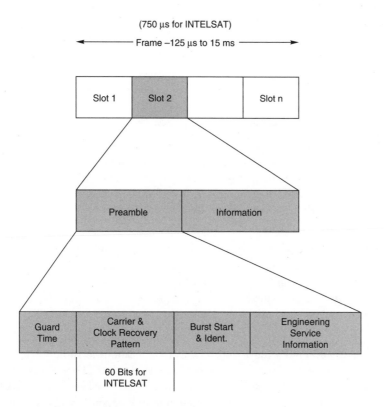

FIGURE 7.19.

TDMA transmission frames.

DEMAND ASSIGNMENT MULTIPLE ACCESS

Using the Demand Assignment Multiple Access (DAMA) technique, each satellite transponder is used much like a telephone switch; that is, a subchannel is assigned only when traffic is available to be carried on it. This is in contrast to the FDMA and TDMA techniques described previously, in which channels are assigned to users permanently, even if there is no traffic demand. DAMA is a variant of FDMA in that a part or all of the transponder is divided into individual channels that can be accessed by all DAMA terminals on the ground that are serviced by the DAMA transponder. A central computer system, or a system of distributed and cooperating computers, on the ground keeps tracks of who gets which channel when. DAMA is particularly useful for loading transponders efficiently when each of several ground sites needs only a few channels.

●
DAMA is similar to FDMA except that channels are not assigned permanently.

PERSONAL COMMUNICATION SERVICES

During the 1970s and 1980s, satellite communications were often thought of as the data communications technology of the future. In fact, many authors wrote about the use of satellite technology eventually replacing the use of most terrestrial communications. This conversion did not occur primarily due to the delays associated with transmitting a signal more than 25,000 miles into the atmosphere and then having that signal retransmitted back to earth. The delay time associated with the use of satellites significantly affects their use for data transfer when data blocks have to be periodically acknowledged. Due to the minimal effect on voice conversations, the use of satellites has taken on a new role as a mechanism for personal communication services.

Within the next few years, several companies are expected to develop satellite systems consisting of 12 to 60 or more non-geo-stationary low and middle earth-orbiting satellites that will provide either continental or near-global communications coverage. Such systems are being developed to support a new type of wireless telephone service that will transmit in the L and Ka-band frequency spectrums and support high-quality voice service as well as facsimile and paging signal transmission.

One of the first satellite-based personal communications services scheduled for operation is the Iridium system from Iridium, Inc. This firm represents a consortium of telecommunication operators and industrial companies originally sponsored by Motorola, Inc., which still has a minority interest in this venture. The first Iridium satellite is scheduled for launch in 1996, and initial service is anticipated to commence in 1998.

The Iridium satellite network is planned to consist of 66 satellites in six orbital planes approximately 480 miles above the earth. Communications to Iridium satellites will be via special Iridium mobile telephones and via conventional telephone systems through the use of satellite earth station gateways that will convert terrestrial signals to the Ka-band for transmission to an Iridium satellite. In addition to Iridium, other major communications firms have announced potentially competitive satellite-based personal communications services. Services announced during 1993 and 1994 for operation later in the decade include TRW's Odyssey and the Loral and Qualcomm's Globalstar satellite-based systems.

What Have You Learned?

1. Light travelling in an optical fiber obeys Snell's law.
2. Light can travel in a multimode optical fiber along several paths, or in a single-mode fiber along only one path.
3. The index of refraction of the glass making up an optical fiber varies across the diameter of the fiber, with the highest index in the middle of the fiber.
4. Fiber-optic system bandwidth is limited by modal delay spreading and material dispersion.
5. Fiber-optic system transmission distance is limited by scattering, absorption, losses at connections, and losses at bends in the cable.

6. Fibers with varying indices of refraction across the fiber are made by heating a preform that has been doped with metal salts such as germanium and phosphorus and drawing it down to a small diameter.

7. Transmitters for fiber-optic systems are light-emitting diodes or semi-conductor injection lasers.

8. Receivers in fiber-optic systems are avalanche photodiodes or integrated p-i-n field-effect transistors.

9. SONET provides a set of standards that enables the fiber-optic transmission systems of interexchange carriers and telephone companies to be interoperable.

10. New services to the home consumer under such terms as video-on-demand and multimedia can be expected to be based on the use of fiber to the home.

11. Satellite transmissions have four uplink bands and four downlink bands.

12. TDMA techniques allow the satellite transmitter to be operated at higher power levels than FDMA.

Quiz for Chapter 7

1. The requirements for a successful transmission system using light are:
   a. Powerful, reliable light source.
   b. Strong glass.
   c. Reliable, low-cost transmission medium.
   d. Powerful amplifiers.

2. The core of an optical fiber has:
   a. A lower index of refraction than air.
   b. A lower index of refraction than the cladding.
   c. A higher index of refraction than the cladding.
   d. None of the above.

3. For single-mode fibers, the core diameter is about:
   a. 10 times the fiber radius.
   b. 3 times the wavelength of the light carried in the fiber.
   c. 15 micrometers.
   d. 10 times the wavelength of the light carried in the fiber.

4. Over a period of 30 years, a kilometer of fiber-optic cable is likely to be broken:
   a. Not at all.
   b. Once.
   c. 10 times.
   d. 2 or 3 times.

5. Deposition of dopants on fiber preforms is done by:
   a. Outside vapor deposition.
   b. Axial vapor deposition.
   c. Inside vapor deposition.
   d. All the above.

6. A light-emitting diode can couple how much power into an optical fiber?
   a. 10 watts.
   b. 10 milliwatts.

c. 100 microwatts.

d. 1 picowatt.

7. Avalanche photodiode receivers can detect bits of transmitted data by receiving:

a. 1 photon.

b. 10 photons.

c. 100 photons.

d. 200 photons.

8. One unsolved problem with satellite systems is:

a. Coverage.

b. Privacy.

c. Bandwidth.

d. Access.

9. The AT&T FT3C fiber-optic transmission system is designed to use how many light wavelengths?

a. 1.

b. 2.

c. 3.

d. 10.

10. The SL Undersea Lightguide system can carry how many two-way voice channels?

a. 10,000.

b. 100,000.

c. 35,000.

d. 760.

11. When the index of refraction is greater in Material 1 than it is in Material 2, the velocity of propagation in Material 1 compared to Material 2 is:

a. Equal or greater.

b. Greater.

c. Lesser.

d. Equal.

12. The different angles of entry of light into an optical fiber in which the diameter of the core is many times the wavelength of the light transmitted are called:

a. Emitters.

b. Modes.

c. Sensors.

d. Refractors.

13. In single-mode fibers, a large fraction of the power is propagated in the:

a. Sheath.

b. Core.

c. Cladding.

d. Air.

14. The loss in signal power as light travels down a fiber is called:

a. Propagation.

b. Scattering.

c. Absorption.

d. Attenuation.

15. The coupling efficiency of an LED light source to an optical fiber with a numerical aperture of 0.2 or more is:

a. 60 percent.

b. 10 percent.

c. 2 percent.

d. 0.1 percent.

16. The FT3C lightwave system contains the following number of fibers:

a. 12.

b. 144.

c. 128.

d. 64.

17. A key advantage of SONET is its capability to enable:

    a. Data to be carried at high operating rates.

    b. The interoperability of optical transmission between interexchange carriers and telephone companies.

    c. Routing of data to the home.

    d. Interconnection of private networks.

18. The number of bytes of overhead in a SONET frame is:

    a. 90.

    b. 9.

    c. 27.

    d. 87.

19. The number of OC-1 signals within a SONET OC-3 signal is:

    a. 3.

    b. 6.

    c. 9.

    d. 12.

20. A geostationary satellite used for communications systems:

    a. Is stationary in the sky.

    b. Rotates with the earth.

    c. Is positioned over the equator.

    d. Remains stationary relative to the earth's surface.

    e. a and c.

    f. b, c, and d.

21. Multiple repeaters in communications satellites are known as:

    a. Transponders.

    b. Detectors.

    c. Modulators.

    d. Stations.

22. In the current frequency assignments, how many frequency bands are there for the uplink frequencies?

    a. 16.

    b. 8.

    c. 4.

    d. 2.

23. The bandwidth required to send 132 voice-grade channels by FDM on an international satellite system is:

    a. 500 MHz.

    b. 10 MHz.

    c. 1320 MHz.

    d. 50 MHz.

24. The capability to provide consumers with video-on-demand:

    a. Will occur by the year 2000.

    b. Depends on the results of field trials.

    c. Is based on fiber to the home.

    d. Is based on the use of satellites.

Protocols and Error Control

About This Chapter

This chapter is about the rules that data communications systems use when communicating with each other, how the systems discover that an error has been made in transmission, and some methods used in correcting those errors. Because there are many data transmission schemes in use (for example, asynchronous and synchronous, half- and full-duplex), many sets of rules, called protocols, and many error detection and correction schemes have been devised. The most common of these techniques are explained in this chapter.

Protocols and Interfaces

A protocol is a set of rules defining the interactions between two machines or processes that are alike or that have similar functions. An interface is a set of rules controlling the interaction of two different machines or processes.

Protocols are agreements between people or processes (usually nowadays the processors are computer programs) about which of them can do what to whom, and when. A protocol is different from an interface. An interface is a set of rules, often embodied in pieces of hardware, controlling the interaction of two different machines or processes, such as a computer and a modem. A protocol, on the other hand, is a set of rules defining the interactions between two machines or processes that are alike or that have similar functions. The difference is illustrated in Figure 8.1. House A and House B look alike but are occupied by a curious set of people. The British engineer on the top floor of house A needs to communicate with another engineer, also British, on the top floor of B. The only telephone, however, is guarded by a Swedish businessman on the bottom floor of each house. The engineer speaks no Swedish, and the Swede no English.

FIGURE 8.1.

Protocols and interfaces.

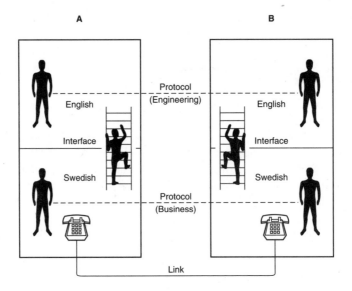

The two engineers, like most people who talk on the telephone, have a routine, worked out over long years, for communicating. The one answering says, "Hullo." The one calling says, "Hullo, this is Reggie." Then the first says, "Oh, hullo, Reggie. How are you, old boy?" This is called a preamble. They then begin discussing Wimbledon, the weather, and even some business. At the end of most sentences, the one being questioned makes a reply, even if it is only a sound rather than a word or sentence. If one party does not hear some sort of reply from the other at fairly short intervals, he might say, "I say, are you still there?" If he still receives no reply, he might terminate the conversation and begin the whole process over. If one party does not understand the other, he says, "What?" and the second party repeats the last sentence. When the conversation is over, the person terminating the call says, "Well, goodbye for now." The called party replies, "Goodbye," and both hang up. The Swedish businessman has a similar technique for conversing with his counterpart. All of these conventional conversational actions make up a protocol. As we will see in the remainder of this chapter, protocols developed for communicating between processes in computers have all the same mechanisms as those used between humans, for exactly the same reasons.

Even though our two engineers can communicate reliably with each other because they have a communications protocol, they still have the problem of having no direct access to the communications channel, which is jealously guarded by the large Swedish businessman. The solution is an interface. The engineers engage a person who stands midway up the stairs and who speaks both engineering English and business Swedish. It is this person's task to relay the conversation from the engineer (speaking in English) to the businessman (listening in Swedish), who relays it over the telephone to his Swedish counterpart in house B, who relays it in Swedish to another person halfway up the stairs, who finally conveys the messages in English to the called party.

This seems like a clumsy and inefficient procedure, and in many respects it is. But it is the same procedure used in millions of data communications systems to allow an applications program, communicating in one set of symbols (perhaps ASCII) and at one rate of symbol production, to communicate through a teleprocessing monitor, using another set of symbols (perhaps EBCDIC) at a vastly different rate, to a line interface program dealing with yet a third set of symbols (bits). The story of standard interfaces is told in Chapter 4, "Asynchronous Modems and Interfaces." The story in this chapter is about protocols.

> ●
> Protocols for machine communication function much like the formats and rules for human conversations, and they are used for the same reasons.

Elements of a Protocol

The basic elements of a communications protocol are a set of symbols, called a character set, a set of rules for the sequence and timing of messages constructed from the character set, and procedures for determining when an error has occurred in the transmission and how to correct the error. The character set consists of a subset that is meaningful to people (usually called printing characters), and another subset that conveys control information (usually called control characters). There is a correspondence between each character and a group of symbols on the transmission channel. For instance, the printing character A might correspond to the binary code 1000001. Several standard codes with equivalent sets of ones and zeros (bits), such as the ASCII discussed in a previous chapter, have been defined over the years. The set of rules to be followed by the sender and receiver gives the meaning, permissible sequences, and time relationships of the control characters and messages formed from the symbols. The error detection and correction procedure allows for the detection of and orderly recovery from errors caused by factors outside the control of the terminal at either end.

> ●
> There are three main elements to any protocol: a character set, a set of rules for message timing and sequence, and error determination and correction procedures.

Teletypewriter and XMODEM Protocols

TTY protocols are the simplest ones in general use. The 58 characters in the character set of one TTY protocol were encoded by a five-bit binary code.

The simplest protocols in general use are the ones associated with the transmission of start-stop or asynchronous data between teleprinter machines. For a long period after the development of the teleprinter, the machines were electromechanically controlled, as discussed in a previous chapter, and protocols had to be appropriate to a very simple mechanical controller in each machine. One of the first teletypewriter (TTY) protocols used a character set containing 58 symbols: 50 printing characters, a space, and seven control characters, as shown in Figure 8.2. These symbols were encoded into a five-bit binary code as shown (the octal representation is shown only for readers familiar with octal).

FIGURE 8.2.
CCITT alphabet No. 2.

Binary	Octal	LTRS	FIGS
00000	00	BLANK	BLANK
00001	01	E	3
00010	02	LF	LF
00011	03	A	–
00100	04	Space	Space
00101	05	S	/
00110	06	I	8
00111	07	U	7
01000	10	CR	CR
01001	11	D	WRU
01010	12	R	4
01011	13	J	BELL
01100	14	N	,
01101	15	F	
01110	16	C	:
01111	17	K	(
10000	20	T	5
10001	21	Z	+
10010	22	L	)
10011	23	W	2
10100	24	H	
10101	25	Y	6
10110	26	P	0
10111	27	Q	1
11000	30	O	9
11001	31	B	?
11010	32	G	
11011	33	FIGS	FIGS
11100	34	M	.
11101	35	X	/
11110	36	V	=
11111	37	LTRS	LTRS

The printing characters are the uppercase letters, the numbers, and 14 punctuation marks. Three control characters allow for carriage return (CR), line feed (LF), and ringing the terminal bell (BELL) to announce a message. Also provided are a NULL (or blank) character (which is not the same as a space) and a WRU character. WRU, which stands for "Who Are You," causes a mechanical device in the teleprinter to send a character sequence identifying that particular terminal. The other two control characters are the FIGS character, which causes the machine to print numbers and punctuation, and the LTRS character, which causes the machine to print the uppercase alphabet. As mentioned in a previous chapter, this character set and associated binary code is commonly referred to as the Baudot code, after Emile Baudot, who invented the first code with symbols of a fixed length.

The protocol for operation of a message system using the Baudot code goes something like this (the procedure varies somewhat according to the operator of the system):

1. A communications channel is connected between the two machines. This might be a temporary dialed connection or a permanent private line.

2. The sending machine sends a WRU, to verify that the receiving machine is the proper one for the message to be sent.

3. The sending machine sends a "Here is…," which is normally the same sequence of characters that is sent when it receives a WRU, to identify the sender.

4. The sending machine sends a preamble or message header that identifies the name and address of the intended message recipient, the date and time entry of the message into the system, the date and time of transmission, and the message sequence number assigned by the sender. In some systems, the sender will use two sequence numbers: one to count the number of messages sent by the sender that day, and the second to count the number of messages sent to the receiver's terminal that day.

5. At the end of the message, the sending machine sends another "Here is…" and another WRU. The second WRU is to determine whether the receiving machine is still connected to the line. If the message is being sent manually, the operator of the sending machine sometimes sends several BELL characters to alert a person at the receiving end that a message is ready for delivery.

This protocol has developed over many years of sending messages manually between individual terminals operated by people. You will note that it has all the elements described in the opening paragraphs: a previously defined set of symbols and corresponding codes suitable for electronic transmission, a preamble, a message, and even a rudimentary error detection procedure (the invocation of the WRU at the beginning and end of the session). The same sort of protocol is used for teleprinter message systems even when one end of the system is a computer, as are all the current public teleprinter networks.

The simple teletypewriter protocol described does not work very well in the presence of even fairly low error rates on the path between the machines. Individual characters can be mutilated in such a way as to cause the receiving machine to begin printing gibberish, and the transmitter will never know. The WRU check at the end of a message ensures only

● Because the simple TTY protocol does not check for errors in the message, even low error rates cause the received message to be gibberish, and the sender does not know of the problem.

that the receiving machine received the WRU correctly and that the circuit is still good in the backward direction. The WRU check says nothing about whether the message got through. To provide better assurance of correct transmission, two more techniques are sometimes used for simple protocols: character parity and echoplex.

Parity

Parity is the technique in which a bit is added to every symbol for the purpose of error detection. It can be either even or odd parity.

This is the Communicator's Creed: "Now abideth faith, hope, and parity, but the greatest of these is parity."

The addition by the transmitter of another bit to the bits that encode a symbol for the purpose of error detection is called parity. The bit is always transmitted, and it is usually set to the value that will cause the coded symbol to have an even number of 1 bits; thus, the scheme is called even parity. The parity bit is recomputed by the receiver. If the newly computed value gives the correct parity, all is well. If not, some indication is given to the receiving terminal, usually by substituting a special error character for the one received.

For an example of parity checking, consider the ASCII character *M*, which has a bit composition of 1 0 0 1 1 0 1 (see Figure 1.5). Because the character has four 1 bits, a 1 bit is added if odd parity checking is used, whereas a 0 bit is used if even parity checking is employed. Figure 8.3 illustrates the formation of the parity bit for odd and even parity checking for the ASCII character *M*.

FIGURE 8.3.

Parity bit formation for ASCII character M.

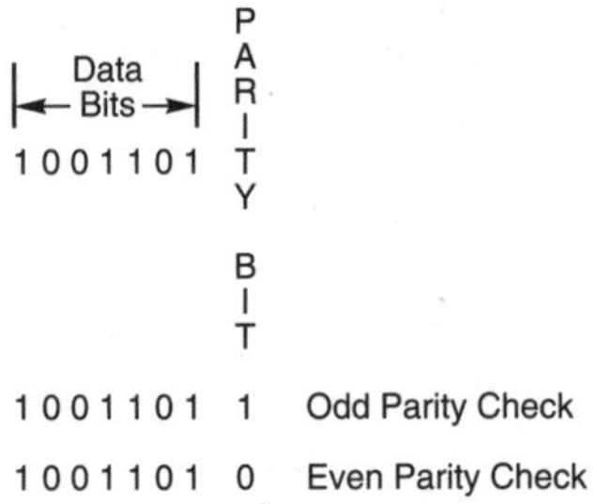

```
               P
               A
  | Data |     R
  |←Bits→|     I
               T
  1 0 0 1 1 0 1 Y

               B
               I
               T

  1 0 0 1 1 0 1  1   Odd Parity Check
  1 0 0 1 1 0 1  0   Even Parity Check
```

Echoplex is an error detection technique in which each character of a message is retransmitted by the receiver back to the originator as it is received.

The parity scheme detects single-bit errors in the transmitted symbols, but not multiple-bit errors. Error correction can occur by the receiver sending a message back that requests retransmission.

Echoplex

Echoplex is perhaps not properly classed as an element of protocols, but we will discuss it here anyway. It is the technique of sending back (or echoing) each character by the receiver as the characters are received. The sender can then see by the copy printed locally whether the characters are making the round trip without being mutilated. When an echoed character is received in error by the original sender, it is not possible to tell whether the data was received correctly at the destination and scrambled on the return path, or whether it was erroneous when received at the original destination. But at least some error indication is immediately available to the sender.

Checksums

In the preceding discussion on parity, the bit required to make the number of 1-bits in an individual character was added to the end of the character and sent along with it. This scheme is sometimes called vertical redundancy checking (VRC), or vertical parity, because if one holds a punched paper tape with its length in the horizontal, each character appears as a vertical column of holes across the tape. It is possible, and is common in some systems, to include a horizontal check character, which performs the parity function for each row of holes in the tape.

Figure 8.4 shows a set of characters represented as holes punched in a tape, with the vertical or character parity bit at the top of each character, and the horizontal or block parity character at the right. The block parity character is usually called a checksum, because it is formed by performing a binary addition without carry of each successive character. It also is sometimes referred to as a longitudinal redundancy check (LRC) character. It is sent as an extra character at the end of each message block. A system that uses both vertical parity and a checksum usually can detect all single-bit errors in a single character and some multiple-bit errors within a single character. In fact, this method of error detection is one of the three types supported by the BiSync protocol described later in this chapter.

●
In addition to character (or vertical) parity, in which a parity bit is added to each character, a block parity character can be added at the end of each message block.

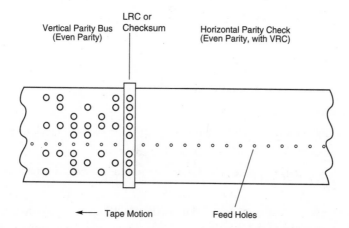

LRC or Checksum
Vertical Parity Bus (Even Parity)
Horizontal Parity Check (Even Parity, with VRC)

← Tape Motion

Feed Holes

FIGURE 8.4.

Vertical and horizontal parity.

XMODEM Protocol

XMODEM protocol has an error-checking technique that can be used between microcomputers. Messages are sent in blocks of 128 characters surrounded by control characters.

The XMODEM protocol was devised by Ward Christensen as a simple error-checking scheme suitable for file transfer operations between microcomputers. It requires that one terminal or computer be set up by an operator or a computer program as the sender and the other be set up as the receiver. After the protocol is started, the transmitter waits for the receiver to send a Negative Acknowledge (NAK) character. The receiver meanwhile is set to send NAKs every 10 seconds. When the transmitter detects the first NAK, it begins sending messages as blocks of 128 data characters, surrounded by some protocol control characters. The beginning of each block is signaled by a Start Of Header (SOH) character. This is followed by a block number character in ASCII, followed by the same block number with each bit inverted. The bit inversion, known as the 1's complement, results in the block number being followed by the 1's complement of the block number. A 128-character piece of the file is sent, followed by a checksum that is the remainder of the sum of all the 128 bytes in the message divided by 255. Mathematically, the XMODEM checksum can be represented as

$$\text{CHECKSUM} = R \left[\frac{\sum_{1}^{128} \text{ASCII Value of Character}}{255} \right]$$

in which R is the remainder of the division process.

Figure 8.5 shows the XMODEM protocol block format.

FIGURE 8.5.

XMODEM protocol block format.

Start of Header	Block Number	1's Complement of Block Number	128 Data Characters	Checksum

The receiver checks each part of the received block:

- Was the first character an SOH?
- Was the block number exactly one more than the previous block received?
- Were exactly 128 characters of data received?
- Was the locally computed checksum identical to the last character received in the block?

If the receiver is satisfied, it sends an Acknowledge (ACK) back to the transmitter, and the transmitter sends the next block. If not, a NAK is sent, and the transmitter resends the block found in error. This process is continued, block by block, until the entire file is sent and verified. At the end of the data, the transmitter sends an End Of Text character. The receiver replies with an ACK, and the session is terminated.

There are several points to be made about the XMODEM protocol. First, it is easy to implement with a small computer, but it does require a computer at each end. Second, it requires manual setup for each file to be transferred. Third, the error detection technique (ordinary sum of the data characters) is unsophisticated and unable to detect reliably the most common type of transmission error, which is a noise burst that can last on the order of 10 milliseconds (the duration of about 12 bits at 1200 bps). Fourth, it is a half-duplex protocol; that is, information is sent, and then the sender waits for a reply before sending the next message. Because operation of the XMODEM protocol generally assumes a full-duplex line, it is inefficient in use of the transmission facility.

In spite of the previously mentioned limitations, the XMODEM protocol and several derivatives are supported by most asynchronous communications programs designed for operation on personal computers. The rationale for the widespread support of those protocols is related to the initial placement of the XMODEM protocol into the public domain. This action allowed software developers to use the protocol without cost. In addition, it provided communications compatibility between programs developed by different vendors, which was extremely important in the 1970s when many software developers preferred to introduce proprietary protocols that worked only when two computer systems used the same software program.

Most of the asynchronous communications programs developed during the early 1980s eventually included XMODEM support. In the late 1980s, several derivatives of the XMODEM protocol gained acceptance due to the increased level of functionality they provided. Some new versions of the XMODEM protocol added CRC error checking, a process described later in this chapter. Other versions provided a full-duplex transmission capability with CRC error detection, further increasing the efficiency of the protocol.

> ●
> Even though the XMODEM protocol is very simple and easy to operate, it requires a computer at each end, and every file to be transferred must be set up manually.

XMODEM DERIVATIVES

If you use an external modem and transfer a file under the XMODEM protocol, you can visually observe two deficiencies of the protocol: its small block size and the half-duplex method of transmission. If you are receiving a file, you will note that your modem's Receive Data (RD) indicator light illuminates for a short time, after which your modem's Send Data (SD) light momentarily illuminates as a flash. This process of RD being on for a second and SD flashing on and off continues until the file transfer is completed or until it aborts if 10 retransmissions occur due to a poor-quality line.

In observing the illumination of SD and RD, you will note that one always follows the other because transmission is half duplex. Thus, after receiving a block of data, your computer stops receiving data and then transmits an ACK or a NAK. By turning off the modem's receiver and turning on its transmitter, the computer creates a small delay. This delay is further increased by the distant computer having to wait for an ACK or a NAK response to the previously transmitted block before being able to resume transmission. In comparison, a few file transfer protocols that support full-duplex transmission enable the simultaneous transmission and reception of data, which increases the effective throughput of the file transfer operation.

When XMODEM was developed during the 1970s, a data block the size of 128 bytes was probably a reasonable size with respect to line quality, because increasing the block size would result in more characters being retransmitted when an error was detected. Beginning in the late 1970s, tens of thousands of miles of fiber-optic cable were installed by communications carriers. Because fiber-optic cable is immune to electromagnetic interference, the probability of transmission errors occurring has substantially decreased. This in turn made the 128-byte block size used by the XMODEM protocol inefficient for modern communications. Although the XMODEM protocol is still very popular, you might want to consider using such derivatives as XMODEM/CRC, YMODEM, and ZMODEM, among others, which provide an enhanced file transfer capability.

XMODEM/CRC

This protocol is the same as the previously described XMODEM protocol with the exception that the checksum is replaced by a polynomial generated CRC whose formation is described later in this chapter. Because the use of a CRC provides a higher level of error detection than the use of a checksum, the use of this protocol reduces the probability of an undetected error in comparison to using the XMODEM protocol.

XMODEM-1K

XMODEM-1K is essentially an XMODEM/CRC protocol that uses 1024-byte (1K) data blocks. For most transmissions, the use of this protocol reduces transmission time in comparison to the use of XMODEM or XMODEM/CRC. The transmission time is reduced because the large block size reduces both the number of line turnarounds and the number of times the transmitting device must wait for a response before sending the next block or retransmitting the previously sent block.

XMODEM-G

The XMODEM-G protocol is a variation of XMODEM-1K developed in recognition of error detection and correction capability being incorporated into many types of modems. The transmission of a file using error detection and correction via modems that have an error detection and correction feature would be inefficient and would introduce additional delays that would adversely affect the efficiency of the file transfer process. In recognition of this problem, XMODEM-G was developed.

XMODEM-G is the same as XMODEM-1K, with the exception of an error detection and correction capability that is omitted. This results in XMODEM-G becoming a "streaming" protocol in which 1K blocks are sent one after another. Although the protocol computes a CRC similar to XMODEM-1K, it is ignored by the protocol. Because this protocol does not provide any error detection capability, it should be used only with modems that have that capability enabled. Otherwise, the transfer of a file occurs without error protection.

YMODEM

Unlike XMODEM and its variations that are limited to transferring a single file, YMODEM supports the transmission of multiple files. Because the protocol enables you to batch a group of files for transmission, many software programs refer to YMODEM as YMODEM BATCH. To provide a multiple file transmission capability, YMODEM uses a header block that carries the filename of each file being transferred, its date of creation or last modification, and the file length.

Figure 8.6 illustrates the basic YMODEM block format, which although similar to XMODEM's has some distinct differences. First, YMODEM replaces the SOH character used by XMODEM with the Start of Text (STX) character. That character informs the receiver that the block contains 1024 data characters. YMODEM can switch to a 128 data character block by replacing the STX character with the SOH character. It automatically does so under certain conditions, such as concluding the transfer of a file when the use of one or more 128 data character blocks is more efficient than the use of one 1024 data character block.

STX	Block Number	1's Complement of Block Number	1024 Data Characters	CRC High Byte	CRC Low Byte

FIGURE 8.6.
YMODEM block format.

A second difference between the XMODEM and YMODEM block formats concerns the block number field. Unlike XMODEM, which commences block numbering at one, YMODEM supports a block number zero, a special block used to transport the filename, its date of creation or last modification, and its length. In addition to the previously discussed capability to transport 1024 data characters per block, another difference between the YMODEM and XMODEM block formats concerns the error detection data contained in the block. As indicated in Figure 8.6, YMODEM contains two bytes of CRC data, resulting in this file transfer protocol having the capability to transport a 16-bit polynomial in place of XMODEM's 8-bit checksum.

Like XMODEM-1K, YMODEM uses 1024-byte (1K) data blocks and is a half-duplex protocol. Some implementations of YMODEM enable you to specify filenames using global characters, such as the asterisk (*) and question mark (?), within the filename and filename extension. Other implementations of YMODEM require you to enter each filename to be batched for transmission. Regardless of the method of specifying filenames, the use of YMODEM enables you to eliminate the delays between one file transfer ending and specifying the name of the next file to be transferred. However, before you use

YMODEM, it is a good idea to check your available disk storage against the storage requirements of the files you want to transfer. Otherwise, you could initiate the transfer of several files and go to the coffee machine only to return and find that the file transfer operation was only partially completed. Unfortunately, YMODEM does not tell you it aborted due to a lack of storage capacity, and you must take a directory listing to determine that there is no available storage left and that the lack of storage caused the file transfer to abort.

YMODEM-G

YMODEM-G can be considered as a batch transfer version of XMODEM-G. That is, YMODEM-G transmits data from one file after another file in 1024 (1K) data blocks without providing an error detection or correction capability. Like XMODEM-G, YMODEM-G should be used only with error-correcting modems.

WXMODEM

The WXMODEM protocol is a full-duplex "sliding window" protocol that allows the transmission of up to four XMODEM 128-byte data blocks before requiring an acknowledgment. This protocol uses a CRC for error checking. It was developed for use on packet switching networks in which the flow of data in small packets that require acknowledgments could adversely affect throughput. By enabling multiple data blocks to be transmitted before requiring an acknowledgment from the receiving device, transmission efficiency is increased. Unfortunately, WXMODEM does not support multiple file transfers.

ZMODEM

The ZMODEM protocol is a full-duplex protocol that supports both 128 and 1024 data block transfers. Unlike the file transfer protocols previously discussed, ZMODEM varies the block size based on the quality of the line determined by the number of retransmission requests received. That is, a poor-quality line indicated by a large number of retransmission requests results in ZMODEM using a 128-byte data block because the small block size requires fewer characters to be retransmitted when an error occurs. Conversely, a good-quality line indicated by a small number of retransmission requests results in ZMODEM using a 1024-byte data block size. Although additional characters will be retransmitted when ZMODEM is using a 1024-byte data block when an error is detected, the low error rate results in a higher level of throughput because most 1024-byte data blocks are received correctly.

In addition to alternating the block size to correspond to the line error rate, ZMODEM enables an interrupted file transfer to be restarted from the point of failure. This can be especially useful because the other protocols require you to restart the file transfer process from the beginning. Two additional features of ZMODEM are its support of multiple file transfers and its support of conventional and extended CRC error checking. Extended CRC checking results in the generation of a four-byte CRC using 32 bits and reduces the probability of an undetected error to below one in many millions of characters.

KERMIT

The KERMIT protocol, developed at Columbia University, was named after Kermit the frog, one of Jim Henson's popular muppets. This protocol differs from the XMODEM series of file transfer protocols primarily due to the characteristics of the operating system used on some mini- and mainframe computers. The XMODEM series and its derivatives were developed for eight-data-bit transfers. Some computer operating systems are limited to seven-bit characters, however, and might not be able to work with ASCII control characters (ASCII 0 through 31) and the delete character (ASCII 127). To provide a file transfer mechanism for such computers, KERMIT was developed.

KERMIT was originally developed as a half-duplex protocol. It uses seven or eight data bits per character. The protocol is designed to convert the eighth bit by stripping it and prefixing the resulting character with another character. Doing so enables operating systems that cannot support eight-bit data characters or certain ASCII control characters to support file transfers in which those characters are disguised.

Since KERMIT was originally developed, many enhancements have been added to the protocol. This protocol now supports multiple file transfers, can operate in a full-duplex sliding window mode, and supports variable block sizes up to 1024 characters per block. Although this protocol is a necessity for accessing computers that cannot handle eight-bit characters or ASCII control characters, it should not be used otherwise. This is because the prefixing of characters significantly adds to the overhead of the protocol and makes it approximately 10 to 20 percent less efficient than the XMODEM protocol, which is the least efficient of all protocols in that series.

SEALINK

The SEALINK protocol was developed by System Enhancement Associates of New Jersey to minimize the effect of delays when transmitting data through a packet network. This protocol is a full-duplex sliding window variation of XMODEM. It uses 128-byte data blocks that are error protected through the use of a CRC. Up to six blocks can be transmitted before an acknowledgment from the receiver is required, which makes this protocol more suitable for use on packet networks that use WXMODEM.

Protocol Selection

The selection of an appropriate file transfer protocol first depends on the protocols supported by your computer and the computer you want to communicate with. Although this limitation might narrow your choice, you might still be faced with a half dozen or more protocols commonly supported from which to make your selection. In doing so, you might want to narrow your choice by considering whether the modem you use and the distant modem you will communicate with support a common error detection scheme, such as MNP Class 5 or the CCITT V.42bis protocol, both of which were described in Chapter 4, "Asynchronous Modems and Interfaces." If so, you might then consider using XMODEM-G if you have a single file to transfer or YMODEM-G if you have multiple files to transfer. Both protocols are "streaming" protocols that do not implement error detection, and their effective use is dependent on enabling error detection in your modem to match the distant modem's method of error detection.

If you previously experienced poor-quality transmission due to communications via an antiquated switchboard in a rundown hotel, an in-progress thunderstorm, or another cause, you might want to consider using ZMODEM. Although many people prefer to use ZMODEM as their first choice because of its full-duplex transmission mode, in actuality, a streaming protocol provides an equivalent to slightly better level of throughput. Where ZMODEM excels is in its capability to restart a transmission at its previous point of failure, alleviating the necessity to retransmit the entire file when transmission impairments result in a break in a transmission session.

If you are using a packet network to access another computer system, consider ZMODEM, SEALINK, and WXMODEM. Each of these three protocols allows many blocks to be unacknowledged, and they are designed to increase throughput when transmission is via a packet network. Because ZMODEM uses a larger data block than either SEALINK or WXMODEM, consider using ZMODEM, if it is available, before using SEALINK or WXMODEM.

If your available file transfer protocols are limited to XMODEM, XMODEM/CRC, and XMODEM-1K, consider XMODEM-1K before XMODEM/CRC, and XMODEM/CRC before the original XMODEM protocol. XMODEM-1K uses 1024-byte data blocks as well as a CRC for error detection and provides a higher throughput than XMODEM/CRC. Although XMODEM/CRC and XMODEM both use 128-byte data blocks, the use of the CRC by the XMODEM/CRC protocol provides a higher probability of data integrity than is gotten from the use of a checksum in the XMODEM protocol.

If you have multiple files to transfer and are considering the use of YMODEM or YMODEM-G, use the latter only if your modem can communicate with the distant modem using a modem error correction protocol. Otherwise, use the YMODEM protocol because it includes an error detection capability based on the use of a CRC.

Three remaining protocols whose uses have not yet been summarized are SEALINK, KERMIT, and ASCII. Because SEALINK uses a CRC for error detection and supports full-duplex transmission, its use provides a higher level of throughput than XMODEM. Unfortunately, its 128-byte data block size negates its performance in comparison to 1024-byte data block protocols. Another limiting factor is its availability, because it does not have a high level of use on many bulletin board systems. Concerning KERMIT, its primary use is for communicating with computer systems whose operating system cannot support the extended ASCII code and ASCII control characters. Because KERMIT strips the eighth bit and prefixes the resulting character with another character, the conversion degrades throughput. Thus, you should use the KERMIT protocol only when absolutely necessary for access to a computer that requires its use.

Because the ASCII protocol has no error detection capability, you might wonder why you should consider its use. The answer to this question is that most electronic mail systems require ASCII input. Thus, if you compose a message offline using a word processor, you should save the file in its ASCII format and then transmit the file when online to the electronic mail system using the ASCII protocol.

To assist readers in comparing the file transfer protocols previously discussed, Table 8.1 compares their key features.

Table 8.1. File transfer protocol comparison.

Protocol	Support Batch	Block Size	Error Detection	Transmission Mode	Data Characters
ASCII	no	n/a	none	n/a	7
XMODEM	no	128	CS	H	8
XMODEM/CRC	no	128	CRC	H	8
XMODEM-1K	no	128/1024	CRC	H	8
XMODEM-G	no	128/1024	none	H	8
YMODEM	yes	128/1024	CRC	H	8
YMODEM-G	yes	128/1024	none	H	8
WXMODEM	no	128	CRC	F	8
ZMODEM	yes	128/1024	CRC	F	8
KERMIT	yes	1024 Max	CRC/CS	H/F	8
SEALINK	yes	128	CRC	F	8

Note: CS = checksum, H = half-duplex, F = full-duplex

Convolutional Coding—Cyclic Redundancy Checks

Convolutional coding attaches a BCC to the end of each message block. The receiver recomputes the BCC and compares it to the one transmitted to determine whether the message was correctly received.

Several schemes have been devised to detect errors in binary communications systems using feedback or convolutional coding. These methods all append information computed at the transmitter to the end of each message transmitted to enable the receiver to determine whether a transmission error has occurred. The added information is mathematically related to the messages and is therefore redundant. The receiver recomputes the value and compares the recomputed number with the number received. If the two are the same, all is well. If not, the receiver notifies the transmitter that an error has occurred, and the message is re-sent. These methods go by the name of Cyclic Redundancy Checking (CRC), and the values appended to the messages are called CRCs or Block Check Characters (BCCs). A CRC is calculated by dividing the entire numeric binary value of the block of data by a constant, called a generator polynomial. The quotient is discarded, and the remainder is appended to the block and transmitted along with the data.

The check character is determined by dividing the total binary value of the entire block by a constant called a generator polynomial.

CRCs usually are computed using multiple section feedback shift registers with eXclusive-OR (XOR) logic elements between each section and at the end. A typical arrangement is shown in Figure 8.6. This register implements the CCITT/ISO High-Level Data Link Control (HDLC) CRC, which is called CCITT-CRC. The circles with a + in the middle represent XOR logic elements. For B = 0 or B = 1, these are the two rules for XOR:

B XOR 1 = 0

B XOR 0 = B

The shift register is initialized to all ones at the beginning of CRC calculation for a message. As each bit of the transmitted characters is applied to the transmission facility, it is also applied at point A of Figure 8.7, and then the entire register is shifted right one bit. As the bits are transmitted and shifted, each 1 bit that appears at A also affects the state of the other XOR elements, and that effect is propagated throughout the register for several bit times after the bit initially appears. Thus, any bit continues to have an effect on the transmitted data for a considerable time after that bit is sent. When the last data bit has been sent, the bits in the CRC shift register are complemented and transmitted.

At the receiver, the identical process is performed, and when the end of the message including the CRC is detected, the CRC is tested for the unique value 0001110100001111. If this value is found, all is well and the CRC register is reset to all ones for the next message. If the special value is not found, the program is notified that a transmission error has occurred, and a negative acknowledgment is returned to the sender.

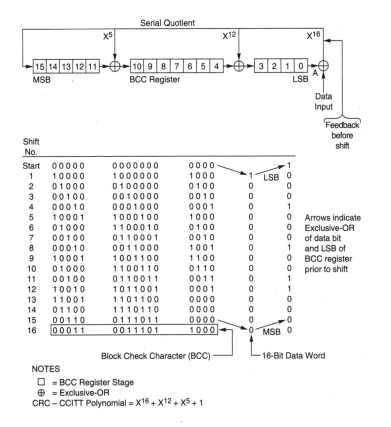

FIGURE 8.7.

Shift register implementation of CCITT-CRC.

NOTES
- □ = BCC Register Stage
- ⊕ = Exclusive-OR
- CRC – CCITT Polynomial = $X^{16} + X^{12} + X^5 + 1$

The CRC process has the advantage that the current state of the shift register is the result of considerable past history. It is therefore unlikely that a burst of errors, such as normally occurs in serial data transmission, will produce a calculated CRC at the receiver that is the same as that which was originally sent. In fact, the 16-bit CRC calculation procedures, CRC-16 and CRC-CCITT, detect all error bursts of 16 bits or less in length. They also detect over 99.9 percent of error bursts of greater than 16 bits. Another advantage of CRC is that it does not require the addition of another bit per character sent as do the VRC and LRC schemes. It does, however, require the sending of one of two (two for CRC-16 and CRC-CCITT) extra characters at the end of each transmitted block.

CRC algorithms are usually implemented in hardware, and integrated circuits have been developed to do the entire process for more than one method (for example, CRC-12, CRC-16, and CRC-CCITT). It is also possible to do the calculations in software, with table lookup techniques providing reasonable performance.

●
The CRC error detection process has a very high rate of success in accurately detecting error bursts of up to 16 bits because of the history held in the shift registers.

Half-Duplex Protocols

A half-duplex protocol is also commonly referred to as a stop and wait protocol. This is because transmission in one direction must stop before transmission in the opposite direction occurs.

Links

Data links, either point-to-point or multipoint, are the data communications equipment and circuits that allow two or more terminals to communicate.

The basic notion in link protocols is that of the data link. A data link is an arrangement of modems or other interface equipment and communications circuits connecting two or more terminals so that they can communicate. Probably the most widely used link protocol is composed of the Binary Synchronous Communications procedures defined by IBM (usually abbreviated as BiSync or BSC). These procedures allow for operation on a data link in one direction at one time. BiSync can be operated on full-duplex circuits, but information still flows in only one direction at a time, so in many cases the advantage of the full-duplex circuit is minimized.

For the purpose of discussion of protocols, the physical form of the link is important in that the procedures for connecting and disconnecting the link might be different depending on whether the link is permanently connected or a dial-up, and also depending on the delay between when a data bit is sent and when it is received. This latter factor is of particular concern on satellite links due to the large difference in round-trip propagation delay between satellite links and terrestrial links. Regardless of the physical form of the link, however, the data is sent over it as a serial stream of symbols encoded as bits, and the control procedures between the ends of the link are affected using the transmission and recognition of the line-control characters or control codes.

POINT-TO-POINT LINKS

A point-to-point link is one that connects only two stations at one time, as Figure 8.8a shows. Point-to-point links can be established on dedicated or dial-up circuits, and they can be half-duplex or full-duplex.

MULTIPOINT LINKS

Multipoint links connect more than two stations at a time, as Figure 8.8b shows. Obviously, some control procedure must be in place to designate which stations can use the link at any one time. For this purpose, one station on the multidrop lines is designated as the control or master station, and all other stations are designated as tributaries or slaves. The control station is the traffic director, designating which stations are to use the link by a polling and selection process. At any instant, transmission on a multipoint link will be between only two stations, with all other stations on the link in a passive receive mode.

FIGURE 8.8.

Point-to-point and multipoint links.

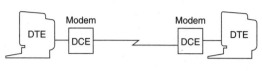

a. Point-to-point

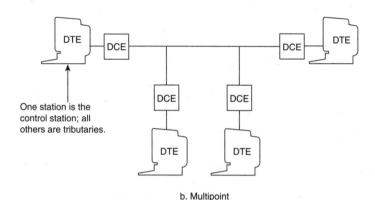

One station is the control station; all others are tributaries.

b. Multipoint

Transmission Codes—Character Sets

BiSync is defined by IBM to accommodate three character sets and their associated binary codes. Each set consists of a set of graphics (letters, numbers, and punctuation), a set of terminal control and format control codes (BELL, Form Feed, WRU, and so forth), and a set of data link control codes (Start of Text, End of Transmission, and so on). The three sets are the Six-Bit Transcode (SBT), Extended Binary Coded Decimal Interchange Code (EBCDIC), and United States of America Standard Code for Information Interchange (USASCII, or more commonly, just ASCII).

● *IBM's BiSync can be used with three character sets: set, EBCDIC, and ASCII.*

The codes differ in number of bits per symbol encoded (six for SBT, seven for ASCII, and eight for EBCDIC), and the different numbers of characters in the character set (64 for SBT, 128 for ASCII, and 144 for EBCDIC). There are significant differences between the sets in such properties as the sorting order between letters and numbers.

Link Control Codes

Link control is affected by the proper recognition of control characters and the taking of appropriate actions. The control codes used in BiSync are defined as listed here:

Synchronous Idle (Syn)—Establishes and maintains synchronization between DCEs. Is used as a filler between data blocks.

Start of Header (SOH)—Identifies the beginning of a block of heading information. Headers are control information (such as addresses, priority, and message numbers) used by the system to process the text part of the message.

● *Various link control codes are used in BiSync to gain control of the data link and ensure that the proper actions occur.*

Start of Text (STX)—Identifies the end of a header and the beginning of a block of text. Text is the part of the message from an applications program that is destined for another applications program and that must pass through the communications system unchanged.

End of Transmission Block (ETB)—Identifies the end of a block started with an SOH or STX. A BCC is sent immediately following an ETB. Receipt of an ETB requires a status reply (ACK0, ACK1, NAK, WACK, or RVI).

End of Text (ETX)—Terminates a block of data started by an STX or SOH that was transmitted as an entity. A BCC is sent immediately following an ETX. ETX also requires a status reply.

End of Transmission (EOT)—Indicates the end of message transmission by this station; the message might have contained one or more blocks. Receipt of an EOT causes all receiving stations to reset. The EOT is also used as a response to a poll when the polled station has nothing to send, and as an abort signal when the sender cannot continue transmission.

Enquiry (ENQ)—Requests a repeat transmission of a response to a message block if the original response is garbled or is not received. ENQ can also indicate the end of a polling or selection sequence, and it is used to bid for the line when the line is a point-to-point connection.

Affirmative Acknowledgment (ACK0 or ACK1)—Indicates correct receipt of the previous block and that the receiver is ready to accept the next block. ACK0 and ACK1 are used alternately, and receipt of the wrong one is an indication of an error in the protocol. ACK0 is the correct response to a station selection (on a multipoint circuit) or a line bid (on a point-to-point circuit).

Wait-Before-Transmit Affirmative Acknowledgment (WACK)—Indicates a temporary not-ready-to-receive condition to the sending station and affirmative acknowledgment of the previously received data block. The normal response to WACK by the sending station is ENQ, but EOT and DLE EOT are also valid. If ENQ is received after sending WACK, the sending station continues to send WACK until it is ready to continue sending data.

Negative Acknowledgment (NAK)—Indicates that the previously received block was received in error and that the receiver is ready to receive another block. NAK is also used as a station-not-ready reply to a station selection or line bid.

Data Link Escape (DLE)—Indicates to the receiver that the character following the DLE is to be interpreted as a control character.

Reverse Interrupt (RVI)—Indicates a request by a receiving station that the current transmission be terminated so that a high-priority message can be sent (such as a shutdown notice). RVI is also an affirmative acknowledgment to the previous block received. In a multipoint circuit, RVI sent from the control station means the control station wants to select a different station. When a sending station receives an RVI, it responds by sending all data that would prevent it from becoming a receiving station.

Temporary Text Delay (TTD)—Indicates that the sending station is not ready to send immediately but wants to keep the line. The receiving terminal reply to TTD is NAK. TTD normally is sent after two seconds if the sender cannot transmit the next block; this control code holds off the normal three-second abort timer at the receiving terminal. The response to TTD is NAK, and TTD can be repeated several times. TTD also is used as a forward abort, by sending EOT in response to the NAK reply.

Switched Line Disconnect (DLE EOT)—Indicates to a receiver that the transmitter is going to hang up on a switched line connection.

Code Sequences

Reference to the ASCII and EBCDIC code charts will reveal no code assigned to several of the control characters mentioned in the preceding listing. Such control codes are represented by two-character sequences of the characters that are defined in the charts. Table 8.2 gives the correspondence between these control characters and sequences of standard characters.

> ●
> Some control characters require a two-character sequence of standard characters.

Table 8.2. Character sequences for BiSync control characters.

BiSync Data Link Character	Character Sequences for Various Code Sets		
	ASCII	**EBCDIC**	**SBT**
ACK 0	DLE 0	DLE 70	DLE -
ACK 1	DLE 1	DLE /	DLE T
WACK	DLE ;	DLE ,	DLE W
RVI	DLE <	DLE @	DLE 2
TTD	STX ENQ	STX ENQ	STX ENQ

Polling and Selection

The active participants on a BiSync link are managed by a control station that issues either a Poll or a Select message addressed to the desired tributary. The Poll is an invitation-to-send from the control to the tributary. This allows the tributary to send any messages desired to the control station. The Select is a request-to-receive notice from the control station, telling the tributary that the control station has something to send to it. The control station thus controls which station has the link, and the direction of transmission.

Stations on the data link are assigned unique addresses that can consist of from one to seven characters. The first character defines the station, and succeeding characters define

> ●
> In a BiSync link, the control station determines which tributary station is active on the link, as well as the direction of transmission.

some part of the station, such as a printer, as required. Some BiSync implementations repeat the station address for reliability purposes.

MESSAGE BLOCKS

Messages consist of one or more blocks of text, called the body of the message, surrounded by synchronization, header and error control characters. The beginning of each block is identified by the STX control character, and all blocks except the last in a message are ended by either an ETB or an ITB character. The last block of the message is ended by an ETX character.

Error Checking

Three types of error detection modes are used by BiSync: an odd parity check of each character including VRC/LRC, a BCC comparison using CRC-12, and a BCC comparison using CRC-16.

BiSync uses three types of error detection: VRC/LRC, CRC-12, and CRC-16. Table 8.3 shows under what conditions each is used. Transparency mode is described later in this section. The VRC is an odd-parity check performed on each character transmitted, including the LRC character at the end of the block. Each bit in the LRC character provides odd parity for the corresponding bit position of all characters sent in the block. Figure 8.9 illustrates the formation of the VRC and LRC for an eight-character data block. Note that the LRC is formed in the same manner as the VRC; however, the LRC covers all characters in the data block, whereas the VRC covers individual characters.

Table 8.3. Type of redundancy check.

Code Set	No Transparency	Transparency Installed and Operating	Transparency Installed but Not Operating
EBCDIC	CRC-16	CRC-16	CRC-16
ASCII	VRC/LRC	CRC-16	VRC/CRC-16
SBT	CRC-12	CRC-12	CRC-12

In BiSync, the LRC character is called the Block Check Character (BCC). It is sent as the next character following an ETB, ITB, or ETX character. The BCC sent with the data is compared at the receiver with one accumulated by the receiver, and if the two are equal, all is well. The BCC calculation is restarted by the first STX or SOH character received after the direction of transmission is reversed (called a line turnaround). All characters except SYN characters received from that point until the next line turnaround are included in the calculation. If the message is sent in blocks with no line turnaround, each block is followed by an ITB, then the BCC. The BCC calculation is then restarted with the next STX or SOH character received.

Character	◄── Data Bits ──►	Character Parity Bit (VRC)
1	1 0 1 0 1 1 0 1	0
2	0 1 1 0 1 0 1 0	1
3	0 1 1 1 0 1 0 1	0
4	1 0 1 0 0 1 0 1	1
5	1 0 0 1 0 0 1 0	0
6	0 1 0 0 1 0 0 1	0
7	1 0 0 1 0 0 1 0	0
8	0 1 1 0 1 0 0 1	1
Block Parity Character (LRC)	1 1 0 0 1 0 0 1	0

FIGURE 8.9.

VRC/LRC parity check.

The Cyclic Redundancy Check codes are used for error checking in the same fashion as the LRC code. If the transmission code set is SBT, the CRC-12 method is used, because each transmitted character is only six bits. For EBCDIC, the CRC-16 scheme is always used. For the ASCII code set, IBM has specified that the VRC/LRC scheme be used in the nontransparency (standard) mode, and that CRC-16 be used in transparency mode. Transparency mode is described in detail in the following discussion.

Message Formats

Information is carried in BiSync as messages. Each message can have several parts: a synchronization sequence, a header, some text, and a block check sequence. Each part is identified by one or more control characters. In the case of messages used only for control, some parts such as the header, the text, or the BCC might be missing.

SYNCHRONIZATION

Unless the transmitter and receiver agree on the exact (to the bit) starting point of a message, they cannot communicate. Achieving this synchronization requires three steps:

1. The modems or other data communications devices at both ends of the circuit must acquire bit synchronization. The methods for doing this were discussed in Chapter 5, "Synchronous Modems, Digital Transmission, and Service Units."

2. The link interface equipment in the DTE must acquire character synchronization. This is done by searching the bit stream for a specific pattern of bits called a Synchronization Character (SYN). In ASCII, the bit pattern for SYN is 0010110. To help insure against recognition of a false SYN, most systems including BiSync require transmission and detection of two successive SYNs before the next step in the synchronization process is taken. The two SYN characters taken as a control set are called a Sync Sequence and are shown in most diagrams as a 0. To ensure that the first and last characters of a transmission are correctly sent, some BiSync stations add a PAD character before the first SYN

●

Establishing the synchronization required between sender and receiver requires a three-step sequence: bit synchronization, character synchronization, and message synchronization.

and after every BCC, EOT, and ACK. This stratagem was devised primarily to overcome hardware limitations in some early hard-wired BiSync terminals.

3. The program operating the protocol must acquire message synchronization. In other words, the program must be able to find the beginning of each message or control character sequence. This is achieved by a program search of the characters received after the sync sequence for a control character that is defined to begin a block of data or control sequence. Such characters are SOH, STX, ACK0/1, NAK, WACK, RVI, and EOT.

HEADING

The SOH character begins the heading used in identifying the message type, numbering priority, and routing.

A heading is a sequence of characters beginning with the SOH character that is used for message type identification, message numbering, priority specification, and routing. Receipt of the SOH initiates accumulation of the BCC (but the SOH is not included in the BCC). The heading can be of fixed or variable length, and it is ended by an STX.

TEXT

The text part of the message contains the information to be sent between applications programs. The text begins with an STX and ends with ETX. Text can be broken into blocks for better error control. Each block begins with an STX and ends with an ETB, except for the last block, which ends with an ETX. The normal end of a transmission is signaled by sending an EOT following the ETX. Control characters are not allowed within the body of a text block. If a control character is detected, the receiving station terminates reception and looks for a BCC as the next two characters.

TIMEOUTS

Four BiSync time-out functions prevent indefinite delays due to data errors or missing line turnaround signals.

Timeouts must be provided by the communications program or terminal to prevent indefinite delays caused by data errors or missing line turnaround signals. Four functions are specified in BiSync for timeouts: transmit, receive, disconnect, and continue.

Transmit timeout is normally set for one second. It defines the rate of insertion of synchronous idle (SYN SYN or DLE SYN) sequences in the data to help maintain bit and character synchronization.

Receive timeout is normally set for three seconds. It carries out a few actions:

- It limits the time a transmitting station will wait for a reply.
- It signals a receiving station to check the line for synchronous idle characters, which indicate that transmission is continuing. The receive timeout is reset each time a sync sequence is received.

● It sets a limit on the time a tributary station in a multipoint circuit can remain in control mode. The timer is reset each time an end signal such as an ENQ or ACK is received as long as the station stays in control mode.

Disconnect timeout causes a station on a switched network to disconnect from the circuit after 20 seconds of inactivity.

Continue timeout causes a transmitting station sending a TTD to send another if it is still unable to send text. A receiving station must transmit a WACK if it becomes temporarily unable to receive within a two-second interval.

Transparent-Text Mode

It is often necessary in communicating between machines to send data that does not represent characters but instead represents some purely arbitrary quantity or object. An example is the binary representation of a computer program. In such a case, it is likely that some of the data will have the same bit pattern as a BiSync control character. Transparent-text mode, sometimes called transparency, allows such data to be sent without being misinterpreted by the communications program. The basic technique in transparency is to precede each true control character with the DLE character, as Figure 8.10a shows. If a DLE bit pattern appears in the text of the message, it also is preceded by a DLE. Thus, a bit pattern is interpreted as a control character only if preceded by a DLE. The resulting message after processing by the link interface program to remove the DLE is shown in Figure 8.10b. Note that any DLE DLE sequence in the text has the first DLE suppressed and the second sent along as part of the data.

●
Data communications often requires the sending of information that is in binary rather than in a character code. A transparent-text mode is used for this purpose.

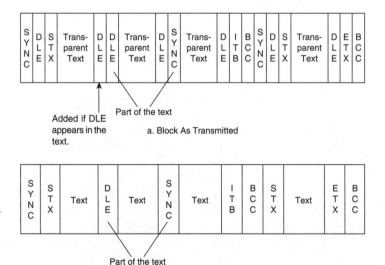

FIGURE 8.10.

BiSync transparency mode.

Full-Duplex Protocols

Online applications using CRT terminals required a protocol for full-duplex operations that contained a powerful error detection and correction system that prevented aliasing.

The Binary Synchronous Communications procedures were devised at a time when most data communications circuits were operated at 2400 bits per second and were two-wire half-duplex circuits connecting remote job entry card reader/printer terminals to mainframes. As online applications using remote CRT terminals became more cost-effective, and as four-wire private line circuits became available, the demand for a communications protocol that could handle full-duplex operations arose. These were the requirements for such a protocol:

- Messages must flow in both directions simultaneously.
- It must be possible to have more than one message in the channel at one time (BiSync allows only one).
- Transparency must be designed in, not tacked on as an afterthought.
- The protocol must allow switched network, half-duplex, and multipoint operation, as well as full-duplex point-to-point.
- The error detection and correction scheme must be powerful and must prohibit the problem of aliasing.

The last condition is a particularly difficult one. Aliasing occurs when a message fragment caused by a transmission error is interpreted as a good message at the receiver; that is, when a bad or broken message "looks like" a good message. This can be a serious problem, especially in critical applications such as funds transfer and military command and control. Much design effort in the international standards organizations and in private companies was devoted to development of protocols that prevented the aliasing problem. This led to the development of three widely used schemes. Two of them were alike in principle and operation and in requiring special hardware but were promulgated by different organizations. The third, developed at Digital Equipment Corporation, uses a different technique but can operate with standard character-oriented line interface equipment.

High-Level Data Link Control Procedures

Protocols to prevent aliasing must determine where a true message block begins and ends and what part of the message is to be included in the CRC. HDLC is one of these.

The critical issue in preventing aliasing is the determination of where a legal message block begins and ends, and exactly what part of the information taken in by the receiver is to be included in the CRC. As a result of work done at IBM by J. Ray Kersey and others in the early 1970s, a protocol was proposed and later adopted as an international standard by the International Standards Organization in 1979. It is called the High-level Data Link Control (HDLC) procedures. In HDLC, the message synchronization indicator (called a Flag) is generated by a hardware circuit, and other hardware circuits prevent any data being transmitted from having the same pattern as the Flag. The Flag then becomes a kind of out-of-band framing signal, much like the break signal in the teletypewriter protocol.

Because the data being transmitted is examined bit by bit to screen out possible aliases of the Flag, HDLC and other similar protocols, such as IBM's Synchronous Data Link Control (SDLC), are referred to as bit-oriented protocols, or BOPs. Unlike BiSync and DDCMP (which will be described later), the text part of messages sent using the HDLC protocol can, in principle, be any arbitrary number of bits long, and HDLC is defined to allow this. In practice, as with BiSync and DDCMP, most implementations of BOPs restrict the text (and in fact all the message including the Flag) to be an integral multiple of the number of bits in a character (almost always eight).

● Data is examined bit by bit in HDLC; thus, it is called a bit-oriented protocol.

In HDLC, all information is carried by frames that can be of three types: information frames (I-frames), supervisory control sequences (S-frames), or unnumbered command/responses (U-frames). Figure 8.11 shows one information frame as a rectangular block divided into its six fields: a beginning Flag (F1) field, an Address (A) field, a Control (C) field, an Information (I) field, a Frame Check Sequence (FCS) field, and a final flag (F2) field. S-frames and U-frames have the same fields except that the I field is left out.

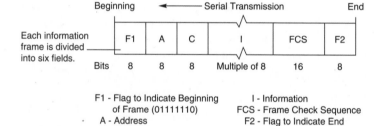

FIGURE 8.11.
HDLC format.

I-frames perform information transfer, and independently carry message acknowledgments, and Poll or Final bits. S-frames perform link supervisory control such as message acknowledgments, retransmit requests, and requests for temporary holds on I-frame transmissions (like a WACK in BiSync). U-frames provide a flexible format for additional link control data by omitting the frame sequence numbers and thus providing a place for an additional 32 command and 32 response functions. The fields in the HDLC frame are used as detailed here:

Flag field—Every frame begins and ends with a Flag, which is the bit pattern 01111110. The same Flag can end one frame and begin the next. Every station connected to a link must continuously search the received data for the Flag.

Address field—In command frames, the address identifies the destination station for the command. In response frames, the address identifies the station sending the response.

Control field—The control field carries commands and responses, according to Figure 8.12.

FIGURE 8.12.

Control field contents.

HDLC Frame Format	Bits in Control Field							
	1	2	3	4	5	6	7	8
I-frame (Information transfer commands/responses)	0	N(S)[1]			P/F[2]	N(R)[3]		
S-frame (Supervisory commands/responses)	1	0	S[4]		P/F	N(R)		
U-frame (Unnumbered commands/responses)	1	1	M[5]		P/F	M		

Notes:

[1]N(S) is the transmitting station send sequence number, bit 2 is the low order bit.

[2]P/F is the Poll bit for primary station transmissions, and the final bit for secondary station transmissions.

[3]N(R) is the transmitting station receive sequence number. Bit 6 is the low-order bit.

[4]S are supervisory function bits.

[5]M are modifier function bits.

> In HDLC, there are six fields in an information frame but only five fields in other frames, which are supervisory control sequences or unnumbered command/responses.

Information field—The information field can contain any sequence of bits, which in principle need not be related to a particular character set or data structure. In practice, the information field is almost always an integral multiple of one character in length, which is usually eight bits.

Frame Check Sequence field—The FCS (or CRC) for HDLC is the CCITT-CRC, as previously discussed.

To ensure that the Flag is unique, the transmitting hardware must monitor the bit stream continually between the beginning and ending Flags for the presence of strings of five one-bits in a row. If such a string occurs, a zero-bit is inserted (called bit stuffing) by the hardware after the fifth one-bit so that the string will not look like a Flag. The added zero-bit is removed at the receiver. This procedure makes any appearance of strings of one-bits greater than five in number a Flag, an error on the transmission line, or a deliberately sent fill pattern between frames of all one-bits. One method of aborting transmission of a frame is to begin transmitting continuous ones.

Specification in the protocol of a unique, hardware-generated Flag pattern and the length of the Address, Control, and FCS fields provides complete transparency for the Information field. The hardware prevents any bit pattern sent by the applications program from having more than five continuous ones, and the hardware-added zeros are stripped from the data stream as it passes through the receiver. Also, the position of the FCS is defined by receipt of the ending Flag so that the residual pattern in the CRC register can be immediately compared with the fixed value (0001110100001111).

The order of bit transmission is defined for addresses, commands, responses, and sequence numbers to be low-order bit first, but the order of bit transmission for the information field is not specified. The FCS is transmitted beginning with the coefficient of the highest order term (x^{15}). An invalid frame is defined as one that is not properly bounded by Flags, or is shorter than 32 bits between Flags. Invalid frames are ignored (in contrast with frames that have a bad FCS, which require a NAK).

HDLC SEMANTICS

The preceding discussion dealt with what is called the syntax of HDLC. The syntax is the definition of the bit patterns and order of sending bits that will make correctly formed messages—that is, those that are legal in the protocol. For you to understand what happens when HDLC is used, however, it is necessary to define the semantic content of messages, or the meanings that should be assigned to correctly formed messages.

The normal sequence of messages in HDLC consists of the transfer of one or more frames containing I-fields from a data source (the transmitting station) to a data sink (the receiving station). The receipt is acknowledged by the sink by sending a frame in the backward direction. The source must retain all transmitted messages until they are explicitly acknowledged by the sink. The value of N(R) indicates that the station transmitting the N(R) has correctly received all I-frames numbered up to N(R)–1. I-frames and S-frames (see Figure 8.12) are numbered, the numbers going from 0 to 7 (for unextended control fields). An independent numbering sequence is carried for each data source/data sink combination. The response from a sink can acknowledge several (but not more than seven) received messages at one time and can be contained in an I-frame being sent from the sink to the source.

A data link consists of two or more communicating stations, so for control purposes it is necessary to designate one station as the primary station, with responsibility for managing data flow and link error recovery procedures. Primary stations send command frames. Other stations on the link are called secondary stations, and they communicate using response frames. Primary stations can send to secondaries using the Select bit in the control field of an I-frame, or a primary can allow a secondary to send by sending a Poll bit.

Secondary stations can operate in one of two modes: a Normal Response Mode (NRM) or an Asynchronous Response Mode (ARM). In NRM, the secondary can send only in response to a specific request or permission by the primary station. The secondary station explicitly indicates the last frame to be sent by setting the final bit in the control field. In ARM, the secondary can independently initiate transmission without receiving an explicit permission or Poll from the primary.

●

A normal message sequence involves sending frames from a transmitting station to a receiving station and having the receiving station acknowledge receipt by sending a frame back to the sender.

Space does not permit covering HDLC in greater detail. The interested reader is referred to International Standards ISO 3309-1979 (E), ISO 4335-1979 (E), and ISO 6256-1981 for the complete definition of the HDLC protocol. There is a data link control procedure standard promulgated by the American National Standards Institute (ANSI) in the United States called Advanced Data Communications Control Procedures (ADCCP), which is functionally equivalent to HDLC.

Synchronous Data Link Control

SDLC, developed by IBM, has the same frame format and is similar in function to HDLC.

The standard full-duplex synchronous data link control protocol used by the IBM Corporation in products conforming to its System Network Architecture is called Synchronous Data Link Control (SDLC). It is functionally equivalent to HDLC, but with these exceptions:

- SDLC information fields must be an integral multiple of eight bits long.

- Current IBM products support only the Unbalanced Normal operation with Normal Disconnected mode class or procedures as defined in ISO DIS 6159 and DIS 4335/DAD1.

- SDLC contains additional commands and responses not defined in the ISO Elements of Procedure, for example, a TEST command and response. Figure 8.13 shows the frame structure of SDLC (which is the same as HDLC), along with the common modes, commands, and responses. A close examination of this illustration will help you understand the SDLC format and the differences between HDLC and SDLC.

Digital Data Communications Message Protocol

At about the same time SDLC was being developed at IBM, George Friend, Steven Russell, and Stuart Wecker were given the task of developing a synchronous protocol at Digital Equipment Corporation. The requirements were similar to those given before full-duplex protocols, but with one important additional item: the protocol must run on existing data communications hardware, and preferably on asynchronous as well as synchronous links. The result was the Digital Data Communications Message Protocol, or DDCMP.

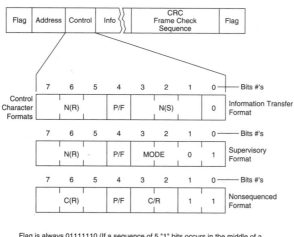

FIGURE 8.13.

SDLC format.

Flag is always 01111110 (If a sequence of 5 "1" bits occurs in the middle of a
transmission, the transmitter "stuffs" a "0" bit and the receiver removes it.)
Address is the Station Address on a particular line
N(S) is Sending Sequence Number = 000 through 111 and then repeats
P/F is Primary Station Poll when = 1 from Primary Station
Secondary Station Final when = 1 from Station on the line
N(R) is Receiving Sequence Number = 000 through 111 and then repeats
Mode is Receive Ready (RR) when 00
Receive Not Ready (RNR) when 10
Reject (REJ) when 01
C/R is Command from Primary Station or Response from Secondary Station
Nonsequenced Information (NSI) = 000-00 ⎫
Set Normal Response Mode (SNRM) = 001-00 ⎪
Disconnect (DISC) = 010-00 ⎬ Commands
Optional Response Poll (ORP) = 100-00 ⎪
Set Initialization Mode (SIM) = 000-10 ⎭

Nonsequenced Information (UI) = 000-00 ⎫
Nonsequenced Acknowledgment (UA) = 110-00 ⎪
Request for Initialization (RIM) = 000-10 ⎬ Responses
Command Reject (FRMR) = 001-10 ⎪
Request Online (DM) = 000-11 ⎭
Info is Information = Variable Length for Information Transfer
Prohibited for Supervisory Format
Variable Length for Nonsequenced Format with NSI
Fixed Format with CMDR
CRC = Cyclic Redundancy Check Remainder

DDCMP is a character-oriented protocol rather than a bit-oriented protocol as is SDLC. Therefore, DDCMP requires no special bit stuffing and destuffing hardware and can be used with various types of line interfaces, including asynchronous units. The method of specifying the length of a message in order to look for the BCC at the right time is inclusion of a 14-bit count field in the header. This is a count of the number of characters in the information field of the message. Because error-free transmission depends on the count field being detected correctly, the header of DDCMP messages is a constant length and has its own BCC, which is checked before setting up to receive the information part of the message. The format of DDCMP messages is shown in Figure 8.14. A detailed study of this figure reveals the bit pattern of the various fields in the frame for different types of messages.

●

DDCMP is character oriented rather than bit oriented.

FIGURE 8.14.

*DDCMP message
format in detail.*

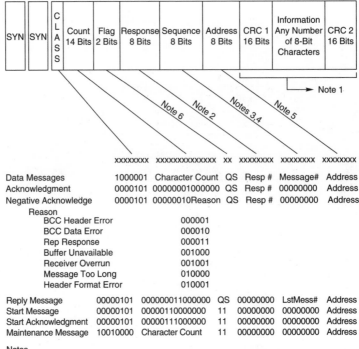

| SYN | SYN | C L A S S | Count 14 Bits | Flag 2 Bits | Response 8 Bits | Sequence 8 Bits | Address 8 Bits | CRC 1 16 Bits | Information Any Number of 8-Bit Characters | CRC 2 16 Bits |

Note 1

Note 6   Note 2   Notes 3,4   Note 5

xxxxxxx xxxxxxxxxxxxxx xx xxxxxxx xxxxxxxx xxxxxxxx

Data Messages	1000001	Character Count	QS	Resp #	Message#	Address
Acknowledgment	0000101	00000001000000	QS	Resp #	00000000	Address
Negative Acknowledge	0000101	00000010Reason	QS	Resp #	00000000	Address

Reason

BCC Header Error	000001
BCC Data Error	000010
Rep Response	000011
Buffer Unavailable	001000
Receiver Overrun	001001
Message Too Long	010000
Header Format Error	010001

Reply Message	00000101	000000011000000	QS	00000000	LstMess#	Address
Start Message	00000101	00000110000000	11	00000000	00000000	Address
Start Acknowledgment	00000101	00000111000000	11	00000000	00000000	Address
Maintenance Message	10010000	Character Count	11	00000000	00000000	Address

Notes

1. Only the Data Message and the Maintenance Message have character counts, so only these messages have the information and CRC2 fields shown in the message format diagram above.

2. "Resp #" refers to Response Number. This is the number of the last message received correctly. When used in a negative acknowledge message, it is assumed that the next higher numbered message was not received, was received with errors, or was unaccepted for some other reason. See "Reasons."

3. "Message#" is the sequentially assigned number of this message. Numbers are assigned by the transmitting station modulo 256; i.e., message 000 follows 255.

4. "LstMess#" is the number of the last message transmitted by the station.

5. "Address" is the address of the tributary station in multipoint systems and is used in messages both to and from the tributary. In point-to-point operation, a station sends the address "1" but ignores the address field on reception.

6. "Q" and "S" refer to the quick sync flag bit and the select bit.

The DDCMP does not require any special hardware to perform successfully on synchronous, asynchronous, or parallel data channels.

DDCMP has two principal advantages and some disadvantages. One advantage is that it is usable without special hardware on asynchronous, synchronous, or even parallel data channels. Another advantage is that the sequence number field allows for up to 255 messages to be outstanding on the channel at one time, a requirement when operating full-duplex channels over satellite links. On the other hand, it does not support a go-back-N or selective reject mode of operation, and it is, in principle, more vulnerable to the aliasing problem than bit-oriented protocols. It also has been mistakenly criticized for inefficiency because of the inclusion of a BCC after the header on the equivalent of I-frames. In fact, for messages of average length, DDCMP is somewhat more efficient than bit-stuffing protocols because of the extra bits added by the hardware in the bit-oriented schemes. In practice, aliasing has not caused noticeable problems with DDCMP.

What Have You Learned?

1. Protocols are rules for communications between processes that are alike. Interfaces are rules for communicating between processes that are different.

2. Data communications protocols are made up of symbols to be communicated, a code set translating those symbols to a binary code, and rules for the correct sequencing of the symbols.

3. Parity is a method of adding redundancy to coded symbols to help detect errors in transmission.

4. XMODEM is a simple protocol used in asynchronous transmission between microcomputers.

5. YMODEM permits multiple files to be transferred between computers.

6. ZMODEM supports the resumption of a file transfer at its point of interruption as well as the dynamic adjustment of the size of data blocks based on the error rate on the line.

7. A Cyclic Redundancy Check is a number calculated from the data transmitted by the sender and recalculated by the receiver that allows the data to be checked for errors in transmission.

8. The most widely used code sets in the United States are ASCII and EBCDIC.

9. Protocols must be suitable for use on dial and private line connections, and for point-to-point and multipoint network arrangements.

10. The most widely used protocols in the United States are TTY, XMODEM, BiSync, SDLC, and DDCMP.

Quiz for Chapter 8

1. Communications protocols always have a:

    a. Set of symbols.

    b. Start of header.

    c. Special Flag symbol.

    d. BCC.

2. The Baudot code uses how many bits per symbol?

    a. 9.

    b. 7.

    c. 5.

    d. 8.

3. When transmitting odd-parity coded symbols, the number of bits that are zeros in each symbol is:

    a. Odd.

    b. Even.

    c. Unknown.

    d. None of the above.

4. In the XMODEM protocol, the sender waits for what character from the receiver before beginning transmission?

    a. WACK.

    b. ACK.

    c. RVI.

    d. NAK.

5. If each character in an XMODEM block has an ASCII value of 50, what would be the value of the checksum added to the block?

    a. 50.

    b. 23.

    c. 41.

    d. 25.

6. Under the YMODEM protocol, block 0 is used to transport:

    a. Error-recovery information.

    b. Two checksums.

    c. Information about the file to be transferred.

    d. A 1024 data character block.

7. The second YMODEM block used to transport a 1100 byte file would use a data field of:

    a. 1024 characters.

    b. 100 characters.

    c. 128 characters.

    d. 64 characters.

8. A streaming protocol:

    a. Provides error detection.

    b. Does not provide error detection.

    c. Uses 64 byte blocks.

    d. Requires a manual setup.

9. An example of a sliding window protocol is:

    a. XMODEM.

    b. YMODEM.

    c. YMODEM-G.

    d. WXMODEM.

10. A protocol that adjusts its block size based on the line error rate is:

    a. XMODEM.

    b. YMODEM.

    c. ZMODEM.

    d. WXMODEM.

11. Which of the following is not a valid rule for XOR?

   a. 0 XOR 0 = 0

   b. 1 XOR 1 = 1

   c. 1 XOR 0 = 1

   d. B XOR B = 0

12. Which of the following BiSync control codes is not defined in the EBCDIC character set?

   a. STX.

   b. ACK0.

   c. ENQ.

   d. TTD.

13. How many messages can be outstanding (unacknowledged) on a BiSync link?

   a. 1.

   b. 2.

   c. 4.

   d. 8.

14. Which code set is used in BiSync when using VRC/LRC but not operating in transparency mode?

   a. EBCDIC.

   b. ASCII.

   c. SBT.

   d. Fieldata.

15. The escape character that identifies control characters in BiSync Transparency mode is:

   a. ESC.

   b. SYN.

   c. DLE.

   d. RVI.

16. One primary difference between DDCMP and SDLC is:

   a. DDCMP does not have a transparent mode.

   b. SDLC does not use a CRC.

   c. DDCMP has a message header.

   d. DDCMP does not require special hardware to find the beginning of a message.

Personal Computer Communications Software

About This Chapter

In this chapter, we turn our attention to software that enables personal computers to communicate via the switched telephone network. In doing so, we will discuss some important communications software features that enable you to control the operation of a modem, emulate a specific type of terminal, transfer binary and ASCII files, and perform other communications functions. Because the best way to become acquainted with personal computer communications software is through the use of a representative program, this chapter uses the popular ProcommPlus communications program from Datastorm Technologies, Inc., for illustrative purposes. Through a series of personal computer screen images, readers are walked through the use of this program to establish a communications session, change dialing directory entries, and perform a file transfer operation.

Communications Program Features

We can get an appreciation for the features built into many personal computer communications programs by discussing their general operation and utilization. First and foremost, the program must be written to operate on the PC platform you use.

Operating System and Operating Environment Support

When considering the potential use of a communications program, you should evaluate both the operating system and the operating environment supported by the program.

Until the late 1980s, there was essentially one operating system for each type of personal computer, which simplified the selection of a communications program. Since then, the Macintosh operating system was significantly revised with the introduction of System 7. In the PC DOS world, Windows and OS/2 operating environments gained widespread acceptance. This means that you might now have to consider whether the communications program was written to work under a specific operating environment as well as a specific operating system.

Although both Windows and OS/2 provide facilities to operate DOS programs, when run in that mode, the program will not support such operating environment features as cursor support, cutting and pasting of information between applications, and the familiar graphical user interface (GUI) of the previously mentioned operating environments.

Modem Support

Due to differences in the design of advanced features into modern modems, their support normally requires the communications program to explicitly support the command set of the modem.

After you select a communications program that satisfies your operating environment and computer platform requirements, you must also consider another important hardware device, the modem you anticipate using. Although most modems support the Hayes Microcomputer Products modem command set, that support primarily references a core set of commands that govern the operation of basic modem functions. As discussed in an earlier chapter, when such features as data compression, flow control, and error detection and correction were added to intelligent modems, vendors incorporated the control of those features in different ways. Some vendors used AT commands, and other vendors used different S Register settings to control new features. This situation resulted in most vendors using proprietary methods to control the operation of modem features beyond the basic modem control functions supported by the standard Hayes modem command set.

Whereas a few years ago the support of the standard Hayes command set was sufficient to operate most modems, today a communications program might include the support of a dozen to fifty or more modems. As an alternative to supporting the command sets used by a large number of modems, some programs provide users with the ability to configure the program to operate with any intelligent modem. In doing so, such programs provide users with a menu of modem functions and enable the entry of the appropriate AT command or S Register setting for each function. Although this requires program users to spend a considerable amount of time looking through a modem manual to locate the command or register setting for each function and then manually enter the function, it also permits the program to support any modem.

Now that we have discussed the relationship of software to the computer platform and modem, we'll turn our attention to the interface between the two devices and the communications program features you might want to consider to control the transfer of data between the devices.

Controlling the Interface

Communications software must provide control over the movement of data between a computer and modem. To help you understand the control features you should consider when examining communications software, we'll examine the flow of data between the two devices and how that flow must be controlled if such modem features as data compression and error detection and correction are enabled.

Figure 9.1 illustrates in schematic diagram format the relationship of the flow of data between a computer and modem. Note that the computer's data transfer rate does not necessarily have to equal the modem's operating rate. In fact, when you use a compression performing modem, you will normally use the communications program to set the computer's serial port to a data rate two to four times the operating rate of the modem. For correct operation during data compression, the data rate into the modem must exceed its operating rate. For example, if a modem has an average compression ratio of 4:1 and an operating rate of 9600 bps, the computer's serial port should be set to transfer data to the modem at four times the modem's operating rate, or 38,400 bps. However, because the compression ratio varies based on the compressibility of data, what happens when the modem cannot compress data or compresses data at a lower compression ratio?

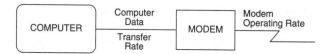

FIGURE 9.1.

Data flow between a computer and a modem.

If data is flowing into the modem at 38,400 bps but the modem compresses data at a rate less than a 4:1 compression ratio, its output is less than its input. This means that within a very short period, the modem's limited buffer storage will overflow and data will be lost. Obviously, modem users do not want this to happen and can prevent this situation from occurring by enabling flow control.

●

For a modem to operate effectively when compressing data, the computer serial port's operating rate must exceed the modem's operating rate.

Flow Control

Flow control can be defined as the orderly regulation of the transfer of data. You can turn on or enable modem flow control via an appropriate command or S Register setting. When turned on, the modem signals the attached computer whenever its buffer fills to a pre-defined level. That signal tells the computer to suspend transmission. When the modem's buffer is emptied to a certain level, it sends another signal to the computer, which disables flow control.

There are three types of flow control supported by most modems: inband signaling, outband signaling, and ENQ/ACK. Inband signaling references the transmission of XON and XOFF control characters. Outband signaling references the modem raising and lowering the Clear to Send (CTS) signal on the RS-232 interface, whereas ENQ/ACK references a signaling method similar to XON and XOFF used primarily by Hewlett-Packard terminal devices. Thus, your communications software that turns your computer into a terminal must support one or more modem flow control techniques to prevent the loss of data when the modem operates in its compressed mode. In addition, flow control becomes a necessity when a modem performs error detection and correction, and transmission errors occur.

Flow control is the orderly regulation of data transfer. To prevent the loss of data, the communications program must be configured to support the method of flow control used by the modem.

This is because the modem must retain blocks of data in memory until they are positively acknowledged. If line errors occur, the modem's buffer rapidly fills as additional data is transferred from the computer to the modem, and the modem cannot purge previously transmitted data from memory. Again the modem will transmit a flow control signal to the computer that the communications program operating on the computer must recognize. Now that we have an understanding of flow control and the relationship between the computer data transfer rate and the modem operating rate, we'll discuss the range of rates supported by communications programs and how those rates are set up.

Operating Rates

The computer data transfer rates supported by most communications programs range from 300 to 38,400 bps. Typically, a 38,400 bps rate is set when a modem operating at 9600 bps has its compression feature enabled. Other computer data transfer rates supported by some communications programs include 57,600 bps and 76,800 bps, which are normally used to support compression performing modems operating at 14,400 and 19,200 bps, respectively.

Prior to setting the computer data transfer operating rate, you should ensure that the modem's serial port is set to auto-baud detect, or you should set it to the computer data transfer rate you want to use. Otherwise, the modem will not be able to recognize the data being transferred to it from the computer due to an interface data rate mismatch.

You set both the modem serial port and the modem operating rate via command codes or S register settings. Both settings are independent of the capability of the communications program because they are dependent on the operating capability built into the modem. Thus, the method by which the communications program enables you to set those operating rates should not be evaluated because the actual settings depend on the modem used.

Dialing Directory

One of the more important features of a communications program is its dialing directory. The basic function of the dialing directory is to enable a user to enter telephone numbers to be dialed as well as to provide a description of each number. Most communications programs expand the functionality of the dialing directory by building into the directory the ability of the user to assign, view, and modify different communications settings. Some of the more common communications settings that are changed through the use of a dialing directory include the operating rate of the computer's serial port, parity, the number of data bits and stop bits per character, the file transfer protocol to be used as a default when performing file transfers, the type of terminal the communications software emulates, and whether or not a script file is associated with the dialing directory. Of those previously mentioned settings, the ones most persons will want to evaluate are the range of serial port operating rates supported, the types of file transfer protocols and terminal emulations included with the program, and the inclusion of a script programming language, as well as the commands supported by the programming language and its ease of use.

The file transfer protocols supported govern your ability to upload and download files from bulletin board systems, other personal computers, and information utilities. Although almost all communications programs support a core set of file transfer protocols, some programs include WXMODEM, ZMODEM, and other protocols that were developed to satisfy one or more communications requirements lacking from other protocols. For example, ZMODEM uses a 32-bit CRC, which reduces the probability of an undetected error to an order of magnitude below other file transfer protocols, whereas WXMODEM facilitates the transfer of files through packet networks.

The types of terminal emulations supported by the communications program govern its capability to communicate with different types of computer systems. This can be extremely important when the program is accessing mainframe and minicomputers that are designed to support certain types of full-screen terminal devices. Those computers transmit special control codes to perform such functions as clearing the screen, moving the cursor to a specific location, displaying different colors, establishing protected fields, and highlighting information. Without the correct terminal emulator, your personal computer will more than likely fail to correctly display information received from a distant computer. In addition, certain keystrokes from your computer will more than likely be received incorrectly at the mainframe or minicomputer when you do not use a correct terminal emulator. This problem occurs because terminal emulators use different key combinations to represent certain control keys, such as IBM program function (PF) keys that are not included on conventional personal computer keyboards.

A script programming language provides you with the ability to automate communications functions, such as logging onto an electronic mail system, checking for new mail, and, if found, downloading the messages in your mailbox. Some communications programs include a script learning capability. This feature enables you to perform the required

> ⬤
> The dialing directory is the key to the functionality of most communications programs because it provides users with the ability to assign, view, and modify different communications parameter settings associated with each telephone number in the directory.

> ⬤
> The terminal emulations supported by a communications program governs its capability to communicate with different types of mainframe and minicomputer systems.

operation once while the program constructs the appropriate script language commands that duplicate the functions manually performed. Thereafter, you can invoke the script to automatically perform the series of manual operations you previously conducted.

The following list shows the communications program features you might want to consider. This list can be used to evaluate the suitability of two or more programs you are considering purchasing or as a mechanism to compare the functionality of a program against your communications requirements.

> Operating system compatibility
>
> Operating environment compatibility
>
> Modem support
>
> Flow control support
>
> Serial port operating rates supported
>
> Number of dialing directory entries allowed
>
> File transfer protocols supported
>
> Terminal emulations supported
>
> Script programming language support

Now that we have reviewed the major features of personal computer communications programs, we'll focus on the use of those features by performing a communications session with a bulletin board system using ProcommPlus.

Using ProcommPlus

ProcommPlus is a comprehensive but easy-to-use communications program when you understand the use of a few Alt key combinations. After you install the program on your computer and invoke its operation, the program displays its name on-screen as it loads, then displays a screen in which only the top and bottom lines display information. This initial program screen is illustrated in Figure 9.2. Although the top line is self-explanatory, the bottom line warrants an explanation for persons not familiar with this program.

The bottom line on the ProcommPlus display can be considered as a status line that indicates the state of key program functions as well as provides users with a prompt concerning the use of the program. That prompt is the message "Alt-Z FOR HELP," which indicates the key combination to press for assistance. Other information displayed on the status line in Figure 9.2 includes the current terminal emulation (ANSI), the transmission mode (FDX), the operating rate, the parity, data and stop bit settings (1200 E71), whether the program's log facility was enabled or disabled (LOG CLOSED), whether each line of information displayed is printed (PRINT OFF), and the status of communications (OFF-LINE). Later in this chapter when we use the program to establish a communications session, we will note how several entries on the status line automatically change.

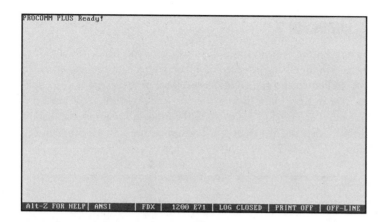

FIGURE 9.2.

Initial ProcommPlus program screen with status information displayed on the bottom line of the display.

ProcommPlus Command Menu

To see the ProcommPlus help facility, press the Alt+Z key combination. Doing so results in the display of the program's command menu, which is illustrated in Figure 9.3. In examining the command menu displayed in Figure 9.3, note that most program functions are invoked by pressing two keys. Because this menu is easy to invoke, it provides a rapid mechanism to "look up" keystrokes required to perform different communications functions without requiring the use of the program's manual. As we examine the use of the program, we will note how several communications functions are easily invoked by pressing a multikey combination.

```
PROCOMM PLUS Ready!
┌────────────────────────────────────────────────────────────┐
│         P R O C O M M   P L U S   C O M M A N D   M E N U   │
├────────────────────────────────────────────────────────────┤
│      ─▶ COMMUNICATIONS ◀─              ─▶ SET UP ◀─          │
│   ── BEFORE ──      ── AFTER ──    Setup Facility .. Alt-S   │
│ Dialing Directory Alt-D  Hang Up ......... Alt-H  Line/Port Setup . Alt-P │
│                   Exit ............ Alt-X  Translate Table . Alt-W │
│   ── DURING ──                     Key Mapping .... Alt-F8  │
│ Script Files ... Alt-F5  Send Files ...... PgUp  ─▶ OTHER FUNCTIONS ◀─ │
│ Meta Keys ....... Alt-M  Receive Files .... PgDn  File Directory .. Alt-F │
│ Redisplay ...... Alt-F6  Log File On/Off  Alt-F1  Change Directory Alt-F7 │
│ Clear Screen ... Alt-C  Log File Pause . Alt-F2  View a File ..... Alt-U │
│ Break Key ....... Alt-B  Screen Snapshot . Alt-G  Editor .......... Alt-A │
│ Elapsed Time .... Alt-T  Printer On/Off .. Alt-L  DOS Gateway .... Alt-F4 │
│   ── OTHER ──                      Program Info .... Alt-I   │
│ Chat Mode ....... Alt-O  Record Mode ..... Alt-R  Clipboard ....... Alt-= │
│ Host Mode ....... Alt-Q  Duplex Toggle ... Alt-E  Monitor Mode ... Ctrl-\ │
│ Auto Answer ..... Alt-Y  CR-CR/LF Toggle  Alt-F3  Toggle Status .. Ctrl-] │
│ Init Modem ...... Alt-J  Kermit Server Cmd Alt-K  Toggle Lines ... Ctrl-- │
│ Reset Terminal .. Alt-U  Screen Pause .... Alt-N  Pulldown Menu Key ... ` │
├────────────────────────────────────────────────────────────┤
│              Press Alt-Z for On-Line Help                   │
└────────────────────────────────────────────────────────────┘
```

FIGURE 9.3.

ProcommPlus command menu screen display indicates the key and key combinations required to invoke different program functions.

As noted in Figure 9.3, the first key combination listed is Alt+D, which invokes the dialing directory. That key combination is listed first in the command menu because the use of the dialing directory provides users with the ability to set communications parameters as well as establish communications sessions using previously specific communications parameter settings.

Dialing Directory

Figure 9.4 illustrates the ProcommPlus dialing directory in which the author entered directory information for all entries except the first, which is the default entry that enables you to dial the bulletin board system of the developer of the program. After you move the highlight bar over an entry in the dialing directory and press Enter, the program transmits the telephone number stored in the entry to the modem for automatic dialing. Because the highlight bar is over the first entry, we'll communicate with the program developer by pressing Enter.

FIGURE 9.4.

ProcommPlus dialing directory screen.

```
DIALING DIRECTORY: PCPLUS.DIR

         NAME                          NUMBER      BAUD PDS D P   SCRIPT
  1 datastorm                     8,3148750503    2400 N81 F D
  2 tymnet                          9,929-0804    2400 E71 F D
  3 mci                         9,,18002346245    2400 O71 F D
  4 frederick engineering         8,301-290-6944  2400 N81 F D
  5 delphi                       9,1,800-3654636  2400 N81 F D
  6 network world                 8,508,620-1160  2400 N81 F D
  7 tymnet                          9,923-7590    1200 O71 F D
  8 Telenet                         9,743-8844    2400 E71 F D
  9 the corner  gh                8,206-242-8574  2400 N81 F D
 10 boyan                         8,410-730-2917  2400 N81 H D

  PgUp Scroll Up     Space Mark Entry      C Clear Marked      L Print Directory
  PgDn Scroll Dn     Enter Dial Selected   E Erase Entry(s)    P Dialing Codes
  Home First Page    D Dial Entry(s)       F Find Entry        X Exchange Dir
  End Last Page      M Manual Dial         N Find Next         T Toggle Display
  ↑/↓ Select Entry   A Add Entry           G Goto Entry        S Sort Directory
  Esc Exit           R Revise Entry        J Jot Notes

  Choice:

 Alt-Z FOR HELP | ANSI |    FDX  |  1200 E71 |  LOG CLOSED |  PRINT OFF |  OFF-LINE
```

Figure 9.5 illustrates the establishment of a communications session using ProcommPlus. Note that certain entries in the status line changed to correspond to the settings in the dialing directory entry invoked. Thus, "2400 N81" indicates that the serial port of the computer is transmitting data at 2400 bps using eight data bits per character, no parity bit, and one stop bit per character. Also note that because a communications session was established, the extreme right of the status line now contains the entry "ON-LINE."

FIGURE 9.5.

Establishing a communications session.

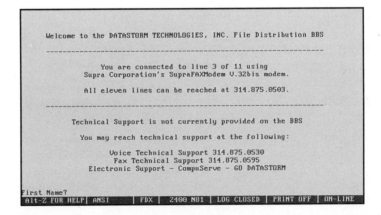

```
   Welcome to the DATASTORM TECHNOLOGIES, INC. File Distribution BBS

   ----------------------------------------------------------------------

                    You are connected to line 3 of 11 using
             Supra Corporation's SupraFAXModem V.32bis modem.

             All eleven lines can be reached at 314.875.0503.

   ----------------------------------------------------------------------

        Technical Support is not currently provided on the BBS

        You may reach technical support at the following:

                Voice Technical Support 314.875.0530
                  Fax Technical Support 314.875.0595
             Electronic Support - CompuServe - GO DATASTORM

 First Name?
 Alt-Z FOR HELP | ANSI |    FDX  |  2400 N81 |  LOG CLOSED |  PRINT OFF |  ON-LINE
```

In the event one or more dialing directory entries do not satisfy your communications requirements, you can use the dialing directory screen to change various communications settings. Figure 9.6 illustrates the previously illustrated dialing directory screen in which the R key was pressed to revise the selected entry. This results in the display of a window labeled "Revise Entry 1," which lists the communications-related features, functions, and settings you can revise. As you move the highlight bar down the second column in that window, certain entries cause other windows to be displayed. When the highlight bar is positioned over the protocol entry, the program displays a window listing the file transfer protocols supported, which enables you to move the highlight bar over a file transfer protocol and press Enter to assign a new protocol to the selected entry in the dialing directory.

The ProcommPlus dialing directory provides users with the ability to store telephone numbers for automated dialing as well as assign various communications parameter settings to each entry.

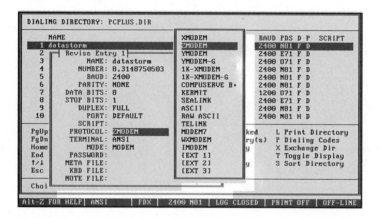

FIGURE 9.6.

Using the dialing directory to change the file transfer protocol assigned to a directory entry.

Figure 9.7 illustrates how you can use ProcommPlus to select or change a file transfer protocol when you are online. Pressing the Page Down key causes the program to display a window labeled "Download Protocols." That window enables you to change a previously established default protocol or press the Enter key to retain the default file transfer protocol.

```
T - TYPE file to your screen
C -┌─ Download Protocols - 227139584 bytes free ├─
A -│
X -│    X) XMODEM                  A) ASCII
O -│    Z) ZMODEM                  R) RAW ASCII
Y -│    Y) YMODEM (Batch)          T) TELINK
G -│    G) YMODEM-G (Batch)        M) MODEM7
S -│    O) 1K-XMODEM               W) WXMODEM
K -│    E) 1K-XMODEM-G             I) IMODEM
W -│    C) COMPUSERVE B+           1) [EXT 1]
Z -│    K) KERMIT                  2) [EXT 2]
   │    S) SEALINK                 3) [EXT 3]
Choo│
    │ Your Selection:    (press ENTER for ZMODEM)
File└─
File Size: 52 Records
 Protocol: XMODEM
Est. Time: 0 mins, 39 secs at 2400 bps

Awaiting Start Signal
(Ctrl-X to abort)

Alt-Z FOR HELP| ANSI    | FDX  | 2400 N81 | LOG CLOSED | PRINT OFF | ON-LINE
```

FIGURE 9.7.

Changing the download file transfer protocol while online is accomplished by pressing the Page Down key and selecting the desired protocol.

After you initiate a file transfer, ProcommPlus automatically provides you with a visual indication of the status of the transfer by displaying a window indicating the progress of the transfer. Figure 9.8 shows the progress of a file transfer when the ZMODEM protocol is used. The window in the right portion of Figure 9.8, which illustrates information about the file transfer, varies with respect to information content based on the file transfer protocol used. Some protocols, such as XMODEM, do not transfer information concerning the file size or its date of creation or last modification. For those protocols, ProCommPlus cannot compute the percentage of the file transmitted nor display the progress of the file transfer visually as a horizontal bar as shown in the lower portion of the window displayed in Figure 9.8. In examining the file transfer window, note that one entry is "Average CPS." By transferring the same file using different file transfer protocols, you can determine which protocol provides you with a higher throughput based on a specific communications environment.

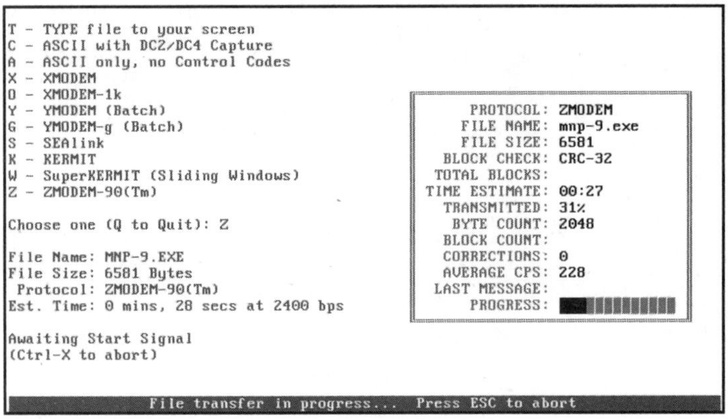

FIGURE 9.8.

The ProcommPlus file transfer window indicating the status of a file transfer using the ZMODEM protocol.

```
T - TYPE file to your screen
C - ASCII with DC2/DC4 Capture
A - ASCII only, no Control Codes
X - XMODEM
O - XMODEM-1k
Y - YMODEM (Batch)                    PROTOCOL: ZMODEM
G - YMODEM-g (Batch)                 FILE NAME: mnp-9.exe
S - SEAlink                          FILE SIZE: 6581
K - KERMIT                         BLOCK CHECK: CRC-32
W - SuperKERMIT (Sliding Windows)  TOTAL BLOCKS:
Z - ZMODEM-90(Tm)                 TIME ESTIMATE: 00:27
                                    TRANSMITTED: 31%
Choose one (Q to Quit): Z            BYTE COUNT: 2048
                                     BLOCK COUNT:
File Name: MNP-9.EXE                 CORRECTIONS: 0
File Size: 6581 Bytes                AVERAGE CPS: 228
 Protocol: ZMODEM-90(Tm)            LAST MESSAGE:
Est. Time: 0 mins, 28 secs at 2400 bps  PROGRESS: ██▌▌▌▌▌▌▌▌

Awaiting Start Signal
(Ctrl-X to abort)

         File transfer in progress...  Press ESC to abort
```

What Have You Learned?

1. Both the support of a specific operating system and the operating environment govern the capability of a communications program to operate on a specific computer platform with a graphical user interface.

2. Support of the Hayes modem command set normally references the operation of basic modem functions. For the control of advanced modem functions, the communications program must support the modem you want to use.

3. For a modem to operate effectively when compressing data requires the computer's serial port operating rate to exceed the modem's operating rate.

4. Flow control is the orderly regulation of data transfer. To prevent the loss of data between a computer and modem requires the communications program to be configured to support the method of flow control used by the modem.

5. The dialing directories of most communications programs provide both a facility to select and dial different telephone numbers as well as the capability to assign specific communications parameter settings to each entry.

6. The terminal emulations supported by a communications program govern its capability to be used to communicate as a full-screen terminal device with minicomputers and mainframe computers.

7. A script programming language permits predefined communications functions to be automated.

8. The capability of a program to display different information concerning the status of a file transfer depends on the protocol used to transfer the file.

Quiz for Chapter 9

1. Hayes Microcomputer Products modem command set compatibility refers to:
   a. The control of basic modem functions.
   b. The control of advanced modem functions.
   c. Flow control.
   d. Data compression.

2. XON/XOFF is:
   a. Seldom used.
   b. Always enabled.
   c. A method of flow control.
   d. A data compression function.

3. To effectively use a compression performing modem:
   a. Set the serial port rate equal to the modem operating rate.
   b. Set the serial port rate higher than the modem operating rate.
   c. Set the serial port rate lower than the modem operating rate.

   d. Set the serial port rate to automatic speed detect.

4. A compression performing modem operating at 14,400 bps that has a 4:1 average compression ratio requires which computer serial port operating rate to effectively operate?
   a. 14,400 bps.
   b. 28,800 bps.
   c. 55,400 bps.
   d. 57,600 bps.

5. An example of outband signaling is:
   a. XON/XOFF.
   b. ENQ/ACK.
   c. RS-232.
   d. CTS.

6. The basic function of a dialing directory is to:
   a. Store address information.
   b. Enable a user to enter telephone numbers to be dialed.
   c. Store communications parameters.
   d. Enable flow control.

7. An example of a file transfer protocol that uses a 32-bit cyclic redundancy check (CRC) is:

   a. YMODEM.

   b. XMODEM.

   c. XYMODEM.

   d. ZMODEM.

8. Information concerning communications parameter settings is displayed on the ProcommPlus:

   a. Main menu.

   b. Status line.

   c. Protocol window.

   d. Log facility.

9. The key or key combination required to be pressed to invoke the ProcommPlus line hang-up function is:

   a. Alt+X.

   b. Page Down.

   c. Alt+Q.

   d. Alt+H.

10. Information concerning the progress of a line transfer displayed by ProcommPlus varies based on:

   a. The file transfer protocol used.

   b. The average CPS.

   c. The date the file was created.

   d. The size of the file.

Alternatives in Local Area Networks

About This Chapter

This chapter begins by describing the characteristics of an ideal local area network (LAN) and the major obstacles to achieving the ideal. The most common types of existing LAN architectures—contention-access-based coaxial cable systems, token passing systems, polled-access-based coaxial cable systems, and frequency-division broadband systems—are discussed through examples of existing LANs. LANs examined in this chapter include the different types of Ethernet networks defined by the Intel, Digital Equipment, and Xerox specification and the IEEE 802.3 standards, Datapoint's ARCnet, and IBM's 4 and 16 Mbps token-ring networks.

What Is a LAN?

A LAN is a data communications facility located within a single building or campus that provides all high-speed switched connections to its terminal processors and peripheral devices.

In its most basic form, a LAN is a data communications facility providing high-speed switched connections between processors, peripherals, and terminals within a single building or campus. Historically, LANs have evolved from the data processing or office processing industry where economics suggest relatively expensive storage devices and printers should be shared by multiple computers. Thus, LANs have evolved partly in response to the emergence of low-cost computing and its need for high-cost peripherals. Indeed, the first-generation LANs were actually one form of distributed computer systems using proprietary high-speed data links between processing nodes and peripheral equipment. A second rationale for the growth in the use of LANs is related to the need of modern organizations for distributed computing. A LAN permits computing power to be directly distributed to the desktop yet permits the desktop user to tap into other computer resources connected to the LAN. This distribution of computer power enables users to be more productive and in many organizations also enables conventional data centers to be eliminated or reduced in size, a process commonly referred to as downsizing.

LAN Versus Other Techniques

A perspective of a local area network as a digital communications facility is shown in Figure 10.1. This illustration depicts the bandwidth versus distance capabilities of three data communications technologies: computer buses, voiceband data links, and LANs. The computer buses are internal to a computer mainframe. They achieve very high data transfers by using high clock rates (for example, a few MHz) and parallel transmission (for example, 32 bits per clock cycle). Such systems are economical and practical only at distances up to a few meters. Voiceband data transmission uses readily available telephone wire pairs with modems. These systems are virtually unlimited in distance, but the standard analog telephone channel usually restricts voiceband data rates to 19,200 bps. From a cost-effectiveness point of view, 9600 bps is very popular for dial-up data communications.

Each of the three data communications technologies have their own particular strengths and weaknesses when considering bandwidth versus distance trade-offs.

As can be seen in Figure 10.1, the capabilities of a typical LAN represent a compromise between long distances and wide bandwidths. Some computer architectures have moved in on the region occupied by LANs by moving away from high-speed parallel buses to more loosely coupled distributed systems. Thus, the LAN region is overlapped on the left edge by distributed computer systems. Similarly, newly developing digital telephone systems are overlapping the LAN region on the bottom by providing moderate data rates (up to a few hundred kilobits per second) as a low-cost addition to basic telephone service.

The distance versus data rate aspect of a local area network depicted in Figure 10.1 actually represents only one level of definition of a LAN. As the market and technology have grown, so has the recognition that a LAN should solve or alleviate more problems pertaining to data communications than merely the data transmission problem. The data communications manager or service organization responsible for a particular building or campus is typically concerned with various applications and associated types of equipment. If these different applications can be supported by one transmission facility, one type of hardware and software interface, and one set of maintenance procedures, total systems costs are reduced, and overall administration is greatly simplified. For example, Figure 10.2 illustrates a local area network serving several independent applications.

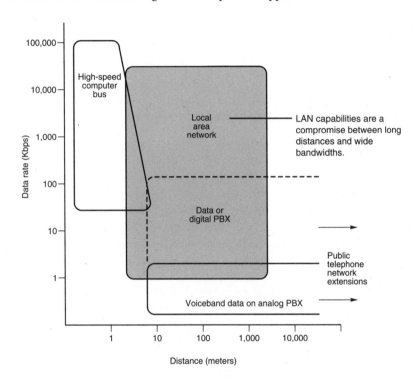

FIGURE 10.1.

Distance versus data rate comparison.

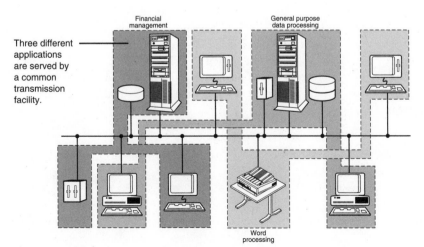

FIGURE 10.2.

Local area network supporting multiple independent applications.

The next section presents the attributes of an ideal local area network—one that is supportive of all applications. In the succeeding sections, present-day LANs are described and compared to the ideal as a means of contrasting one type of LAN with another.

The Ideal LAN

The ideal LAN should provide the same ease of access and equipment utilization that is found in a building's AC circuit.

The ideal LAN would be an information distribution system that is as easy to use as the conventional AC power distribution system in a building. Thus, adding a data terminal, processor, or peripheral to a local area network should require nothing more than plugging it into a conveniently located access port. When plugged in, it should communicate intelligently with any other device on the network. This ideal system is summarized by the features that make the AC power system so easy to use:

- One-time installation
- Widespread access
- Application independence
- Excess capacity
- Easy maintenance and administration

The features identified in this list have been developed over the years to minimize life-cycle costs for supplying AC power within a building. Although the costs of a typical installation can be reduced by wiring only to locations with immediate electrical needs, the costs of only small amounts of rewiring to supply additional locations at a later date would more than offset the initial savings. To achieve a one-time installation, it is necessary to provide widespread access—that is, an electrical outlet virtually everywhere one might be needed. Furthermore, the capacity at every outlet is generally greater than the needs of the electrical appliances that connect to it. Adding wiring or rewiring becomes necessary only for particularly high-power consuming devices (for example, those needing 240 volts or dedicated, high-current circuits).

If an information distribution system were available with all the desirable properties listed previously, it would mean that telephones, data terminals, printers, and storage devices could be moved as easily as unplugging and plugging in a lamp. Moreover, the equipment could be supplied by various vendors. Although such an ideal system does not now exist, local area networks of several forms represent some of the first steps in the development of such a system.

Major Obstacles to the Ideal LAN

The major obstacles to overcome in the development of the ideal system are summarized in the following sections.

There are four major obstacles that must be overcome in the development of the ideal LAN.

NO SINGLE STANDARD

Due to the continually changing status of LANs and the competitive nature of the vendors, various local area network standards exist—both official and de facto. The situation is improving, however, because even the dominant suppliers who have been protecting their proprietary interfaces are being pressured by a maturing market to release interface specifications.

DIVERSE REQUIREMENTS

The communications needs of a modern office building include voice, video, high-speed data, low-speed data, energy management, fire alarm, security, electronic mail, and so forth. These systems present transmission requirements that vary greatly in terms of data rates, acceptable delivery delays, reliability requirements, and error rate tolerance.

COSTLY TRANSMISSION MEDIA

Being able to deliver tens of megabits per second to one device and only a few thousand bits per second to another implies that the lower rate devices are burdened with a costly transmission media. The best economic solution must involve a hierarchical network design (one with stepped levels of capacity) that allows twisted pair connections for low and medium data rate devices (a low step) feeding into a backbone high bandwidth transmission system (a higher step such as coaxial cable or optical fibers).

SOPHISTICATED FUNCTIONAL REQUIREMENTS

Providing a network with the desired data rates and distances is only one item that must be considered in the data communications problem. Before one data device can communicate intelligently with another, numerous higher level communications functions must be compatible. These include codes, formats, error control, addressing, routing, flow control, configuration management, and cost allocations.

The ISO Model

A formal hierarchical identification of all data communications network functions has been established by the International Standards Organization (ISO) and referred to as the ISO Model for Open Systems Interconnection (OSI). This model, shown in Figure 10.3, identifies seven distinct levels of functional requirements pertaining to data communications networks. The lower three levels of this model were originally proposed by CCITT to encourage vendor commonality in interfacing to public packet switching networks. This standard, designated as the CCITT recommendation X.25, is described in detail in Chapter 11, "Architectures and Packet Networks," along with the ISO model.

FIGURE 10.3.

The ISO Model for Open Systems Interconnection.

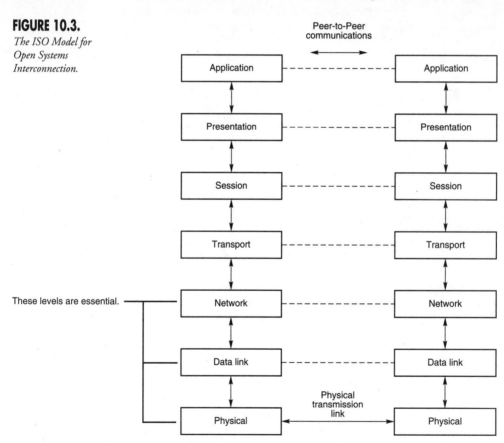

Realization of the ideal LAN would require all levels of functions included in the OSI standard. However, not all levels of the OSI standard need to be implemented to provide effective communications in a LAN. If only the lower levels of the standard exist, a LAN can usefully support the multiple applications shown in Figure 10.2. In essence, the transmission media and lower level interfaces are common so that data can be exchanged within virtual subnetworks—for example, the financial management group indicated in Figure 10.2.

LAN Standards

Local area network standards (as with other communications standards) get established by two groups: dominant manufacturers who attract plug-compatible competitors, and official standards organizations. The leading official standards organization for LANs in the United States is the IEEE 802 Standards Committee. This committee has several working groups responsible for establishing these LAN standards:

- 802.1—Coordinating the interface between OSI Levels 1 & 2 with the five higher level layers
- 802.2—Logical data link standard similar to HDLC and ADCCP
- 802.3—CSMA/CS standard similar to Ethernet
- 802.4—Token bus standard
- 802.5—Token-ring standard

Logical Link Control—IEEE 802.2

To accommodate multiple LAN access methods, the IEEE 802 standards committee separated the OSI Data Link Layer into two sublayers: a logical link control (LLC) sublayer and a media access control (MAC) sublayer, as shown in Figure 10.4. Under working group 802.2, the LLC control procedures have been defined to be basically the same as the CCITT X.25 Link Access Procedure HDLC in a balanced mode (LAPB). The balanced mode is used for peer structured networks wherein any station can originate communications directly with any other station.

Two basic types of services are provided within 802.2 LLC. The type 1 service involves unacknowledged "connectionless" operation wherein the source station sends a message to another station (or stations) without having established a logical connection for sequencing and acknowledging messages. This mode of operation is intended for transmission of messages that are not essential and for systems in which higher levels provide error recovery and sequencing functions (as in Ethernet).

●
A formal data communications hierarchy model containing seven levels of functional requirements has been established by the International Standards Organization.

●
The IEEE 802 standards committee separated the OSI Data Link Layer into LLC and MAC layers.

●
LLC control procedures are similar to CCITT's X.25 Link Access Procedure HDLC in a balanced mode.

FIGURE 10.4.

Relationship of IEEE 802 partition to ISO reference model.

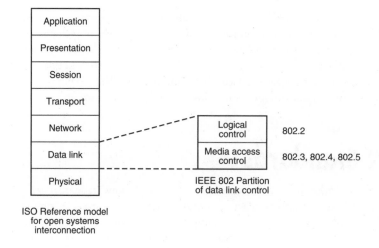

ISO Reference model
for open systems
interconnection

The type 2 service is the more conventional balanced data communications service that establishes logical connections between two LLCs. Each LLC can send and receive both messages and responses. Each LLC also has the responsibility of ensuring complete and accurate deliveries of its outgoing messages.

CSMA/CD—IEEE 802.3

The IEEE 802.3 standard defines the MAC sublayer for Carrier Sense Multiple Access/ Collision Detection and a corresponding physical layer for connection to baseband co-axial cable and twisted pair wiring. The standard is basically patterned after the Ethernet specification.

Variations in the physical layer allow signaling rates of 1, 5, and 10 Mbps. A multidrop coaxial cable segment is limited to 500 meters (with 100 stations) rather than 1500 meters in Ethernet, but there can be as many as five coaxial segments in an IEEE 802.3 system. Later in this chapter, we will examine in detail the original Ethernet and the IEEE 802.3 standards to include network architecture and frame formats.

Token Passing Ring Access— IEEE 802.5

The IEEE 802.5 standard defines a token passing ring method in which access to a shared medium is obtained by the passing of a token. The token, which is a predefined sequence of bits, provides a receiving workstation on a token-ring LAN with the right to transmit a frame or a sequence of frames onto the ring.

When a workstation receives a free token, it builds a frame that includes the destination address of its transmission, its source address, and an information field, as well as a frame check sequence. The latter is used for frame verification similar to the manner in which a CRC or BCC is used. As the frame circulates around the ring, each workstation examines the destination address. If the destination address matches the address of the workstation, the workstation receives data from the information field and sets a field in the frame to indicate the successful receipt of the frame. As the frame continues around the ring, it returns to the originator, which notes the successful transfer of information in the frame. The originator now generates a new token, which provides other workstations with the capability to gain access to the transmission medium.

Ethernet (CSMA/CD)

Although Ethernet was not the first data communications network to technically qualify as a local area network, it is the most important because it represents the first major product offering with nonproprietary communications interfaces and protocols. Using an experimental design developed in a Xerox Corporation research laboratory, Xerox, Digital Equipment, and Intel teamed to define some commercial products based on jointly published communications standards. This action has invited other manufacturers to develop compatible products. The marketing strategy has been successful enough to establish the Ethernet interface as a standard even on systems utilizing transmission media different from the baseband coaxial cable originally specified for use in Ethernet.

> ●
> Ethernet, which uses baseband coaxial cable as its carrier medium, was a joint effort by Xerox, Digital Equipment, and Intel. Ethernet was the first commercially available LAN.

The Ethernet architecture is based in concept on the Aloha satellite communications network developed at the University of Hawaii. The Aloha system allows multiple distributed devices to communicate with each other over a single radio channel using a satellite as a transponder. One station communicates with another by waiting until the radio channel is idle (determined by carrier sensing) and then sending a packet of data with a destination address, a source address, and redundant check bits to detect transmission errors. All idle stations continuously monitor incoming data and accept those packets with their address and valid checksums. Whenever a station receives a new packet, the receiving station returns an acknowledgment to the source. If an originating station receives no acknowledgment within a specified time interval, it retransmits the packet under the assumption that the previous packet was interfered with by noise or by a transmission from another station at the same time. (The latter situation is referred to as a collision.) Ethernet employs the same basic system concept, originally using coaxial cable for distribution throughout a building or campus.

Physical Layer

The transmission media of Ethernet was originally restricted to the use of conventional "thick" coaxial cable using baseband transmission at 10 Mbps. Other media now used for Ethernet transmission includes "thin" coaxial cable and twisted-pair wire. Both types of coaxial cable media support the use of a bus technology, and the use of twisted-pair wire requires the use of a star topology for an Ethernet LAN.

Baseband transmission implies that data is transmitted without the use of a carrier and with only one channel defined in the system. In comparison, broadband signaling results in the bandwidth of the media subdivided by frequency into multiple channels that can support the concurrent transmission of different types of signals, such as voice, data, and video. Figure 10.5 illustrates the operation of baseband and broadband signaling. Under the IEEE 802.3 set of LAN network standards, a broadband Ethernet referred to as 10BASE-36 was standardized. Later in this chapter, we will compare Ethernet to the IEEE 802.3 series of standards.

FIGURE 10.5.

Baseband versus broadband signaling.

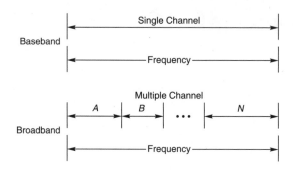

When a station is transmitting, it uses the entire 10 Mbps capacity of the system. Data is encoded using a Manchester code as shown in Figure 10.6. This line code provides a strong timing component for clock recovery because a timing transition always occurs in the middle of every bit. In this type of coding, each bit period is divided into two complementary halves. A negative-to-positive voltage transition in the middle of the bit period designates a binary "1," whereas a positive-to-negative transition represents a binary "0." The Manchester line code has the additional property of always maintaining equal amounts of positive and negative voltages. This method prevents the build-up of a DC component, which simplifies the implementation of decision thresholds in the data detectors.

● Baseband signaling results in one signal on a cable, whereas broadband signaling supports multiple simultaneous signaling on a cable.

● The Manchester code provides a form of carrier in its continuous transition. Multiple stations can enter or leave the line without causing traffic interruptions by using passive taps.

Although the data are not transmitted with a carrier per se, the continuous transitions of the Manchester code provide the equivalent of a carrier, so the channel is easily monitored for activity (for example, by a carrier sense technique). Multiple access to the coaxial cable is provided by passive taps, thereby allowing station connections (called drops) to be added or removed without disrupting traffic in the system.

Another requirement of the transmission link and its associated access electronics is that while transmitting, a transceiver must be capable of detecting the existence of another active transmitter. This is referred to as collision detection. Thus, the three basic steps for accessing an Ethernet are denoted CSMA/CD (Carrier Sense, Multiple Access with Collision Detection).

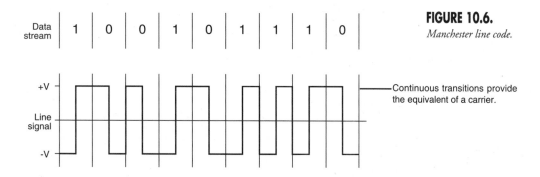

FIGURE 10.6.

Manchester line code.

The capability to detect collisions allows colliding stations to release the channel after using it for only a short period. A conventional Aloha system (one without collision detection), on the other hand, transmits entire messages without knowing whether a collision has occurred. Because an Ethernet station checks for carrier presence before transmitting, collisions occur only if two stations begin transmitting within a time interval equal to the propagation delay between the stations. By restricting the maximum distance between transceivers on a bus-based coaxial cable LAN to 2500 meters, the collision window is limited to 23 microseconds (μs), including amplifier delays.

When a station begins transmitting, it can be sure that no collision will occur if none is detected within a round-trip propagation of 46.4 μs. Because one bit time is 0.1 μs at 10 Mbps, the collision detection decision is made within 464 bit times. The maximum length of a frame is 12,144 bits; thus, the collision detection feature detects a collision very early in the frame to save significant transmission time that would be wasted if the entire frame were transmitted before detection.

Whenever a collision occurs, all colliding stations detect the condition and wait individually random amounts of time before retrying the transmission. Thus, the stations do not wait for acknowledgment timeouts to trigger a retransmission. (Acknowledgments are unnecessary at this level of the protocol but might be used at a higher level to ensure that the message was received at the final destination.) The method of waiting random amounts of time before transmitting reduces the probability of repeated collisions. In heavy traffic conditions, the average delay before retransmission begins to increase after 10 unsuccessful attempts. After 16 collisions, no further attempts are made to transmit that message, and the station is notified of the error by the transceiver.

In preparation for transmitting a data frame, the physical layer must insert a 64-bit preamble so that all receivers on the network can synchronize to the data stream before the desired data frame begins. The preamble consists of alternating ones and zeros, ending in two ones to signify the start of a frame.

A transceiver must be able to detect any other active transmitters on the line while it is transmitting. This is collision detection.

Physical Layer Interface

Standard Ethernet transceiver cable connectors are 15-pin D-shell connectors (MIL-C-24308 or equivalent). The transceiver has a male connector, whereas the station apparatus has a female connector. Thus, the interconnecting cable must have one connector of each type. These are the pin assignments:

1. Shield
2. Collision Presence +
3. Transmit +
4. Reserved
5. Receive +
6. Power return
7. Reserved
8. Reserved
9. Collision Presence –
10. Transmit –
11. Reserved
12. Receive –
13. Power
14. Reserved
15. Reserved

Figure 10.7 illustrates the relationship of Ethernet hardware components required to connect a workstation to a bus-based coaxial cable. The interface board or adapter card is normally installed in a system expansion slot within the system unit of a personal computer. That board or card is also known as a controller and is often referred to as an Ethernet controller.

FIGURE 10.7.

Relationship of Ethernet hardware components.

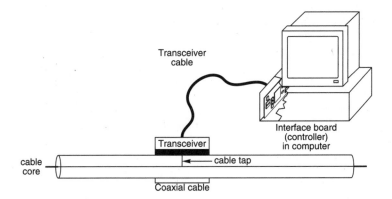

The Ethernet controller formats data from the computer into frames for transmission via the transceiver cable to the transceiver. The transceiver converts unipolar digital signals generated by the computer into Manchester encoded digital signals. In addition, the transceiver is responsible for detecting collisions by examining the voltage level on the cable. That is, when the voltage level rises beyond its normal nominal height, it indicates the occurrence of a collision.

Data Link Layer

The data link layer is primarily concerned with message packaging and link management. It is largely independent of the medium-dependent physical channel. The message packaging function includes

● Framing: Identifying the beginning and end of a message.

● Addressing: Specified fields for source and destination addresses.

● Error checking: Redundant codes for detecting channel errors.

The format of an Ethernet frame is shown in Figure 10.8. The preamble consists of the repeating sequence 101010... for 8 bytes or 64 bits and announces the occurrence of the frame. The preamble's generation and removal are functions of the physical layer. Similarly, the end of a frame is provided by the removal of the carrier sense signal detected by the absence of a bit transition following the last bit of the frame check sequence. Notice that frame sizes must be an integral number of bytes, ranging from 72 to 1526 bytes. (At 8 bits per byte, that's 572 to 12,208 bits.) The TYPE field is reserved to indicate which of several possible higher level protocols might be in use.

> The data link is concerned with message frame format, message addressing, and error checking, and as such is largely independent of the medium-dependent physical channel.

8 Bytes	6 Bytes	6 Bytes	2 Bytes	46-1500 Bytes	4 Bytes
Preamble	Destination Address	Source Address	Type	Data	Frame Check Sequence

FIGURE 10.8.
Ethernet data link frame format.

System Configurations

Besides the single cable system indicated in Figure 10.7, other Ethernet configurations are possible in which several multidrop segments (possibly one in each of several buildings) are interconnected with point-to-point cables and repeaters. Figure 10.9 shows a typical configuration of a multisegment system. The following specifications apply:

> By using point-to-point cables and repeaters, several multidrop segments can be connected to add flexibility to Ethernet systems.

Maximum Lengths:

1500 meters of multidrop cable

1000 additional meters of point-to-point cable between cable segments

300 additional meters in six transceiver cables

50 meters in a single transceiver cable

Maximum Number of Stations:

1024

FIGURE 10.9.

A typical large-scale Ethernet configuration.

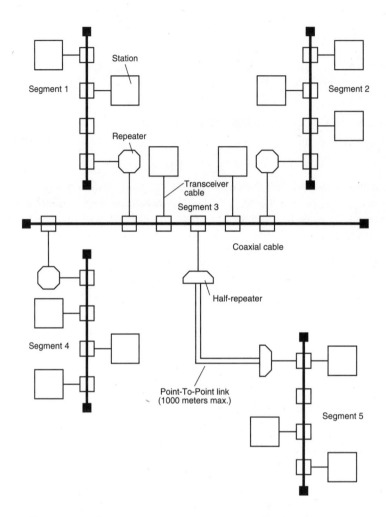

Other Ethernet Networks

In actuality, when referring to Ethernet, we reference a group of networks based on the CSMA/CD access protocol. The original Ethernet standard defined by Xerox, Digital Equipment, and Intel operated at 10 Mbps over a bus-based thick 50 ohm coaxial cable. When Ethernet was standardized by the IEEE 802.3 committee, five additional "Ethernet" standards were promulgated.

Table 10.1 compares the operational characteristics of each IEEE 802.3 network standard to the original Ethernet standard.

Table 10.1. Ethernet and IEEE 802.3 network characteristics.

Operational Characteristics	Ethernet	10BASE-5	10BASE-2	1BASE-5	10BASE-T	10BROAD36
Operating rate Mbps	10	10	10	1	10	10
Access protocol	CSMA/CD	CSMA/CD	CSMA/CD	CSMA/CD	CSMA/CD	CSMA/CD
Type of signaling	baseband	baseband	baseband	baseband	baseband	broadband
Data encoding	Manchester	Manchester	Manchester	Manchester	Manchester	Manchester
Maximum segment length (meters)	500	500	185	250	100	1800
Stations/ segment	100	100	30	12/hub	12/hub	100
Media	50 ohm coaxial (thick)	50 ohm coaxial (thick)	50 ohm coaxial (thin)	unshielded twisted pair	unshielded twisted pair	75 ohm coaxial
Topology	bus	bus	bus	star	star	bus

The IEEE uses the general format "s type l" to develop the name of each CSMA/CD network. Here, "s" references the speed in Mbps; "type" indicates the type of signaling, either BASE for baseband or BROAD for broadband; and "l" generally indicates the maximum segment length in hundreds of meters. For example, 10BASE-5 denotes the standard for a 10 Mbps baseband LAN that has a maximum segment length of 500 meters and uses the CSMA/CD access protocol. Readers should note that "l" does not always indicate the maximum segment length or an accurate maximum segment length. For example, 10BASE-2 has a maximum segment length of 185 meters, and 10BASE-T, in which T indicates the use of twisted-pair wiring, has a maximum segment length of 100 meters.

● The IEEE 802.3 committee defined five additional types of CSMA/CD networks.

Under the IEEE 802.3 standard, a few minor changes occurred to the Ethernet frame illustrated in Figure 10.8 that resulted in the incompatibility of equipment designed for use in computers based on the original Ethernet specification and the IEEE 802.3 frame format.

Figure 10.10 illustrates the IEEE 802.3 data link frame format. In comparing that format to the Ethernet data link frame format illustrated in Figure 10.8, note that the Preamble field was reduced to seven bytes, and a Start of Frame Delimiter field was added under the IEEE 802.3 frame format. The Start of Frame Delimiter field is actually a continuation of the preamble, with the sequence 10101011. However, the ending two bits are 11 rather than the 10 contained in the Ethernet Preamble field.

Another difference between the two frame formats is the replacement of the Type field by a Length field in the IEEE 802.3 frame. Here the length field specifies the number of bytes that follow that field as data.

● Under the IEEE 802.3 frame format, the Ethernet Type field was replaced by a Length field.

FIGURE 10.10.

IEEE 802.3 data link frame format.

IEEE 802.3

Preamble	Start of Frame Delimiter	Destination Address	Source Address	Length	Data	Frame Check Sequence
7 bytes	1 byte	2/6 bytes	2/6 bytes	2 bytes	46-1500 bytes	4 bytes

10BASE-5

> The IEEE 10BASE-5 network standard resulted in changes in terminology of hardware used in the original Ethernet network.

Although a 10BASE-5 network follows the same configuration rules as the original Ethernet network, certain changes in terminology cause some confusion to many persons. To alleviate that potential confusion, Figure 10.11 illustrates the changes in terminology between the original Ethernet 50 ohm coaxial cable bus-based network and the IEEE 802.3 10BASE-5 bus-based network.

As indicated in Figure 10.11, the controller under 10BASE-5 is now referred to as a NIC (pronounced "nick"), or network interface card. The transceiver cable is now known as an AUI, or Attachment Unit Interface, and the transceiver is called a MAU (pronounced to rhyme with "cow") of media attachment unit.

FIGURE 10.11.

Terminology changes between Ethernet and IEEE 10BASE-5.

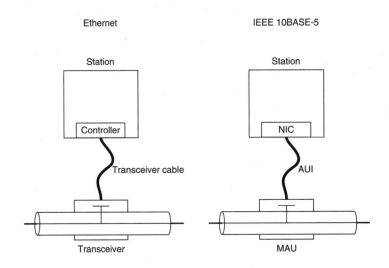

Legend:
AUI = Attachment Unit Interface
MAU = Media Attachment Unit
NIC = Network Interface Card

Most 10BASE-5 NICs include both a DB-15 and a BNC connector. The DB-15 provides a connection to the AUI, whereas the BNC permits the use of the NIC on a 10BASE-2 network. Thus, the dual connectors permit the use of the NIC on two types of 802.3 standards.

10BASE-2

A 10BASE-2 network is based on the use of thin coaxial cable that provides a degree of cabling flexibility not obtainable with the thick coaxial cable used with a 10BASE-5 network. In addition, the use of thin coaxial cable makes cabling more economical. A 10BASE-2 workstation is connected to the thin coaxial cable by BNC connectors, which are also referred to as barrel connectors.

Figure 10.12 illustrates the cabling of stations to a 10BASE-2 network. This type of Ethernet network permits a maximum of 30 stations per cable segment. You can extend a 10BASE-2 network through the use of inter repeater cable segments (IRCS), or you can combine 10BASE-2 and 10BASE-5 networks, although you must ensure when doing so that you do not violate any cabling rules. Refer to the book *Ethernet Networks,* written by Gilbert Held and published by John Wiley & Sons, for specific information concerning Ethernet IEEE 802.3 cabling restrictions and the interconnection of different types of IEEE 802.3 networks.

●

A 10BASE-2 network is limited to 30 stations per segment and uses thin coaxial cable for the transmission media.

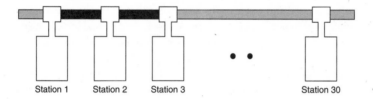

Station 1　Station 2　Station 3　　　　Station 30

FIGURE 10.12.

Cabling a 10BASE-2 network.

10BASE-T

Another series of configurations is obtainable through the use of 10BASE-T, which is a more modern standard that allows the construction of 10 Mbps Ethernet LANs over unshielded twisted-pair wire. Under the 10BASE-T standard, which is also referred to as the IEEE 802.3i standard, workstations are cabled using twisted-pair wire to medium access units (MAUs). Each MAU normally has a built-in attachment interface unit (AIU) that can be cabled to a coaxial transceiver attached to a coaxial cable. Thus, workstations can be configured in a star topology and cabled to a bus structured backbone cable that serves to interconnect MAUs. Figure 10.13 illustrates a hybrid Ethernet media configuration in which personal computer workstations are cabled to MAUs via the use of twisted-pair wire. The MAUs in turn are connected to a coaxial cable that not only links MAUs, but in addition provides access to a mainframe computer.

FIGURE 10.13.

Hybrid Ethernet media configuration.

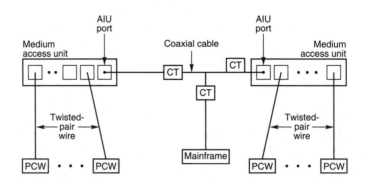

Legend

PCW = Personal Computer Workstation

AIU = Attachment Interface Unit

CT = Coaxial Transceiver

Token Passing Networks

Token passing networks provide access to the network by only one station at a time—the one with the token that is ready to send a message.

Because access to a CSMA network involves a certain amount of contention (competition) between stations trying to send a message at the same time, the behavior of the network must be analyzed and controlled statistically. Token passing networks, on the other hand, provide a different access procedure. Access is determined by which station has the token; that is, only one station at a time, the one with the token, is given the opportunity to seize the channel. The token is passed from one idle station to another until a station with a pending message receives it. After the message is sent, the token is passed to the next station. In essence, a token passing network is a distributed polling network.

Token topologies can be either a token passing ring or a token passing bus; each has its own peculiar strengths and weaknesses.

Two basic topologies (configurations or arrangements) exist for token passing networks: token passing rings and token passing buses. In a token passing ring, shown in Figure 10.14, the closed loop topology defines the logical topology (that is, the order in which the token is circulated). A token passing bus, shown in Figure 10.15, has more operational flexibility because the token passing order is defined by tables in each station. If a station (for example, a printer) never originates communications, it will be a terminate-only station, and it need not be in the polling sequence. If a station needs a high priority, it can appear more than once in the polling sequence.

Besides the operational differences between bus and ring topologies, there are other major contrasts, included in the following list:

- A ring requires an active interface module in series with the transmission link. A bus uses a passive tap like a CSMA system.

- The point-to-point nature of a ring's transmission links implies that the signal quality is easily controlled. Multiple taps in a linear bus system, on the other hand, each contribute to signal distortions.

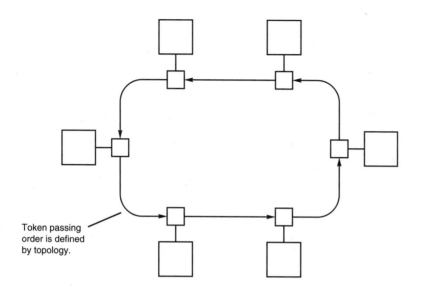

FIGURE 10.14.

Token passing ring.

Token passing
order is defined
by topology.

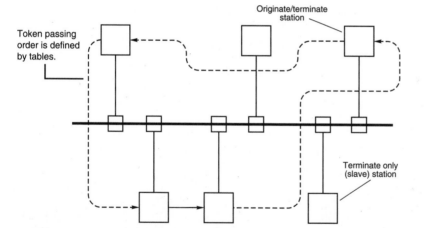

FIGURE 10.15.

*Representative access
sequence in token
passing bus.*

Originate/terminate
station

Token passing
order is defined
by tables.

Terminate only
(slave) station

● A ring has no inherent (built-in) distance limitation (as does the bus) because there is no delay dependence in its operation, and the access taps at each station serve as regenerative repeaters to the digital signals.

● A bus allocates the entire channel to an active device. The channel of a ring can be subdivided into time division multiplexed subchannels for time-continuous lower data rate applications. Figure 10.16 shows a ring with time division multiplexed subchannels. Such a system, also referred to as a loop, typically requires a unique control node to define framing for the subchannels. Access to the TDM channels is distributed by passing tokens.

FIGURE 10.16.

*Time division
multiplex loop.*

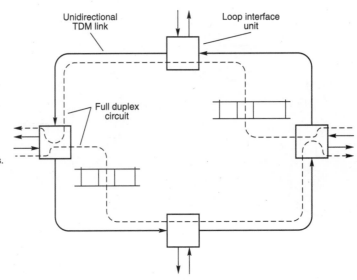

The ring topology is ideally suited to the particular capabilities of fiber-optic transmission. As discussed in a previous chapter, optical fibers provide very wide bandwidth and complete elimination of electrical interference, but they are presently practical only as point-to-point transmission links.

ARCnet

ARCnet is a type of token passing bus. Its topology is a hybrid bus/star.

The forerunner of token passing networks in the United States is the Attached Resource Computer Network, ARCnet, developed by Datapoint Corporation. Initially, the network and protocol were kept proprietary, but the data link protocol, interface specs, and even integrated circuits were made publicly available in 1982. Functionally, the ARCnet is a token passing bus, but the physical topology, shown in Figure 10.17, is a hybrid bus/star. Rather than distribute taps along a linear bus as suggested in Figure 10.15, the ARCnet uses hubs with individual ports to connect Resource Interface Modules (RIMs) to the transmission media.

The hub-based architecture is an effective means of controlling the signal quality because the hub isolates each RIM port from the main coaxial cable. Unidirectional (one-way) amplifiers in the hubs provide zero insertion loss and suppress reflections because only one direction of transmission is enabled at a time. Amplifier switching is possible because a token passing network only transmits in one direction at a time.

RG62 coaxial cables with a baseband transmission rate of 2.5 Mbps are used to connect the hubs and RIMs in an ARCnet.

Physical Layer

The ARCnet interconnects the hubs and RIMs with RG62 coaxial cable using baseband transmission at 2.5 Mbps. Although 2.5 Mbps is a relatively low data rate, ARCnet uses inexpensive coax and can be configured (laid out) with as much as four miles between stations. The cable length between a hub and a RIM is limited to 2000 feet, but a four-mile span can have up to a maximum of 10 hubs in a series path.

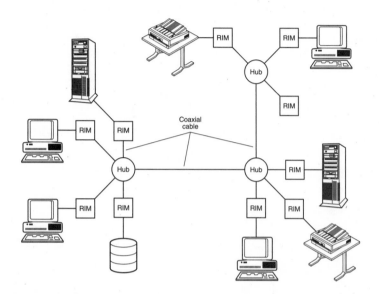

FIGURE 10.17.

Representative ARCnet configuration.

Link Protocol

The ARCnet employs five basic message formats, as shown in Figure 10.18. The first four formats are used for control messages; the fifth carries data between stations. All address fields consist of eight bits, which restricts the number of stations to 255 (address 0 is reserved as a broadcast address to all stations). As indicated in Figure 10.18, the destination address (DID) is duplicated with every message for error protection.

There are five basic message formats used in link protocol—four control messages and one data carrier. Eight bits are used in all address fields.

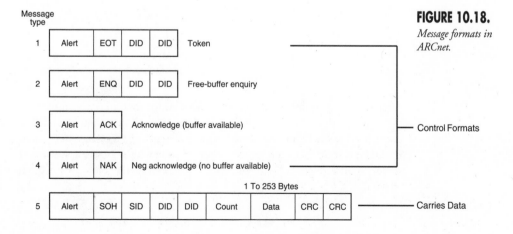

FIGURE 10.18.

Message formats in ARCnet.

A logical flow diagram of the token passing procedure implemented in every RIM is shown in Figure 10.19. On receiving a token (message type 1) with the proper address, a RIM chooses one of two paths, depending on whether it has transmit data pending. If data is pending, the RIM sends a free-buffer request (message type 2) to the desired destination RIM enquiring whether it is ready to receive. The destination RIM responds with an ACK (message type 3) if it has buffer space available, or a NAK (message type 4) if it does not have buffer space available.

FIGURE 10.19.

Flow diagram of token passing procedure in ARCnet.

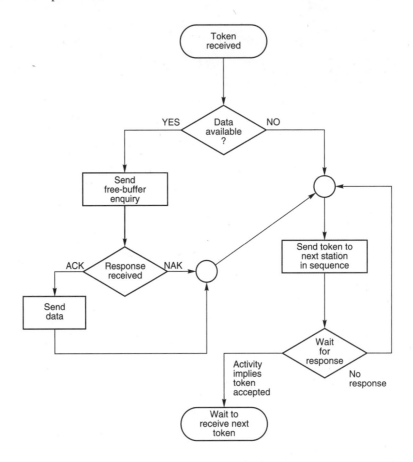

After a RIM has transmitted its data or determined that it cannot, it passes the token to the station with the next higher address. After sending the token, the RIM monitors the channel to see whether it is accepted. The occurrence of a message type 1, 2, or 5 indicates the token is accepted. No response on the channel within 74 µs implies that the intended station is off-line, and the token should be passed to the station with the next highest address.

IBM Token-Ring Network

In the mid-1980s, IBM introduced its token-ring network based on the use of token passing. This token-ring network uses a logical ring topology that is physically wired as a star, with workstations connected to a wiring concentrator known as a multistation access unit (MAU). MAUs are cabled to each other to form a ring, in effect resulting in a star-ring topology for the token-ring network.

Figure 10.20 illustrates the wiring of workstations to each MAU. Each workstation uses a twisted-pair connection for "ring-in" and a second twisted pair for "ring-out," with the data flowing from station to station in one direction to represent a logical ring. In addition to functioning as a central wiring point, the MAU also controls access of each workstation to the LAN. This is accomplished by the use of relays in each MAU port, enabling the MAU to simply short the relay to bypass a workstation. To get access to the LAN, a workstation raises a 5-volt signal that causes the MAU to open the relay on the port and add the workstation to the ring. This technique enables all inactive stations on a ring to be automatically bypassed, which serves to maximize LAN performance.

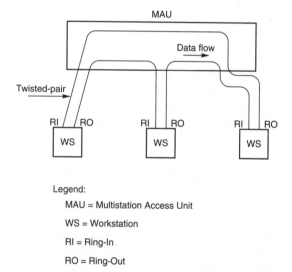

FIGURE 10.20.

Wiring workstations to a MAU.

Although three workstations are shown connected to one MAU in Figure 10.20, in actuality, up to eight workstations can be connected. A token-ring network is expanded to support additional workstations through the use of additional MAUs, with the MAUs interconnected to form a ring.

IBM, as well as several third-party manufacturers, produces token-ring adapter cards that can be installed in personal computers to allow PCs to be cabled to MAUs. The original IBM token-ring network operated at 4 Mbps and supported a maximum of 72 device connections, which is the equivalent of interconnecting nine MAUs. This network, for which 4 Mbps token-ring adapter cards are used in PCs, can use shielded or unshielded twisted-pair wiring. A second IBM token-ring network operates at 16 Mbps and extends the support of devices to 250 but requires the use of shielded cable. The 16 Mbps network requires the use of 16 Mbps token-ring adapter cards. Although IBM and third-party manufacturers market 4/16 Mbps token-ring adapters that can operate at either data rate, all devices on a LAN must be set to operate at either 4 or 16 Mbps. This means that users migrating from a 4 Mbps token-ring network to 16 Mbps must change all adapters for the LAN to operate at the higher rate.

Network Expansion

As previously mentioned, you can expand a token-ring network by adding one or more MAUs and connecting the ring-out (RO) port of one MAU to the ring-in (RI) port of another MAU. The original IBM MAU, known as the 8228, contained 10 ports, of which 8 provided connections to workstations because one was the ring-in port and another was the ring-out port used for network expansion. When an organization had many workstations to be connected to a token-ring network, it would have to get a number of 8228s and cable the RI and RO ports of each device together. In addition, one or more racks might be required to install the 8228s to facilitate cabling of workstations to ports on each 8228. Recognizing the problems associated with the cabling and rack mounting of individual 8228s, both IBM and third-party hardware vendors developed different types of products that essentially represent multiple 8228 MAUs. One such product is the IBM 8230 control access unit.

A control access unit is expanded by the use of lobe attachment modules to support additional workstations on a token-ring network.

The control access unit (CAU) can be considered an expandable MAU. The basic unit consists of a control unit and one lobe attachment module where the latter device provides the capability to cable individual workstations to the 8230. The 8230 is expanded by the addition of one or more lobe attachment modules. Figure 10.21 illustrates the expansion of a token-ring network through the use of a MAU and CAU. Here it was assumed that many workstations were clustered in one portion of a floor in a building and that eight workstations were clustered at another location on the same floor. Note that only two long-distance cables are required to connect the MAU and CAU. In comparison, if one CAU were used, you would require the installation of eight long-distance cables to connect the workstations located in the upper-right portion of Figure 10.21 to the CAU. Thus, the appropriate use of MAUs and CAUs can reduce cabling requirements, which can be an important consideration when conduits do not have room for the installations of a large number of additional cables.

Bridges

Bridges are devices that connect LANs at the ISO data-link level. In a token-ring network, a local bridge can be used to connect two adjacent token-ring LANs into one LAN. One example of a local bridge is an IBM PS/2 Model 55 personal computer containing two token-ring adapter cards, with each card cabled to the MAU of a local token-ring net-work. Figure 10.22 illustrates the use of a local bridge to connect two token-ring networks.

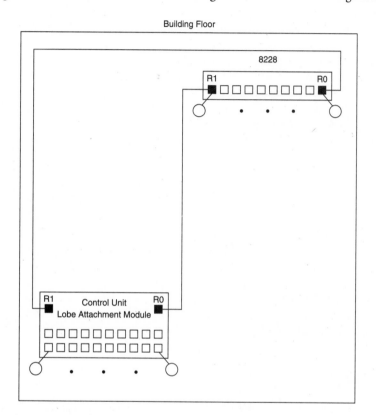

FIGURE 10.21.

Ring construction using a MAU and CAU.

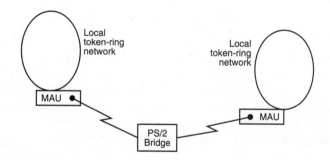

FIGURE 10.22.

Using a local bridge.

Local and remote
bridges can be
used to interconnect
LANs.

A second type of bridge is a remote bridge. This type of bridge is used to connect token-ring networks located at a distance from one another that requires interconnection via the use of a communications carrier transmission facility. When two LANs are connected by remote bridging, a remote bridge must be installed on each LAN. In place of a second token-ring adapter, each remote bridge would contain a serial communications port, allowing the device to be connected to a modem or a DSU/CSU, which, in turn, would be connected to an analog or digital transmission facility. The remote bridge examines addressing information in each token-ring frame and upon recognition of an address on the distant LAN routes the frame via the serial port of the device onto the communications carrier transmission facility linking the remote LANs together. Figure 10.23 illustrates the use of remote bridges to interconnect two LANs located remotely from one another.

FIGURE 10.23.

Using remote bridges.

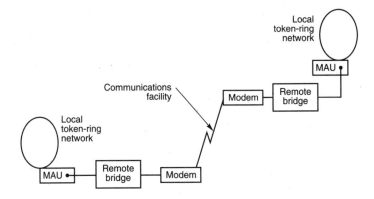

Routers

Routers operate at the network layer of the ISO Reference Model and permit support of several functions that bridges are not capable of providing due to their operation at the data link layer. Two additional functions that routers can perform include dynamic path assignment and frame fragmentation.

The capability to dynamically assign different paths permits routers to use alternative paths in the event a communications circuit becomes inoperative. In addition, this capability enables routers to perform a dynamic load balance of communications traffic when alternative routes are available between networks. This capability can reduce or eliminate the potential effect of congestion when too much traffic from one network destined to another exceeds the transmission capability of a single communications circuit.

Frame fragmentation permits routers to interconnect dissimilar LANs easily. For example, a 4 Mbps token-ring network has a maximum frame length of 4500 data bytes, whereas a 16 Mbps token-ring network has a maximum frame length of 18,000 data bytes. When connecting the two networks through the use of bridges, you would have to set software configuration parameters on each workstation on the 16 Mbps token-ring LAN to limit the maximum frame length to 4500 data characters to permit interoperability between networks. In comparison, if routers are used, they can fragment frames exceeding 4500 data characters originating on the 16 Mbps token-ring network into multiple frames for transmission on the 4 Mbps token-ring network. Because it's easier to configure one router than to configure numerous workstations connected via bridges, the use of routers can simplify network interoperability.

Gateways

To provide an interconnection capability for accessing mainframe computers, IBM markets several products that can be equipped with token-ring adapters and function as gateway devices. Two examples of such products are the IBM 3174 control unit with token-ring adapter (TRA) and the IBM 3725 token-ring interface coupler (TIC). The 3174 control unit can be located locally or remotely from a mainframe computer and allows up to 32 terminal devices to share access to the mainframe over a common cable or transmission facility. When equipped with a TRA the 3174 can serve as local or remote LAN gateway for accessing an IBM mainframe.

Because the maximum data rate of a 3174 is 56 Kbps, the use of a TRA on that device can result in degraded performance if too many LAN users attempt to access the mainframe simultaneously. To provide an increased level of gateway access, the IBM 3725 or 3745 front-end processor (FEP) can be equipped with a TIC, which allows the FEP to be directly connected to a 4 or 16 Mbps token-ring network. Figure 10.24 illustrates several methods by which the IBM 3174 control unit and the IBM 3725 front-end processor can provide token-ring network users with access to an IBM mainframe computer.

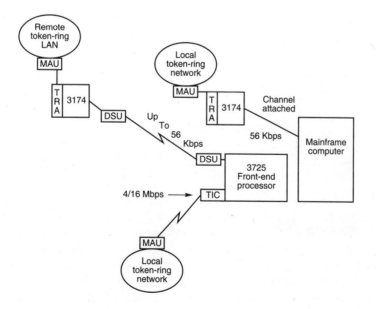

FIGURE 10.24.

Gateway access to an IBM mainframe.

Broadbent Networks

Frequency division multiplexing over wide bandwidth coaxial cables is used by broadband local area networks to transmit on multiple channels. This technique was developed by the cable TV industry.

Broadband local area networks use wide bandwidth coaxial cables with frequency division multiplexing (FDM) to establish multiple channels within a system. The FDM channels are typically 6MHz wide following the standards and technology developed by the CATV (cable TV) industry. Because the usable bandwidth of a CATV cable is 300 to 400 MHz, there can be as many as 50 to 60 separate channels. Often separate FDM channels are used for separate applications.

The power and attraction of a broadbent network is evident in Figure 10.25. Notice that the transmission system supports not only a data network, but also closed-circuit TV distribution, point-to-point voice telephone circuits, and point-to-point data circuits.

Use of a broadband system for data transmission requires modems in the physical interface equipment. If the modems are assigned to a fixed frequency (channel), the associated station can communicate only with other stations assigned to the same frequency. If frequency agile modems (modems that have a tuner to allow changing channels) are used, the stations can switch between the FDM channels to gain access to much larger networks.

FIGURE 10.25.

Broadband LAN supporting multiple services.

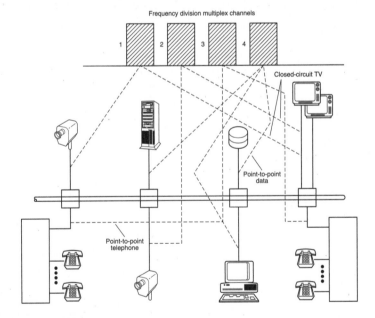

Single-cable systems use a dual-frequency architecture; one frequency for sending, one for receiving on the same cable.

Physical Layer

Broadbent LAN systems utilize either one or two cables routed to every station. Single-cable systems are patterned after customary CATV systems where the FDM channels are separated into two groups as shown in Figure 10.26. One group of frequencies carries signals from the transmitter of all station interfaces to a frequency translation module referred to as the head end. The head end amplifies the received signals and shifts them to the second group of frequencies, and then they travel back along the cable to the receivers of every station interface. Thus, a single channel in a functional sense requires a pair of FDM channels in a physical sense. The dual-frequency architecture permits the use of unidirectional amplifiers as shown in Figure 10.26.

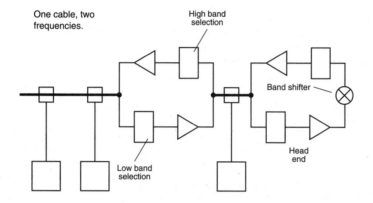

FIGURE 10.26.

Dual-frequency single-cable broadband network.

An alternative to the dual-frequency approach is the dual-cable architecture shown in Figure 10.27. Each station interface transmits on a particular channel in one cable and receives on the same channel in the second cable. The head end no longer provides FDM group translation; in fact, it might be nothing more than a passive cable-to-cable connection.

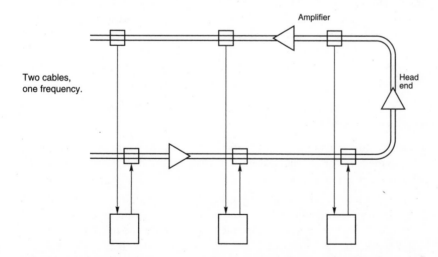

FIGURE 10.27.

Dual-cable/single-frequency broadband network.

Whichever physical architecture is used, the advantage of unidirectional amplification appears in the maximum distance specifications of broadbent networks. Distance limits of 5 to 30 miles are typical except in cases where access protocols like CSMA/CD restrict the allowable propagation times.

Data Link Layer

There is no single standard for broadband networks. Only the FDM channels have been given specific frequency assignments to allow interface with CATV systems.

Due to the flexibility and multiple services supported by broadband networks, no one standard configuration or agreement on operation has come about or is likely to come about that explicitly defines the entire use of the bandwidth on the cable. For example, under 10BROAD-36, the CSMA/CD protocol is specified for use on defined channels with the use of radio frequency (rf) modems to modulate data at assigned frequencies. However, this standard does not define other signals that can be carried on the same cable. The only thing that appears to be a standard is the assignment of FDM channels, which must be standardized to interface with CATV systems. Suppliers of data communications services on broadband cables generally have decided to use the data link protocols of the baseband systems. In particular, both Ethernet and ARCnet access protocols are available for rf channels on a broadband network. Thus, the OSI goal of separating the physical layer from the higher layers has proven to be useful by allowing data communications suppliers these options.

Voice and/or Data PBX

As LAN technology has been developing, PBXs have been evolving and using more digital electronics in voice switched services.

The local area networks described in the preceding sections have evolved primarily from the data processing or office equipment industry; therefore, they are strongly influenced by data communications applications. At the same time that LAN technology has been developing, voice telephone systems called private branch exchanges (PBXs) have been incorporating more and more digital electronics as a means of providing switched voice service. As shown in Figure 10.28, the conventional PBX architecture utilizes dedicated twisted-pair wires from every station to the central node (switch). Connection requests are signaled by an off-hook signal and dialed digits or "hot line" addresses stored in the memory of the switch controller. After a connection is established, the associated transmission channels are dedicated to that connection for its duration.

The data PBX depicted in Figure 10.28 provides an economical solution to several data communications problems:

- A terminal can be switched to different computers (CPUs) for different applications, to modems for external dial-up connections, or to data multiplexers for efficient use of external leased lines.

- The distance between the computer ports and the data terminals is extended to as much as several thousand feet. The standard EIA specification for the RS-232 interface is limited to 50 feet (although RS-232 interfaces are often used over longer distances).

- The switch acts as a port concentrator; that is, many external device ports can be handled by a few computer ports. The switch accomplishes this by connecting only active terminals to the computer ports. This greatly reduces the number of ports required in each computer.

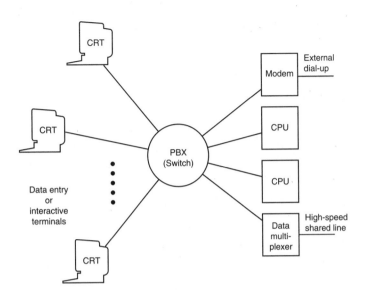

FIGURE 10.28.

Representative application of a data PBX.

Although twisted-pair wires are relatively inexpensive and easy to install, they restrict the capacity of the data channels to a range of 50 Kbps to 1 Mbps, depending on distance. Thus, the data PBX is a viable solution for data entry and medium rate interactive terminal communications, but not for high-speed processor-to-processor communications.

Integrated Voice/Data PBXs

Beginning in the mid-1970s, PBXs began utilizing digital technology in their switching matrices because, despite the cost of voice digitization at line interfaces, the total switch cost is lower due to economics in the matrix. More recently, the point of digitization has begun to move from within the central equipment to the voice stations themselves. These are the main motivations for digitizing in the instruments:

> To easily multiplex control information (which is inherently digital) onto the same pair or pairs of wires that carry the voice signals (typically 64 Kbps). This allows sophisticated multiline telephones to operate over one or two pairs of wires. Conventional analog telephone systems use expensive 25-pair cables for multiline key sets.

> To multiplex data channels on the same pairs of wires used for voice so that one installation can simultaneously provide voice and data communications.

Initially, the digital instruments could be cost-justified only in sophisticated applications. As the cost of digital instruments decreased, however, it became possible to cost-justify an all-digital system, thus providing 64 Kbps digital channels at every location of a telephone. The widespread presence of 64 Kbps digital channels makes it easier to add other digital transmission services, as shown in Figure 10.29.

● PBXs are not capable of effectively handling high-speed processor-to-processor communications because of the 50 Kbps to 1 Mbps transmission rate range.

● Digitization of PBX Systems will enable control information to be multiplexed onto the voice signal wires, allowing only one or two wires to handle multiple lines rather than the normal 25 pairs.

FIGURE 10.29.

Integrated voice/data PBX with digital instruments.

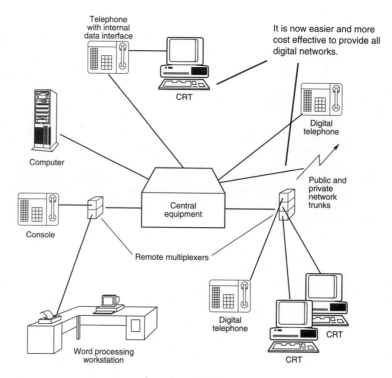

LAN Comparisons and Trends

Each of the LAN system architectures presented in the previous sections has unique technical and operational advantages and disadvantages. The following paragraphs contrast the systems in terms of the properties of an ideal LAN.

One-Time Installations

The overall goal of a one-time installation is not satisfied in practice by any of the LAN architectures. Even a telephone system, which is a necessity in every building, typically requires significant rewiring as people move, if only from one side of an office to another.

Widespread Access

Before widespread access becomes a reality for an information distribution network, the cost of significant numbers of unused ports must be reduced. Even though telephone twisted pairs are relatively inexpensive, unused telephone ports typically represent a significant hidden cost in terms of the electronics interfaces that the wires are connected to in the central equipment. Distributed access architectures such as CSMA or token passing do not produce hidden costs for unused ports as long as the maximum number of ports is not exceeded.

Application Independence

A major prerequisite for an information network to support multiple applications is the support of higher level data communications functions. The suppliers of coaxial-cable-based LANs are generally most advanced in this regard, although it is more a matter of market orientation than a technology difference. The CSMA and token passing systems also provide a high data rate for those applications that need it.

Excess Capacity

In one sense, the CSMA or token passing architectures are ideal because the entire capacity of the system is available at every port. A port can use as much bandwidth as it needs. On the other hand, this feature limits the system capacity. If the total bandwidth requirements of the stations exceed the system bandwidth, the needed expansion is either very costly or impossible.

In contrast, circuit switched (PBX) architectures can be expanded almost without limit. The bandwidth delivered to every port remains unchanged as more stations are added.

Easy Maintenance and Administration

The most difficult systems to maintain are the broadband systems because of the tight gain requirements of the amplifiers and equalizers. From a data communications point of view, the integrated voice/data PBX is the easiest to maintain because well-established procedures already exist for the voice services. Furthermore, PBX suppliers are accustomed to providing turnkey system support for the life of the installation. However, due to product background, they typically do not support higher level communication requirements.

No presently available single LAN system architecture can economically satisfy the needs of all communications within a building or campus. Nor is it likely that one system will ever evolve to economically fulfill these needs. Thus, there will always be a need for either separate systems tailored to specific applications or possibly hybrid systems employing the best features of selected individual architectures. One such hybrid architecture that is beginning to evolve is shown in Figure 10.30. This illustration depicts an integrated voice/data PBX that collects terminal traffic and switches it onto high-speed multiplexed computer to PBX interfaces (CPIs). Communications between processors (CPU) and their shared high-speed peripherals is best accomplished with a high-speed coaxial cable or fiber-optic LAN. The advantage of the configuration in Figure 10.30 is that low-speed, short messages to and from the terminals are not contending for the high-speed facility optimized for file transfers.

●
No single LAN system architecture has sufficient capabilities to fulfill all possible needs. Each has its own special qualities and technical advantages and disadvantages.

FIGURE 10.30.

Hybrid PBX/LAN network.

A hybrid system allows tailoring to specific needs.

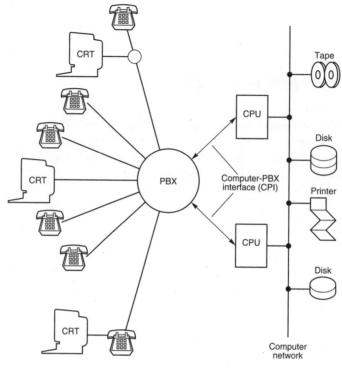

Voice/Computer access network

What Have You Learned?

1. LANs provide high-speed switched connections between such data equipment as computers, storage devices, printers, word processors, and display terminals at distances up to a few thousand meters.

2. The usefulness of a LAN is maximized if it provides higher level data communications support in addition to basic transmission and switching functions.

3. Communications functions within a network should be partitioned in a hierarchical manner to isolate the implementation of major functional components from each other.

4. Myriad LAN architectures are possible, but these are the most prevalent:
   a. Contention-access-based coaxial cable systems (for example, Ethernet).
   b. Token passing systems (for example, IBM token-ring network).
   c. Polled-access-based coaxial cable systems (for example, ARCnet).
   d. Frequency division broadband systems based on cable television technology and practice.

5. Some of the incompatibilities that traditionally arise in LAN equipment supplied by different vendors are being resolved by IEEE standards committee 802.

6. The IEEE 802.3 standard is really a set of standards that define several types of CSMA/CD LANs.

7. Digital PBXs for telephone switching are being designed to carry data in addition to basic telephone service. Although these systems do not provide the very high rates of a conventional LAN, they represent a very economical alternative to a LAN for moderate date rate switched connections.

Quiz for Chapter 10

1. Which of the following transmission systems provides the highest data rate to an individual device?
   a. Voiceband modem.
   b. Local area network.
   c. Computer bus.
   d. Digital PBX.

2. Which of the following systems provides the longest digital transmission distances?
   a. Voiceband modem.
   b. Local area network.
   c. Computer bus.
   d. Digital PBX.

3. Which of the following options is a characteristic of a LAN?
   a. Parallel transmission.
   b. Unlimited expansion.
   c. Low cost access for low bandwidth channels.
   d. Application-independent interfaces.

4. Which of the following transmission media is not readily suitable to CSMA operation?
   a. Radio.
   b. Optical fibers.
   c. Coaxial cable.
   d. Twisted pair.

5. Which of the following functions is not provided as part of the basic Ethernet design?
   a. Access control.
   b. Addressing.
   c. Automatic retransmission of a message.
   d. Multiple virtual networks.

6. Which of the following options is not a useful property of a Manchester line code for an Ethernet?
   a. Continuous energy.
   b. Continuous clock transitions.
   c. No DC component.
   d. No signal change at a 1 to 0 transition.

7. Which of the following data communications functions is generally provided for in a LAN?

    a. Data link control.

    b. Applications processing.

    c. Flow control.

    d. Routing.

8. The purpose of the preamble in an Ethernet is:

    a. Clock synchronization.

    b. Error checking.

    c. Collision avoidance.

    d. Broadcast.

9. The difference between the Ethernet frame preamble field and the IEEE 802.3 Preamble and Start of Frame Delimiter fields is:

    a. 1 byte.

    b. 1 bit.

    c. 8 bits.

    d. 16 bits.

10. A 10BASE-2 network is limited to:

    a. 20 bytes per data field.

    b. 30 stations per segment.

    c. 40 segments.

    d. 50 feet of cable.

11. Which of the following features is possible in a token passing bus network?

    a. Unlimited number of stations.

    b. Unlimited distances.

    c. Multiple time division channels.

    d. In-service expansion.

12. Which of the following features is not possible in a token passing loop network?

    a. Unlimited number of stations.

    b. Unlimited distances.

    c. Multiple time division channels.

    d. In-service expansion.

13. Which of the following LAN architectures can be expanded to the greatest total system bandwidth?

    a. Digital PBX.

    b. CSMA/CD baseband system.

    c. Token passing network.

    d. Broadband cable system.

14. Which of the following systems is the most capable of servicing a wide range of applications?

    a. Digital PBX.

    b. CSMA/CD baseband system.

    c. Token passing network.

    d. Broadband cable system.

15. Which of the following options is a characteristic of a token passing ring as opposed to a token passing bus?

    a. Signal quality control.

    b. Passive interface (tap).

    c. Flexible polling sequence.

    d. Priority access capabilities.

16. Which of the following options is not a characteristic of the hub architecture of ARCnet?

    a. Directionalized transmission.

    b. RIM port isolation.

    c. Zero insertion loss amplifiers.

    d. Alternate routing.

17. A router operates at:

    a. The data link layer.

    b. The application layer.

    c. The network layer.

    d. The segmentation layer.

18. Which of the following items cannot be provided in a broadband LAN?

    a. Frequency agile modems.

    b. Closed-circuit TV.

    c. Voice circuits.

    d. Fiber-optic transmission.

19. Which of the following features is not possible in a digital (data) PBX using twisted pair transmission?

    a. Computer port concentration.

    b. 64 Kbps data circuits.

    c. High-speed file transfers.

    d. Transmission up to several thousand feet.

20. Which of the following options is not a motivation for digitizing a voice signal in the telephones of a digital PBX?

    a. Simplified control signaling.

    b. Lower cost telephones.

    c. Fewer wire pairs.

    d. Multiplexed voice and data channels.

Architectures and Packet Networks

About This Chapter

This chapter deals with several data networking architecture concepts—that is, the way data networks are arranged or structured. These include the concept of architectural levels or layers. Without emphasizing architectural structure or terminology, previous chapters have actually described data networking and switching on two different levels: the physical level and the link level. Packet networks, which involve a third architectural level, are discussed in this chapter. The CCITT X.25 standard packet switching architecture is described; then the Open Systems Interconnection (OSI) Reference Model is explained along with its relationship to X.25 and other systems.

Protocol Layering

A protocol is a set of rules governing a time sequence of events that take place between peer entities—that is, between equipment or layers on the same level.

Physical Layer

In a previous chapter, we discussed the mechanical, physical, electrical, logical, and functional relationships between the various wires and signals in a serial interface and how the bits of data are passed through them between Data Terminal Equipment (DTE) and Data Circuit-terminating Equipment (DCE). We showed, for example, that bits passing through the transmit data wire from a source DTE should eventually pass through a receive data wire to a sink DTE. These are called physical layer or level one protocols.

Level one protocols deal with the physical layer of data communication, or the passing of the bits through the wires to and from DTEs. Link protocols cover a higher level of architecture; they are concerned with all aspects of maintaining order within the link.

Link Layer

In a previous chapter, we discussed means by which various fields, such as address, text, and error checking, can be present within the same bit stream. Several specific link protocols were discussed, showing techniques that are used to define (without any possibility of confusion) the boundaries of the fields within a bit stream, send information to a specific terminal on a multipoint link, check for and correct transmission errors, and generally maintain order within the line.

Architecturally speaking, link protocols are at a higher level (a more "intelligent" level) than physical protocols; yet all of the information used in the link protocol is actually contained in the bit stream transmitted through the serial interface. Conceptually, we speak of the link protocol fields as embedded (contained within) or layered within the physical protocol bits.

Network Layer

The highest level of protocol architecture is the network layer. This layer is used to route data link-to-link through a network.

At the third architectural level is the network layer. Protocols at this layer can be used to route data from link to link through a network containing intelligent nodes called packet switches. The method by which this routing and associated administration takes place is called the network layer protocol. The network layer protocol information, called the packet header, is embedded in the information field of a link-level frame. The packet switch uses part of this information to route the data to the next link, and so on. The packet header, together with the user data, is called a packet.

Packet Networks

Packet networks function with the help of special intelligent switching nodes. A network node joining three or more links is called a DSE.

A packet network is a special kind of data network containing intelligent switching nodes. Packet networks have the following general characteristics:

- Before transmission, each data message is segmented into short blocks of specified maximum length, and each block is provided with a header containing addressing and sequencing information. Each packet becomes the information field of a transmission at the link protocol level which usually contains error control capabilities.

- The packets are passed very quickly from node to node, arriving in a fraction of a second at their final destination.

- The node computers do not archive (store) the data. Messages are "forgotten" by the sending node as soon as the next node checks for an error (if required), and acknowledges receipt.

The terms DTE and DCE have been discussed previously. In packet networks, an additional term is introduced: the Data Switching Exchange (DSE). A DSE is a network node joining three or more links. Figure 11.1 shows the relationship between DTEs, DCEs, and DSEs in a packet network. The point where the serial interface cable connects to the DCE is sometimes referred to as the network gateway.

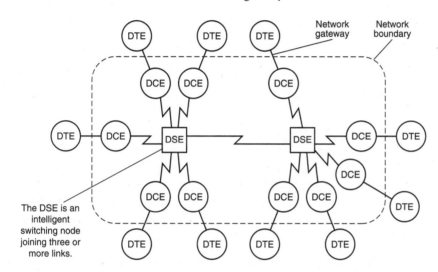

FIGURE 11.1.

Two-node packet network.

Unlike level one switching, in which a specific link is dedicated to a particular message or group of messages, data packets are forwarded from DSE to DSE in such a way that packets from many sources and to many sinks can pass through the same internode link at different moments during the same short period.

Advantages of Packet Switching

Depending on the situation, packet switching can offer several possible advantages over other data communications techniques:

● For data applications in which the amount of traffic between terminals cannot justify a dedicated circuit, packet switching might be more economical than transmission over private lines.

● For applications in which data communication sessions are shorter than a minimum chargeable time unit for a telephone call, packet switching might be more economical than dialed data.

● Because destination address information is inherently a part of the packet, a large number of messages can be sent to many different destinations as fast as the source DTE can turn them out. Depending on the type of packet service being used, there might not be any connection time delay before transmitting packets containing actual data.

● Packet switching can offer significant advantages over other data communications techniques.

- Because of the intelligence built into the network (that is, computers at each node), dynamic routing of data is possible. Each packet travels over the route established by the network as the best available path for that packet at that time. This characteristic can be used to maximize efficiency and minimize congestion.

- Built-in intelligence also facilitates a "graceful degradation" property of the packet network, because whenever there is a failure of a link or node, packets can be automatically rerouted around the defective portion of the network.

- Because of the intelligence within the network, a rich array of basic communications services is possible. Examples include error detection and correction, message delivery verification, group addressing, reverse billing, message sequence checking, and diagnostics.

X.25 Packet Systems

The CCITT X.25 standard for packet switching systems is one of the most significant networking architectures affecting data communications for the present and the foreseeable future. The X.25 standard is actually only a part of a much larger collection of CCITT recommendations on public data networks. To fully understand the subject, one must study the entire "X" series.

The X.25 standard itself describes the physical, link, and network protocols in the interface between the DTE and DCE at the gateway to a packet switching network. At first glance, the concept of describing a packet network in terms of gateway parameters might seem peculiar, but from the users' point of view, it's all that's needed. In voice telephone network terms, if we were to collect all the standards relating to the physical, electrical, logical, and functional properties of local loops and their signals into one document, we would have the telephone network equivalent of X.25. As shown in Figure 11.2, X.25 relates a data terminal to the gateway of a packet network in precisely the same way that local loop signaling standards relate a telephone to the central office of a telephone network.

The primary emphasis of the X.25 standard is to describe what a terminal and its associated network must be able to do, not to describe the terminal and network themselves.

If we had never seen a telephone or placed a telephone call, our knowing all there is to know about a local loop and its signaling wouldn't teach us much about the design of the telephone or of the network—but we would know how to use them. Similarly, the X.25 standard describes neither the data terminal nor the packet data network, but X.25 reveals a great deal about what the terminal and the network must be able to do. It is for this reason that the X.25 has taken on so much importance.

As already mentioned, the X.25 standard specifies three separate protocol layers at the serial interface gateway. The physical-layer characteristics of X.21 (or X.21bis) are specified as the physical layer protocol ("bis" is the Swiss/French equivalent of "alternate form"). X.21 uses a 15-pin synchronous interface, which has not enjoyed enthusiastic acceptance in the United States because of the popularity of RS-232 and V.35, which existed before X.21.

In recognition of this fact, the CCITT has endorsed X.21bis as a suitable alternative. X.21bis specifies V.24/V.28 (essentially the equivalent of RS-232), X.26/IS-4902 (essentially the equivalent of RS-449), and V.35 at their appropriate respective bit rates. Because U.S. vendors generally provide RS-232 or V.35, no change is required.

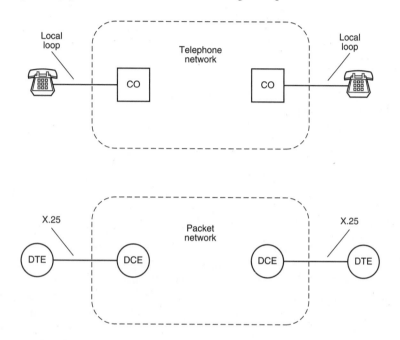

FIGURE 11.2.

Analogy between X.25 and the total specifications for a local loop.

Link Level

At the link level, the protocol specified is a subset of HDLC, referred to in X.25 terminology as LAPB (Link Access Procedure Balanced). (An older version of X.25 used a link protocol called LAP, which has been essentially phased out.) LAPB provides for two-way simultaneous communication between the DTE and DCE at the network gateway. LAPB frame structure is identical to that of SDLC, which was explained in a previous chapter. The delimiter (flag), abort, idle channel, transparency (zero insertion), frame sequencing, flow control, and error control mechanisms are identical to those of SDLC. The differences in the LAPB procedures and the SDLC procedures are mainly in the areas of line control and addressing; these topics will be covered later.

●

The protocol at the link level, LAPB, provides for two-way simultaneous communications between the DTE and DCE at the network gateway.

Network Level

The packet level of X.25 is the network level, and it is transmitted as an information field in the command frame. At least three octets are used in the header.

The network level of X.25 is referred to in the standard as the packet level. All X.25 packets are transmitted as information fields in LAPB information command frames. A packet contains at least a header of three or more octets. (An octet is a group of eight bits.) Most packets also contain user data, but some packets are only for control, status indication, or diagnostics. (The preceding terms will be explained in later text and illustrations.) The maximum amount of user data that can be included in a data packet is determined by the network vendor but is usually 128 octets.

Capabilities of X.25

The X.25 standard, together with its references, specifies two essential services that must be offered by carriers to be in full compliance with the standard. These services are Virtual Call Service and Permanent Virtual Circuit Service.

VIRTUAL CALL SERVICE

Virtual connections are made and disconnected by using special, nondata-carrying packets that have a unique bit stream. In a virtual connection, no fixed physical path actually exists in the network.

In Virtual Call Service (VC), a virtual "connection" normally must be established first between a logical channel from the calling DTE and a logical channel to the called DTE before any data packets can be sent. Establishment of a virtual connection is precisely the functional equivalent of placing a telephone call before beginning a telephone conversion. The virtual connection is established and disestablished using special packets that have unique bit streams but usually contain no data. After the connection has been established, the two DTEs can carry on a two-way dialog until a "clear request packet" (disconnect) is sent.

The VC connection is referred to as "virtual" because a fixed physical path does not exist through the network. The intelligence in the network simply relates a specified logical channel number at one DTE to that at the other DTE.

A given DTE can have many logical channel numbers active in the same X.25 interface at the same time. (That statement was important. Read it again.) After a virtual connection has been established, say, between logical channel #319 on one DTE and #14 on another DTE, then the actual data packet headers need refer only to logical channel numbers. The intelligent network keeps up with their conversational relationship; that is, a data packet from logical channel #319 at the one DTE will appear on logical channel #14 at the other, with the network performing the conversion. Further details on this subject will be given later.

PERMANENT VIRTUAL CIRCUIT SERVICE

Permanent Virtual Circuit (PVC) service is the functional equivalent of a private line service. As in VC, no end-to-end physical pathway exists; the intelligent network relates the respective logical channels of the two DTEs involved. No special packets are sent by the DTE to establish or disestablish connections. A PVC is established by requesting it in writing from the carrier providing the packet network service, and it remains in effect until disestablished by written request. Terminals between which a PVC has been established need only send data packets on the carrier-assigned logical channels as required. Because a DTE can have many logical channels active at the same time within the X.25 interface, some can be assigned as PVCs whereas others are used for setting up VCs as required—all in the same X.25 interface!

For both VC and PVC, the network is obligated to deliver packets in the order submitted, even if the physical path changes due to circuit loading, failure, or whatever. Costwise, the relationship between VC and PVC is similar to that between long-distance telephone and private line services. Other standard packet network features, such as error control and diagnostics, are equivalent for VC and PVC.

> ●
> After a PVC has been established, only data packets are sent between the terminals on the carrier-assigned logical channels.

FACILITIES

In CCITT terminology, a facility is an optional feature offered with a service, sometimes at extra cost. X.25 specifies a rich array of facilities for VC and PVC services. In any case, the final choice of services and facilities is up to the customer.

Examples of facilities for VC service are fast select, incoming calls barred, outgoing calls barred, closed user group, and reverse billing. Fast select gives the user the ability to send and receive data to and from a number of different remote stations very quickly and efficiently without actually establishing regular virtual connections. Such a capability has many potential uses for distribution of electronic mail, polling of inventories, and so on.

> ●
> Facilities are optional features available to customers to customize VC service.

LAPB Procedures

Space does not allow for a complete discussion of the link layer protocol of X.25; the following information, however, provides general knowledge of the LAPB procedures. A thorough treatment is included in the X.25 standard, and examples of operation are included in ISO 4335 Addendum 2.

LAPB provides for two-way simultaneous transmission on a point-to-point link between a DTE and a DCE at the packet network gateway (see Figure 11.1). Because the link is point-to-point, only the address of the DTE or the address of the DCE can appear in the A (address) field of an LAPB frame. These addresses are shown in Figure 11.3. The A field refers to a link address, not to a network address. The network address of the destination terminal is embedded in the packet header (PH), which is part of the I field.

FIGURE 11.3.

Commands versus responses in LAPB.

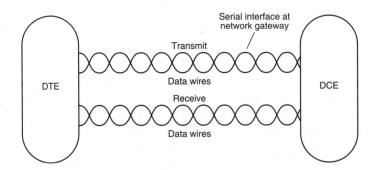

Frames in transmit data wires contain
A = 10000000 for commands and
A = 11000000 for responses.

Frames in receive data wires contain
A = 11000000 for commands and
A = 10000000 for responses.

Commands and responses can be made by both the DTE and the DCE. The function of a frame depends on the direction it is moving and the value of A.

Both stations (the DTE and the DCE) can issue commands and responses to each other, as shown in Figure 11.3. Whether a frame is a command or a response depends on a combination of two factors:

- In which direction it is moving—that is, whether it's on the transmit data wires from the DTE or the receive data wires toward the DTE.

- What the value of A is.

Because of the addressing scheme, there can be no uncertainty even if frames are moving in opposite directions at the same time between DTE and DCE.

Table 11.1 and Table 11.2 show the legitimate commands and responses in the LAPB frame, along with their respective control octet values. Explanations of the abbreviations and terms are given in the following paragraphs.

Table 11.1. LAPB commands.

Command Name	Content of Control Octet Bit Number			
	876	5	432	1
I (Information)	N(R)	P	N(S)	0
RR (Receiver Ready)	N(R)	P	000	1
RNR (Receiver Not Ready)	N(R)	P	010	1
REJ (Reject)				
SABM (Set Asynchronous Balanced Mode)	001	P	111	1
DISC (Disconnect)	010	P	001	1

Table 11.2. LAPB responses.

Response Name	Content of Control Octet Bit Number			
	876	**5**	**432**	**1**
RR (Receiver Ready)	N(R)	F	000	1
RNR (Receiver Not Ready)	N(R)	F	010	1
REJ (Reject)	N(R)	F	100	1
UA (Unnumbered Acknowledgment)	011	F	001	1
DM (Disconnect Mode)	000	F	111	1
FRMR (Frame Rejected)	100	F	011	1

EXPLANATION OF LAPB COMMANDS AND RESPONSES

During LAPB operation, most frames are commands. A response frame is compelled when a command frame is received containing P = 1; such a response contains F = 1. All other frames contain P = 0 or F = 0.

SABM/UA is a command/response pair used to initialize all counters and timers at the beginning of a session. Similarly, DISC/DM is a command/response pair used at the end of a session. FRMR is a response to any illegal command for which there is no indication of transmission errors according to the frame check sequence (FCS) field.

I commands are used to transmit packets—that is, in the I field. Packets are never sent as responses. N(S) is a three-bit packet counter capable of counting from 0 through 7 (000 through 111 in binary). After seven packets have been sent, the counter simply rolls over to 000 again for the next value of N(S).

While N(S) counts packets sent from one end of the link, the value of N(R) indicates the next value of N(S) expected to be returned from the other end of the link. By updating the value of N(R), a station acknowledges correctly received packets in the same way as SDLC frames are acknowledged. For example, if a DTE sends an I command (a packet) for which N(S) = 5 and P = 1, and the DCE returns an RR response with N(R) = 6 and F = 1, the DTE knows that the packet was received correctly. If N(R) = 5 and F = 1, the packet was received incorrectly. No more than seven unacknowledged packets can be outstanding, because an ambiguity would result.

●
Most frames in LAPB operations are commands. Response frames are issued only when a command frame with P = 1 is received.

In checkpointing, a type of LAPB error detection, RR is the response by a station that has no packets to send but must answer a compelled response.

RR is what a station sends when it needs to send something but has no packets to send. For example, a compelled response to an I command might be an RR with F = 1. This procedure is called checkpointing. Checkpointing is one of the techniques that LAPB makes available for error detection.

REJ is another way of requesting transmission of frames. RNR is used for flow control to indicate a busy condition. It prevents further transmissions until cleared by an RR.

Packet-Level Procedures

The most interesting feature of X.25 is the network (packet) layer protocol. Remember that the packets are contained in the I command frames at the link (frame) level and that each packet has a header of at least three octets. Most, but not all, packets contain user data; other packets are used for control, status indication, or diagnostics. Figure 11.4 illustrates the general layout of X.25 packet headers.

FIGURE 11.4.

General layout of X.25 packet headers.

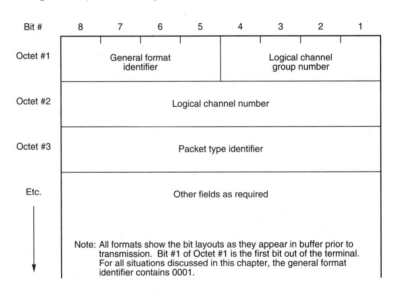

DATA PACKETS

Data Packets are packets in which Bit #1 in Octet #3 of the header has a value of 0. A data packet can have up to 128 octets of user data.

A packet that has 0 as the value of Bit #1 in Octet #3 of the header is a data packet. Data packet headers normally contain three octets. A standard X.25 data packet contains up to 128 octets of user data following the header. Figure 11.5 illustrates the layout of a typical data packet. This chapter is not intended to cover all possible ramifications and extensions of X.25. There is, for example, the provision for modulo 128 P(S) and P(R) counters, each of which requires seven bits. A data packet header in such a system would require a minimum of four octets.

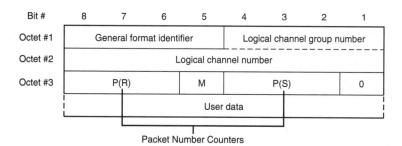

FIGURE 11.5.

Typical CCITT X.25 data packet.

It was pointed out earlier that X.25 specifies two essential services: Virtual Call (VC) and Permanent Virtual Circuit (PVC). After a VC has been set up, the operation of data packets under VC service is identical to that under PVC. In the paragraphs that follow, operation under PVC will be described first, then the additional concerns of VC, such as call setup, will be described.

Theoretically, every X.25 gateway interface can support up to 16 logical channel groups, each containing up to 256 logical channels, for a grand total of 4096 simultaneous logical channels per gateway. It is up to the company that establishes the networks to say how many it will actually support in each type of service—that is, PVC and VC.

Notice in Figure 11.5 that Octet #3 of the data packet header contains two 3-bit fields, P(S) and P(R), and a 1-bit field, M. M is the "more data" mark. When M has a value of 1, additional data packets will follow that are to be considered as a unit; when it has a value of 0, no more packet will follow in this unit. P(S) and P(R) are data packet counters, each of which can vary from 000 through 111 (0–7). The counters roll over to 000 again after passing 111. (These are not the same as N(S) and N(R) discussed earlier.) Only data packets have a P(S) counter; there will be a P(S) in each data packet sent across the DTE to DCE interface at the network gateway (Figure 11.1) and a P(S) in each data packet sent from DCE to DTE at the network gateway.

By definition, P(R) is the amount of the next expected value of P(S) from the other direction on that logical channel (this will be explained in a moment). The values of P(S) and P(R) relate to each other within a logical channel at the network level in exactly the same way that N(S) and N(R) relate to each other on a point-to-point link. The Ns are not related to the Ps, however, because the Ns refer to all packets sent in a link, and the Ps refer only to data packets sent in a particular logical channel within that link.

The use of P(S) and P(R) is illustrated in Figure 11.6. A sequence of two-way simultaneous (full-duplex) transmissions of data packets within a logical channel across a DTE/DCE interface at a packet network gateway is illustrated. In this illustration, each rectangle represents a packet. The first number in the rectangle is the value of P(S), and the second is the value of P(R) in that packet's header. Inspection of the sequence in Figure 11.6 will confirm two facts already implied:

●

There are three parts to Octet #3 of the data packet header: two 3-bit fields, P(S) and P(R), and a 1-bit field, M. When M is 1, more data packets are to follow as a single unit.

●

The values of P(S) and P(R) are related within a logical channel at the network level. P(R) is the amount that P(S) is expected to be in the next packet that is coming from the other direction on that particular logical channel.

- The values of P(S) in a particular direction in a logical channel proceed in numerical order: 0, 1, 2, 3, and so forth.

- The value of P(R) sent in a packet is not updated to i until the entire packet whose value of P(S) is i − 1 has been completely received error free. Such update is an acknowledgment of all packets in that logical channel through P(S) = i − 1.

FIGURE 11.6.

Values of P(S) and P(R) for a sequence of data packets.

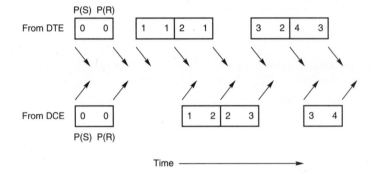

The dynamic establishment and disestablishment of a VC using special packets is very similar to that of placing and terminating a telephone call on the public telephone network, as indicated in Table 11.3 and Table 11.4. Inspection of these tables reveals that seven new packet names have been introduced. An event occurring on one side of the network is usually paired with a complementary event on the other side. For example, a Call Request Packet from calling DTE to DCE at one interface results in an Incoming Call Packet from DCE to called DTE at another interface. Table 11.5 shows the packet type identifiers (Octet #3 of the header) for these pairs of packet types.

Table 11.3. Network analogies for call establishment.

Telephone Network	X.25 Packet Network
Place call	Send "Call Request" Packet
Hear telephone ring	Receive "Incoming Call" Packet
Pick up handset of ringing phone	Send "Call Accepted" Packet
Hear "Hello"	Receive "Call Connected" Packet
Fail to answer ring	Send "Clear Request" Packet*
No answer, busy, or fast busy	Receive "Clear Indication" Packet
Hang up	Send "Clear Confirmation" Packet*
*With causes shown in packet	

Table 11.4. Network analogies after establishment of call.

Telephone Network	X.25 Packet Network
Hang up to disconnect	Send "Clear Request" Packet
Hear other person hang up	Receive "Clear Indication" Packet*
Hang up after other person hangs up	Send "Clear Confirmation" Packet
Call disconnected by network	Receive "Clear Indication" Packet*
*With causes shown in packet	

Figure 11.7 shows a "normal" sequence of a VC setup, two-way simultaneous data transfer, and terminal-initiated disconnect. Note that the four packet type identifiers of Table 11.5 are simply passed through the network without the network modifying them.

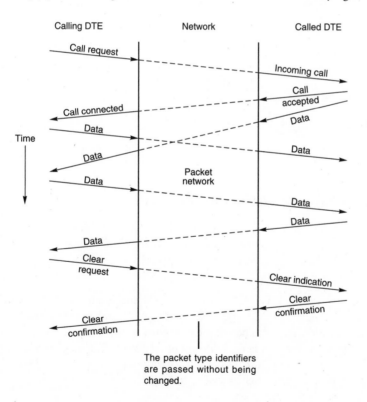

FIGURE 11.7.

A "normal" VC sequence.

Table 11.5. Packet type identifiers for call setup and clearing.

DTE to DCE	DCE to DTE	Octet #3
Call Request	Incoming Call	0 0 0 0 1 0 1 1
Call Accepted	Call Connected	0 0 0 0 1 1 1 1
Clear Request	Clear Indication	0 0 0 1 0 0 1 1
DTE-Initiated— Clear Confirmation	Network-Initiated— Clear Confirmation	0 0 0 1 0 1 1 1

Figure 11.8 shows what happens when a VC does not complete. If the VC is refused by the called DTE, the called DTE sends Clear Request. If the VC is refused by the network, the calling DTE receives Clear Indication.

FIGURE 11.8.

VC not completed.

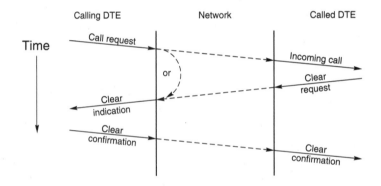

CALL REQUEST/INCOMING CALL PACKETS

The headers of the Call Request/Incoming Call pair of packets are the most complex of the various header formats. They contain not only the basic three octets shown in Figure 11.4, but also destination addressing and facility selection information. In certain cases, they also contain user data.

The logical channel numbers (LCNs) and logical channel group numbers (LCGNs) for PVC service are assigned by the carrier from the ranges of numbers that the carrier decides to designate for PVC service. The numbers assigned to opposite ends of a given logical channel do not have to be the same. Different numbers could be assigned to the opposite ends of the channel, and the intelligent switches within the network would make the appropriate conversions as the packets pass to and fro.

The numbers assigned to the ends of a logical channel do not have to be the same. The intelligent switcher will make the appropriate connection as required regardless of the end numbers.

In the case of VC service, the numerical values of logical channels at the opposite inter-faces are never the same; the network always converts these numbers to and fro. The channel numbers used are assigned from a pool of numbers available at the time of call setup.

In placing a Call Request, a calling DTE selects the highest logical channel number that does not exceed a limit specified by the carrier and that is not already being used on an-other VC. The network then pairs the selected logical channel number with that VC from that calling DTE. At the destination end, the network selects the lowest logical channel number that is not less than a limit specified by the carrier and that is not already in use with that called DTE. The network then pairs that logical channel number with that VC to that called DTE. The two DTEs engaged in PVC or VC transactions never know (or care) which LCGN or LCN is being used by the other DTE/DCE interface.

> The logical channel numbers used in VC service come from a pool of numbers available when the call is made. The numbers at the opposite interfaces are different.

VC DESTINATION ADDRESSING

The DTE Address field in the Call Request/Incoming Call Packet format contains digits that are handled much like telephone numbers, with up to 14 digits on international VCs. The arrangement of these 14 digits is given in X.121. For domestic calls, fewer digits are required.

There are many other details in X.25 that cannot be covered here, and the list of facilities and diagnostic codes continues to grow. Refer to the standard for details.

Value-Added Services

X.25 describes a highly flexible basic point-to-point service through a public network. To the user whose terminals operate in the X.25 packet mode, have a significant amount of traffic to send to many locations, and connect via a DTE/DCE serial interface to an X.25 network gateway, X.25 has few shortcomings. For the user who cannot meet all these cri-teria, X.25 does have limitations. Enhanced (value-added) service offerings, such as those provided by AT&T Information Systems, Sprint (formerly GTE Telenet), BT Tymnet (formerly Tymnet), and others, seek to address these and other matters:

> Enhanced, or value-added, services are provided by some carriers to overcome some of the shortcomings of X.25 that can arise when a terminal does not meet some prerequisites for full X.25 use.

- Broadcast services (sending the same data at the same time to many receivers).
- Dial access. (Because the DTE/DCE interface is intended as a two-way simulta-neously synchronous gateway, packetmode access normally cannot be provided via the public telephone network.)
- Conversion to lower speed start-stop transmission for low-volume terminals.
- Code and protocol conversion services.

The CCITT has provided guidance with regard to the third item, as will be shown later.

The X Series of Recommended Standards

Services, facilities, terminals, and interfaces are covered by CCITT sections X.1 through X.39. Network architecture, transmission, switching, and all remaining areas are covered by sections X.40 through X.200.

As stated earlier, X.25 is part of the "X" series of recommended standards for public data networks being made public by the CCITT. The X series is classified into two categories: X.1 through X.39, which deal with services, facilities, terminals, and interfaces; and X.40 through X.199, which deal with network architecture, transmission, signaling, switching, maintenance, and administrative arrangements. From a packet network user viewpoint, the most important X standards are given in the following list with their titles and brief descriptions.

X.1—International User Classes of Service in Public Data Networks. Assigns numerical class designation to different terminal speeds and types.

X.2—International User Services and Facilities in Public Data Networks. Specifies essential and additional services and facilities.

X.3—Packet Assembly/Disassembly Facility (PAD) in a Public Data Network. Describes the packet assembler/disassembler that normally is used at a network gateway to allow connection of a start-stop terminal to a packet network.

X.20bis—Use on Public Data Networks of DTE Designed for Interfacing to Asynchronous Duplex V-Series Modems. Allows use of V.24/V.28 (essentially the same as EIA RS-232).

X.21bis—Use on Public Data Networks of DTE Designated for Interfacing to Synchronous V-Series Modems. Allows use of V.24/V.28 (essentially the same as EIA RS-232) or V.35.

X.25—Interface Between DTE and DCE for Terminals Operating in the Packet Mode on Public Data Networks. Defines the architecture of three levels of protocols existing in the serial interface cable between a packet-mode terminal and a gateway to a packet network.

X.28—DTE/DCE Interface for a Start-Stop Mode DTE Accessing the PAD in a Public Data Network Situated in the Same Country. Defines the architecture of protocols existing in a serial interface cable between a start-stop terminal and an X.3 PAD.

X.29—Procedures for the Exchange of Control Information and User Data Between a PAD and a Packet Mode DTE or Another PAD. Defines the architecture of protocols behind the X.3 PAD, either between two PADs or between a PAD and a packet-mode terminal on the other side of the network.

X.75—Terminal and Transit Call Control Procedures and Data Transfer System on International Circuits Between Packet-Switched Data Networks. Defines the architecture of protocols between two public packet networks.

X.121—International Numbering Plan for Public Data Networks. Defines a numbering plan including code assignments for each nation.

Interrelationships Between X Standards

Figure 11.9 shows the interrelationships between many of these X standards. In summary: X.25 specifies the relationship between a packet-mode DTE and a packet network. X.28 specifies the relationship between a start-stop (asynchronous) DTE and an X.3 PAD that must reside between a nonpacket DTE and a packet network. X.29 specifies additional relationships above those in X.25 that a packet-mode DTE must satisfy when communicating with a nonpacket mode DTE through a packet network and PAD. X.29 also covers the relationships between two PADs when two nonpacket mode DTEs are communicating through a packet network.

The CCITT envisioned the X.3 PAD as being within the packet network—that is, behind the DCE. The 1980 version X.3 covers the PAD only for start-stop (asynchronous) terminals, but it leaves open the future possibility of covering other nonpacket terminals, for example, IBM BSC. Several stand-alone X.3 PADs are now marketed for connection of various start-stop and non-start-stop DTEs to packet networks.

Many X standard sections give details on other sections or add depth to specific areas of concern. In some cases, a section describes conditions that must be met before other sections become applicable.

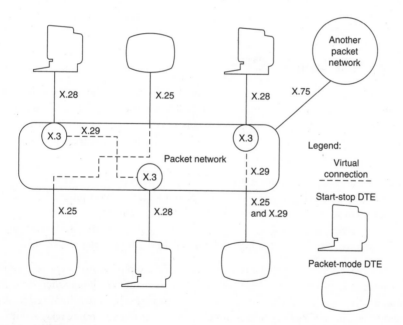

FIGURE 11.9.

Relationships between some X interface standards.

Frame Relay

Although X.25-based packet networks have gained widespread acceptance, their data handling capability in an era of increasing use of fiber-optic cable represents a severe limitation. The growth in the installation of fiber-optic cable for the transmission of voice, data, and video between communications carrier central offices has reduced the potential of transmission errors to fewer than 1 in 10^9 bits from the rate of 1 in 10^5 typically encountered on analog transmission facilities. However, the use of X.25 packet networks results in the flow of packets through numerous data switching exchanges, with each DSE performing error checking and sometimes performing flow control procedures, both of which introduce delays that adversely affect the throughput of data.

Although X.25 error-checking procedures were necessary when packet networks were established using analog leased lines to interconnect DSEs, for many communications applications in which data flows over fiber-optic cable, the use of a series of error checking procedures is both unnecessary and detrimental to developing high-speed transmission that effectively uses available bandwidth. Recognizing this limitation to X.25, a form of fast packet switching referred to as frame relay was developed.

Frame relay can be considered as a logical progression of X.25 packet switching. Under frame relay, most error checking and flow control functions performed in an X.25 network are eliminated. As a result, frame relay transmission occurs at data rates up to the 1.544 Mbps DS-1 rate, which are significantly higher than are obtainable using X.25 packet networks.

FRAME RELAY COMPONENTS

The connection of a computer or data terminal to a frame relay network involves the installation of various hardware components as well as knowledge of features unique to this data transport mechanism. From a physical perspective, the connection from a customer premise to a frame relay service provider is quite similar to the connection used for other types of services provided by communications vendors.

Figure 11.10 illustrates a typical connection from a customer premise to a frame relay service provider's nearest serving office. Note that communications equipment located at the customer premise can be any type of frame relay compliant device, such as a front-end processor, multiplexer, or router. The router illustrated in Figure 11.10 is assumed to provide each workstation on the LAN with access to the frame relay network.

Any frame relay compliant device that is to include a front-end processor, multiplexer, or router can be connected to a frame relay service.

The CSU/DSU converts unipolar digital signaling into a bipolar format for transmission on the local digital access line as described in a previous chapter. Although there is no reason why an analog local access line cannot be used to provide access to a frame relay service, present service provider policy is to commence the access rate to a frame relay service at 56 Kbps via a digital leased line. The local access line is routed to the serving telephone company office, where it is connected to the frame relay service provider's point of presence (POP), assuming that the service provider is a long-distance carrier. Recently, several local carriers announced frame relay service offerings which enable organizations that require the transmission of data only within a limited geographic area to have their frame relay service requirements performed by a local carrier, assuming that the carrier is cost competitive. Regardless of the frame relay service provider, the local access line can transport in effect multiplexed data representing two or more destinations that are routed as virtual circuits by the frame relay service provider.

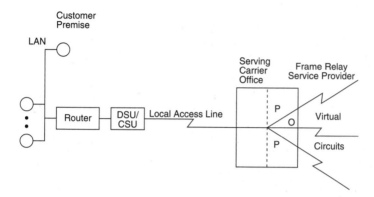

FIGURE 11.10.

Frame relay components.

Similar to the use of an X.25 packet network, the use of a frame relay service enables organizations to route data to many locations via the use of a single leased line. To illustrate this concept, consider the four-site frame relay network shown in the top portion of Figure 11.11. In this example, an organization with four geographically distributed LAN locations installed four frame relay access lines to connect each location to a frame relay access provider. Here, as requirements for transmission between locations occur, the mesh structured network of the service provider is used to get virtual circuits between each location. Note that only four routers, with one port per router, are required to get the capability to transmit between any location. In comparison, the use of leased lines to establish an organizational frame relay service would require six leased lines and 12 router ports, as indicated in the lower portion of Figure 11.11.

In establishing a frame relay service, it is important to distinguish between the operating rate of the frame relay port connection and what is referred to as the committed information rate (CIR). The port operating rate defines the highest possible speed you can achieve into the frame relay service. That rate also represents the maximum operating rate of any virtual circuit originating from the access line.

The carrier's frame relay network will carry traffic from many organizations. This means that at times the service provider's facilities might not be available to transport the full data rate flowing into the frame relay service.

FIGURE 11.11.

Comparing the use of a frame relay service to constructing a frame relay network.

Using a Frame Relay Service Provider

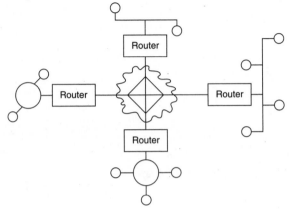

Establishing a Frame Relay Network

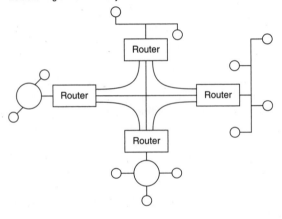

The committed information rate represents the minimum data transfer rate obtainable on a frame relay service.

Frame relay service providers for a fee will guarantee a minimum end-to-end transmission rate for each permanent virtual circuit required between your premise and distant locations. That minimum rate is referred to as the committed information rate (CIR). The higher the CIR, the higher level of performance, albeit at a higher cost.

During most of the day, the data rate transported by the frame relay service might equal the port operating rate of equipment connected to the service. However, during certain periods of time, many users subscribing to the service might require transmission through common portions of the carrier's network facilities that exceeds the capacity of intranetwork circuits. At that time, the carrier periodically drops frames of different subscribers until the aggregate data rate between the congested locations can be carried by the available bandwidth. In doing so, the frame relay service provider will not lower the operating rate of each virtual circuit below the CIR, because the CIR defines the minimum end-to-end transmission rate of each virtual circuit. Because equipment connected to the frame relay service is responsible for end-to-end data integrity, the originating device simply retransmits dropped frames.

To provide equipment connected to the frame relay service with notification that congestion is occurring, bits known as forward error congestion notification (FECON) and backward error congestion notification (BECON) are used within a frame. As congestion occurs, the frame relay service will set the FECON and BECON bit positions before actually dropping frames. Those settings alert equipment to the fact that congestion is occurring in the network.

COST COMPARISON

A comparison of the costs associated with the use of a frame relay service can involve an investigation of the pricing structure of many elements. Most frame relay service providers charge a frame relay port fee based on the operating rate of the interface to the service as well as a fee for the CIR subscribed for. Some service providers bill for each CIR for each permanent virtual circuit, whereas other service providers bill for a bandwidth allocation that represents the sum of the CIRs for all virtual circuits. Other charges that frame relay providers might bill for include a fixed charge per virtual circuit, a usage charge based on frames transmitted, and a distance charge based on the length of virtual circuits.

Open Systems in Interconnection Reference Model

In 1983, the International Organization for Standardization (ISO) culminated six years of intensive effort to develop and publish a guideline—a reference model—for describing data communications architectures. The resulting document, International Standard #7498, has been redrafted by the CCITT using its own terminology, and the redraft has been designated CCITT X.200. The generic name for both documents is Open Systems Interconnection Reference Model (OSI/RM)—usually called simply OSI.

OSI is not a protocol nor does it contain protocols. What OSI does is define a consistent language and boundaries for establishing protocols such that systems that abide by its rules should be "open" to one another—that is, able to communicate.

Decades of frustration caused by incompatibility between competitive or geographically distinct communications systems have created such an appetite for the establishment of cooperative systems that there is a virtual stampede toward global standardization of data communications architectures. Many standard committees in several organizations are now engaged in the development of protocols for the various layers in the numerous systems to which OSI will apply.

● OSI/RM is a reference model for data communication architectures. It has been redrafted by the CCITT and designated CCITT X.200.

● OSI defines a consistent language and boundaries for protocols so that systems that follow OSI can communicate with one another. However, OSI itself is not a protocol.

OSI Layers

OSI defines a complete architecture having seven layers. There is no specific reason why it is seven rather than six or eight; the functions that must be performed just happened to fall into roughly seven groupings. The lowest three layers (physical, link, and network) correspond closely to the physical, link, and packet levels of X.25. Protocols have been and are being developed for other kinds of systems, such as facsimile, integrated voice/data networks, videotex, and so forth. Even if the protocols were never written, OSI has had a tremendous impact in standardizing the way we view communications.

These are the official names of the seven layers, from top to bottom:

7. Application   3. Network

6. Presentation   2. Link

5. Session   1. Physical

4. Transport

Each successive step up the list takes one to a higher level of system supervision. In terms of the protocols, lower levels involve successively more embedded headers. Figure 11.12 shows how the seven levels relate for a system whose lower three layers correspond to X.25. (In this case, NH is the packet header.) The concept of layers was previously discussed in Chapter 10, "Alternatives in Local Area Networks."

FIGURE 11.12.

Seven embedded layers of OSI.

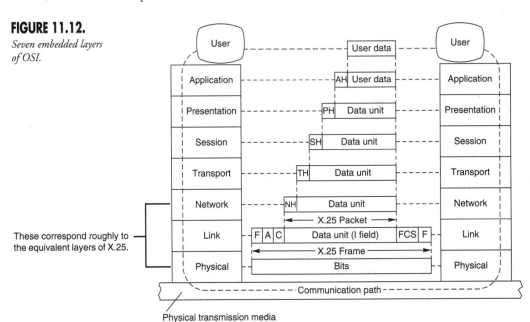

These correspond roughly to the equivalent layers of X.25.

An Analogy

Whenever people communicate, whether by computer or verbally, they invoke protocols at all seven levels of OSI. Without going into the laborious details and vocabulary of the OSI standard, we will illustrate the OSI categorizations of the seven levels from top to bottom for a typical telephone call.

1. *Physical Layer Concerns*—These are the actual sounds being uttered into the mouthpiece and heard from the receiver.

2. *Link Layer Concerns*—Talk when you're supposed to and listen when you're supposed to. Ask for a repeat if there is something you don't understand. Tell the other party to slow down if he's talking too fast.

3. *Network Layer Concerns*—Dial the number and listen for call-progress signals. Redial if you get a busy signal or if cut off. Disconnect when the conversation is completed.

4. *Transport Layer Concerns*—What is the most cost-effective way to handle this call (or these calls) consistent with priorities? What long-distance carriers should be used?

5. *Session Layers Concerns*—Can this situation be handled in one call or several? Will other people need to be brought in at different times? Who will control the discussion in a multiparty conversation? Who will reestablish the call if we're cut off?

6. *Presentation Layer Concerns*—Are we talking the same language and dialect?

7. *Application Layer Concerns*—Am I talking to the right person? Who is paying for this call? Is this the best time to talk, or should I call back later? Does the other party have a pencil and paper to take notes?

Anyone who has used a telephone in everyday business situations can relate to all seven levels of the reference model just described. By reflecting on X.25, the reader should be able to identify the analogies to the packet, link, and physical layer protocols.

● The basic requirements to establish, maintain, and terminate communications without error are similar whether verbal or computer communications are being used.

What Have You Learned?

1. When protocols are layered, the higher level layers are embedded inside fields of less intelligent layers.

2. Packet switching involves fast store-and-forward computers at each network node.

3. X.25 is an international standard packet switching architecture specifying three layers of protocols at the network gateway.

4. When properly used, X.25 networks provide a fast, reliable, accurate, flexible, and cost-effective data communications alternative.

5. X.25 specifies two services: Virtual Call service is analogous to a telephone call; Permanent Virtual Circuit service is analogous to a private line.

6. X.25 doesn't provide for dial access or for start-stop transmission, but enhanced services do.

7. A single X.25 interface can handle many logical channels at the same time.

8. X.25 is but a part of a larger group of CCITT standards on public data networks.

9. X.25/X.121 provides for an extremely large worldwide population of terminals.

10. Frame relay is a form of fast packet switching in which error checking and flow control is minimized.

11. Open Systems Interconnection is a reference architectural model that is revolutionizing the way we view telecommunications.

Quiz for Chapter 11

1. The electrical state of the control leads in a serial interface is a concern of:
   a. The physical-layer protocol.
   b. The link-layer protocol.
   c. The network-layer protocol.
   d. None of the above.

2. The X.25 standard specifies a:
   a. Technique for dial access.
   b. Technique for start-stop data.
   c. Data bit rare.
   d. DTE/DCE interface.

3. The X.25 standard is:
   a. Required for all packet switching networks.
   b. A recommendation of the CCITT.
   c. A complete description of a public data network.
   d. Used by all packet terminals.

4. The X.25 standard for packet networks is analogous to:
   a. PBX standards for a telephone network.
   b. Handset standards for a telephone.
   c. Local loop standards for a telephone network.
   d. Switching standards for a telephone network.

5. The value of the "A" field in an LAPB frame specifies:
   a. The calling DTE for a virtual call.
   b. The called DTE for a virtual call.
   c. The data sink for a VC or PVC.
   d. One of the two ends of a serial interface.

6. A group of packets from a source through an X.25 packet system to a sink:

    a. Arrives in the same order sent for VC, but not PVC.

    b. Arrives in the same order sent for PVC, but not VC.

    c. Arrives in the same order sent for both VC and PVC.

    d. None of the above.

7. The value of $N(S)$ is related to the value of $P(S)$ as follows:

    a. $N(S) - P(S)$ = number of outstanding packets.

    b. $N(S) - P(S)$ = number of outstanding frames.

    c. $N(S) - P(S)$ = number of active logical channels in a link.

    d. They are not related.

8. A protocol is a set of rules governing a time sequence of events that must take place:

    a. Between peers.

    b. Between nonpeers.

    c. Across an interface.

    d. None of the above.

9. The OSI Reference Model defines the functions for seven layers of protocols:

    a. Including the user and communications medium.

    b. Not including the user or communications medium.

    c. Including the communications medium but not the user.

    d. Including the user but not the communications medium.

10. The X.25 standard covers how many OSI layers:

    a. 3.

    b. 4.

    c. 7.

    d. None.

11. Architecturally, link protocols are at a level:

    a. Lower than physical protocols.

    b. Higher than physical protocols.

    c. The same as physical protocols.

    d. None of the above.

12. A data packet is a packet header together with:

    a. A network layer.

    b. An administrative layer.

    c. User data.

    d. A packet switch.

13. A network node joining three or more links is a:

    a. DSE.

    b. DTE.

    c. DCE.

    d. DTE and DCE.

14. The X.25 standard specifies how many separate protocol layers at the serial interface gateway:

    a. 8.

    b. 2.

    c. 4.

    d. 3.

15. The LAPB frame structure and the frame structure of SDLC are:

    a. Opposite.

    b. Identical.

    c. Reversed.

    d. None of the above.

16. Establishing a virtual "connection" is functionally equivalent to:

    a. Placing a telephone call prior to a conversation.

    b. Connecting a virtual memory.

    c. Physically connecting a DTE and DCE.

    d. None of the above.

17. In X.25 network layer protocol, the data packets normally contain:

    a. One octet of header plus data.

    b. Two octets of header plus data.

    c. Three octets of header plus data.

    d. Four octets of header plus data.

18. The frame relay committed information rate represents:

    a. The maximum data rate on the network.

    b. The steady state data rate on the network.

    c. The minimum data rate on the network.

    d. The interface data rate.

19. The number of circuits required for the connection of equipment at four locations to each other is:

    a. 2.

    b. 4.

    c. 6.

    d. 8.

20. The number of ports required for the connection of equipment at four locations to each other is:

    a. 3.

    b. 6.

    c. 9.

    d. 12.

21. Notification of the occurrence of congestion in a frame relay service occurs through the:

    a. Committed information rate.

    b. Forward error congestion notification.

    c. Backward error congestion notification.

    d. Both b and c.

22. The OSI reference model is:

    a. Worthless.

    b. A protocol.

    c. Not a protocol.

    d. None of the above.

23. Layer 1 of the OSI model is the:

    a. Link layer.

    b. Physical layer.

    c. Network layer.

    d. Transport layer.

24. The applications layer of the OSI
model is the:

    a. Seventh layer.

    b. Sixth layer.

    c. Fifth layer.

    d. Fourth layer.

Network Design and Management

About This Chapter

The user's terminal is the source and sink of all user data, but good network design and management is usually necessary to make data communications networks usable and affordable. The term "network design" refers to the selection of various circuit parameters and to the selection and interconnection of various devices to accomplish design goals.

This chapter covers the goals, principles, and tools of efficient network design and management. Many of the administrative principles of network management, such as planning and budgeting, are similar to other kinds of management. The technical aspects to be discussed here include network design goals and throughput timing, networking devices, interconnection, fault isolation, fault correction, and quality assurance.

Any network, no matter how simple or complex, can be incorporated into a larger network. The approach of this chapter is to start with the principles of good network design for basic point-to-point networks, establishing a solid basis for these, and then to discuss some of the technologies for building more complex networks.

Network Design Goals

To achieve an optimum cost of a data network versus application balance, factors other than equipment cost must enter into the final cost determination.

The greatest motivation for network design is cost. Cost includes a multitude of factors other than the prices of the terminals and networks. For example, the costs of local area networks are usually justified on the basis of higher speed, because the time of the people and computers who use these networks is expensive. In other situations, communications reliability is the basic cost justification. In many cases, the failure of a data communications system to function properly when needed can cost a business far more than the price of the system.

If price were no object, most data networks would be a simple point-to-point channel. Indeed, if a point-to-point channel can be kept busy at a reasonably high bit rate for transmitting data that's worth sending, it might be the most cost-effective way to handle a particular data communications task.

On the other hand, many data applications cannot cost-justify dedicated channels because of insufficient quantity or priority of the data. In such cases, it is sometimes possible to combine data from more than one source into a single long-haul transmission path by use of multiplexers and other networking devices. Although the use of such techniques might allow cost justification of the application, the addition of equipment is likely to reduce reliability and to increase the time and effort required to find and correct a problem.

The underlying objective of data networking is to strike a satisfactory balance between the accurate, timely, and secure delivery of user data and total cost. The term "satisfactory" implies that the user who is paying for the delivery system is satisfied with it.

Accuracy

Previous chapters have discussed the subject of accuracy in terms of error control. Not all data transmissions are required to be error-free; for example, overseas telex messages and cablegrams that contain human-language messages do not suffer loss of meaning if a word is occasionally misspelled. On the other hand, the transfer of accounting information between financial institutions requires a high level of accuracy.

The timely delivery of data involves the amount of data to be transmitted, the importance and priority of the information, the average rate of transfer of error-free data, and the availability of the network to the user.

Timeliness

Timeliness involves four general aspects, which are discussed in the following sections.

AMOUNT OF DATA

Obviously, the amount and priority of data will have an impact on the throughput rate required, but cost must be considered in establishing these parameters. In some extreme situations, the amount of data might be so great that the best way to transfer it will be by physically transporting truckloads of magnetic tape! At the other extreme, a satisfactory "networking" solution might be a simple low-speed transmission over a dialed point-to-point telephone channel.

PRIORITY OF DATA

As a general rule, the importance and frequency of testing is directly proportional to the importance and priority of the data. An Italian proverb asserts, "Good things cost less than bad ones." Although this proverb doesn't apply universally to data communications, it does remind us that the best solution isn't always the cheapest. There are numerous situations, for example in industrial process control and manufacturing, in which a total failure of a data link could cost a company more than $10,000 an hour. In such cases, reliability, testing, and planning for alternative methods obviously are of extreme importance.

INFORMATION THROUGHPUT RATE

The information throughput rate, properly known as the Transfer Rate of Information Bits (TRIB), will be covered in detail in the next section. Basically, TRIB is the average rate of transfer of the actual error-free bits of user data, not counting overhead bits.

AVAILABILITY OF THE NETWORK

Availability of the network is determined by three factors: access time, mean time between failures (MTBF), and mean time to restore service (MTRS). For private lines and permanent virtual circuits, access time is of no concern; for dialed connections and virtual calls, the time delay to establish the call might be significant in comparison with the transmission time if the amount of data is small. MTBF usually refers to the time between "hard" (permanent) failures, but if the error rate becomes high enough, the TRIB can nosedive even though the connection still exists. MTRS might involve a temporary restoration, as in the case of dialed backup for a private line, or it might simply refer to repair time if no alternative service is available.

Security

Security is receiving increasing attention as data communications is used more and more for significant and important matters of everyday life. Many sources of information are now available that cover this area in detail. Besides the physical aspects of security, data communications security involves both privacy and authentication. Privacy refers to secrecy (use of codes) and protection from unauthorized access (use of passwords). Authentication has to do with ensuring that a data message hasn't been tampered with between source and sink, and with verifying that the sender of the message is as claimed.

As more and more confidential and proprietary information is being transmitted through data communications systems, the security of this information becomes more important.

In certain kinds of transmissions, authentication is more important than any other aspect of networking mentioned so far. For example, a Swiss bank receiving an international telex from another bank containing instructions to transfer funds between accounts will be interested in knowing whether extra zeros have been added to the amount, whether account numbers have been modified, and whether the claimed source of the message is authentic.

In summary, data network design involves a complex series of interrelated judgments involving these and other factors:

1. Cost of delivery system	6. Reliability
2. Priority of the data	7. Testing
3. Response time required	8. Contingency Planning
4. Throughput rate	9. Privacy
5. Accessibility	10. Authentication

Transfer Rate of Information Bits

● The TRIB is a result of several factors other than the data link bit rate. In almost all cases, the TRIB is less than the bit rate at the serial interface.

As mentioned earlier, TRIB is sometimes called the information throughput rate. By definition,

$$\text{TRIB} = \frac{\text{Number of information bits accepted by the sink}}{\text{Total time required to get those bits accepted}}$$

Due to the burst nature of most data transmission, TRIB has meaning only as an average over a period. Although the data link bit rate has a lot to do with TRIB, other factors might at times have as much or more influence. For example, if the channel is noisy, a higher bit rate might increase the error rate to such an extent that the TRIB actually goes down.

TRIB is almost always less than the bit rate at the serial interface. (In a few sophisticated data compression systems, the TRIB might appear to exceed the actual interface bit rate because the receiver puts out more bits than were actually transmitted.) Two other parameters that usually affect TRIB are transmission overhead and delays. Both of these parameters are closely tied to the coding and blocking of the data and to the protocols used. For example, if the protocol requires that acknowledgment of a block must be received by the sender before the next block is transmitted, round-trip delays will be added to the denominator of the TRIB definition given previously. In such instances, block length and delays can have a substantial effect on TRIB. Besides bit rate, these are the factors that should be considered in estimating TRIB:

● The major parameters that adversely affect the TRIB are transmission overhead and delays.

1. Noninformation bits sent with the data. These include:

   a. Start and stop bits if asynchronous transmission is used.

   b. Parity bits if ASCII code is used.

    c. Redundant (or "stuffed") zeroes if a bit-oriented link protocol (SDLC/ HDLC) is used.

    d. Filler bits used by teleprocessing system utilities to fill out partial data blocks, if any.

2. Noninformation characters in the message stream. Depending on the link protocol used, these might include:

    a. Sync characters or flags.

    b. Address characters.

    c. Control characters (STX, ACK, and so on) or control byte.

    d. Error-checking characters (BCC or FCS).

    e. Transparency characters (DLE) and pads.

3. Noninformation messages required in the administration of the link protocol. These are the initialization, connect, disconnect, polling and status messages, and so forth. They usually are not counted in TRIB calculations if the sessions are sufficiently long for them to have a negligible effect.

4. Carrier turn-on delay. This is the period of time between request-to-send from the terminal and clear-to-send from the modem. It is also known as "modem turnaround time." It is required only when a modem is operating with a switched carrier on a circuit that cannot support the bit rate of the modem two ways simultaneously, such as a dialed connection at 4800 bps. It also applies to at least the remote (secondary) stations, and sometimes to all stations, on a multipoint circuit. The amount of the delay, if any, is programmed into the modem at the time of installation, based on the modem manufacturer's recommendations for the particular circuit type and bit rate. It can be from a few milliseconds to a few hundred milliseconds.

5. Modem propagation delay. All synchronous modems operating on voice-grade circuits buffer the data on both transmit and receive. Depending on bit rate, the delay can be in the range of 2 to 10 milliseconds (ms) per modem.

6. Circuit propagation delay. Microwave radio signals, including communication satellite signals, and signals in optical fibers travel at near the speed of light. Electrical signals in local wires and cables travel somewhat slower. Also, many local telephone systems contain buffers of various types. As a rule of thumb, estimate 6 ms for local equipment on each end, and 1 millisecond for each 150 miles of cross-country terrestrial circuit. This gives [12 + (miles/150)] milliseconds for terrestrial one-way delay. Depending on latitude and longitude, satellite signals travel 45,000 to 50,000 miles in propagating from one satellite earth station to another; they also are buffered in the satellite and in the earth stations. As a rule of thumb, estimate 350 ms from user-to-user (one way), including terrestrial links between respective earth stations and users.

●

TRIB also is affected by transmission delays, buffer delays, response time computations, number of filler bits, and the transmission error rate.

7. Other propagation delays due to buffering. Most devices used in creating complex networks for data communications store groups of received bits in buffers before retransmitting those bits on the next link. Multiplexers, concentrators, and other types of communications processors are examples of such devices. Depending on the number of bits so buffered and the circuit length, the buffer delays in some systems can exceed all other propagation delays in the transfer of data. Buffer delays are normally included in the equipment specifications provided by the manufacturer.

8. Computation time for response and other interlock time delays. Although the time for data calculations normally wouldn't be considered in TRIB, processing time required to check for transmission errors and fabricate an appropriate response should be included because it is a communications function. Also, systems that allow multiple blocks to be sent between acknowledgments often require time gaps or filler bits between successive blocks.

9. Error rate. For blocked data, if the error rate is not large, it is usually sufficient to estimate TRIB by first assuming no errors, then making an adjustment based on the block error rate (BLER). For example, if 1 percent of the blocks contain an error, the block error rate is said to be 1 percent. This means that 1 percent of the blocks will need to be retransmitted; thus, the TRIB will be lowered by approximately 1 percent due to errors.

Example of TRIB Calculation

Problem: How long will it take to transmit 10,000 records a distance of 500 miles every day on a dialed connection at 4800 bps using BSC protocol? There are 80 EBCDIC characters per record, and 2 records per block; thus, there are 5000 blocks containing 160 characters. What is the TRIB?

The first step in calculating TRIB is to determine the propagation delays.

Solution: Because the connection is dialed at 4800 bps, the carrier must be switched, which means there will be a carrier turn-on delay in each direction for each block (one for data, one for acknowledgment). From the modem manufacturer's recommendations, this is established as 100 ms. Other delays include the following types:

- Circuit propagation delay, which for a terrestrial 500 mile circuit would be about 15 ms.

- Modem propagation delay, which according to the modem operation manual is 4 ms.

- Computation delay, which according to measurements on the actual terminals is 10 ms for the receiving terminal and negligible for the transmitting terminal.

Assume that each data transmission block includes

1	leading pad character
4	sync characters
1	STX character
160	data characters (2 records at 80 characters each)
1	EOB or ETX character
2	character lengths of BCC
1	trailing pad
170	characters

Thus, each block has 170 characters including overhead, but not counting DLE characters that would be sent if transparency is required. If each character requires 8 bits, the transmission time actually needed to send a data block at 4800 bps will be

$$\frac{170 \times 8}{4800} = 283 \text{ ms}$$

Assume that each acknowledgment block includes

1	leading pad character
4	sync characters
2	character lengths of ACK0/ACK1
1	trailing pad character
8	characters (all overhead)

The transmit time actually needed to send an acknowledgment block will be

$$\frac{8 \times 8}{4800} = 13 \text{ ms}$$

Including delays, the round-trip time to send 1 block will be

100	ms near-end carrier turn-on
283	ms data block transmission
4	ms transmit modem propagation
15	ms circuit propagation
4	ms receive modem propagation
10	ms sink terminal calculation
100	ms far-end carrier turn-on
13	ms acknowledgment block transmission
4	ms transmit modem propagation
15	ms circuit propagation
4	ms receive modem propagation
552	ms or 0.552 second round-trip time per block

● The next step is to determine the character count in the data block and acknowledgment block, and the transmission time required at the data rate.

● The calculation is completed by combining all delay times to get round-trip time per block, which results in the total time for all blocks. The total time divided into the actual data bits transferred gives the TRIB value.

The total time needed to send 5000 blocks, neglecting retransmissions due to errors, is 0.552 × 5000 = 2760 seconds, or 46 minutes. If we assume that 1 percent of the blocks will contain at least 1 bit in error, then the time will be lengthened by about 1 percent. The actual number of information bits transmitted is 160 characters per block × 8 bits per character × 5000 blocks = 6,400,000 bits. If errors are not counted, then:

$$\text{TRIB} = \frac{6,400,000 \text{ bits}}{2760} = 2319 \text{ bits/sec}$$

Maximizing TRIB

It will be noted that the TRIB in the example just given is less than half of the modem bit rate of 4800 bps! Major factors contributing to this poor result were the modem carrier turn-on delay (modem turnaround) and the fact that acknowledgment of each block had to be received before the next block could be transmitted. (Note that the total of these times accounted for almost 40 percent of the round-trip time.)

Persons who are unfamiliar with the type of calculation just illustrated often assume that the best way to improve throughput is to increase modem speed. To attempt such a remedy in this example would probably result in lower (not higher) TRIB, because it is likely that the modem turnaround, modem propagation delay, and error rate all would be higher. Not only would the modems cost more, but also the dialing and redialing required to get a connection that would operate satisfactorily at a higher rate would be both time-consuming and frustrating to the operator—if it would work at all.

One possible approach to improvement of TRIB in the example shown might be to eliminate modem turnaround entirely by installing full duplex modems. Still another approach to TRIB improvement might be to change to a different protocol. SDLC is capable of allowing acknowledgment of up to seven frames with only one response. However, to change from BSC to SDLC link protocol would require expensive software and probably hardware modifications in both terminals.

The best way to improve the TRIB in this case would be to increase block length. Assuming sufficient buffer capacity in both terminals, an increase of block length from 2 records to 10 records would result in a total round-trip time of 1.619 seconds per block, with only 1000 blocks required to be sent. The total time needed would be 27 minutes, a daily saving of 19 minutes of long-distance calling. The new TRIB would be 3953 bps, an increase of 70 percent.

> **Caution:** Increasing block length always increases the block error rate because there is a greater exposure to the probability of error in a long block. For a block length increase of 500 percent, the BLER will increase by roughly the same factor. In the example, if the block error rate had really been 1 percent before (very high for such a short block), it would be about 5 percent now. This would erode some of the time saving.

●
Several actions can be taken that would improve the TRIB. Installing a two-way simultaneous channel might provide the desired improvement, if the added expense of a private line is justified.

●
Other possible approaches to improving TRIB performance include changing to a different protocol or increasing block length.

Optimum Block Length

Figure 12.1 illustrates how block length affects TRIB, all other factors being equal. For very short blocks, the TRIB is low (as illustrated in the previous calculations) because overhead is a significant proportion of the total transmission. For very long blocks also, the TRIB is low because there is a significant probability of error within the block, and most blocks have to be retransmitted. Somewhere between the extremes, there is a block length, L_M, which yields maximum TRIB. Whether L_M is optimum depends on several factors besides TRIB:

- If the error rate is low, the value of L_M might be so large as to be impractical, particularly for an interactive data system in which fast response is more important than throughput.

- Quite often, the memory capacity of the terminals is not sufficient to handle a block length of L_M.

- The utility programs that actually perform the blocking of data usually won't allow a precise match with L_M.

- Long-term changes in error rates and delays make precise matching impractical anyway.

●
Exact matching to the optimum block length often is not practical because of what the blocking program can accomplish or because long-term changes in error rates and delays cause the optimum block length to change.

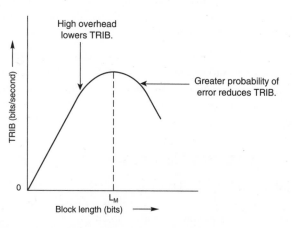

FIGURE 12.1.

Block length (L_M) for maximum TRIB.

Regardless of these considerations, the network designer should make reasonable estimates of TRIB, be aware of the major impairments to faster TRIB, and ensure that the combination of factors is "best" for each situation.

Networking Devices

Several types of special-purpose devices exist for improving cost-effectiveness of data networks. The basic purposes and advantages of the main types are given in the paragraphs that follow. Refer to Chapter 6, "Multiplexing Techniques," for detailed information concerning the operation and utilization of multiplexers.

Multiplexers

Both the FDM and the TDM have advantages and disadvantages that must be considered to determine which to use in a particular application.

Multiplexers are devices that allow the combination of several data channels independently into one physical circuit. Data streams so combined can be separated and recovered at the opposite end of the system. There are two main types: frequency-division multiplexers (FDMs) and time-division multiplexers (TDMs). FDM has the advantage that it can be used on multipoint circuits, but the individual channels usually must each be for start-stop data. TDM can be used if all channels are point-to-point and generally allows faster bit rates and potentially more channels than FDM at less cost.

TDMs are of two types: classical (or dumb) TDMs and statistical (or smart) TDMs. Dumb TDMs should be used if the duty cycles of the data channels to be multiplexed are relatively high. A high duty cycle means that the channel is actually carrying bits most of the time. Because dumb TDMs send even idle (marking) bits when a channel becomes inactive, they waste a lot of potential capacity when the duty cycles are low.

Whenever usage statistics indicate low duty cycles as the normal mode of utilization of most of the channels to be multiplexed, a statistical multiplexer system is usually a good choice. These devices send only data bits (no idle bits), so they can appear to have a higher total bit rate than the actual rate if there is a high percentage of idle bits coming from the terminals.

Modem Sharing Devices

Modem sharing devices allow several terminals to share the serial interface of one modem.

Modem sharing devices (MSDs) do just that: they allow several remote terminals at one site on a common multipoint circuit to share a single modem at that site. MSDs do not multiplex; they simply provide a means of sharing the serial interface of one modem among several terminals.

A useful networking device is the protocol converter—a microprocessor that converts data from one protocol to another.

When a modem sharing unit is used, transmission occurs via polling and broadcast. To understand the operation and utilization of a modem sharing unit (MSU), consider Figure 12.2, in which three terminals share access to a common modem via an MSU.

Line Bridging Devices

Line bridging devices allow two or more analog circuits to be shared as one. Bridges are not multiplexers. They allow one modem to be used with circuits to more than one destination. Telephone companies and users can use bridges to create multipoint analog circuits from point-to-point segments.

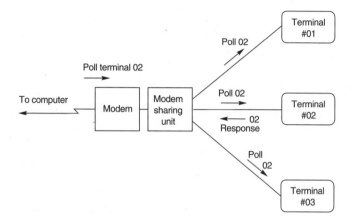

FIGURE 12.2.

Modem sharing unit enables transmission via polling and broadcasting.

Modem Eliminators

Modem eliminators are used to connect two DTEs together directly. They also are called null modems.

Protocol Converters

Protocol converters are microprocessors that convert data operating in one protocol, say start-stop ASCII, to another, say IBM BSC. A dial-up X.3 PAD for converting start-stop to X.25 is an example of a protocol converter.

Interconnection of Networking Devices

The preceding section contained only a partial listing of devices intended to interconnect digital serial interfaces. Space does not allow a discussion of the numerous possible alternative requirements in the actual interconnection of leads between devices, terminals, modems, and so forth.

Probably the best advice that can be given is to study the equipment manuals and the interface standards themselves. As an alternative, the reader is referred to the book *Data Communications Networking Devices, Third Edition,* by Gilbert Held, published by John Wiley & Sons, for specific information concerning the operation and utilization of more than 25 networking devices. Fortunately, all standard digital serial interfaces have been designed so that no actual damages can be caused by interconnecting two devices

●

When actually making the physical connections between the various types of networking devices, be sure that all equipment manuals and interface standards are thoroughly understood.

incorrectly. In the case of uncertainty, a programmable break-out box (discussed in the next section) can be a handy tool for trying different combinations until the connection works.

In addition to the physical mating of pins and receptacles when connecting two serial interfaces together, particular attention should be given to:

- Which is the device (Source) of signal and which is the receiver (sink) of signal. Each pin-receptacle pair must contain one of each. For example, pin 2 of an RS-232 connector involves a driver in a DTE and a receiver in a DCE.

- Stand-alone TDMs are generally schizophrenic; that is, the terminal ports each behave as DCEs communicating with DTEs, and the trunk port behaves as a DTE communicating with a DCE. TDMs generally are manufactured with female receptacles on all ports, both terminal and trunk, requiring male-to-male cables between the trunk port and trunk DCE. When such a TDM port is being extended by use of a remote channel, special care must be given to control, data, and timing leads. The TDM manual should be read to get specific information.

- Whenever synchronous devices are interconnected, special attention should be given to clocking. Remember that the DCE is normally the source (driver) for both the transmit clock and the receiver clock. However, when two DCEs are interconnected, one DCE must accept external clocking, and it must be an internal switch setting. The presence of clock pulses on the external clock pin is not sufficient to make a modem accept external clocking.

- Digital transmission systems normally will not accept external clocking, because their timing comes from a central network clock.

Fault Isolation

Fault detection usually is pretty easy; fault isolation is more complicated. The first question is, "Is the problem in a terminal or in the communications system?" Troubleshooting data terminals is beyond the scope of this book. If the terminals pass self-test procedures, but still will not communicate, chances are good that the problem is in the communications system.

Loopback Tests

In the loopback test, which is a basic data communications fault isolation technique, faults are successively isolated by the process of elimination.

One of the basic techniques for isolation of faults in data communications is the loopback test. In a loopback, the output at the far end of a system or subsystem is connected to the input of the return path. Then the output of the return path is examined in relation to the input to the outgoing path.

Figure 12.3 illustrates how successive loopbacks can be used to isolate a fault on a single point-to-point data link that uses an analog circuit. The local modem is first self-tested using an analog loopback at its far terminals (point A). If it passes the test, the loop is removed from the local modem. Then the local modem and the analog circuit are tested together using a remote analog loopback at the near terminals (point B) of the remote modem. If that test also appears satisfactory, then the remote analog loop is removed and the entire data link is tested end-to-end round trip using a digital loopback at the far terminals (point C) of the remote modem. (Loopbacks at points B and C are useful only if the channel is full-duplex.) Using a process of elimination, the location of the fault can be narrowed to the local modem, the analog circuit, or the remote modem.

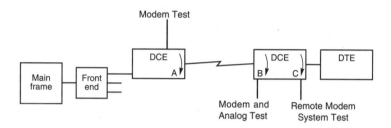

FIGURE 12.3.

Loopback test points.

Loopbacks cannot determine which side of a path, outgoing or return, is faulty, but only the person who has to repair it really needs that information. End-to-end tests can distinguish the direction of the fault, but that often requires at least modest training of a person at the remote site.

CAUTION NUMBER ONE

Know what is being tested when performing a self-test on a device. As with terminals, no self-test ever tests all the circuitry. For example, Figure 12.4 shows that a self-test of a modem doesn't check data continuity through the line transformers and through the RS-232 interface circuitry. The latter problem can be very treacherous. Whenever practical, use external tests to be sure.

CAUTION NUMBER TWO

Most analog data circuits are designed to operate with a substantial drop in signal level from input to output; for example, there is a 16-dB loss each way in a private-line voice-grade circuit to be used for data. When an analog loopback is performed at the remote end without inserting gain at that point, the input signal for the return path is 16 dB lower than it should be. Such a low-level signal can cause both the analog return path and the local modem receiver to operate improperly, perhaps giving a false indication. Many systems that provide for remote analog loopbacks automatically insert gain in the loopback path to avoid this problem. If the modems used in the test depicted in Figure 12.3 are not so equipped, a different procedure should be used. For example, perform a self-test on each modem, and then with an assistant at the far end, perform an end-to-end test.

One should not only know what parameters of the faulty device can be tested, but also know the capabilities, limitations, and special requirements of the test system/equipment.

FIGURE 12.4.

Some modem circuitry is not tested in self-test.

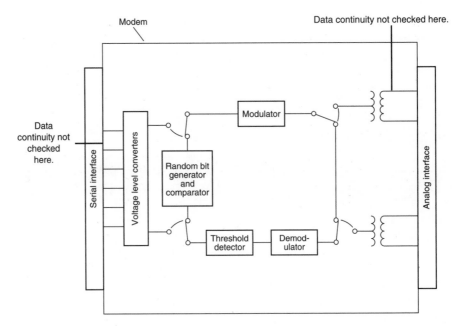

Switches are shown in self-test position

Data Communications Test Equipment

Test equipment enables network technicians and users to observe the state of the DTE-DCE interface circuits, as well as the composition of data on a circuit. In this section, we will examine the operation and initialization of light types of test equipment.

AMPLIFIER-MONITOR

A wide variety of test equipment is available to assist in the detection and isolation of faults in data communication systems.

The self-contained, battery-operated audio amplifier-speaker-monitor, sometimes called a "watergate box," is readily available at retail electronic supply stores for around $20 or less. It not only is useful for detecting modem carrier and changes in modem output signals, but it's also the easiest way to detect a noisy circuit or to tell whether a modem is putting out tone-dial or pulse-dial signals. It can also be used to monitor call progress and answer-back tones on dialed data links.

BREAKOUT BOX

The basic specialized data-testing device is the breakout box, so named because it provides access to individual leads in the serial interface between a DTE (such as a terminal) and a DCE (such as a modem). Prices range from about $60 to $250 for breaking out the

25 leads of an RS-232 interface. Price depends on ruggedness, whether the unit is programmable (leads can be crisscrossed), and whether data activity can be observed directly without a voltmeter. The higher priced units feature built-in battery power, full tri-state LED monitoring of leads, programmability, ruggedness, and DIP switches to open the circuits of individual leads. They might also provide positive and negative test voltages.

BIT ERROR RATE TESTER

The next step up in acquisition of specialized data test equipment would be a bit error rate tester (BERT). RS-232 BERTs range in price from under $500 to around $3000, depending on whether block error (BLERT) and error-second measurements are to be included, whether start and stop bit insertion/deletion is required (if asynchronous multiplexers are in the circuit), and various automatic indicator features. Some models also feature programmable message generators for checking out teleprinters. High-speed BERT/BLERTs in the multimegabit-per-second range can cost much more.

DECIBEL METER

If analog voice-grade circuits are used extensively, a decibel (dB) meter is a wise investment for checking transmit and receive levels. A basic dB meter costs around $200. Persons considering purchase of a dB meter should consider a combination unit. Excellent portable meters with digital display are available. Such a meter that can read dBm, relative dB, frequency, relative frequency, voltage, current, and resistance costs about $400 to $500. Such an expenditure is not recommended unless testing on analog circuits is expected to be a common occurrence.

OSCILLOSCOPE

A multichannel oscilloscope (or "scope") with x-y inputs can be used in conjunction with a breakout box for observing serial interface signals and in conjunction with a modem for detecting certain impairments on analog circuits. Examples of the use of a dual-trace scope in the RS-232 interface would be to measure modem turnaround time, to check for crosstalk interference between timing leads, and to observe degradation of signals in long serial interface cables.

With synchronous modems having signal-space (constellation) pattern generators, an x-y oscilloscope becomes a powerful instrument for detecting phase hits, phase jitter, amplitude hits, harmonic distortion, dropouts, and impulse noise in analog circuits. With other modems, a scope can be used to observe eye patterns for harmonic distortion, phase jitter, and certain types of hits.

●
An oscilloscope, used within a breakout box for access, is an important error isolation and testing tool.

Scopes that are suitable for these purposes generally cost in the range of $800 to $3000, depending on compactness, maximum data rate, and number of channels.

VOICE FREQUENCY TEST SET

A voice-frequency test set permits measurement of frequency response, noise, and distortion of voice-grade analog circuits.

For the really serious user of data over voice-grade analog circuits, a voice frequency test set is a device that can quantify the major parameters of a voice-grade analog circuit. Standard capabilities include frequency response (amplitude received versus frequency for constant amplitude transmitted), C-message noise in dBrnc, C-message notched noise (S/N) in dB, and audio monitoring. Costs can range from $1500 upward, depending on the degree of automation in the tests and additional test functions provided. Although the less expensive units do not provide for measurement of envelope delay distortion (one of the two parameters affected by C-conditioning), large amounts of delay distortion often are accompanied by large amounts of attenuation distortion, which is much easier to measure. Voice frequency test sets normally should be used in pairs to provide end-to-end testing.

DATA LINK CONTENT MONITOR

A data link content monitor monitors and displays signals crossing the serial interface. Some allow specified sequences to be stored for later analysis.

Many large users of data communications have painfully discovered that the general-purpose computer is not an efficient device for debugging data link and network protocols. Nor is it the best device for bit error rate testing of wideband data channels, T1 multiplexers, and the like. The computer time, programmer time, and other expensive resources saved in a single project often can pay for the purchase of test equipment to cover these areas.

One equipment category is the basic RS-232 data link content monitor at approximately $1000 to $6000. This device simply monitors and displays signals passing across the serial interface. The display is normally in terms of characters, if appropriate, or it can be in binary or hexadecimal in the case of uncoded data. Pricing varies with the number of codes, the type of display, the capability to trap (or freeze) and display specific sequences, the amount of memory, scrolling of trapped memory contents, speed of the device with and without recording in memory, and whether the conditions of various nondata leads in the serial interface are recorded with the data for later analysis.

SIMULATOR

Monitor devices are excellent for diagnosing protocol problems in data links, but they are not efficient for system development. This function is best handled by a simulator. Such a device can be user-programmed to simulate a computer port, remote terminal, or network gateway in order to "exercise" the hardware/software system being developed.

Simulators are actually special-purpose computers utilizing easy-to-learn high-level programming languages. They also can be programmed to operate effectively as content monitors, BERTs, and BLERTs. Prices range from $1000 to $25,000, depending on protocols supported, speed, serial interfaces supported, amount of memory, type of display, ease of programming, and portability. The more sophisticated units provide simulation up through the packet level (OSI Level 3) of X.25/X.75 protocols.

●
Because a simulator is actually a special-purpose computer, it can be programmed to simulate a computer port, remote terminal, or network gateway for system development.

PROTOCOL ANALYZER

The protocol analyzer is the most sophisticated type of data communications test equipment currently marketed. The protocol analyzer gets its name from the major function it performs—protocol analysis. In doing so, the protocol analyzer monitors the bit stream flowing on a communications circuit or a LAN cable and decodes the bits into characters that represent the format and information content of the protocol. When designed explicitly for use on LANs, the protocol analyzer is usually referred to as a LAN analyzer. When designed for use on LANs and WANs, the protocol analyzer is referred to as an enterprise analyzer. For example, a protocol analyzer monitoring an HDLC transmission would convert the bit sequence 01111110 to a flag character and then indicate the start or end of a frame of information. Other features incorporated into most protocol analyzers include the capability to analyze several communications protocols, perform data simulation, and carry out BERT and BLERT testing.

Most protocol analyzers include a built-in breakout box, a keyboard, online storage, and a display in a common housing. Due to the almost ubiquitous status of personal computers, some protocol analyzer manufacturers designed their products as adapter boards that are inserted into the system unit of a PC. When acquired as an adapter board, the protocol analyzer uses the keyboard, online storage, and display of the computer, significantly reducing the cost of the analyzer. Prices of protocol analyzers range from $1500 for devices manufactured on adapter boards for use in personal computers to more than $25,000 for stand-alone protocol analyzers designed to decode the most recent protocols, such as signaling on the ISDN D channel.

Figure 12.5 illustrates a Digilog 800 protocol/performance analyzer. This device contains a color monitor, hard disk, and floppy disk, as well as a full-function keyboard. In addition to decoding a number of protocols, the Digilog 800 provides numerous performance statistics based on line monitoring of different protocols. The screen shown in Figure 12.5 is a "fill in the blank" menu system that enables operators to easily develop programs and get performance measurements or decode different protocols.

FIGURE 12.5.

*Digilog 800 protocol/
performance analyzer.*

Figure 12.6 illustrates a recently introduced hand-held and very portable protocol ana-lyzer manufactured by Frederick Engineering of Columbia, Maryland. Referred to as the ParaScope 64M, this protocol analyzer can be cabled to any PC DOS computer's parallel port to use the processing power of the computer to execute the vendor's software, which turns the computer into a protocol analyzer.

The ParaScope 64M illustrated in Figure 12.6 can be used to monitor standard RS-232 communications at data rates up to 19,200 bps or V.35/RS-449 communications at data rates up to 64,000 bps. The light-emitting diodes and switches located in columns in the middle of the ParaScope 64M provide users with a breakout box capability to monitor and open and close circuits on a monitored interface. However, the primary use of the ParaScope 64M is as a protocol analyzer, providing users with the ability to monitor the flow of data, create programs to operate on the monitored data, and display the results of the execution of programs.

The Frederick Engineering ParaScope 64M was developed as an extension of that vendor's Feline series of protocol analyzers. The Feline series was developed as adapter cards de-signed for insertion into conventional PCs and laptop and notebook computers, as well as software that operated on each computer. A special hardware interface box referred to as a pod is cabled to the adapter card installed in the computer. The pod is very similar to the ParaScope 64M in that it contains connectors for monitoring the interface between a DTE and DCE and converts the voltage level of the monitored circuit to the transistor-to-transistor logic (TTL) voltage level used internally by computers. The ParaScope 64M differs from the Feline pod in that it incorporates the adapter card logic, alleviating the necessity to install an adapter card in a computer. This makes the ParaScope 64M ideal for use with modern notebook computers that lack an expansion slot to accommodate the insertion of an adapter card.

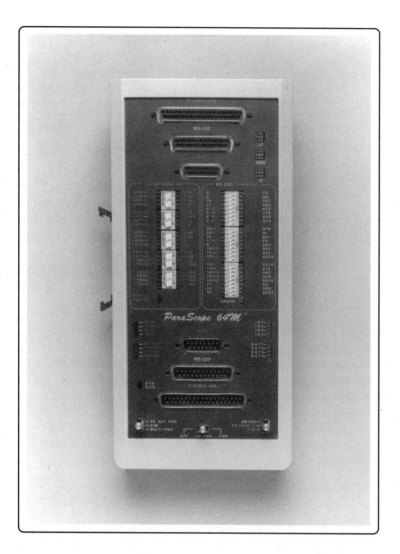

FIGURE 12.6.

The Frederick Engineering ParaScope 64M protocol analyzer.

The integration of the Feline adapter card into the ParaScope 64M results in its capability to be used with Feline software. To illustrate the utility of the system gotten from the use of Feline software and ParaScope 64M hardware, we'll examine some of the features of the software. Figure 12.7 illustrates a split-screen Feline display in which the upper portion of the screen defines information about the interface being monitored and the status of timers and counters. Timers and counters can be considered as memory locations in the computer operating Feline software that accumulate specific timing or counting values based on the execution of a program you create using Feline. In the next section, we will examine the creation of a small program and illustrate its execution on monitored data. The lower portion of Figure 12.7 contains a window that indicates the DCE and DTE data flow across the monitored interface.

●

The ParaScope 64M is cabled to the parallel port of a DOS computer, which executes Feline software that results in the computer becoming a protocol analyzer.

FIGURE 12.7.

Feline protocol analyzer software split-screen display.

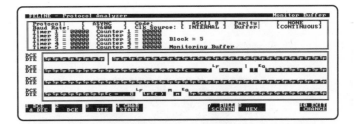

If you examine Figure 12.7, you will note that control and nonprintable characters are indicated by mnemonics, such as Lf for line feed, and Sp for space character. The lower line across every Feline display screen indicates the function key values assigned to a specific screen. For example, to remove the split screen and display monitored data in a full screen, you would press the F7 key, which is assigned to the generation of a full-screen display.

PROGRAM DEVELOPMENT

Figure 12.8 illustrates the creation of a program that counts the number of spaces encountered on the DTE side of a monitored interface. When you select Feline's program mode of operation, your display is initially filled with a series of blank steps and function key value assignments. As you press appropriate function keys when the cursor is placed in a step, you assign one or more program instructions to the step. In Figure 12.8, step 1 waits until a space is encountered on the DTE side of the line, and then the program jumps to step 2. In step 2, counter 1 is incremented, and step 3 simply branches the program back to step 1. Thus, when data is monitored using this program, the value in counter 1 indicates the number of spaces encountered on the DTE side of the line.

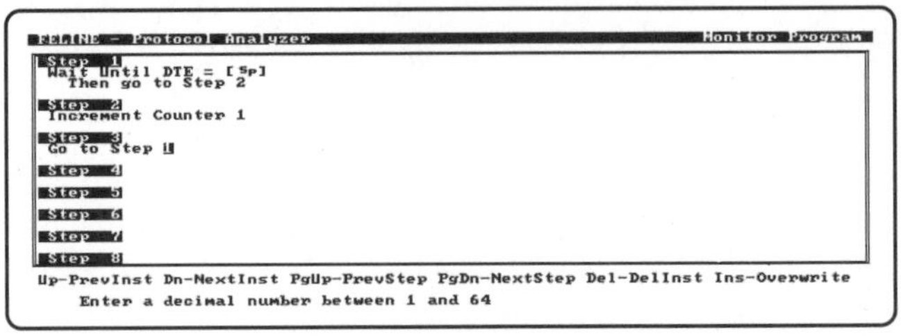

FIGURE 12.8.

Creating a program to count spaces on the DTE side of the line.

Now that we have created a program, we'll again monitor the line and examine the value assigned to counter 1. Figure 12.9 illustrates the Feline split-screen display resulting from monitoring a 9600 bps line after we created the program previously illustrated in Figure 12.8. Note that when the screen was captured for printing, a total of 2810 spaces on the DTE side of the line were encountered because that is the value assigned to counter 1. Although the program is not very sophisticated, it provides an indication of how you can create a program and use the program when monitoring a line. If users were reporting throughput problems on a particular circuit during a file transfer operation, you might consider developing a program to count negative acknowledgments. Because each NAK results in the retransmission of a previously transmitted block, a high level of NAKs would indicate that retransmissions due to line errors are resulting in a low level of data throughput.

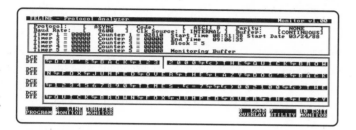

FIGURE 12.9.

Monitoring with a program that counts spaces on the DTE side of the line and assigns the number of spaces to counter 1.

NETWORK CONTROL SYSTEM

Many companies that operate large complex data networks have found the timely isolation of faults to be so important as to cost-justify the installation of a centralized network control system, as depicted in Figure 12.10. Such systems commonly use the low end of the frequency spectrum of the voice-grade circuit to carry a signal interrogation and reporting "side channel." Such systems add significantly to the cost of each modem in the system.

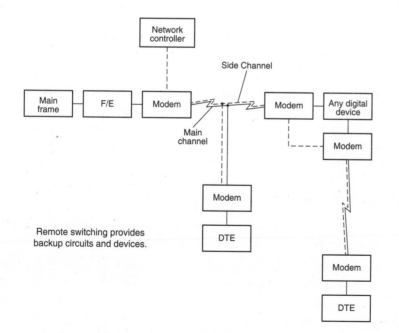

FIGURE 12.10.

Network control system.

In a large complex data network, it might be cost effective to add a centralized network control system to assist in fault detection and isolation.

A modem that is addressed by the central unit can be commanded to perform certain tests and report the results back for display or recording. Such tests as continuity, level of received signal, and condition of an RS-232 lead can be accurately conducted without interrupting or modifying data flow. Other tests, such as self-tests and loopbacks, do cause interruption of data flow. Many of the more sophisticated systems can be user programmed to perform interruptive tests automatically during off-hours when actual interruption of data is unlikely. Test results can be automatically logged and compared with former test results to detect changes in circuit parameters.

Network control systems usually have a scheme for remote switching of circuits and devices to provide backup in the event of failures. The combination of remote testing and remote backup of data communications network control systems based on digital interrogation and reporting is now beginning to replace the analog systems.

Restoration of Service

Providing reliable service restoration promptly and economically is a challenging task.

Given enough planning and money, prompt and reliable restoration of data communications service is easy, but to make it economical is a little harder.

The planner for data communications backup should consider the following questions:

- What is the frequency and length of downtime to be expected?
- Can steps be taken to decrease the frequency and length of downtime without incurring additional costs; that is, are you getting what you already are paying for?
- What will be the extra costs incurred due to complete outage of the service for the frequency and duration indicated?
- Can these extra costs be reduced by a reduced-capability backup—for example, backing up a 9600 bps private line using a 2400 bps dialed connection?
- What are the actual costs of all relevant backup schemes? Include the cost of personnel time as well as the cost of backup. The cost of backup must include the operating costs, such as dialed connection charges, as well as initial investment and installation costs.

Getting the Most for the Money

Before a backup technique is designed and implemented, a review of current procedures might improve the frequency and duration of downtime.

- Is there ongoing positive communication not only with the people in the user's own organization, but also with suppliers of equipment and services?

● Do users have a thorough knowledge of the capabilities and limitations of all data communications system facilities, software, and hardware at their disposal, particularly the capabilities and limitations of self-contained test features?

● Are there well-designed restoration procedures that are agreed to in advance by all concerned that are strictly followed?

● Are new systems benchmark tested as they are placed in service, and then tested on a regular schedule to detect changes in circuit parameters?

● Are exception (failures) documented, and are repeat offenders discovered?

● Is there an ongoing in-house training program to ensure that each individual in the organization can properly handle all appropriate parts of the above five points for those portions of the system within his or her purview?

> Existing system performance often can be improved by closely examining the existing system and established procedures.

RAPPORT WITH SUPPLIERS

Central to any cost-effective service-restoration program is a firmly established positive rapport with all major suppliers of equipment and services—especially with key individuals such as telephone company (telco) personnel. Many data-link failures can be traced directly or indirectly to a breakdown in people-to-people communications between vendors and users. For example, in the case of an organization such as a telephone company with many levels of personnel that deal with the customer, the rapport between supplier and customer must exist at all levels: Data technicians should be on a first-name basis with telco testboard personnel, technician supervisors with testboard supervisors, the data communications operations manager with the telco network operations manager, and so on. When such rapport exists, several symptoms will be apparent:

> Close personal rapport between supplier and customers at all levels is of utmost importance to the smooth, efficient restoration of service of a communications system.

● Employees on both sides will be more helpful and understanding, especially in high-pressure situations.

● Information on new testing and quality assurance techniques will flow easier. The user will gain a better understanding of the built-in test capabilities in the vendor's services and equipment. In fact, technicians on both sides will be eager to share their excitement over some new piece of test gear or a new discovery.

● Better confidence in each other's abilities will emerge and will give rise to more of a supplier-user team approach.

● The vendor employee will often render assistance above and beyond what is required and expected.

Data communications managers who succeed in cultivating this kind of rapport with their major vendors consider it among their greatest assets. In particular, they are careful to establish and follow good procedures for the testing of systems and proper reporting of problems to the vendor. Inherent in this process is the careful development of an escalation and reporting system.

Escalation and Reporting

Through meetings with all concerned, the data communications manager should develop a very specific escalation schedule. This schedule should show exactly who becomes involved at increasing levels of authority, what calls are placed, and at what levels when a particular type of problem fails to show progress toward resolution after a specific time lapse. All persons involved in this schedule should be involved in its development, should "sign-off" on it, should have a personal copy of the finished product, and should have a cause for negative feelings whenever it is invoked.

Before asking for help from higher levels or from the vendor, it is absolutely vital that the user exhaust all means at his disposal to make use of test facilities available to him—especially self-tests. Remember the story about the little boy who cried "wolf"? Nothing can damage credibility and rapport faster than to blame the vendor when the problem is with another vendor or is in-house.

Personnel responsible for data subsystem and system testing must be thoroughly familiar with self-tests and their limitations, and with the meaning of any other tests for which they have equipment. Troubles should be reported only after such testing has been adequately documented, and escalation should be invoked only after the lack of progress in problem resolution has been documented.

Such documentation of problems and their resolution should be permanently recorded and reviewed with the vendor at regular intervals. This review aids in spotting areas of recurring difficulties and possibly degrading facilities and components, so these can be serviced before a "hard" failure occurs. This is why the benchmarking of newly acquired facilities is important.

Finally, appreciation should be expressed when appropriate. Nothing will make an employee of a vendor work harder for a user than an appreciation letter to his boss for good work done in the user's behalf.

> ● Clearly established procedures must be developed to ensure that the proper level of management is involved in the correction of problems in a timely manner.

> ● The personnel involved in system and data subsystem testing should be thoroughly familiar with the capabilities and limitations of the tests and the test equipment.

Backup Techniques

Even the best procedures will not totally eliminate failures of circuits and equipment. When priority of data requires backup during the repair process, decisions must be made in the areas of providing spare parts for on-premise equipment (such as multiplexer boards and power supplies), providing complete standby devices (such as modems), providing an alternative physical communications medium (such as dialed backup), and determining who will do what when a failure occurs.

In high-priority situations, it isn't uncommon to find that duplicate hot-standby private lines back up the regularly used private lines. In such cases, it's important that the backup be provided via diversely routed circuits, even to the extent of using different entry points into the user's building.

> ● Thought must be given to backup systems to keep priority lines in at least partial operation while repairs are being made. In high-priority situations, a duplicate hot-standby private line is often used.

The majority of backup plans provide for dialed backup, often with reduced capability. The following factors should be considered:

● Backup on the public telephone network is generally limited to 19,200 bps.

● Depending on several factors, including distance from the modem to the central office, satisfactory dialed connections at 19,200 bps might not be attainable, requiring fallback to 9600 or 4800 bps.

● If full-duplex backup is required at bit rates greater than 9600 bps, two calls might be required. This doubles the cost of providing backup. Some users provide only half-duplex backup for a full-duplex circuit; however, this type of fallback might require changing the link protocol option selections whenever backup is invoked.

● If the circuit to be replaced is multipoint, full backup will require simultaneous calls to each remote site that is affected—that is, six calls to fully back up a three-drop full-duplex circuit. Some users provide backup of a multipoint line to only one remote site at a time, which reduces the number of dialable lines required in the data center.

Suppliers of network control systems generally have system-integrated provision for remotely controlled backup and switching of circuits, modems, multiplexers, or anything else money can buy. For the less sophisticated user, stand-alone devices are available from a number of suppliers.

Figure 12.11 illustrates a typical stand-alone arrangement to provide remotely controlled full-duplex dialed backup of a multipoint circuit. The central site bridge provides for simultaneous transmission and reception on the private line and each pair of central office business lines. Because of the high cost for usage of a multiplicity of dialed connections, most users prefer manually dialed backup to ensure control over long-distance charges.

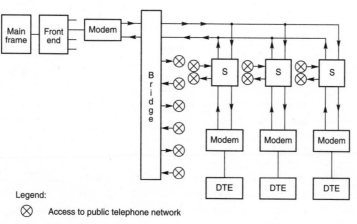

FIGURE 12.11.

Dialed backup of a multipoint analog circuit.

Legend:

⊗   Access to public telephone network

S   Back-up switch

——▶   One-way analog channel

There are several schemes for the operation of the "S" switches in Figure 12.11. One typical scheme for operation of one "S" switch is as follows:

1. The central site technician places a call on one business line to the appropriate line connected to an "S" switch. The switch "answers" the call and places the call on "hold," starting an abort timer.

2. The operator places a second call to the other line. If the call comes in before the abort timer runs out, the switch answers and connects the modem to both dialed lines; if not, it aborts the first call.

3. The "S" switch reverts to the private line if either no modem carrier is detected within a specified interval or the carrier is interrupted. More sophisticated types of "S" switches require reception of special coded commands both for switching away from the private line and for returning to it.

Some high-priority systems require the capability to substitute another path for both the private line and the remote DCE. Figure 12.12 shows such a configuration. The operation is similar to that in Figure 12.11, except for the position and arrangement of the switch within the circuit. As indicated in the drawing, this arrangement is also useful for backing up a digital link.

> There are several methods that can be used to provide dialed backup service. In high-priority situations, alternative paths should be provided for both the private line and the remote DCE.

FIGURE 12.12.

Dialed backup of a digital link.

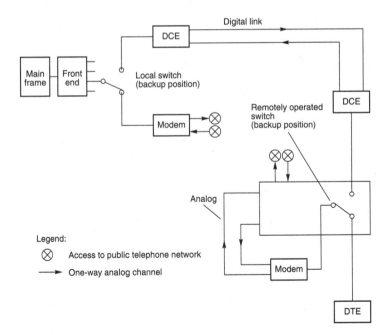

What Have You Learned?

1. The underlying objective of data networking is to strike a balance between the accurate timely delivery of user data and total cost.

2. Any network, no matter how simple or complex, can be incorporated into a large network. A larger network cannot be optimized until its component parts are individually optimized.

3. Information throughput rate involves many factors besides the modem bit rate.

4. Classical time division multiplexers provide a powerful tool for combining data transmission link requirements into a smaller number of higher speed links. Statistical TDMs can be even more powerful if the duty cycles of individual links to be combined are low.

5. Frequency division multiplexers can be useful if the links involve low-speed multipoint data transmission.

6. Other useful networking devices include sharing devices, modem eliminators, and protocol converters.

7. Loopbacks are a common and simple technique for testing data communications components and networks.

8. Test equipment for data communications falls into two generic categories: digital testing and analog testing.

9. The capability to create programs that operate against monitored data can be used to isolate different types of communications problems.

10. Good network design includes appropriate planning for contingencies and procedures for restoring service.

11. Dialed backup is a common technique for restoring service on analog and digital transmission systems.

Quiz for Chapter 12

1. Which of the following is not considered a primary objective of data networking?

   a. Security.

   b. Packet switching.

   c. Timeliness.

   d. Accuracy.

2. On a point-to-point data channel using an analog circuit, TRIB is:

   a. Higher than the modem bit rate.

   b. Equal to the modem bit rate.

   c. Lower than the modem bit rate.

   d. Not related to the modem bit rate.

3. The block length that gives maximum TRIB:

   a. Increases as the error rate increases.

   b. Decreases as the error rate increases.

   c. Isn't related to error rate.

   d. Is called the optimum block length.

4. Smart TDMs:

   a. Are always better than dumb TDMs.

   b. Are always better than FDMs.

   c. Are the same as modem sharing devices.

   d. Might be better than dumb TDMs if the data terminals have a low duty cycle.

5. FDM devices can operate:

   a. On multipoint analog data channels.

   b. More efficiently than dumb TDMs.

   c. More efficiently than smart TDMs.

   d. Like modem sharing devices.

6. Protocol converters are:

   a. The same as multiplexers.

   b. The same as TDMs.

   c. Usually operated in pairs.

   d. Usually not operated in pairs.

7. Null modems are a type of:

   a. Modem eliminator.

   b. Modem.

   c. Multiplexer.

   d. Protocol converter.

8. A basic technique for isolating data communications faults is:

   a. Calling the telephone company.

   b. Performing a loopback test.

   c. Calling the DTE service department.

   d. Simulating the system on a special-purpose computer.

9. The main purpose of a data link content monitor is to:

    a. Determine the type of switching used in a data link.

    b. Determine the type of transmission used in a data link.

    c. Detect problems in protocols.

    d. Measure bit error rates.

10. The most sophisticated type of data communications test equipment is the:

    a. Simulator.

    b. Protocol analyzer.

    c. DTE.

    d. Breakout box.

11. Full-capability dialed backup of a multipoint full-duplex 4800 bps private line having 4 remote drops requires:

    a. 4 calls.

    b. Either 4 or 8 calls.

    c. 8 calls.

    d. Can't tell.

12. An example of a portable protocol converter is the:

    a. ParaScope.

    b. Datascope.

    c. UniScope.

    d. UltraScope.

13. An example of a protocol converter counter value is:

    a. Bit delay.

    b. ACK/NAK delay.

    c. ACK/NAK count.

    d. Data rate.

ISDN

About This Chapter

ISDN, which is the acronym for Integrated Services Digital Network, augurs the potential for the development of a universal digital network that provides integrated voice and data on common telephone company facilities. In this chapter, we'll examine the idea behind ISDN, its architecture, and some of the benefits that can be expected from it in the not-too-distant future.

Concept

The need to transmit human speech resulted in the development of a telephone system that was originally designed for the transmission of analog data. Although the telephone system satisfied the basic need to transmit human speech, its design required the conversion of digital signals produced by computers and terminals into an analog format for the transmission of digital data. This conversion was awkward and expensive because modems were required at both ends of a telephone channel to do the digital-to-analog and analog-to-digital conversions.

A rapid decrease in the cost of semiconductors and the evolution in digital signal processing resulted in the application of digital technology to the telephone network. In the 1960s, telephone companies began to replace the electromechanical switches located in their central offices with digital switches. By the early 1970s, several communications carriers were offering end-to-end transmission services. In these services, unipolar digital data from terminals and computers was converted first into a modified bipolar digital format. Then, through a series of digital repeaters in the network, the data was transmitted to its destination. At its destination, data was converted back to its original unipolar digital format. The unipolar-to-bipolar signal conversion enabled the telephone company to space repeaters farther apart, reducing the construction cost of the digital network. Figure 13.1 illustrates the use of amplifiers and repeaters on analog and digital circuits.

The amplifier used on analog circuits amplifies the entire signal, including any signal impairments. The digital repeater, also known as a data regenerator, regenerates a new digital pulse, eliminating any distortion to the pulse that occurs as it travels on a digital circuit.

Because analog amplifiers increase the size of an analog signal to include any previous distortion, whereas digital repeaters regenerate a digital pulse and eliminate any previous distortion to the digital signal, the error rate on a digital network is significantly lower than that on an analog facility. In addition, the devices required to perform the unipolar-to-bipolar and bipolar-to-unipolar signal conversion are much less expensive than the modems required for signal conversion on analog facilities.

FIGURE 13.1.

Amplifiers versus repeaters.

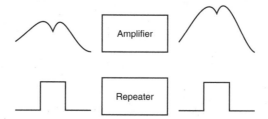

By the mid-1980s, most telephone companies had incorporated a large amount of digital technology into their plant facilities so that a significant portion of the lines connecting telephone company central offices transported speech in digital form, although speech continued to be carried in analog form from the subscriber to the central office. At the central office, speech is digitized for transmission over the backbone network of the telephone system. Similarly, at the central office closest to the destination of the telephone conversation, the digitized speech is reconverted into its analog format, then transmitted to the subscriber's telephone.

The progression of telephone systems in the use of digital technology forms the basis for ISDN. Thus, ISDN can be viewed as an evolutionary progression in the conversion of the analog telephone system into an eventual all-digital network, enabling both voice and data to be transported end to end in a digital format.

Besides integrating voice and data, ISDN provides a level of communications capability above that obtainable with conventional analog technology. When voice and data are integrated, subscribers will be able to talk on the telephone and use a computer or terminal at the same time over a common subscriber line. For business, this capability should improve the productivity of office workers and reduce the cost of wiring buildings and offices because there should be no need to install separate wires to each desk for voice and data. Thus, ISDN offers subscribers a level of efficiency beyond that obtainable through the utilization of conventional facilities.

For individual subscribers, ISDN can result in the offering of a series of new functions accessible to their homes over existing telephone wire. Electronic meter reading, slow-scan video, electronic mail, and other applications can be expected to be offered to individual subscribers and businesses.

ISDN Architecture

Two methods of access to ISDN have been defined—Basic access and Primary access. ISDN Basic access deals with the connection and operation of individual telephone instruments and terminals to the digital network. Primary access governs the method by which many Basic access subscribers can be connected to the network over a common line facility.

Basic Access

Basic access defines a multiple-channel connection that is derived by the time division multiplexing of data on twisted pair wiring. This multiple-channel connection links an end-user terminal device directly to a telephone company office or to a local Private Automated Branch Exchange (PABX). Figure 13.2 illustrates the channel format of the ISDN Basic access method.

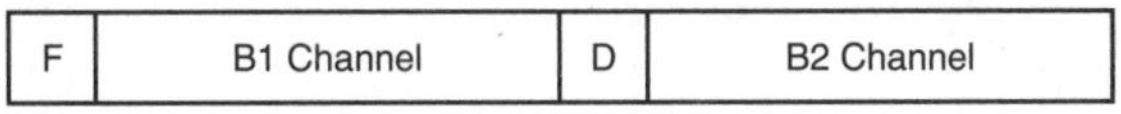

F	B1 Channel	D	B2 Channel

FIGURE 13.2.
ISDN Basic access channel format.

B channels are 64 Kbps each.

D channel is 16 Kbps.

2B + D service is a 144 Kbps data stream.

When framing (F) and multiplexing overhead is considered, the actual data rate of a Basic access channel is 192 Kbps, which is the interface transmission rate of the line.

As shown in Figure 13.2, Basic access consists of two bearer (B) channels and a data (D) channel. The three channels are multiplexed by time onto a common twisted pair wiring media. Each bearer channel can carry one digitized voice conversation or data stream at a transmission rate of 64 Kbps. Digitized voice in ISDN is encoded by sampling voice signals 8,000 times per second and encoding each sample in 8 bits, which results in a 64 Kbps data rate. The inclusion of two bearer channels enables Basic access to provide the subscriber with the ability to simultaneously transmit data and conduct a voice conversation on one telephone line or to be in conversation with one person and receive a second telephone call. In the latter case, assuming subscribers have an appropriate telephone

●
Under the Basic access format, up to three channels can be used to provide simultaneous data streams.

instrument, they could put one person on hold and answer the second call, all on one line! With analog technology, two physical lines are required. In fact, a Basic access ISDN line can be used to connect up to eight different devices that can be independently accessed via one standard telephone circuit. This expanded access is permissible because the D channel is designed to control the B channels through the sharing of network signaling functions and for the transmission of packet switched data.

To illustrate the expanded capability of ISDN Basic access over conventional telephone service, consider Figure 13.3. Figure 13.3a indicates how you might connect a telephone, fax machine, and computer modem to the public switched telephone network via the installation of three separate telephone lines between your home or office and the telephone central office. Figure 13.3b shows the same equipment connected to a Basic access ISDN line, which, in effect, is one telephone line onto which digitized data is multiplexed. Note that although up to eight devices can share access to the same ISDN Basic access line, only two devices can simultaneously operate at 64 Kbps because only two B channels are contained on a Basic access line. It is anticipated that the capability to transmit packet switched data will enable the D channel to be used to provide many new applications, including monitoring home alarm systems and reading utility meters on demand.

FIGURE 13.3.

ISDN Basic access versus conventional telephone access.

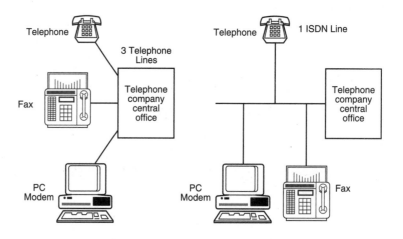

a. Conventional telephone access   b. Using ISDN Basic access

Primary Access

Primary access is a multiplexing arrangement whereby a grouping of Basic access users shares a common line facility. Primary access is designed to directly connect a PABX to the ISDN network. This access method eliminates the need to provide individual Basic access lines when a group of terminal devices shares a common PABX that could be connected directly to an ISDN network via a single high-speed line. Because of the different methods used to multiplex digitized voice conversations between telephone company offices in North America and Europe, two Primary access standards have been developed.

In North America, Primary access consists of a grouping of 23 B channels and one D channel to provide a 1.544 Mbps composite data rate. This data rate is more commonly known as the standard T1 carrier data rate, which was described in Chapter 6, "Multiplexing Techniques." The D channel in Primary access, and each B channel, operates at 64 Kbps. Multiplying 24 channels by 64 Kbps results in a data rate of 1.536 Mbps, which is precisely 8 Kbps fewer than the T1 carrier's 1.544 Mbps data rate.

A North American T1 carrier consists of 24 digitized voice channels. Each voice channel is sampled 8,000 times per second, and 8 bits are used to encode the digitized value of each sample. Thus, a 64 Kbps data rate is required to transmit a digitized voice conversation. To permit synchronization of the T1 signal, a single bit, known as a framing bit, is added to the data stream. The framing bit represents 24 channels, as illustrated in Figure 13.4. One sample of 24 channels of digitized voice is therefore represented by 193 bits. Because the sampling occurs 8,000 times per second, the data rate of a T1 carrier is $193 \times 8,000$, or 1.544 Mbps.

● The T1 carrier used in North America is not the same as that used in Europe due to different methods of signaling.

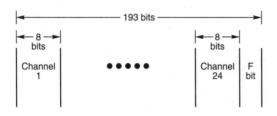

FIGURE 13.4.
The T1 frame.

In Europe, the T1 carrier consists of 30 digitized voice channels and 2 separate signaling channels. Because each channel operates at 64 Kbps, the resulting T1 carrier data rate is 2.048 Mbps.

ISDN Implementation Standards

ISDN implementation standards address the lower three layers of the OSI Reference Model described in a previous chapter. The CCITT defined a series of standards that govern both basic and primary rate physical layer interfaces, as well as the D channel link layer and call setup procedures over the D channel that take place at the network layer level of the OSI Reference Model. Figure 13.5 illustrates the relationship of ISDN implementation standards to the OSI Reference Model. As indicated in Figure 13.5, two sets of standards, I and Q, govern the implementation of ISDN. The I standards govern the physical connection of ISDN-compatible equipment to ISDN circuits, and the Q standards govern the transmission of D channel setup data and information. The Q.921 standard defines the frame structure for transmitting information on the D channel, as well as the contents of the fields of the frame. The Q.931 standard defines the call control procedures used for call setup and teardown, the message structure used to carry call procedure information, and the types of messages that can be transported at the network layer. Readers are referred to CCITT ISDN Q-series standards for specific information concerning call establishment procedures and data formats on the D channel, as well as the framing format used to transport information on that channel.

FIGURE 13.5.

Relationship of ISDN to the OSI Reference Model.

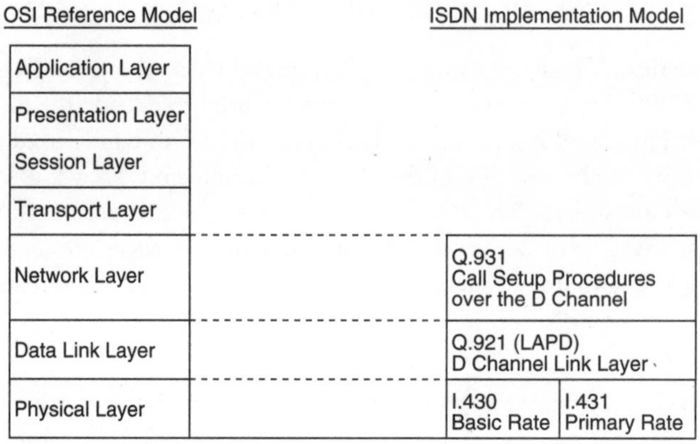

OSI Reference Model	ISDN Implementation Model	
Application Layer		
Presentation Layer		
Session Layer		
Transport Layer		
Network Layer	Q.931 Call Setup Procedures over the D Channel	
Data Link Layer	Q.921 (LAPD) D Channel Link Layer	
Physical Layer	I.430 Basic Rate	I.431 Primary Rate

Network Characteristics

The major characteristics of an ISDN network follow and form the basis of businesses, and telephone companies' desire for the development of this new network.

ISDN integrates voice, data, and video services.

ISDN has a digital end-to-end connection that provides high transmission quality.

ISDN has improved and expanded services because of B and D channel data rates.

ISDN is more efficient and productive.

ISDN offers advances in device connectivity.

The digital nature of ISDN integrates voice, data, and video services, which eliminates the need for subscribers to get separate facilities for each service. Because an ISDN network is designed to provide end-to-end digital transmission, pulses can be regenerated easily throughout the network, resulting in the generation of new pulses to replace distorted ones.

In comparison, analog transmission facilities use amplifiers to boost the strength of transmission signals, but they also increase any impairments in the analog signal. Because regeneration is superior to amplification, digital transmission has a lower error rate and provides a higher transmission signal quality than an equivalent analog transmission facility.

Basic access provides three signal paths on a common line, and ISDN, too, offers to subscribers the potential of improvements and expansion to existing services. For existing services, current analog telephone line bandwidth limitations preclude data transmission rates more than 19.2 Kbps occurring on the switched telephone network. In comparison, under ISDN, each B channel can support a 64 Kbps transmission rate, whereas the D channel can operate at 16 Kbps. In fact, if both B channels and the D channel were in simultaneous operation, a data rate of 144 Kbps would be obtainable on a Basic access ISDN circuit, exceeding by a factor of seven the current analog circuit data rates.

Because each Basic access channel consists of three multiplexed channels, different operations can occur simultaneously without requiring the subscriber to acquire separate multiplexing equipment. Thus, a subscriber could receive a call from one person, transmit data to a computer, and have a utility company read his or her electric meter, all at one time. With the ability to conduct as many as three simultaneous operations on one line, the subscriber gains efficiency and productivity. Efficiency should increase because one line now can support several simultaneous operations, whereas the productivity of the subscriber can increase because of the ability to receive telephone calls and conduct a conversation while transmitting data.

Advances in device connectivity to the ISDN network can be expected to occur in two areas. At the physical interface, an eight-pin modular plug and jack will provide a common interface that will enable devices to be portable between jacks. This will eliminate special cabling and, usually, additional telephone company installation charges for the movement of devices between offices. Digital telephones and other instruments can be expected to have an intelligent reporting capability. When a telephone is moved from one office to another, simply plugging it into a jack will result in it reporting its extension and location to a PBX. This capability will permit employees who are moving within an organization to immediately receive telephone calls at their new locations without waiting for the company to reprogram the PBX.

Telephone Equipment and Network Interface

A key element of ISDN is a small set of compatible multipurpose user-network interfaces developed to support a wide range of applications. These network interfaces are based on a series of reference points for different user terminal arrangements that define these interfaces. Figure 13.6 illustrates the relationship between ISDN reference points and network interfaces.

The ISDN reference configuration consists of functional groupings and reference points at which physical interfaces can exist. The functional groupings are sets of functions that can be required at an interface, whereas reference points are employed to divide the functional groups into distinct entities.

FIGURE 13.6.

ISDN reference points and network interfaces.

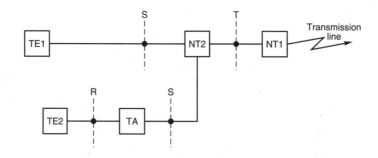

TE1   (Terminal Equipment 1) type devices comply with ISDN network interface.

TE2   (Terminal Equipment 2) type devices do not have an ISDN interface and must be connected through a TA (terminal adapter) functional grouping.

NT2   (Network Termination 2) includes switching and concentration equipment that performs functions equivalent to layers 1 through 3 of the OSI reference model.

NT1   (Network Termination 1) includes functions equivalent to layer 1 of the OSI reference model.

The TE (Terminal Equipment) functional grouping is composed of TE1 and TE2 type equipment. Digital telephones, conventional data terminals, and integrated voice-data workstations are examples of TE equipment. TE1 type equipment complies with the ISDN user-network interface and permits such equipment to be connected directly to an ISDN "S" type interface that supports multiple B and D channels.

The NT2 (Network Termination 2) functional group includes devices that do switching and data concentration functions equivalent to the first three layers of the OSI Reference Model. Typical NT2 equipment can include PABXs, LANs, terminal controllers, concentrators, and multiplexers.

> The Terminal Adapter (TA) can be expected to play a key role in the use of ISDN because it permits equipment with a non-ISDN interface to be connected into an ISDN network.

The NT1 (Network Termination 1) functional group is the ISDN digital interface point and is equivalent to layer 1 of the OSI Reference Model. Functions of NT1 include the physical and electrical termination of the loop, line monitoring, timing, and bit multiplexing. In Europe, where most communications carriers are government-owned monopolies, NT1 and NT2 functions can be combined into a common device, such as a PABX. In such situations, the equipment serves as an NT12 functional group. In comparison, in the United States, the communications carrier can provide only the NT1, whereas third-party equipment would connect to the communications carrier equipment at the T interface.

The last interface that occurs at reference point U is a two-wire connection (Basic access) or four-wire connection (Primary access) between the customer premises (NT1) and the carrier's central office. From this reference point to the central office, data flows in a special compressed transmission format (2B1Q) in which 2 binary bits (2B) are encoded in one quaternary symbol (1Q). When transmission occurs in the 2B1Q format, up to four signal levels can occur, with each level defining the encoding of two bits of data. Table 13.1 indicates the relationship between the four allowed signaling states and the composition of the encoded pairs of bits. Figure 13.7 illustrates an example of 2B1Q coding (top) and the resulting relationship between the quaternary symbol and the encoded binary pairs.

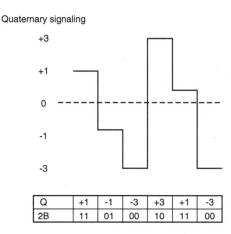

Q	+1	-1	-3	+3	+1	-3
2B	11	01	00	10	11	00

FIGURE 13.7.

2B1Q encoding example.

Table 13.1. 2B1Q relationship.

Quaternary Signal Level	Encoded Bit Values
−3	00
−1	01
+3	10
+1	11

Through the use of 2B1Q encoding, the Basic access 144 Kbps data rate is achieved via a 4-kilobaud rate. This allows the large base of conventional copper pair wiring previously installed between customer premises and communications carrier central offices to be used to support ISDN transmission.

Refer to the CCITT I recommendation series for detailed information about ISDN reference points and network interfaces.

By providing a set of standardized network interfaces, both pre- and post-ISDN terminals will be able to share the benefits of using ISDN. Pre-ISDN terminal devices will be connected to ISDN facilities by Terminal Adapters, which will convert a non-ISDN interface (R) into an ISDN interface (S). With several well-publicized field trials of ISDN being conducted in the United States and abroad, it is only a matter of time until commercial ISDN offerings become available for selection by many analog telephone subscribers. Similar to the manner in which "plastics" was used as the all-encompassing word of the future in a popular 1960s movie, "ISDN" can be expected to be its replacement for the late 1990s.

What Have You Learned?

1. ISDN can be viewed as an evolutionary process because communications carriers have been converting their facilities to digital technology since the 1960s.

2. Access arrangements to the ISDN network include Basic and Primary access.

3. The multiple channels on one ISDN physical line are gotten through time division multiplexing.

4. Multiple channels on one ISDN physical line permit multiple voice or voice and data transmission to occur at the same time on a common circuit.

5. The Basic access D channel on which data is transmitted in packet form can be expected to be used for such new applications as monitoring of home alarm systems and reading of utility meters, as well as for the transmission of signaling information to control the operation of the B channels.

6. Non-ISDN equipment can be connected to ISDN lines through the use of terminal adapters.

Quiz for Chapter 13

1. The data rate of the ISDN Basic access B channel is:
   a. 32 Kbps.
   b. 64 Kbps.
   c. 144 Kbps.
   d. 192 Kbps.

2. The data rate of the ISDN Basic access D Channel is:
   a. 64 Kbps.
   b. 16 Kbps.
   c. 8 Kbps.
   d. 144 Kbps.

3. The equation that defines the composition of an ISDN Basic access line is:
   a. 2B + D.
   b. B + D.
   c. B + 2D.
   d. 2B + 2D.

4. In North America, the equation that defines the composition on an ISDN Primary access line is:
   a. 30B + D.
   b. 2B + D.
   c. B + D.
   d. 23B + D.

5. The network interface that will permit equipment without an ISDN interface to be connected into an ISDN interface is known as:
   a. TE1.
   b. TE2.
   c. TA.
   d. TE.

6. The number of channels on which different operations can occur simultaneously on one ISDN Basic access line is:

    a. 1.

    b. 2.

    c. 5.

    d. 3.

7. Digital telephones and integrated voice-data workstations are examples of what type of ISDN equipment?

    a. TE.

    b. TA.

    c. NT2.

    d. TP.

8. The transmission of data on an ISDN line between a customer's premises and a carrier's central office is encoded using:

    a. Quadrature amplitude modulation.

    b. 2B1Q encoding.

    c. Hexadecimal encoding.

    d. Octal encoding.

Glossary

2B1Q   An encoding technique used on ISDN lines in which two binary bits (2B) are encoded in one quaternary (1Q) symbol.

Amplifier   A device used to increase the strength of an analog signal.

Analog Signal   A signal, such as voice or music, that varies in a continuous manner. Contrast with digital signal.

ASCII (American Standard Code for Information Interchange)   A 7-bit code established by the American National Standards Institute to achieve compatibility between data services. Equivalent to the international ISO 7-bit code.

Attenuation   The difference between transmitted and received power due to transmission loss through equipment, lines, or other communication devices.

Bandwidth   The frequency range between the lowest and highest frequencies that are passed through a component, circuit, or system with acceptable attenuation.

Baseband   The frequency band occupied by a single or composite signal in its original or unmodulated form.

Baseband Signaling   A method of signaling in which only one signal occurs on the transmission media at any point in time.

Basic Access   The method whereby individual telephone instruments and terminals will be connected to a digital network.

Baud   A unit of signaling speed equal to the number of signal events per second. Not necessarily the same as bits per second.

Binary Coded Decimal (BCD)   A system of binary numbering where each decimal digit 0 through 9 is represented by four bits.

Binary Synchronous Communications (BSC or BiSync)   A communication protocol developed by IBM that has became an industry standard. It uses a defined set of control characters and control character sequences for synchronized transmission of binary coded data between stations in a data communications system.

bis Meaning second in Latin, this term is used as a suffix to denote a secondary version of a CCITT modem standard.

Bit Contraction of binary digit. The smallest unit of information. A bit represents the choice between a one or zero value (mark or space in communications terminology).

Bit Rate The speed at which bits are transmitted, usually expressed in bits per second. Not necessarily the same as baud rate.

Block A sequence of continuous data characters or bytes transmitted as a unit. A coding procedure is usually applied for synchronization or error control purposes.

bps (bits per second) A measure of the information transfer rate of a data channel.

Bridge A device that connects LANs at the ISO data link level.

Broadband Signaling A method of signaling in which multiple signals share the bandwidth of the transmission media by the subdivision of the bandwidth into channels based on frequency.

Buffer A storage device used to compensate for a difference in rate of data flow, or time of occurrence of events, when transmitting data from one device to another.

Byte A binary element string operated on as a unit and usually shorter than a computer word. Eight-bit bytes are common.

Carrier A signal suitable for modulation by another signal containing information to be transmitted. The carrier is usually a sine wave for analog systems.

CCITT (Consultative Committee for International Telephone & Telegraph) A standards-making body whose recommendations are more closely followed in Europe than North America.

Channel, Voice Grade A channel, generally with a frequency range of about 300 to 3400 Hz, suitable for transmission of speech or data in analog form. Data transmission rates of 9600 bps can be achieved by modulation techniques that produce a baud rate of 2400.

Character A letter, figure, number, punctuation, or other symbol contained in a message or used in a control function.

Character Set The characters that can be coded and/or printed by a particular machine.

Code A set of unambiguous rules specifying the way in which characters can be represented.

Committed Information Rate The minimum operating rate supported by a frame relay service.

Common Carrier A company that furnishes communication services to the general public and that is regulated by appropriate state or federal agencies.

Conditioning, Line The addition of equipment to a leased voice-grade channel to improve analog characteristics to allow higher rates of data transmission.

Constellation Pattern The pattern gotten from plotting the location of each bit combination modulated by a modem through phase and amplitude changes.

Contention The facility provided by the dial network or a port selector that allows multiple terminals to compete on a first-come-first-served basis for a smaller number of computer ports.

Data Communications Equipment (also Data Circuit-Terminating Equipment) (DCE) The equipment that provides the functions required to establish, maintain, and terminate a connection, and provides the signal conversion required for communication between data terminal equipment and the telephone line or data circuit.

Data Terminal Equipment (DTE) A computer or business machine that provides data in the form of digital signals at its output.

dBm Decibel referenced to one milliwatt. Used in communications circuits as a measure of signal power. Zero dBm equals one milliwatt into a specified impedance, often 600 ohms.

Decibel (dB) A logarithmic measure of the ratio between two powers, P_1 and P_2. The equation is $dB = 10 \log_{10} P_2/P_1$.

Delay Equalizer A corrective network that is designed to make the phase delay or envelope delay of a circuit or system substantially constant over a desired frequency range.

Delay, Propagation The time required for a signal to travel from one point to another in a component, circuit, or system.

Demodulation The process of recovering data from a modulated carrier wave. The reverse of modulation.

Dial-Up Line A communications circuit that is established by a switched circuit connection using the telephone dial network.

Dialing Directory A module in a communications program that permits telephone numbers and descriptions of those numbers to be entered. Selecting an entry in the dialing directory results in the program dialing the number associated with the entry.

Dibit A group of two bits. In four-phase modulation, such as differential phase shift keying (DPSK), each possible dibit in encoded as one of four unique carrier phase shifts. The four possible states for a dibit are 00, 01, 10, and 11.

Digital Repeater A data regenerator that, on the detection of the rise of a digital pulse's leading edge, regenerates the pulse.

Digital Signal   A discrete or discontinuous signal; one whose various states are identified with discrete levels or values.

Distortion, Delay   Distortion resulting from nonuniform speed of transmission of the various frequency components of a signal through a transmission medium. Also called group delay.

Distortion, Harmonic   The result of nonlinearities in the communication channel that cause harmonics of the input frequencies to appear in the output.

Distortion, Linear (or Amplitude)   An unwanted change in signal amplitude so that the output signal envelope is not proportional to the input signal envelope, but no frequency related distortion is involved.

Echo Suppressor   A device that allows transmission in only one direction at a time. They are inserted in telephone circuits to attenuate echoes on long-distance circuits. They are not desirable in data communications circuits because they increase the turnaround time.

Equalization   The process of reducing the effects of amplitude, frequency, and/or phase distortion of a circuit by inserting networks to compensate for the difference in attenuation and/or time delay at various frequencies in the transmission band.

Filter   A network designed to transmit electrical signals having frequencies within one or more frequency bands and to attenuate signals of other frequencies.

Flow Control   The orderly regulation of the flow of data by the use of special characters (inband signaling) or control signals at the RS232 interface (outband signaling).

Frame Relay   A packet switched service that does not provide for error detection and correction, resulting in minimal routing delays.

Frequency Division Multiplexer   A device that divides the available transmission frequency range into narrower bands, each of which is used for a separate channel.

Frequency Response   The change in attenuation with frequency relative to the attenuation at a reference frequency. Also called attenuation distortion.

Frequency Shift Keying (FSK)   A form of frequency modulation commonly used in low-speed modems in which the two states of the signal are transmitted as two separate frequencies.

Full-Duplex   Refers to a communications system or equipment capable of simultaneous two-way communications.

Gateway   Hardware and software that permits devices located on a local area network to access the facilities of another network.

Half-Duplex   Refers to a communications system or equipment capable of communications in both directions, but in only one direction at a time.

Handshaking Exchange of predetermined codes and signals between two data terminals to establish a connection.

Inband Signaling A method of flow control in which a device transmits a character (usually an XOFF) to inform another device to suspend transmission and another character (usually an XON) to resume transmission.

Interface A shared boundary defined by common physical interconnection characteristics, signal characteristics, and meanings of interchanged signals.

Intermodulation Noise Spurious frequencies, such as sum and difference frequencies, which are the products of frequencies transmitted through a nonlinear circuit.

ISDN (Integrated Services Digital Network) A future offering designed to provide a universal digital network that will permit the integration of voice and data on a common telephone company facility.

Jitter A tendency toward lack of synchronization caused by mechanical or electrical changes.

Kilostream A digital network that operates in the United Kingdom.

Line (1) A circuit between a customer terminal and the central office. (2) The portion of a transmission system, including the transmission media and associated repeaters, between two terminal locations.

Link A circuit or transmission path, including all equipment, between a sender and a receiver.

Local Area Network A communications network that is restricted to a small geographical area, usually within a building or on a campus, and that has cabling normally installed and/or controlled by the organization that operates the network.

Loop, Local The pair of wires between a customer terminal and the central office.

Loopback Test A test of communications link performed by connecting the equipment output on one direction to the equipment input of the other direction and testing the quality of the received signal.

Mark One of the two possible states of a binary information element. The closed circuit and idle state in a teleprinter circuit. See Space.

Modem (MOdulator/DEModulator) A type of DCE that at the transmitting end converts digital data to an analog signal for transmission on telephone circuits. A modem at the receiving end converts the analog signal to digital form.

Modulation The process of varying some characteristic of the carrier wave in accordance with the instantaneous value or samples of the intelligence to be transmitted. Amplitude, frequency, and phase are the characteristics commonly varied.

Multiplex   To interleave or simultaneously transmit two or more messages on a single channel.

Multistation Access Unit   A device that enables workstations on a LAN to be cabled in a star configuration.

Noise   Random electrical signals, introduced by circuit components or natural disturbances, which tend to generate errors in transmission.

Outband Signaling   A method of flow control in which an RS232 control signal (usually Clear to Send) is lowered to inform a device to suspend transmission and raised to inform a device to resume transmission.

PABX (Private Automatic Branch Exchange)   A device that is installed on a customer's premises and that permits a large number of telephones to automatically access the switched telephone network by using a smaller number of lines connecting the PABX to the telephone company network.

PBX (Private Branch Exchange)   Telephone switching equipment dedicated to one customer and connected to the public switched network.

Personal Computer   A computer with processing power based on a microprocessor and designed primarily for use by one person.

Polling   The individual selection of multiple terminals by a controller to allow transmission of traffic to/from all terminals on a multidrop line in an orderly manner.

Port   An interface on a computer configured as data terminal equipment and capable of having a modem attached for communication with a remote data terminal.

Primary Access   A multiplexing arrangement whereby many ISDN Basic access subscribers can be connected to a digital network over a common line facility.

Protocol   The rules for communication between like processes, giving a means to control the orderly communication of information between stations on a data link.

Protocol Analyzer   A device that decodes a bit stream being monitored into characters that represent the format and information content of a transmission protocol.

Redundancy   The portion of the total information contained in a message that can be eliminated without loss of essential information.

Repeater   A communications system component that amplifies or regenerates signals to compensate for losses in the system.

Serial Transmission   A method of information transfer in which the bits comprising a character are sent in sequence one at a time.

Slow Scan Video   The process whereby still video images are transmitted frequently to provide the appearance of video motion.

Space One of the two possible states of a binary information element. The open circuit or no current state of a teleprinter line. See Mark.

Start Bit or Element The first bit or element transmitted in the asynchronous transmission of a character to synchronize the receiver.

Statistical Multiplexer A multiplexer that uses the idle time of connected devices to carry data traffic from active devices.

Stop Bit or Element The last bit or element transmitted in the asynchronous transmission of a character to return the circuit to the at-rest or idle condition.

Symbol The graphical representation of some idea that is used by people. Letters and numbers are symbols.

TA (Terminal Adapter) A device that is used to permit equipment with a non-ISDN interface to be connected to that digital network.

TE1 (Terminal Equipment 1) Devices that comply with the ISDN network interface and can be connected directly to the digital network.

TE2 (Terminal Equipment 2) Devices that do not have an ISDN interface and must be connected by using a TA (terminal adapter) to the digital network.

ter Meaning third in Latin, this term is used as a suffix to denote a third version of a CCITT modem standard.

Terminal Emulation Software or firmware that enables a personal computer or terminal to duplicate the screen attributes of a terminal.

Time Division Multiplexer (TDM): A device that permits the transmission of two or more independent data channels on a single high-speed circuit by interleaving the data from each channel on the circuit by time.

Transmission, Asynchronous Transmission in which each information character is individually synchronized, usually by the use of start and stop elements.

Transmission, Synchronous Transmission in which the sending and receiving instruments are operating continuously at substantially the same frequency and in which the desired phase relationship can be maintained by means of correction.

Trellis Coded Modulation A modem modulation process in which one or more redundant bits is added to each group of bits used to generate a signal change. The extra bit or bits permits only certain sequences of signal points to be valid, resulting in a lowering of the error rate.

Turnaround Time The actual time required to reverse the direction of transmission from sender to receiver or vice versa when using a half-duplex circuit. Time is required for line propagation effects, modem timing, and computer reaction.

UART (Universal Asynchronous Receiver/Transmitter) A device that performs asynchronous communication functions by converting parallel digital output from a DTE into serial bit transmission and vice versa.

XMODEM A half-duplex file transfer protocol limited to transmitting one file at a time.

YMODEM A half-duplex file transfer protocol that supports the transfer of multiple files.

ZMODEM A full-duplex file transfer protocol that supports the transfer of multiple files and enables a previously interrupted transmission to be resumed at the point of interruption.

Bibliography

A History of Engineering & Science in the Bell System: The Early Years (1875-1925), Whippany, NJ: Bell Telephone Laboratories, Inc., 1975.

Bell Laboratories Record, Whippany, NJ: Bell Telephone Laboratories, Inc., November 1980.

Bellamy, John. *Digital Telephony*, New York: John Wiley & Sons, Inc., 1982.

Bigelow, Stephen. *Understanding Telephone Electronics, 3rd Ed.*, Carmel, IN; Sams, a division of Macmillan Computer Publishing, 1983.

Black, Uyless. *Computer Networks Protocols, Standards, and Interfaces*, Englewood Cliffs, NJ: Prentice Hall, Inc., 1993.

Black, Uyless. *Data Networks*, Englewood Cliffs, NJ: Prentice Hall, Inc., 1989.

CCITT Recommendations V.29, X.21, and X.25, CCITT, Geneva, C.H.

Doll, Dixon. *Data Communications; Facilities, Networks and Systems Design*, New York: John Wiley & Sons, 1978.

EIA Standard RS-232-C (and others), Electronic Industries Association.

Freeman, R.L. *Telecommunication System Engineering*, New York: John Wiley & Sons, Inc., 1980.

Freeman, R.L. *Telecommunication Transmission Handbook, 2nd Ed.*, New York: John Wiley & Sons, Inc., 1981.

General Information—Binary Synchronous Communications, IBM Publication Nr. GA27-3004, IBM Systems Development Division, Publications Center.

General Information—IBM Synchronous Data Link Control, IBM Publication Nr. GA27-3093-2, IBM Systems Development Division, Publications Center.

Held, Gilbert. *Data Communications Networking Devices, 3rd Ed.*, New York: John Wiley & Sons, 1993.

UNDERSTANDING

Held, Gilbert. *Data Compression, 3rd Ed.,* New York: John Wiley & Sons, 1991.

Held, Gilbert. *Digital Networking,* New York: John Wiley & Sons, 1991.

Held, Gilbert. *Ethernet Networks,* New York: John Wiley & Sons, 1994.

Held, Gilbert. *Mastering PC Communications Software,* New York: Van Nostrand Reinhold, 1993.

Held, Gilbert. *Testing and Troubleshooting Data Communications Networks, 2nd Ed.,* New York: Van Nostrand Reinhold, 1992.

Held, Gilbert. *The Complete Modem Reference, 2nd Ed.,* New York: John Wiley & Sons, Inc., 1994.

IEEE Transactions on Communications, IEEE Communications Society, August 1980, Vol. COM-28.

Kreager, Paul. *Practical Aspects of Data Communications,* New York: McGraw-Hill Book Co., 1983.

Martin, James. *Telecommunications and the Computer,* Englewood Cliffs, NJ: Prentice Hall, Inc., 1969.

McNamara, John E. *Technical Aspects of Data Communications, 2nd Ed.,* Digital Press, 1982.

Members of the Technical Staff and the Technical Publications Department. *Engineering and Operations in the Bell System,* Whippany, NJ: Bell Telephone Laboratories, Inc., 1977.

Members of the Technical Staff. *Transmission Systems for Communications, Revised 4th Ed.,* Whippany, NJ: Bell Telephone Laboratories, Inc., 1971.

Notes on the Network, American Telephone & Telegraph Co., 1980.

Owen, Frank E. *PCM and Digital Transmission Systems,* New York: McGraw-Hill, Inc., 1982.

Parameters of Telephone Network Design, IBM Publication Nr ZZ-11-3201-0, IBM World Trade Corp., Jan. 1977.

Sherman, Kenneth. *Data Communications: A User's Guide,* Reston Publishing Co., 1981.

Stauffer, J.R. *IEEE Journal on Selected Areas in Communications,* Vol. SAC-1, No. 3, April 1983.

Tanebaum, Andrew S. *Computer Networks,* Englewood Cliffs, NJ: Prentice Hall, Inc.

Index

C

E

G

H

M

O

P

Q

S

T

VRC (vertical redundancy checking), 245

VRC/LRC method for BiSync error detection, 260

VSM (vestigal sideband modulation) in 9600 bps modems, 163-164

W

WACK (Wait-Before-Transmit Affirmative Acknowledgement) link control code, 258

WAN (wide-area network), 28

waveguide (bounded media), 77

wavelength multiplexing (fiber-optics), 221-222

weather information networks, 33

Western Electric (WE) 201
    phase coding, 157

Western Electric (WE) 208
    phase coding, 161-162

Western Union Telegraph Company, 5

Windows (DOS operating environment), 21, 276

wire pairs, 73-75

wpm (words per minute) in teleprinter speed, 33

WRU (Who Are You) character, 243

WXMODEM protocol, 250
    dialing directory, 279

Wyse WY-50 terminal, 51

X

X.1 standard, 340

X.2 standard, 340

X.3 standard, 340

X.20bis standard, 340

X.21 recommendation, 129-130

X.21bis standard, 340
    physical layer protocol for X.25 packet systems, 328

X.25 standard
    data packets, 334-338
    delay, 342
    facilities, 331
    frame relay, 341-345
    LAPB, 329-334
    network (packet) layer protocol, 334-339
    packet switching, 328-339
    Permanent Virtual Circuit service, 331
    value-added services, 339
    Virtual Call Service, 330

X.25bis standard, 340

X.28 standard, 340

X.29 standard, 340

X.75 standard, 340

X.121 standard, 340

X.200 guideline, 345

XMODEM protocol, 246-251, 402

XMODEM-1K protocol, 248

XMODEM-G protocol, 248-249

XMODEM/CRC protocol, 248

XON/XOFF (data flow control method), 139

XOR logic elements (Cyclic Redundancy Checking), 254

Y

YMODEM protocol, 249-250, 402
    block number field, 249
    global character file specifcation, 249

YMODEM-G protocol, 250

Z

ZMODEM protocol, 250-251, 402
    block size alternation, 250
    dialing directory, 279
    extended CRC checking, 251
    multiple file transfer, 251
    restarting file transfers, 250

Answers to Quizzes

Chapter 1

1. d	7. b
2. b	8. a
3. a	9. c
4. c	10. c
5. c	11. c
6. b	12. b

Chapter 2

1. c	12. c
2. a	13. c
3. b	14. a
4. b	15. b
5. c	16. c
6. c	17. a
7. d	18. c
8. a	19. b
9. a	20. a
10. b	21. c
11. c	22. a

Chapter 3

1. c	8. d
2. a	9. a
3. b	10. c
4. d	11. c
5. d	12. b
6. b	13. c
7. b	14. c

Chapter 4

1. c	8. c
2. a	9. b
3. b	10. a
4. a	11. c
5. b	12. b
6. c	13. c
7. c	

UNDERSTANDING

Chapter 5

1. d	8. c
2. b	9. b
3. c	10. c
4. c	11. d
5. d	12. d
6. c	13. b
7. a	14. c

Chapter 6

1. b	9. b
2. c	10. a
3. c	11. c
4. c	12. c
5. a	13. a
6. d	14. d
7. c	15. a
8. d	

Chapter 7

1. a and c	13. c
2. c	14. d
3. b	15. c
4. d	16. b
5. d	17. b
6. c	18. c
7. d	19. a
8. b	20. f
9. c	21. a
10. c	22. c
11. c	23. b
12. b	24. c

Chapter 8

1. a	9. d
2. c	10. c
3. c	11. b
4. d	12. b and d
5. d	13. a
6. c	14. b
7. c	15. c
8. b	16. d

Chapter 9

1. a	6. b
2. c	7. d
3. b	8. b
4. d	9. d
5. d	10. a

Chapter 10

1. c	11. d
2. a	12. d
3. d	13. a
4. b	14. d
5. c	15. a
6. d	16. d
7. a	17. c
8. a	18. d
9. b	19. c
10. b	20. b

Chapter 11

1. a	13. a
2. d	14. d
3. b	15. b
4. c	16. a
5. d	17. c
6. c	18. c
7. d	19. c
8. a	20. d
9. b	21. d
10. a	22. c
11. b	23. b
12. c	24. a

Chapter 12

1. b	8. b
2. c	9. c
3. b	10. b
4. d	11. c
5. a	12. a
6. d	13. c
7. a	

Chapter 13

1. b	
2. b	
3. a	
4. d	
5. c	
6. d	
7. a	
8. b	